ASEAN and China

ASEAN and China
An Evolving Relationship

EDITED BY
**Joyce K. Kallgren, Noordin Sopiee,
and Soedjati Djiwandono**

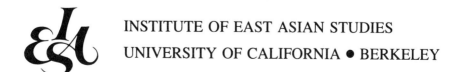

INSTITUTE OF EAST ASIAN STUDIES
UNIVERSITY OF CALIFORNIA • BERKELEY

A publication of the Institute of East Asian Studies, University of California, Berkeley. Although the Institute of East Asian Studies is responsible for the selection and acceptance of manuscripts in this series, responsibility for the opinions expressed and for the accuracy of statements rests with their authors. Correspondence may be sent to: Publications, Institute of East Asian Studies, University of California, Berkeley, California 94720.

The Research Papers and Policy Studies series is one of several publications series sponsored by the Institute of East Asian Studies in conjunction with its constituent units. The others include the China Research Monograph series, the Japan Research Monograph series, the Korea Research Monograph series, and the Indochina Research Monograph series. A list of recent publications appears at the back of the book.

Contents

Introduction

JOYCE K. KALLGREN

ASEAN'S views of China are positive yet cautionary in tone. On one hand, there are benefits to be derived from successful Chinese modernization but, on the other, common concern over the pressures that may result if and when the People's Republic of China becomes a major regional power. Considering these overlapping possibilities in light of economic and political issues, there are differing scenarios that the ASEAN countries may have to deal with in the coming decade and by the year 2000.

The scenarios follow from two related but separate series of questions. First, is China making progress in its modernization efforts and will it continue to do so? And, second, what are the likely consequences of such progress for the region, especially ASEAN, and with respect to specific bilateral relations?

China scholars have assumed that modernization is a desirable outcome. Successful achievement of the Four Modernizations, namely, agriculture, industry, science and technology, and defense, is considered a "plus," with perhaps some dispute over the significance of defense. Assessments differ on the extent of current progress and in anticipation of future problems. How stable is the political leadership espousing the reforms, and how solid the transitional mechanism for a new generation of reformers? How successful has China been in integrating new technology into an often conservative industrial framework? How attractive would a return to China be for foreign-trained Chinese intellectuals? How is China financing the industrial effort? What are the consequences of the growing foreign trade sector? What development lessons, if any, may be drawn by countries in the region from the Chinese experience? These questions in varying forms are commonly addressed in the research efforts of Western European and American scholars.

They are also the object of study by ASEAN scholars as well but with an important addition, namely, what are the consequences of Chinese developments on the political, economic, and strategic situations of the ASEAN countries? Some of China's neighbors—in private if not in public—wonder about the short- and long-term consequences of PRC policies. In the short run, the effort to move effectively and efficiently into the ranks of the developed states has resulted in setting aside or at least moderating some of its foreign policies deemed objectionable by its neighbors, cutting back on military spending, and reducing armed forces, all in the cause of ambitious but realistic goals set for the year 2000.

But what will success mean in the long run? Where will China turn for markets? From what countries will it import? What effect will a modernized Chinese navy have on the security considerations of China's neighbors, who may have claims to islands that the Chinese seek? What role and prominence in the Southeast Asian region will China want to play? What influence, if any, will it seek to exert on the ethnic Chinese minorities scattered throughout Southeast Asia in newly established nations? What will be the consequences of its presence for the larger powers in the area: the Soviet Union? the United States? even possibly India?

In January 1987 the Kuala Lumpur Institute of Strategic and International Studies with the cooperation of the Centre of Strategic and International Studies, Jakarta, and the Institute of East Asian Studies, University of California, Berkeley, convened a conference to discuss many of these issues. The chapters in this book, representing efforts from that conference, address various aspects of the Chinese modernization process and its likely consequences. First are discussions on political leadership, then economic matters, China's military policies, its policies on ethnic Chinese in the region, its role in regional problems, its bilateral relations with the ASEAN countries, and, finally, U.S.-USSR-PRC relations and their likely consequences for the region.

With the exception of the chapter on Vietnam, the bilateral discussions are by scholars in the region. Most of the Americans focus on Chinese developments, with limited comment on the implications for ASEAN. On the other hand, the ASEAN scholars always deal with the two basic issues: the positive potential from Chinese modernization and the negative scenario that may follow renewed Chinese economic and military strength.

Many of these analyses are colored by the ongoing Vietnam-Kampuchea turmoil. The lack of progress by January 1987, when border clashes between China and Vietnam were in progress during the conference, may account for much of the pessimism here, more than would be the case in mid-1988. But the struggle in Kampuchea, intervention by the Vietnamese, Chinese support for the Khmer Rouge, and the different scenarios for expediting a Vietnamese withdrawal from the region are themes that emerge in most of the chapters.

For, if there is one area in which ASEAN has taken the lead—and thus demonstrated its effectiveness in regional matters—it is in the diplomatic problems arising from the Kampuchean-Vietnamese conflict. ASEAN has presented the region's views in the United Nations. It has also taken some action to explore and to some extent support the idea of a zone of peace, freedom and neutrality in the region. In addition, there is some limited trade cooperation among the member states, though the organization does not, in fact, function as an Asian European Economic Community. In contrast to ten years ago, ASEAN's image and presence have developed considerably, but outside of the Kampuchean problem, its effectiveness in regional matters has yet to be fully realized.

Readers will inevitably differ with some of the viewpoints of the various authors. For the most part, they have been given considerable leeway in expressing their views and the preferred facts to support them. The result provides a range of judgments about Chinese intentions but leads to occasional duplication as authors defend their positions. This is especially true for the discussion of Vietnam and Kampuchea. Scholars in the region writing about Chinese relations with a frontline state that is ethnically Chinese or has a large Chinese minority express their views with differing degrees of intensity. A sense of their perspective might have been lost had too severe editorial constraints been placed upon their manuscripts. Readers should also keep in mind that little updating was possible after January 1988, especially in respect to Vietnam and Kampuchea. Nor has it been possible to incorporate references to the Sihanouk discussions in December 1987 and January 1988. Keeping these qualifications in mind, let us turn to the views expressed by these participants in the Kuala Lumpur conference on the evolving relationship between a modernizing China and the ASEAN community.

The first group of authors focuses primarily on the internal experiences of the Chinese when viewed from political, economic, and military perspectives, the heart of any appraisal of Chinese progress. Kenneth Lieberthal addresses the nature of the change, with special emphasis on the political component. He categorizes the types of reform, regimes, and leadership that such models seem to develop. The political and economic possibilities range from a corrupt regime (corruption considered as the core characteristic of such a system), to radical reform, moderate reform, an abandonment of reform, and, finally, to system breakdown. Against this backdrop he discusses the issues of leadership succession, the inputs from economic reforms, and the effects of certain foreign problems such as Hong Kong. Lieberthal foresees the probability of radical reform some ten to fifteen years hence but concludes that ''two factors—succession politics and a sluggish response to the search for foreign markets—make the interim prospects for moderate reform or abandonment of reform more likely.''

Professor Abhinya Rathanamongkolmas, in her emphasis on political leadership, sets forth three alternatives in terms of schemes of economic development—left, right, and moderate. She addresses the forty-year history of the leadership and lists by time period salient political and economic events. From her perspective the PRC is now in a "moderate" period where "managerial modernizers" constitute the new leadership. As with Lieberthal the matter of transition is of key importance. Rathanamongkolmas also discusses the implications for Southeast Asian security of the role of ethnic Chinese and concludes with a judgment that is roughly congruent with Lieberthal, though her categories differ. She believes that the desire to develop its economy, together with a still "inadequate military capability" will compel China to maintain a low nonaggressive profile. Her conclusion places emphasis upon the leadership component: "National interest will cause China to maintain and promote amicable relations, a policy likely to be continued as long as the managerial modernizers dominate Chinese politics."

Economic reforms in the post-Mao period are analyzed by K. C. Yeh and Reynaldo Ty y Racaza. Yeh addresses the difficult issues that may limit continued success, especially persistent inflationary pressures. He outlines the impact of a "high-growth" scenario for China because it would be most significant for Southeast Asia, specifically trade. Yeh concludes, therefore, that the "impact of China's economic reform on the strategic environment is likely to be a mixed blessing."

This view contrasts with Reynaldo Ty y Racaza's summary of China's economic achievements and current policies and their implications for ASEAN. An observation about potential conflict notwithstanding, he is more optimistic about Chinese-ASEAN relations—"It seems likely then that China and the ASEAN countries may sustain relatively harmonious economic relations," concluding with a call for cooperative efforts against forces that may block China's and ASEAN's development as well as that of other Third World countries.

Military policies follow as important consequences of political and economic modernization policies. Though Chinese modernization efforts have resulted in officer retirements and a reduction in the total number of armed forces, the matters of China's military intentions and capability remain crucial concerns for ASEAN as an entity and for its constituent members. Here also there is a division of views, though not as sharp as one might expect. In a thoughtful and detailed discussion, Harlan Jencks outlines the strategic considerations of the ASEAN region in light of Chinese military modernization and concludes with some judgments about future Chinese-Vietnamese relations. Despite his acknowledgment of efforts to upgrade their military preparedness, Jencks tends to be moderate in his expectations.

Stephen Leong, for his part, also discusses many aspects of Chinese modernization but is more inclined to stress the possible aggressive scenarios that may result. In that sense, the two discussions balance each other to some degree, whereas Edward Ross's views are somewhat apart. Ross sets forth the nature of American military assistance policies for China in a reassuring manner with a view to explaining their limitations and to stressing the defensive character of some items and programs. This chapter was updated to December 1987 and includes a valuable chronology of U.S.-China relations.

If military policies and accompanying strategic considerations are of primary importance for regional discussions, the role of ethnic Chinese in the region and likely policies of the PRC ranked second at the conference. This issue was the central concern of Robert Ross and Chan Ngor Chong. Ross surveys the various countries in the region as well as Chinese policies toward the overseas Chinese and concludes that there are no direct security issues posed by the overseas Chinese but that ''Beijing's pursuit of the economic resources of Chinese abroad does heighten the valid domestic security concerns of the host countries.'' Chan addresses the problem thoughtfully, focusing on the pre-1976 period with due regard for changing domestic problems that impact on overseas Chinese policy. He also looks briefly at the differing economic roles of the various Southeast Asian Chinese communities. Whereas Ross notes the possible complications for China as its strength and capacity for action increase, Chan Ngor Chong stresses the key role of the leadership in the countries of residence.

Setting the stage for the later discussions on China's bilateral relations in Southeast Asia, Jusuf Wanandi provides a general survey of the region, reminding readers of the perception by the ASEAN countries of China as a threat. Size, population, and cultural dominance, as well as propinquity, virtually ensure that reality. More interesting now is Wanandi's judgment that the ASEAN members remain ahead of the Chinese in their current stages of development as they deal with a future agenda of crucial issues, namely, territorial sovereignty, overseas Chinese, party-to-party relations, economic competition, and the Kampuchean conflict.

Although Wanandi recognizes economics as an important reality, Chia Siow-Yue gives a more comprehensive discussion of economic relations between ASEAN in general and its component nations, emphasizing the relationship between ASEAN's essentially market economies and the still largely planned Chinese economy. Chia sees ASEAN as more dependent upon China as a source of imports than of exports. She believes that China can play a significant role in helping ASEAN diversify its trade and be less dependent on developed market economics. Chia also recognizes, however, that ASEAN has been experiencing a widening deficit in its trade with China despite efforts to achieve a balance. She thinks that the economic benefits for ASEAN from a prosperous and economically vibrant China far outweigh the costs and that China like Japan can become an engine of growth in the region. Such economic development—for Chia, as well as for other authors here—depends upon nonideological development.

In the bilateral analyses, we can discern several common themes, many of which are related to issues raised by previous authors. Edgardo Maranan finds relations between China and the Philippines largely problem-free. Concentrating on its own economic and political recovery, the Philippines may view the Chinese experience as a useful model. Indonesia, on the other hand, remembers its clashes with China during the coup efforts by Indonesian communists and is more inclined to focus upon the development of trade with political normalization still some way off. Hadi Soesastro illuminates the difficulties confronting the Chinese and Indonesians in their efforts to improve trade and concludes that since formal diplomatic relations cannot be restored until the Chinese Communist Party abandons "its policy of interfering in communist movements in Southeast Asia," current trade efforts should focus on the ways and means of improving informal trade relations. The author does not seem optimistic of a positive outcome.

For Singapore and Malaysia, the overseas Chinese problem is weighed against the obvious attractiveness of increased Chinese trade and commercial relations, particularly in recent years when economic growth in both ASEAN countries has slowed. In the case of Singapore, economic and political relations with China have improved (though normalization has not occurred), but a constant theme in Chin Kin Wah's chapter is his concern that Singapore continue to stay ahead in the rush toward development and that China honor its commitments to economic modernization. In the case of Malaysia (Bahari), economic ties are attractive, but there is a great deal of anxiety because of the racial divisions in the society. Though attracted by the commerce and business with China that would be desirable for a country that has suffered a decline in markets for its raw materials, Malaysia's deep-seated fear of Chinese dominance is still a consideration in both government and scholarly circles.

The chapters by Sukhumbhand Paribatra and Douglas Pike with respect to Thailand and Vietnam, respectively, shed light on current strategic and military considerations as well as on long-term developments. Sukhumbhand notes the development of military relations and personal connections that would seem to accompany the transshipment of arms to the Kampuchean guerrillas. Pike outlines geographic realities and is evenhanded in arguing that both Vietnam and China have contributed to the difficulties that characterize their relations. He is not optimistic about an early resolution.

In the concluding essay on the relations among the Soviet Union, the United States, and China, Robert Scalapino notes the marked degree of fluidity that characterizes relations among the three powers but comments that priority seems to be given to economic matters and development—an observation borne out by the other discussions. Scalapino recognizes the continued doubt among the ASEAN countries about Chinese intentions, as well as about the Soviet Union's. His assessment of Chinese and Soviet relations with the United States emphasizes gradualism. Indeed, in his conclusion, Scalapino reaffirms the economic focus, sets aside the prospects for political convergence, and notes that with the changes in communist governments, great power accommodation, though partial and tentative would ''appear to be in the offing. And among the available alternatives, this is the best one for the smaller states, including those in Southeast Asia.''

Taken together, the views expressed here illustrate how pervasive are regional fears of Chinese power and at the same time the attractiveness of the obvious economic potential of a modernized China. A note of realism characterizes even the most optimistic appraisals. At present, the Kampuchea struggle serves to unite the nations of the region in their efforts to resolve the conflict. Differences in perspective between frontline states such as Thailand and island nations such as Indonesia are still present, but they are more muted in light of a positive Chinese effort in Southeast Asia.

The world powers are still present in Southeast Asia. The links between Vietnam and the Soviet Union are threatening to the PRC. American interests and its presence are both sought but are also sources of concern. When the Kampuchea problem is resolved, sustaining the power and leadership of ASEAN will become an urgent task. The authors set forth various problems that may heighten centrifugal forces; they are less effective in establishing the means whereby ASEAN can sustain its ability to provide a regional response to new challenges.

Though historical themes recur throughout these pages, reminding readers of the capacity of nations to transfer longtime fears into current difficulties, it is also true that the countries of ASEAN show considerable ingenuity in developing economic policies to resolve potential problems with China while hoping to profit from Chinese progress. This fact suggests the possibility of continued progress toward forging new relationships between China and ASEAN.

PART ONE

Political Leadership in China: Implications for Southeast Asia

1. Implications of China's Political Situation on ASEAN

KENNETH LIEBERTHAL

China's policies directed toward the ASEAN countries since 1978 have been closely linked to the PRC's domestic priorities, with the important exception of the spinoffs of China's Vietnam strategy. Other chapters in this volume examine the various policy developments in China's relations with the ASEAN countries. These developments thus warrant only brief mention here as a basis for discussing which Chinese domestic priorities are of greatest importance for underpinning a constructive Chinese policy toward ASEAN in the future.

In broad terms (and with some important exceptions), China has been playing a more constructive role in Southeast Asia during the 1980s than was previously the case. Specifically, the PRC has sharply reduced its support for subversion in the area. This includes a virtual halt in physical support to Southeast Asian communist parties and revolutionary movements. It also encompasses cessation of verbal encouragement for these politically subversive movements.[1] Indeed, China's own turn away from Maoism has itself greatly reduced the role of the PRC as a source of ideas and an energizing model for radicals in other Asian countries.

This retreat from subversion has been coupled with a policy of seeking improved state-to-state relations. Among the ASEAN countries this effort has, perhaps, borne the most fruit with Thailand. Nevertheless, China has proved willing to increase substantially its contacts with ASEAN states with which it does not have formal diplomatic ties, and it has sought to nudge each of these relationships toward normalization. Foreign Minister Wu Xueqian's April 1985 trip to Indonesia to commemorate the thirtieth anniversary of the Bandung conference exemplifies this effort.[2]

---

[1]See, e.g., William R. Heaton, "China and Southeast Asian Communist Movements: The Decline of Dual Track Diplomacy," *Asian Survey*, vol. 22, no. 8 (August 1982), pp. 779–800.
[2]Wayne Bert, "Chinese Policy Toward Burma and Indonesia," *Asian Survey*, vol. 25, no. 9 (September 1985), pp. 963–80. See also Eric Teo Chu Cheow, "New Omnidirectional Overtures in Thai Foreign Policy," *Asian Survey*, vol. 26, no. 7 (July 1986), p. 747, which calls China, "the new de facto patron of Bangkok" (the older patron is the United States).

3

China has, additionally, sought improved economic ties with the ASEAN states. This effort has focused primarily on luring investment from, and increasing trade with, overseas Chinese in the region, although it has also extended beyond the overseas Chinese community.[3] China's role in the region has not, of course, been totally benign during the 1980s. Its dispute with Vietnam has put obstacles in the way of a potential settlement in Kampuchea and has de facto had the effect of increasing the Soviet Union's presence in Southeast Asia. China also retains the potential to be a more assertive and disruptive force in the region, both indirectly and via its overseas Chinese populations in the area.

On balance, though, the trends in Chinese policy toward the ASEAN countries since the end of the 1970s have been preferable to the nature of the PRC's policy in this region in earlier years. China's size, the existence of overseas Chinese communities, and other factors will always make people in the ASEAN countries somewhat cautious about PRC policies throughout the area. But given the range of realistic possibilities, recent Chinese policy has been relatively constructive (again, setting Vietnam aside).

The core questions for this chapter thus are twofold: First, how will the domestic priorities that have supported policy toward ASEAN in recent years fare in Chinese politics over the coming years? And second, how will the repercussions for ASEAN vary with different scenarios for the future development of domestic Chinese politics?

Prospects for Chinese Developments

The Reform Programs in China

Chinese politics since 1978 have allowed for considerable experimentation in the search for a viable framework for "reform."[4] In the wake of the ideologically supercharged atmosphere of Mao Zedong's last decade, the changes wrought since 1978 have been bold and, sometimes, disruptive and disorienting. In analyzing these changes and their future, however, it is important to appreciate that two basic (and some-

---

[3]Chinese Vice Premier Tian Jiyun articulated the goals of improved economic and political relations with ASEAN during his October 11–28, 1986, visit to Singapore, Malaysia, the Philippines, and Thailand. See Xinhua English-language service on these dates. Chinese trade figures with the ASEAN countries through 1983 are provided in *Zhongguo dui wai jingji maoyi nianjian, 1984* (Yearbook of China's Foreign Trade, 1984) (Beijing: China Foreign Trade Publishing House, 1984), p. 4.

[4]This section draws on Kenneth Lieberthal, "The Future of Reform in China," *AEI Foreign Policy and Defense Review*, vol. 6, no. 3, pp. 3–10.

what overlapping) reform efforts have been articulated and debated during this period. One, the "moderate" agenda, seeks simply to make the socialist economic and political system work more efficiently and equitably. The other, a "radical"[5] approach, seeks to alter core premises of the socialist system itself. Neither reform approach has produced an accepted canon or dogma.

In broad terms, the moderate concept of reforms incorporates the following general policy elements and trends. First, moderate reformers envision broad institutional changes in the direction of reducing the scope of administrative responsibility of the party apparatus, sharply curtailing the military's role in domestic political and economic affairs, cutting back on political coercion (and thus reining in the public security and propaganda organs that previously played central roles in coercing the populace), and bolstering the resources and authority of the State Council units that run the economy. In sum, these institutional changes are designed to shift China from a totalitarian to an authoritarian system[6] by restructuring both relations among the major ruling bureaucracies and relations between the political organs themselves and the society.

Second, the moderates have tried to bring younger, better educated individuals into leading positions. This effort has produced major personnel turnover in leading positions at both provincial and central levels in the party, state, and military hierarchies. In general, those moving into key leadership positions have more technical training than did the older cadres they are replacing.[7]

Third, moderates are making greater use of material incentives to enhance efficiency and are utilizing market forces to guide production and distribution where the state cannot effectively directly manage these functions. The most important initiative in this category is the de facto decollectivization of agriculture that began at the end of the 1970s and became the dominant feature of agricultural production during the early 1980s. The startlingly successful results of this policy provided enormous momentum for the extension of the reform effort into the urban economy. There, material incentives in the form of bonuses have joined with other measures (such as greatly reducing the number of

---

[5]"Radical" is used here to mean a willingness to make major breaks with the recent past. It does *not* connote leftism.

[6]Michel Oksenberg and Richard Bush, "China's Political Evolution: 1972–1982," *Problems of Communism*, vol. 31, no. 5 (September-October 1982), pp. 1–19.

[7]A. Doak Barnett, "Ten Years After Mao," *Foreign Affairs* (Fall 1986), pp. 47–48, provides basic figures on these changes.

items directly controlled by the national economic plan) to reduce substantially the extent to which administrative decisions made in Beijing structure the choices and activities of urban workers and managers. These measures have been accompanied by concerted efforts to bring about a sectoral shift in economic growth in favor of light industry and agriculture at the cost of some growth in heavy industry.[8]

Fourth, the moderates have also supported opening the country in a limited way to the international economy, including importing and utilizing foreign capital and technology. They look to the international arena for capital, technology, some managerial skills, and for export markets. The moderates have proven willing to tolerate greater regional inequalities within China as a natural consequence of this turn abroad and priority on rapid economic growth.[9]

Finally, the moderates support policies to promote economic growth based on a rational utilization of scarce resources. These include, for example, increasing the use of feasibility studies in the decision-making process[10] and improving the academic quality of the educational system. In sum, the moderate variant of the reforms is itself quite ambitious.

China since 1978 has basically implemented this moderate set of initiatives. While these initiatives have not yet fully run their course, the major part of this approach had been put into place by the end of 1984. To the moderate reformers, much of the effort required in the future would amount to fine tuning these basic ideas. The available evidence suggests that virtually all current leaders in the Politburo, Secretariat, and State Council Standing Committee agree that the above policy thrusts, at a minimum, are necessary. There is some disagreement, though, over how far many of them should go.

The more ambitious radical reform agenda builds on the above initiatives but is premised on the notion that more fundamental components of China's system must change if the country is to achieve wealth and power over the coming decades. The radical reformers thus have supported the above initiatives since 1978, but they regard them as simply necessary stepping stones to more basic changes. While there is no program to which the radical reformers have all agreed, some of their fundamental ideas have found their way repeatedly into the Chinese

---

[8]See esp. the articles by K. C. Yeh and by Robert M. Field in *China Quarterly*, no. 100 (December 1984).

[9]"Regional Belts: Rich Get Richer," *China Economic Letter*, vol. 2, no. 18 (September 22, 1986), pp. 1–6.

[10]Kenneth Lieberthal and Michel Oksenberg, *Bureaucratic Politics and Chinese Energy Development* (Washington, D.C.: U.S. Government Printing Office, 1986), esp. ch. 6.

press and journals dating back to the late 1970s. These in their totality would move China a major step toward a market economy.

Some of the core ideas of the radical reformers are the following. First, change the nature of ownership of major enterprises so that the managers of these firms no longer look to state administrative organs as their ultimate bosses. Second, substitute interdependence for enlightened self-reliance in China's conceptualization of its relations with the international economy. This would see the international arena as more than a last-resort source of imports aimed at import substitution goals and would, rather, recognize an international division of labor and the energizing effects of internationally based competition.[11] Third, rather than seek to make planning more effective, fundamentally alter the relative role of planning and of the market in favor of the latter. Fourth, create labor, capital, and land markets, as well as markets in intermediate products. And finally, greatly enhance the role of the banking system at the cost of the power of the planning, finance, and ministerial systems in governing the economy.[12]

In short, the radical reformers want to undertake initiatives that could alter in rather basic ways the relationship of the state to the economy and the nature of ties between China and the outside world. In many ways, the crux of the issue that divides moderate from radical reformers is their different perceptions of the repercussions of the market. Former party general secretary Hu Yaobang, Zhao Ziyang, and Tian Jiyun (to name some key radical reformers) believe the market provides discipline, efficiency, and incentives for innovation. By contrast, Chen Yun, Yao Yilin, and Li Peng, all of whom are moderate reformers, see in the market more chaos than efficiency and therefore want to permit the market to determine production and distribution only when the state cannot itself handle these well. Thus, to the more moderate reformers, the market is an arena that produces anarchy and inequity as much as it engenders efficiency and innovation.

Deng Xiaoping is the obvious omission from this list. He is clearly the most radical reformer among the powerful elder statesmen (including also Chen Yun, Peng Zhen, Li Xiannian, Bo Yibo, Yang Shangkun,

---

[11]See Zhang Yunling, "International Economic Environment and China's Development," paper presented to the Conference of [Chinese] Scholars of International Relations (Houston: June 20–22, 1986).

[12]Major elements of the radical reformers' ideas are presented in *Renmin ribao*, March 28, 1986, in Foreign Broadcast Information Service (hereafter FBIS), *Daily Report, China*, April 10, 1986, pp. K1–6. For a trenchant critique of the moderate reforms by an advocate of radical reform, see Yang Xiaokai, "Zhongguo di jingji tizhi gaige" (Reform of China's economic system), *Zhishi fenzi* (July 1985), pp. 38–45.

and Wang Zhen), but it stretches the evidence to state that Deng is wholly a radical reformer, even though he has provided support and protection for the radical reformers since the late 1970s.[13]

Looking to the future, there are some important policies that both the moderate and the radical reformers support. Both, for example, agree on the importance of bringing younger, better educated cadres into positions of responsibility. Both groups, moreover, basically support continuation of one-party rule by the Chinese Communist Party (CCP) in a politically less coercive system. Neither group, therefore, sees political pluralism and Western-style democracy as desirable, near-term goals of the reforms (although the more radical reformers would probably feel comfortable with a less strict cultural regime than would the moderate reformers).

The major political differences between moderate and radical reformers thus lie in the political ramifications of their respective economic programs. The radical reformers would push the changes in power among key bureaucratic institutions much farther than would their more moderate counterparts. The radical reformers would also permit more wide-ranging and less fettered interactions with the international arena and greater disparities of wealth at home. These different basic policy thrusts would bring with them important implications for the relative power of various party and government bodies, the relative wealth of various regions and of different sectors of the populace, and the cultural and social dynamics of life in China.

Probable Political and Economic Futures

The range of possible political and economic futures for the PRC remains broad.[14] The reforms have produced significant changes, such as decollectivization of agriculture, that cannot be reversed without extraordinary effort in the future. These same reforms have, however, generated tensions and frustrations to the extent that there is serious question about the momentum still remaining behind the reform effort.

---

[13]On Chen Yun and Deng Xiaoping, see their respective speeches to the September 1985 National Party Conference: *Beijing Review* 30 (September 1985), pp. 15–20. On Tian Jiyun and Li Peng, see *Zhengming*, no. 93 (July 1, 1985), pp. 6–8, in FBIS, *Daily Report, China*, July 10, 1985, pp. W3–5. On Li Peng, see also Xinhua, December 13, 1985, in FBIS, *Daily Report, China*, December 18, 1985, pp. K17–18; and Dong Xusheng, "Zhongguo weilai: Liu Su pai yu liu Mei pai di da bodou" (China's future: the big struggle between those who studied in the USSR and those who studied in America) *Zhongguo zhi chun* (China spring), no. 11 (1985), pp. 1–16.
[14]This section draws on Michel Oksenberg and Kenneth Lieberthal, "Forecasting China's Future," *National Interest*, no. 5 (Fall 1986), pp. 18–27.

And, as explained above, there is an important level of disagreement among the leaders as to the desirable nature and scope of future reforms.

In broad terms, there appear to be five realistic scenarios for the development of China over the coming decade. Each of these posits a distinctive set of relationships among the political system, economy, and society. While they are not, strictly, different points on a continuum of outcomes, they do incorporate a trend from minimum to maximum centralized and unified government administrative control over the economy.[15] The scenarios are as follows.

Corrupt Regime. The attempt at reform escapes political control. The price reform necessary for the radical reform program occurs, but widespread corruption prevents a functioning market economy from emerging. Authoritarian rulers at the national and local levels rule by means of systematic corruption and cronyism through a party that has lost any sense of discipline or purpose. While some degree of corruption is almost necessary under most of the five scenarios,[16] in this variant, corruption becomes a core characteristic of the entire system. On a larger scale, China comes to resemble Marcos's Philippines in its last years, or several other African and Asian states.

Radical Reform. The reforms proceed along the radical reform path, and a historical compact is reached between the political and economic elite in which each in effect cedes a legitimate sphere of autonomy to the other. The party ceases to be an ideological instrument of mobilization and instead plays an integrating function, as the Mexican Institutional Revolutionary Party eventually did after that revolution. The role of the market expands dramatically, although its overall parameters remain subject to various macroeconomic control measures. The PRC develops a relationship among the state, the economy, and the society that is somewhat comparable to that on Taiwan in the early 1980s.

Moderate Reform. The reforms basically stall in their present moderate phase, and the radical reforms are never fully implemented. A mixed system, largely planned but with a circumscribed role for the marketplace, continues. The party remains in perpetual quest for its proper role, and promoting ardent nationalism becomes potentially attractive both as a raison d'être for the party and as a vehicle for relieving systemic tensions. An economic elite emerges through the opportunities for entrepreneurship that the system permits, but it exists in

---

[15]The sole exception is system breakdown, the fifth scenario.
[16]Samuel Huntington, *Political Order in Changing Societies* (New Haven: Yale University Press, 1968), pp. 59–71.

uneasy tension with the politicians and bureaucrats. The major reforms undertaken to date, such as the open door and the decollectivization of agriculture, basically remain in place. Radical reformers may continue to try to promote their program, but the system as a whole remains, in broad terms, similar to that in 1987.

Abandonment of Reform. Deng's successors retract many of the reforms implemented by their predecessor. The state reasserts itself. Foreign trade and investment come under tighter central government control, capital investment is again almost fully within the state plan, and ideological and cultural policies become more restrictive. The Communist Party justifies its preeminent position by claiming to represent the purity of the revolution, specifically by its ability to protect the country from cultural, economic, and military "aggression." The political elite, in short, reasserts its control over the destiny of the economy and society. This scenario represents some retreat from even the moderate reform tendencies and would likely entail a more strident nationalism. Direct foreign access to the society and the economy would diminish.

System Breakdown. As has occurred in many developing countries, there is a systemic breakdown. Not only the political elite but the leaders of other hierarchies (military or economic) prove unable to control and direct amorphous social forces. The catalyst that would initiate such a crisis is unpredictable, as is the nature of the upheaval itself. But the existing structure of authority proves incapable of coping with the challenge and collapses. The Cultural Revolution and its aftermath constituted, in a sense, something approaching such a state of affairs, though one deliberately induced by the nation's top leader and one from which recovery proved possible. Such a phenomenon is unlikely to recur, but the history of modern China as well as of other developing countries suggests that the ability of the political system to absorb all the forces it has unleashed cannot be taken for granted.

These alternative scenarios having been sketched out, it should be acknowledged that a single, consistent line of development toward any one of them is unlikely. Indeed, as explained below, it seems likely that the immediate post-Deng era may see several years of moderate reform or abandonment of reform, quite possibly then followed by a renewed period of radical reform.

Further, it is not clear that the entire country will experience a similar process of change. The nature of interaction between the political and economic realms is likely to vary from region to region in a country as diverse as China. For example, Guangzhou in the south, with its robust entrepreneurial activity, is certainly different from the still bureaucratically controlled atmosphere of Beijing.

Nonetheless, recognizing that the scenarios represent rather simplified tendencies, it is possible to hazard predictions about the likely outcome ten to fifteen years hence. At present, there is only a marginal chance for the emergence of a corrupt regime (although substantial levels of corruption might occur under almost any of these scenarios). Even less likely is the chance of a systemic breakdown. What looks most likely are the outcomes that cluster around the remaining three scenarios, and thus the remainder of this analysis focuses exclusively on these three possibilities. Of the three, radical reform appears the most likely over the long run. But moderate reform is almost equally likely. The one remaining scenario, abandonment of reform, is over the long run the least likely of the three, but it is still a very possible outcome, especially in the short term.

The key factors that will determine the type(s) of regime(s) that will emerge during the coming fifteen years or so can be grouped into several broad, interrelated categories: (1) the succession, (2) the economic results of reform, (3) the economic response of the outside world, (4) the management of the Hong Kong and Taiwan issues, and (5) the international security environment.

The Succession. Deng Xiaoping has attempted to arrange for an orderly succession, but events in 1986–87 damaged this effort. Deng in early 1987 demanded that his protégé, Hu Yaobang, resign the party general secretary post. This demand was made in part in response to pressures from more conservative party elders, some of whom had (in theory) retired from politics several years earlier. The increased role of such old men throughout 1987 highlighted the very limited extent to which Deng had succeeded in institutionalizing and regularizing Chinese politics at the apex. The likely result is that the succession will prove more difficult—and the pressures on the radical reformers more powerful and persistent—than had appeared to be the case as late as 1986.

Initially, the succession is likely to pass to radical reformer Zhao Ziyang, but Deng Xiaoping and his associates have also identified a "third generation" of successors—Vice Premiers Li Peng and Tian Jiyun on the government side, the Secretariat members Hu Qili and Qiao Shi in the party. These leaders, however, appear to be divided between moderate and radical reforms. Both their own public remarks and the Hong Kong rumor mill suggest that Tian and Hu are more radical than are Li and Qiao.

In addition, the recently retired Chen Yun, Peng Zhen, and Li Xiannian appear to be less sympathetic than Deng is to the ideas of the radical reformers. Should Deng precede them in death, they might be able to influence the succession arrangements so as to limit future reforms, especially after their surge of activity during 1987.[17] Second, the real strength of annointed successors only becomes clear in the event, and the abilities of Zhao are yet to be fully tested. Third, the true beliefs of the third generation and their ability to avoid debilitating power struggles are yet to be proven.

Finally, and perhaps most significantly, Deng has yet to finalize the succession at the apex of the military. Indeed, he has retained the command of the People's Liberation Army (PLA) in his own hands as chief of the pivotal CCP Military Affairs Committee (MAC). Some evidence indicates that in 1986 Deng sought to make Hu Yaobang head of the MAC—and that military resistance to this effort contributed to Hu's political disgrace. Deng succeeded in 1987 in making Zhao Ziyang the first ranking vice chairman of the MAC. While this was a major step in securing Zhao's position, it did not fully resolve civilian-military tensions. The military could increase the possibility of abandonment of reform.

On balance, these uncertainties must be viewed in the context of the very substantial progress Deng has made, not just at the apex but at the ministerial level and in the provinces, in installing people who appear committed to either moderate or radical reform. It is possible that before he dies Deng will succeed in bequeathing to the nation a succession arrangement that can avoid abandonment of reform. The succession arrangements help give the radical reform scenario its plausibility; the uncertainties prompt weight being given to the possibilities of moderate reform or abandonment of reform.

Economic Results of Reform. Nothing succeeds like success. To the extent that the reforms continue to produce high but controlled economic growth rates, the likelihood of radical reform grows.

Since 1979, the Chinese economy has performed remarkably well. Per capita national income has risen nearly 7 percent a year. Except for setbacks in grain production in 1985 and 1986 due to inclement weather and a drop in sown acreage, agricultural production has grown an astounding 5 percent per year. The value of exports has expanded from $13.66 billion in 1979 to $26.46 billion in 1985. Imports increased from $15.67 billion to $40.24 billion over the same period.[18] The visual impressions of growth are there, too, both in urban and nearby rural areas: a better fed and clothed populace, a building boom, traffic jams, dirtier air, a crushing demand upon leisure time activities. To be sure, the growth is uneven. Some cities, such as Shanghai, do not appear to

---

[17]Peng Zhen may prove especially important in this regard.

[18]*China Macroeconomic Newsletter*, vol. 2, no. 4 (February 24, 1986), p. 6.

be growing as rapidly, and areas of severe poverty continue to exist in arid, mountainous, or remote regions of the country.

In fact, the main problems confronting the reformers have been those indicative of an overheated economy: inflation, government deficits, rapid drawdown of foreign currency, the import of luxury consumer goods to sop up disposable income, and high rates of capital construction (sometimes in economically unsound investments). These problems prompted the leaders to retrench and step back from the reforms on several occasions, most noticeably in late 1980 and again in 1985–86.[19]

The growth pattern can be linked to the alternative scenarios. Should growth exceed 10 to 12 percent for a sustained period, the possibilities of the corrupt regime scenario would grow. The economy might be expanding more rapidly than the political system could absorb and order. Population shifts into urban areas, acute shortages of inputs in high demand, and other factors would greatly increase the opportunities for—and payoffs from—corrupt official behavior. Continued real growth at 5 to 10 percent even as radical reform measures are tried should enhance prospects for the radical reform scenario, as such growth would legitimize price reform and other disruptive policies while keeping the situation under reasonably sound control. A slowdown of growth would make it increasingly difficult for the reformers to resist those who seek greater stability and predictability. Thus, growth of under 5 percent could enhance the short-term prospects for abandonment of reform.[20] But over the longer term, abandonment of reform itself is probably incapable of stimulating a higher rate of growth in China's increasingly complex economy. Pressures for moderate or radical reform would then grow.

The key near-term question, then, is whether the growth can be sustained within the 5 to 10 percent range while more radical measures are tried. As far as preventing excessive growth is concerned, the leaders have already demonstrated their capacity to retrench when needed. Their tools, however, are blunt ones; and retrenchments tend to be almost too restrictive, generating a boom-bust cycle.[21] Moreover, some economic sectors are difficult to reach and cool off, especially locally funded capital construction. As the leaders recognize, they lack the monetary and fiscal

---

[19]*China Macroeconomic Newsletter*, vol. 2, no. 5 (March 10, 1986).

[20]This is a widely held view among Chinese leaders and economists. It reflects the extent to which all reformers have based their legitimacy on the promise that their measures will raise the standard of living of the people.

[21]*China Macroeconomic Newsletter*, vol. 2, no. 5 (March 10, 1986).

tools to regulate the economy in as refined and surgical a fashion as they would like. (These tools may develop over time, as the taxation, banking, and accounting systems are modernized.)

As to sustaining growth above 5 percent, the prospects are good. Agriculture will not be able to sustain its 1980–84 record, which is partially attributable to unusually good weather from 1982 to 1984 and partially to the unrepeatable gains from decollectivization and the introduction of new incentives. However, the industrial sector retains great promise. Measures can be taken to alleviate bottlenecks in transportation, communication, and energy. Managerial inefficiencies can be gradually reduced. Over the long run, environmental constraints (water and air quality) and inadequately trained manpower—the result of long neglect of the educational system and its drastic dislocation during the Cultural Revolution—may prove to be more fundamental obstacles to sustained growth. But most foreign economists agree that the ingredients are in place for sustained growth above 5 percent per year, assuming no gross political or social turmoil. Here, too, is cause for assigning somewhat higher probability to the radical reform scenario.

External Response. The reformist development strategy assigns high priority to the acquisition of foreign technology, equipment, and capital. The Seventh Five-Year Plan projected a 40 percent increase in foreign trade (with the quiet hope that it may reach 50 percent).[22] It originally anticipated a total capital flow to China through foreign investments, foreign aid, borrowing at concessional and commercial interest rates, drawings on the International Monetary Fund (IMF), and so on of roughly $30 to $40 billion during the same five years, from 1986 to 1990.

Yet it must be stressed that an important portion of the projected growth depends on the infusion of capital and technology from abroad, and in this the figures for 1986 and 1987 were disappointing. Moreover, the Chinese expect to secure increased access to foreign markets in order to pay for their imports. They wish to keep their borrowing at commercial interest rates at a minimum and to avoid heavy indebtedness or problems in their current accounts.

The reform program would be adversely affected by a reimposition of strict foreign controls over technology flow to China, protectionism in the outside world, or a continued decline in the interest of foreign firms in investing or establishing co-production arrangements in China. There seems little likelihood of a tightening up on Chinese access to foreign technology; indeed, the trend is strongly in the other direction. But a

---

[22]"Details of the Seventh Five-Year Plan," *Summary of World Broadcasts* FE/8235/C1 (April 17, 1986), pp. 1–34.

note of caution is necessary with respect to the other considerations. China earned roughly 20 percent of its foreign exchange from petroleum exports in 1980–85; with the drop in world energy prices, it must compensate for the loss through an intensified effort to expand export of manufactured commodities.[23] China has incurred trade deficits since 1985, and it may be facing a chronic balance-of-payments problem.[24] To date, it has relied heavily on textiles; overall export performance since 1985 has been below expectations. Uncertainties in this area give some weight to the moderate-reform or even abandonment-of-reform future.

Further, many foreign firms are wearying of the battles of establishing co-production arrangements.[25] While China has done a great deal to create a hospitable climate for foreign firms, the problems of doing business—in terms of bureaucratic impediments, coping with inconsistent policies and high costs, and repatriating earnings—are discouraging. China is not yet competitive with many East and Southeast Asian countries, and Chinese expectations of a foreign rush to its gates have not been met. In addition, some of the measures to attract foreign firms, such as the special economic zones (SEZs), are quite controversial within China. At some point alleged Western and Japanese inadequacies and the reform efforts to attract the foreigner to China could come under attack. Hence, the prognosis has to be hedged, and some weight has to be given to the moderate-reform or even the abandonment-of-reform future.

Management of Hong Kong and Taiwan Issues. Related to the problems caused by external factors is that of how the leaders continue to manage the Hong Kong and Taiwan issues. Deng Xiaoping and his associates have made great strides in planning for the transfer of Hong Kong to Chinese sovereignty in 1997 and in reducing tensions with the authorities on Taiwan. The aplomb with which they have handled these thorny issues has been an important factor in maintaining business confidence to invest on the mainland itself. Since 1978 the Chinese leaders have demonstrated pragmatism, patience, and persistence in pursuit of their objectives toward Taiwan and Hong Kong.[26]

---

[23]"Manufacturing Exports Offset Oil Revenue Loss," *China Macroeconomic Newsletter*, vol. 2, no. 15 (July 28, 1986), pp. 1–3.
[24]*China Economic Trends* (Washington, D.C.: Rock Creek Research, Spring 1986), pp. 87–108.
[25]James Sterba, "Firms Doing Business in China Are Stymied by Costs and Hassles," *Wall Street Journal*, July 17, 1986.
[26]See, e.g., the series of articles on Hong Kong in *China Business Review*, vol. 12, no. 5 (September–October 1985), pp. 30–46.

Can these interrelated issues continue to be well managed? As the 1997 transfer date comes closer, unease in Hong Kong will surely rise and increased migration will occur. How will the mainland respond to these predictable jitters? Under the slogan "one country, two systems," the stated intent is to allow Hong Kong to retain a separate, capitalistic economy and to enjoy administrative autonomy. Yet the CCP and the PLA will exist in Hong Kong, and many mainland ministries and corporations will have subordinate units there.[27]

Things could go awry. Demands by the citizens of Hong Kong to participate in decisions about their own political future could elicit tension-inducing efforts by the mainland to limit freedom of expression, for example. Or the Chinese leaders may prove unable to restrain their bureaucracies from seeking to enter the Hong Kong economy in disruptive fashion. After all, what has enabled Hong Kong to retain its competitive edge in world trade has been its raw capitalism: ineffective firms are not subsidized, they go bankrupt. With the growing PRC presence, this aspect of the Hong Kong economy is already beginning to change. The stakes are so high that the leaders of China will probably continue to manage the situation carefully and to prevent a catalytic event from disrupting the plans for Hong Kong and hence the opening to the outside world.

Similarly, a process of reconciliation between Taiwan and the mainland is beginning to unfold. Indirect trade, scientific exchanges in international settings, and journeys to native places from Taiwan via Hong Kong or Japan are all occurring. But the progress is fragile and the issue remains deeply emotional. Should this progress be disrupted—for example, through inadvertent American or Japanese intervention in a process that is occurring through Chinese initiatives—the skeptics of reform would use this nationalistic issue to flail their opponents. Destabilizing political developments on Taiwan could also force this issue to a head in the direction of a hardening of policy—with potentially wide-ranging repercussions—in Beijing.

The International Security Environment. Both economically and psychologically, the radical reform program rests on an assumption that astute diplomacy can keep China out of military conflict over the coming decade and more. Any sharp deterioration in China's security environment would create pressures toward the reassertion of state control over the economy, greater resources devoted to heavy industry, and a more nationalistic political program designed to justify the resulting sac-

---

[27]John P. Burns, "The Process of Assimilation of Hong Kong (1997) and the Implications for Taiwan," *AEI Foreign Policy and Defense Review*, vol. 6, no. 3, pp. 19–25.

rifices in the standard of living. Depending on the size and nature of the external threat, pressures for abandonment of reform, or at least for adhering to moderate versus radical reform, could result.

There are, in sum, continuing uncertainties about China's future political and economic developments. The above analysis indicates that the current Chinese leadership can at best exercise limited influence over the five major factors that may shape the type of system the PRC develops over the coming years.

Assuming that the five factors introduced above develop in a fashion that is, on balance, neither wholly favorable nor completely unfavorable to the radical reformers, China will probably in the late 1980s and early 1990s experience a period of some political and economic retrenchment.[28] Such a retrenchment might appear to resemble abandonment of reform, but the new regime would probably fairly soon move back to moderate reform.

This prognosis is based on several considerations: that there will be a time directly after Deng Xiaoping's demise when it will be politically difficult to muster the authority to undertake bold new initiatives; that concerns over corruption and increasing foreign influence will make a harder line on these issues an attractive position in the jockeying for the succession; that China's transition, already under way, into a country with substantial foreign debt will generate political strains among the elite that will make temporary retrenchment attractive; that the initial results of growing implementation of the radical reforms (e.g., some factory closings, inflation, and greater regional inequality) will generate pressures for retrenchment and stability; and, perhaps most importantly, that during the coalition building that will characterize the succession period, it will appear to each of the contenders too risky to promote reform policies that would undercut the power of major bureaucracies.

Over the longer run, however, China will experience the pressures that stem from its location at the center of the fastest growing region in the world over the coming decades. Thus, a Chinese system that does not encourage technological upgrading and dynamic interaction with the international economy will probably produce an increasing level of domestic dissatisfaction at both popular and elite levels. The pressures for rapid growth will continue, and much of this growth will have to be

---

[28]The following paragraphs assume that Deng's effective political demise occurs in the next few years.

intensive rather than extensive.[29] The radical reform prospects should thus increase in the early to mid-1990s.[30]

The long-term need for economic growth, therefore, sustains the probability of radical reform ten to fifteen years hence. However, two factors—succession politics and a sluggish external response to the search for foreign markets—make the interim prospects for moderate reform or abandonment of reform more likely. The external security environment and Hong Kong and Taiwan developments loom as potentially difficult obstacles on the way to radical reform.

Implications for China's Role vis-à-vis ASEAN

The above uncertainties render judgments about the impact of future domestic Chinese developments on Southeast Asia and ASEAN necessarily quite tentative. As indicated above, China's reform effort to date (essentially the moderate reform regime) has produced a foreign policy that has generally been favorable for the ASEAN countries. The dynamics of this reform have created strong incentives for the PRC to play a constructive role vis-à-vis the ASEAN countries in both the political and economic arenas. At the same time, limitations inherent in this effort to date have prevented the PRC from developing the dynamic efficiency that might enable it to become a serious challenger to the export markets of most ASEAN countries. In a subtle fashion, the same cross-pressures generated by very incomplete reforms may also have indirectly contributed to limiting the role of the United States in contributing to China's military might and in encouraging more active Chinese involvement in Southeast Asian security affairs.

In short, when evaluating China's posture toward ASEAN, it is important to recognize that many of the benefits stemming from developments in recent years grow not only from the fact that China has embarked on reforms but also from the fact that these reforms have been limited. They have, on balance, nurtured a period of relatively quiescent Chinese nationalism, created considerable willingness to try to become an attractive target for foreign investment, encouraged a basically benign foreign diplomatic policy (other than toward Vietnam), and

---

[29]See, e.g., Bruce Reynolds, "China in the International Economy," in *China's Foreign Relations in the 1980's*, ed. Harry Harding (New Haven: Yale University Press, 1984), pp. 71–106.

[30]This prognosis assumes that the international economic, security, and Taiwan and Hong Kong issues do not develop in a way that drives the PRC toward abandonment of reform.

yielded relatively slow progress in becoming competitive in international markets for manufactured products.

While nothing ever remains wholly the same, the above analysis of probable internal developments in China makes it seem likely that roughly the same basic situation will continue for the coming five to ten years. This prognosis could be upset by two developments. First, Deng Xiaoping might remain active throughout this time and successfully promote considerable movement to the radical reform regime during this time. Second, any combination of the above elements could produce a sharp turn toward abandonment of reform during a succession, with accompanying growth of more virulent Chinese nationalism. These two developments pose potentially quite different challenges to the ASEAN countries.

The Challenge of Radical Reform

China has begun measures to implement the radical reform program, although at present these remain minor in their impact on the overall political system and urban economy. For example, some limited development of capital markets has occurred, and in September 1986 Beijing announced that prices of major consumer manufactures would henceforth be set free from government controls.[31] The PRC has also taken widely publicized measures to attract foreign capital and technology, in the process allowing foreign vendors greatly increased access to Chinese end users.

As of late 1987, however, the Chinese system still provides enormous protection for domestic industries from foreign competition. The bureaucratic and economic policies in place also provide vastly insufficient incentives for domestic firms to meet the exacting and rapidly evolving demands of the international market. Fundamental reform policies now under discussion—a bankruptcy law, free labor market, and so forth—are necessary components of a reform that would potentially make the PRC's firms compete effectively abroad.[32]

Major political and administrative changes thus are required to create the diversity and dynamism that are necessary for becoming a major competitive force in the Asian and world economies. These changes necessarily entail painful adjustments both by members of the elite in affected bureaucracies and on a broader social level. It will thus require either a strong political commitment by a man as powerful as is Deng to force these changes through or, over a much longer period, a far more

---

[31]*China Economic Letter*, vol. 2, no. 19 (October 6, 1986).
[32]Yang Xiaokai, "Zhongguo di jingji tizhi gaige."

dramatic demonstration that anything less than these changes will prevent China from making progress on closing the gap that separates it from many of the other countries in the region.

If China should fundamentally loosen the fetters of the socialist bureaucracies that currently manage the economy, the potential exists for very rapid and dynamic growth in four major regions: in the northeast, along a corridor from Dalian to Shenyang; in the north, centering on Beijing and Tianjin; in the lower Yangtze, from Shanghai westward through Nanjing and perhaps to Wuhan; and in the southeast, centered on the Pearl River delta. These regions, each with its own distinctive mix of economic strengths, could well bring roughly two hundred million Chinese into the orbit of the modern Asian economy over the coming three decades. The impact on the ASEAN countries would be substantial and unsettling.

Strictly economic challenges aside, a robust and dynamic growth of these regions in China would produce a great strengthening of the country as a whole in the international arena. Greater active diplomatic involvement throughout Asia would be one very likely result of this development. Again, the level of discomfort in the ASEAN countries may grow. This observation is likely to be true even though China would, under radical reform, avoid a resurgence of virulent nationalism and of revolutionary fervor.

The Challenge of Abandonment of Reform

Abandonment of reform almost certainly sharply reduces any direct competitive economic threat that China would pose to the ASEAN countries. This posture would, however, carry with it a far greater risk that tensions in the system would produce a stronger and more assertive type of nationalism as a key force in the dynamics of Chinese politics.

The risks for ASEAN of this greater Chinese nationalism are difficult to assess, since the nationalism might seek any of several different outlets. It could, for example, produce a more assertive posture toward the United States and Japan, especially since it would be combined with a pullback from domestic economic reforms and a reassertion of a more Soviet-type economic and cultural system. This reversion to a more traditional socialist system characterized by stronger nationalistic impulses need not preclude a warming relationship with the Soviet Union, with unsettling effects in Southeast Asia.

Other dynamics of assertive Chinese nationalism could affect the PRC's policies toward the overseas Chinese in Southeast Asia, toward state-to-state relations with countries in the region, and toward assistance to destabilizing forces in the area. The range of possible actions is simply too broad to analyze without specifying the particular combination of circumstances that produce and sustain the abandonment of reform—a task beyond the scope of this paper.

Conclusion

The above analysis leads to three broad conclusions. First, during the years directly after Deng Xiaoping's demise (assuming that this period begins before the radical reforms have been implemented), China will probably go through a period of moderate reform or abandonment of reform. Second, over a longer term, the chances of a resurgence of radical reform will grow, to the extent that this becomes the most likely future one or two decades hence (assuming that the external economic and security environments remain conducive to this). And third, what has been termed here moderate reform holds the most favorable prospects for the ASEAN countries,[33] as this creates strong incentives for China's constructive engagement of the region while limiting the PRC's ability to compete in unsettling fashion with the ASEAN economies.

---

[33]Analysis of the implications for ASEAN of the much less likely corrupt regime or system breakdown scenarios is beyond the scope of this chapter.

2. Political Leadership and Development in China

ABHINYA RATHANAMONGKOLMAS

For a long time to come, at least for the 18 years until the end of the century, we must bend every effort to do the following four things: restructure the administration and the economy and make our cadre ranks more revolutionary, younger in average age, better educated, and professionally more competent; strive to build a socialist civilization which is culturally and ideologically advanced; combat economic and other crimes that undermine socialism; and rectify the Party's style of work and consolidate its organization on the basis of a conscientious study of the new Party's Constitution. These will be the most important guarantees that we keep to the socialist road and concentrate our efforts on modernization.

Deng Xiaoping
Opening speech at Twelfth CCP Congress
September 1, 1982

It is obvious that there have been socioeconomic and political changes in the People's Republic of China since Deng Xiaoping resumed his leadership role. These changes reflect an attempt to combine the struggle for equality with the struggle for economic modernization. It appears that this combination is difficult to achieve, for economic modernization has received more emphasis than social equality.[1] The social differentiation and material incentives that Mao Zedong attempted to eradicate continue to exist.

In the communist system, the degree to which economic development/modernization correlates with internal political change is still a matter of debate. However, many scholars insist that political change in the communist regime is more or less an unavoidable consequence of economic development, "since changes in the economic base inevitably required changes in the political superstructure."[2] This chapter assumes that change in the means of economic development has an impact on the leadership. Development is considered to be one factor

---

[1] For the details on racial inequality in China, see David M. Lampton, "New 'Revolution' in China's Social Policy," *Problems of Communism* (September-December 1979): 16–33.
[2] H. Gordon Skilling, "Group Conflict and Political Change," in Chalmers Johnson, ed., *Change in Communist Systems* (Stanford, Calif.: Stanford University Press, 1970), pp. 229–32.

influencing the performance of the political system, thus indirectly affecting the pattern of structural change.

Development of China's Economy

To understand present economic strategies in China, we must focus attention on past policy decisions. Since 1949, the Chinese have faced economic problems. Deng's attempt to establish economic development as a national priority can be traced back to the early 1960s. At that time, Deng was labeled a "revisionist," or "rightist," because of his idea that economic distribution should be "to each according to his ability," a view in direct opposition to that of Chairman Mao. Deng was forced from the Chinese political scene for almost a decade.

The demarcation of the Two Line Struggle, between the "leftist" idea of Mao and the "rightist" idea of Liu Shaoqi and Deng,[3] reflects the differing conceptions of the two groups concerning man and human nature. The revolutionary experiences of the Maoists taught them to believe that man and human nature were active, capable, and self-propelling entities. On the other hand, the followers of Liu Shaoqi tended to view man as reactive and passive in the face of stimuli from external forces, especially with regard to technology and economic development. In their eyes, material incentives and rewards were an essential part of the strategy to motivate man to participate in development and the nation-building process. The differences between the two camps served as a framework for postulates about the goals, the processes, the climates, and the actors of development.

The goal of development, in both the leftist and rightist views, is concerned with the availability and growth of consumer goods and basic industry. However, the leftists emphasize equity in growth—"to each according to his need." This emphasis leads to mass organization and mass participation as a development policy. In contrast, the rightists emphasize the efficiency of growth. The emphasis on the rational allocation of resources guides the rightists to choose a developmental policy that yields the highest return. Therefore, the most efficient forms of production—for example, a reliance on expertise, capital investment, and high-technology—are employed.

The leftists focus on the spiral process of accumulating capital, skills, and technologies for development through "self-sufficiency." This process involves scattering resources and intensive labor. From the

---

[3]Jack Gray, "The Two Roads: Alternative Strategies of Social Change and Economic Growth in . . . China," in Stuart R. Schram, ed., *Authority, Participation, and Cultural Change in China: Essays by a European Study Group* (London: Cambridge University Press, 1973).

rightists' point of view, rapid, efficient development results from a high rate of capital investment and technology-intensive techniques.

These contradictions contribute to the differentiation of the two lines in terms of the developmental climate and actors involved. The leftists prefer masses as developmental actors to the rightists' use of skilled and educated persons. Allowing the masses to participate in the developmental process, for the leftists, is not just for the purpose of production but also for individual learning and self-transformation. These ideas are linked to the developmental climate. The leftists sacrifice "order" for the "transformation" seen in the case of the Great Cultural Revolution; the rightists insist on the discipline of organization in transformation in order to avoid social disorder.

With these two development views in mind, many scholars believe that politics in China during the Cultural Revolution through the downfall of the Gang of Four was a power struggle to legitimize a specific strategy.[4] Whether this is the whole truth or not, China could not move into the post-Mao period without carrying over some conceptions. Hence, when Deng resumed his leadership position in 1976, he brought his former rightist strategy for economic development. Combined with some leftist ideology, this strategy is now viewed as the "moderate" line.[5] China has experienced a series of swings in its primary political and economic schemes as characterized in Table 1.

The moderate line of economic development in China appears, now, in the well-known policy of Four Modernizations. Through the variables listed in Table 2,[6] one can see that this moderate line is a deviation from the left line of Mao, which was considered the socialist approach for development. The use of the world market mechanism and of material incentives are proof that this strategy does not rely on a rigid conception of socialist economy in order to reach the goal of equal distribution to the masses. Instead, the leaders are willing to employ many different conception methods to secure "the big pie" for the socialist state. In short, while Mao worried about the means of economic development,

---

[4]For examples, see the works of Parris Chang, *Power and Policy in China*, 2d ed. (University Park and London: Pennsylvania State University Press, 1978); Joseph W. Esherick and Elizabeth J. Perry, "Leadership Succession in the People's Republic of China: Crisis or Opportunity?" *Studies in Comparative Communism* 16:3 (Autumn 1983): 171–77.

[5]For these varied interpretations, see the Bulletin of Concerned Asian Scholars, ed. *China from Mao to Deng: The Politics and Economics of Socialist Development* (New York: M. E. Sharpe, Inc., 1983).

[6]I would like to thank Dr. Jean C. Robinson, Department of Political Science, Indiana University at Bloomington, for her contribution to this table.

Table 1

Political and Economic Events by Time Period

Years	Characteristics of Events
1950–54	Employed the Soviet model for economic development: emphasized expertise and minimized reliance on mass mobilization
1955–56	Moved slightly to the "left": idealized collectivization and mass mobilization for both economic and political goals
1956–57	Shifted to the "rightist" line of development, organizing One Hundred Flowers Movement giving political freedom and using political mass mobilization campaign
1958–60	Great Leap Forward Movement: stressed mass participation in political and economic change
1961–65	Returned to the "right" line, emphasis on commerce and central planning for economic development, increased bureaucracy, more freedom to intellectuals
1966–69	Extreme "left" line, antitechnology, antispecialist
1969–76	Slow amalgamation of the "left" and the "right" lines of economic development
1976 to present	Carrying the "moderate" line

Deng worries about the results. The Deng policies and results influence patterns of recruitment.

New Status of Leadership

Changes in leadership patterns are a consequence of the changes in economic development. Illustrating the change in the Chinese view on economic value of development, Deng said:

> [T]o accelerate economic growth, it is essential to increase the degree of specialization of enterprise, to raise the technical level of all personnel significantly and train and evaluate them carefully, to greatly improve economic accounting in the enterprises, and to raise labour productivity and rates of profit to much higher levels. Therefore, it is essential to carry out major reforms in the various branches of the economy with respect to their structure and organization as well as to their technology.[7]

---

[7]Deng Xiaoping, "The Working Class Should Make Outstanding Contributions to the Four Modernizations," speech at the Ninth National Congress of Chinese Trade Unions, in *Selected Works of Deng Xiaoping* (1975–82) (Beijing: Foreign Languages Press, 1984), pp. 146–47.

Table 2

Pattern of Economic Development in China

In terms of:	Left	Right	Moderate
Motive force	Ideology	Organization	Organization
Method of organization	Enthusiasm (via mass mobilization)	Discipline	Discipline
Leadership style	Mass line	Party	Party and mass
Forces of production	Human	Science/ technology	Science/ technology
Form of education	Red	Red/expert	Expert
Division of labor	Generalist	Expertise	Expertise
Economic emphasis	Agriculture/ heavy industry	Industry	Agriculture/ industry
Type of growth	Labor intensive	Capital intensive	Labor/capital intensive
Implementation of start	Dialectical	Planning	Planning/market
Start of participation	Decentralization to immediate level	Centralization	Centralization/ decentralization
Incentive	Moral/group	Individual	Individual material/ consumption goods
Economic foreign relations	Self-reliance/ isolation	Soviet/socialist camp	World market

This is in essence a demand for technical expertise to perform functional specialization. The emphasis on the role of the generalists in Mao's era has been changed (see Table 2), followed by changes in the form of education. The personnel for this new economic development scheme are expected to contribute their specific skills and techniques derived from a new form of formal higher education and from a socialization in a modernizing society. These cadres tend to be younger than prior Chinese cohorts and to be intellectuals with higher education levels.

Along the moderate line of economic development, the need to promote growth requires expertise in science and technology as well as managerial ability. This development policy encourages professionalization in occupations. Moral incentives have been deemphasized and sometimes replaced by the use of materials and consumption goods. The school system thus becomes the major avenue to upward mobility.

These conditions help create circumstances for the emergence of technocrats in the Chinese communist system. Furthermore, they influence the pattern of elite recruitment and change "revolutionary" to "modernization-oriented" values as the basis for selecting cadres to carry out programs of economic reform.

These "technocrats" or "managerial modernizers" or "revisionists" or members of a "new class,"[8] therefore, must also possess certain administrative and personal abilities. This Chinese new class can be seen in the leadership categorization found in the Chinese Communist Party (CCP) document of October 1983, after the Twelfth Party Congress. Here, the CCP made the following decisions. Those who are aged about seventy years or more are the first echelon. They are old revolutionaries who "should retire to an advisory role." The second echelon, aged about sixty years old, is recognized as containing the day-to-day adminstrators. The third echelon contains the future leaders in training, aged about thirty-five to forty-five years old.[9] Thus, the members of the new class are the young experts.

The government in the post-Mao period has tried to ease the disparity of educational opportunities occurring between those in urban and rural areas. However, urban dwellers enjoy more advantages than their rural counterparts.[10] The continued implementation of a policy for economic growth that stresses specialization will certainly aggravate the interprovincial and urban-rural inequities. Yet, it seems that the present Chinese leaders prefer economic modernization to social equality. As

---

[8]These terms are different but possess similar characteristics. See William A. Welsh, "Elites and Leadership in Communist Systems: Some New Perspectives," review article in *Studies in Comparative Communism* 9:1–2 (Spring-Summer 1976): 165–66; David S. G. Goodman, "The National CCP Conference of September 1985 and China's Leadership Changes," *China Quarterly* 105 (March 1986): 127; Lowell Dittmer, "Chinese Communist Revisionism in Comparative Perspective," *Studies in Comparative Communism* 13:1 (Spring 1980): 20–39; Milovan Djilas, *The New Class: An Analysis of the Communist System* (New York: Praeger, 1957), pp. 37–69.

[9]Goodman, "National CCP Conference," pp. 128–29.

[10]Lampton, "New 'Revolution,' " p. 31.

Dittmer points out, "[T]his may be justified in theoretical terms by arguing that a more egalitarian social order will inevitably follow modernization in accordance with the logic of historical determinism, but that equal distribution requires first that there be sufficient surplus to redistribute, and the accumulation of a surplus in turn depends upon industrialization."[11]

Consequently, inequalities in the opportunity to gain leadership status may provoke a conflict. Moreover, communist systems do not easily mediate conflict. Violence may occur again in the resolution of power struggles. Past experience suggests that Deng will try to avoid this situation. In an attempt to prevent it, Deng has engaged in efforts to promote restructuring of the political regime.

We see a shift away from command, dogmatic modes of action toward procedural and empirically oriented modes. "Learn truth from facts" means that organizations and cadres are to persuade rather than coerce. We see the restructuring of the Party's leadership from a charismatic to a more oligarchical one. The charismatic pattern of Mao is to be followed by a collective leadership that emphasizes experts and political managers. A significant degree of functional or expert autonomy is to be granted to scientists and artists.[12]

The political change just described is connected to the process of succession in China—that is, the consolidation of the power of Deng and his colleagues. The technique employed to continue the new policies as well as to stabilize the political system was revealed in the streamlining of provincial leadership in the spring of 1983 and in the subsequent reforms at the provincial level and below.[13] The creation of the Central Advisory Commission as an honorary halfway house for veteran leaders of the "revolutionary generation" made the 1983 provincial transfer of power less difficult. It should be noted that the new breed of administrative specialists who are to become provincial leaders has two or more areas of expertise.[14] However, Mills reminds us that political reliability remains a far more important qualification for high office than technical expertise.[15]

---

[11]Dittmer, "Chinese Communist Revisionism," p. 30.
[12]These three conceptions are derived from Kenneth Jowitt, "Inclusion and Mobilization in European Leninist Regimes," in Jan Triska and Paul Cocks, eds., *Political Development in Eastern Europe* (New York: Praeger, 1977); and Richard Lowenthal, "On Established Communist Party Regimes," *Studies in Comparative Communism* 7:4 (Winter 1974).
[13]William deB. Mills, "Leadership Change in China's Provinces," *Problems of Communism* (May-June 1985), pp. 39–40.
[14]Goodman, "National CCP Conference," p. 129.
[15]deB. Mills, "Leadership Change," pp. 29–30.

In conclusion, a need for younger technical experts to administer state activities is compatible with some economic values of capitalism. This need leads to a new pattern of succession and to the transformation of the "revolutionary generation." The emergence of a class of "managerial modernizers" with some bourgeois characteristics is inevitable. There is no value consensus between the "revolutionaries" and the "managerial modernizers," but political change brought about by a new recruitment pattern strengthens the managerial modernizers.

New Type of Leadership and Southeast Asia

The reaction to capitalist economic values can be seen in the prescriptions for and implementations of Chinese economic policy. The conception of the Four Modernizations and the strategy of "to each according to his work" are the ends and means China is using to reach higher growth.[16] "Equity" is considered the equal opportunity to enjoy the fruits of economic growth in satisfying basic human needs. Chinese society would like to improve its economic position, and its citizens are capable of learning to operate the machines and to follow the scientific procedures that might lead to such improvement.

If we consider the political behavior of the present Chinese leaders, we will find that some behavior may be compatible with the economic plan. Some Chinese leaders emphasize the diffusion of new economic cultures and institutions such as free competition and connections to the world market. There is stress on the role of technocrats as the major developmental actors. With respect to military matters, some post-Mao policies advocate lower personnel levels and reduced budgetary allocations. The recent reduction in military expenditure, the retirement of troops and officers, and a renewed stress on professionalism are examples of this tendency.[17]

The willingness to experiment with "capitalist" means of economic development in the socialist states suggests that antagonistic contradictions between capitalist and socialist values are not inevitable. The diffusion of these values may lead to the replacement of conflict with "peaceful coexistence" in the international community. The economic and social policies pursued since 1978 indicate a strong potential for China to use the world market for its increased economic growth. The turning of China's attention to long-deferred tasks of restructuring the

---

[16]For details of these conceptions, see Xue Muqiao, *China's Socialist Economy* (Beijing: Foreign Languages Press, 1981).
[17]*The Nation* (Bangkok), October 9, 1986, p. 4.

economic system, raising the living standard of the population, upgrading the technological level of Chinese industry, and reducing the size of the Chinese military establishment may help make "peaceful coexistence" a reality in Southeast Asia. Intensified intellectual and commercial exchanges between the member states of the capitalist system and China will increase. All of these activities may help realign the international power balance in the region as well as facilitate diverse forms of commerce between the two systems.

This discussion of development does not adequately explain the increasingly amicable relations between China and Southeast Asia. China's national security must be of concern as well. The Sino-Soviet struggle shows signs of improvement through the resumption of economic, cultural, and personnel exchanges. However, three obstacles to Sino-Soviet normalization—for example, the Sino-Soviet border conflict, the Kampuchean problem, and the Soviet invasion of Afghanistan—still limit progress. Despite some efforts to improve the relationship between China and the Soviet Union, normalization is still a long way off. The Soviet Union remains a security threat to China.[18] In order to lessen this threat, China's foreign policy toward Southeast Asia must aim to develop friendly ties and support.

The interests of China in Southeast Asia are to develop economic relations with the region in order to assist its own development program, and to counter efforts by the Soviet Union to consolidate "regional hegemonism." Hampering these goals are the worries of Southeast Asian nations over Beijing's support for revolutionary movements in the region and the problem of the overseas Chinese. (Other chapters in this volume discuss these problems.) Present Chinese leaders recognize those obstacles and are trying to reduce them. There have been efforts to minimize China's ties to Southeast Asian revolutionary movements: they completely shut down the "Voice of Thai People" of the Thai Communist Party on July 7, 1979,[19] and the "Voice of the Malayan Revolution" of the Malayan Communist Party on June 30, 1981.[20]

---

[18]Jonathan D. Pollack, "China's Changing Perceptions of East Asian Security and Development," *Orbis* (Winter 1986): 774–75.

[19]Thai Friend Group in Europe, *Crisis in Present Progressive Thais* (in Thai) (Bangkok: Sarn Muan Chon Publishing, 1982), p 161.

[20]Donald H. McMillan, "The Maintenance of Regional Security in the Southeast Asian Region: China's Interests and Options," in T. B. Millar, ed., *International Security in the Southeast Asian and Southwest Pacific Region* (Queensland: University of Queensland Press, 1983), p. 251.

China will, nonetheless, continue its support of revolutionary movements. This support issue is of importance in China's domestic politics as continued evidence of the Chinese Communist Party's commitment to revolutionary struggle.[21] The growth of the Chinese government role in policy in contrast to that of the Party has implications for Southeast Asia. Recent information suggests that the growth of government authority in all levels lessens the Party's role in daily government and economic affairs. In a circular published on October 30, 1986, the Central Committee of the CCP and the State Council called on rural party officials to cease running all the practical affairs of government and to concentrate on the Party line, both principle and policy.[22] Nevertheless, with the collective leadership, China will avoid linking "government-to-government" with "party-to-party" relationships with Southeast Asian countries.

The main concern of Southeast Asian governments is the problem of national security, because most of the local Communist Party members in the region are assumed to be ethnic Chinese. In addition, Beijing's ambiguous position on the legal status of some of the overseas Chinese community makes matters difficult.[23] The problems of Indonesia in 1965 are well remembered by Southeast Asian leaders. Moreover, many Southeast Asian governments are unable to determine the extent of support for Communists among their overseas Chinese residents.

The interest of China in the overseas Chinese in Southeast Asia has an economic component. The ethnic Chinese, numbering about 18 million, hold economic rather than political power. They are the top investors and traders, and provide a reservoir of professional expertise and skilled manpower that could contribute to China's economic development. The problem for Southeast Asian governments is whether or not the links of overseas Chinese to their ancestral home are incompatible with loyalty to the states in which they now reside.

Besides being the source of manpower and financial support, Southeast Asia can provide raw materials and technological know-how on a basis compatible with Chinese economic interests. The Southeast Asian region is a promising market for Chinese export goods and services as well as joint investments. However, the conservative Chinese

---

[21]Ibid., p. 252.

[22]*The Nation* (Bangkok), October 31, 1986, p. 9.

[23]For more details on how the issue of nationality relates to ASEAN security, see Purificacion Valera-Quisumbing, "ASEAN and China: Some Policy and Security Concerns," *Foreign Relations Journal*, 1:1 (January 1986): 123–50; and McMillan, "The Maintenance of Regional Security," pp. 253–54.

bureaucratic attitude toward international trade and investment remains a barrier to China's own economic development. The Chinese government is trying to modify its system to attract foreign investors and improve relations with foreign governments. Nevertheless, fear of China still seems to deter many Southeast Asian governments from fostering closer economic ties.

The desire to develop its economy, and the inadequate military capability to safeguard its security interests in the region, compel China to maintain a low, nonaggressive profile in its relations with Southeast Asian nations. National interest will cause China to maintain and promote amicable relations, a policy likely to be continued as long as the managerial modernizers dominate Chinese politics.

PART TWO

China's Economic Reforms:
Implications for Southeast Asia

3. China's Economic Reform

K. C. YEH

China's economic system is now undergoing fundamental changes, the outcome of which could have profound implications for China's own economic future as well as for other countries'. At this stage the reform is far from complete. Nonetheless, the goals and the broad outline of the reform program have been made clear by the leadership, and after eight years of experimentation, profiles of the new economic system are beginning to take shape. Meanwhile, many other countries are observing the development in China with great interest. It would be useful to take stock of the progress of the reform movement, to assess its prospects, and to evaluate its potential impact on other economies.

To this end, this chapter addresses two sets of issues concerning China's economic reform. The first deals with the reform movement itself. What is the purpose and nature of the reform, what has been accomplished so far, and where is it heading? The second set of issues concerns the international impact of China's economic reform. How might a postreform China with varying degrees of success affect the economic environment in Southeast Asia?

Purpose of Economic Reform

The purpose of China's economic reform is to improve overall economic efficiency by building a "socialist commodity economy" to replace the command economy that has been in existence since 1949. The basic elements that distinguish the old system from the new are summarized in Table 1.[1]

Essentially, the command economy is a highly centralized planned system in which economic activities are coordinated mainly by direct

---

[1] The organizational structure and degree of concentration of decision-making authority varied in the past. For a historical account of the evolution of China's economic system during 1949–78, see Zhou Taihe, *Dangdai Zhongguo de jingji tizhi gaige* (Reform of the economic system in contemporary China) (Beijing: China's Social Sciences Publishing House, 1984), pp. 1–158. The old system as described here refers to an abstract model that approximates the operational norm in the pre-1979 period. For a brief description of the workings of the system in the early 1970s, see Joan Robinson, *Economic Management in China* (London: Anglo-Chinese Educational Institute, 1975); and Liu Guoguang, "Zhong-guo shehuizhuyi jingji de liang da biandong" (Two major changes in China's socialist economy), *Xinhua wenzhai* (New China digest), no. 8 (1986), p. 49.

Table 1

Command Economy Versus Planned Commodity Economy

Basic Features	Command Economy	Planned Commodity Economy
Ownership pattern	Public ownership only	Public ownership predominant, with limited private and foreign ownership
Decision-making power	Highly concentrated in the hands of the state; decisions based on planners' preferences	Enterprises, households, and state share power; decisions based on multilevel preferences
Coordinating mechanism	Mandatory planning and direct allocation by the state	Markets and prices and guidance planning
Economic organization	Enterprises as administrative organs of the state; hierarchical structure of enterprises under various departments and local governments	Enterprises as independent economic entities; lateral economic ties among enterprises
Incentive system	Incentive system based on ideological mobilization; egalitarianism in income distribution	Incentive system based on material reward; lets some people become rich first

administrative means, its management is divided among departments and regions, and its income is distributed on an egalitarian basis. Prices and markets play virtually no role in resource allocation.

This system is patterned after the Soviet model, but it also has its origin in China's own wartime experience, both of which emphasize centralized decision making and direct allocation of resources. But China's decision to adopt a highly centralized system in the 1950s was not without economic justification. At that time China's transportation and communications systems were so backward and the legal framework so primitive that conditions for an efficient market system were lacking. Meanwhile, the party network had an efficient channel of communication and command through which the central authorities could obtain the necessary information for centralized decision making and to enforce policy implementation. Furthermore, the low per capita income and the lack of entrepreneurs limited the capacity to save and the incentive to invest. Therefore, the state had to assume the role of the entrepreneur, and it aggressively collected the agricultural surplus by compulsory measures and transformed it into industrial capital.

Although the organizational structure of the Communist Party provided an institutional framework that made the command system in China feasible, the system was not an efficient one. Indeed, the highly centralized command economy has many defects. It inhibits the vitality of the enterprises because the managers are not motivated to manage the enterprises (or communes) efficiently or to innovate. The most important success indicator in measuring a manager's performance is, the extent to which he fulfills or overfulfills his output quota. His efforts are therefore geared primarily toward this goal, disregarding production costs and quality control. The tensions and rigidity of the system put additional pressure on the manager to accelerate growth of output, encouraging him to hoard more raw materials, labor, and capital than necessary. He is not motivated to innovate because there is little reward for innovation, and there is the risk that a development program may jeopardize his meeting the production quota. If he makes a profit, all of it goes to the state budget. If he incurs a loss, the state subsidizes him. In short, there is no reward or penalty for his performance insofar as efficiency is concerned.

For the individual worker or peasant, there is no incentive to work hard because under the egalitarian principle of income distribution, his income would not increase if he does. Nor would he lose his job if he does not.

For the economy as a whole, the product mix determined by the planners often does not match the pattern of demand of the industrial users and consumers. The hierarchical network of control results in departmentalization, which in turn encourages self-sufficiency within the department and localities, thus sacrificing the economic benefits from specialization and economies of scale. The irrational price system inevitably misguides the planners in resource allocation. For example, the allocation of investment funds can hardly be optimal if capital costs are totally neglected.

Rough estimates of growth of total factor productivity in China during 1952–82 indicate that it was on average low by comparison with other developing countries,[2] suggesting inefficiencies in the use of capital and labor inputs and lack of technological advance. Supporting evidence of widespread inefficiencies includes large consumption of energy per unit of output, low agricultural yields, high incremental fixed capital-output ratios, large shares of increase in stocks in total gross capital formation compared with those of other developing countries, and huge subsidies to state-owned enterprises with financial losses. It is primarily to eliminate these inefficiencies and to improve productivity that the leaders have decided to reform the economic system.

Elements of the New System

The basic elements of the new system are listed in Table 1. To recapitulate, the model system is a planned market-oriented economy based on public ownership. Its specific features include the following:

1. Various ownership systems coexist, but public ownership remains predominant.
2. Enterprises, households, and individuals are independent economic entities with their own decision-making power, responsible for their profits and losses, and competing with one another.
3. The state regulates the market through economic, legal, and limited administrative means, and the market guides the enterprises. There are not only commodity markets but also factor markets and money markets. Prices are market-determined.
4. Income is distributed among enterprises and workers on the basis of more pay for greater efficiency and more pay for more work.
5. The functions of the government and enterprises are separated so that the enterprises are no longer administrative subordinates of various departments and local governments, and they are free to develop economic ties across departmental or regional boundaries.

---

[2]World Bank, *China: Long-Term Issues and Options* (Washington, D.C.: World Bank, 1985), p. 9.

The Reform Movement: Progress, Problems, and Prospects

How far has the current economic system been restructured along the lines of the new model? The reform movement began with changes in the rural economic organization in 1979. By the early 1980s the process of replacing the commune system with household farming was completed. Economic decision making has been largely shifted from the party cadres managing the communes, brigades, and production teams to the farm households. Rural markets multiplied in size and number. Prices of most agricultural products have been decontrolled. In 1985 state monopoly of the purchase and marketing of farm products was replaced by the contract system.

The economic effects of the rural reform are quite profound. The sweeping changes have greatly enlivened the rural economy. Agricultural output and productivity have increased markedly since 1978. The proportion of farm output sold at market prices trebled during the period 1978–84.[3] Rural industry, commerce, transport, and services rapidly developed, absorbing large quantities of surplus labor released from agriculture. In particular, the growth of rural industry was phenomenal.

In the urban economy, however, the progress of reform has been slow. The urban reform movement went through two stages. In the first stage, 1978–84, institutional changes were largely experimental and thus gradual. In the second stage, 1984 to date, a set of guidelines for reform was introduced.[4] To implement the reforms, the leaders have adopted the incremental or sequential approach, taking into consideration the uneven economic development in different regions, the shortage of management personnel, and political resistance from vested interests.

Up to now China has not had a detailed, comprehensive blueprint for reform.[5] However, the broad objectives and principal tasks have been clearly specified in the party's 1984 Decision and the Seventh Five-Year Plan.[6] At the present stage, the focus of the reform program is on enterprise reform, probably because of China's success with rural

---

[3]State Statistical Bureau, *Statistical Yearbook of China 1985* (Hong Kong: Economic Information and Agency, 1985), pp. 24, 479.

[4]For an account of the early stage of urban reform, see Zhou Taihe, *Dangdai Zhongguo*, pp. 159–209. For the decisions of the party, see Chinese Communist Party, *Decision of the Central Committee of the Communist Party of China on Reform of the Economic Structure* (Beijing: Foreign Languages Press, 1984).

[5]*Jiefang ribao* (Liberation daily), June 6, 1987, p. 3.

[6]Chinese Communist Party, *Decision of the Central Committee*; and Zhao Ziyang, "Explanation of the Formulation of the Proposed Seventh Five-Year Plan," *Beijing Review*, 28(40) (October 7, 1985) pp. i–xiv.

reform, which focused on motivating the farm households. The immediate goal of urban reform is to revitalize the enterprises. The method is to decentralize the economic decision-making power to provide the enterprise managers with the incentive, responsibility, and authority to operate efficiently. Within the framework of the state's mandatory plans and guidelines, the manager has the power to work out his own production and sales plans, to hire and dismiss workers, to decide on the size of bonuses, and to set prices within limits. The state also allows the enterprise to keep a portion of its profits after paying taxes. These changes require the manager to assume the role of entrepreneur, independent of the control of the party secretary under the new director responsibility system.

In reality, however, enterprise reform has not been very successful.[7] The enterprises have been granted only limited autonomy. Although the portion of total profits and taxes retained by the enterprise increased, the proportion retained was only 14.3 percent in 1984.[8]

The decentralization of decision-making power by itself is not sufficient to revitalize the enterprises. The manager's power has little use unless there are options open to him. His choices will not really maximize profits or minimize costs unless they are based on a set of rational prices. Hence, the reform program calls for other institutional changes to complement enterprise reform. The first and foremost of these changes is the development of markets and price reform. For most consumer goods and farm products the ration system has been abolished. Some capital goods are being sold on the market. Markets for technology and capital are beginning to appear. Labor markets have not yet developed possibly because the concept is alien to the Marxist doctrine that labor is not a commodity and therefore not tradable, and also because there are technical constraints such as housing shortages and institutional barriers restricting the individual's freedom of choice. In any event, by the end of 1984, there were 990 trading centers for daily use products, 646 trading centers for agricultural and sideline products, and 320 centers for producer goods. In addition, there were over 60,000 rural and urban markets.[9] At the same time, the number of commodities directly distributed by the state dropped sharply, from 256 items in 1980 to 23 in 1985.[10] In

---

[7] Liu Guoguang, "Zhongguo jingji tizhi gaige de huigu yu qianzhan" (Reform of China's economic system: Retrospect and prospect), p. 3; *Caijing wenti yanjiu* (Studies in financial and economic problems), no. 3 (1986), *Wen hiu pao*, August 10, 1987, p. 2.
[8] Liu Guoguang, "Zhongguo jingji tizhi gaige," p. 3.
[9] Ibid., p. 4.
[10] Ibid.

short, commodity markets and, to a lesser degree, factory markets have begun to emerge.

Together with the development of markets, price reform has also taken place. Over the period 1979–84, price reform was focused on the adjustment of irrational prices. For example, in 1979 the procurement prices of farm products were raised sharply and the sales prices of eight nonstaple foods in the cities were also raised. Subsequently, the prices of fuels and certain raw materials such as pig iron and rolled steel have been increased. The prices of some consumer goods such as cigarettes, beer, liquor, and cotton textiles were adjusted upward; some others such as those of synthetic fabrics were adjusted downward. In 1984 freight rates and passenger fares for railway and water transportation were raised.

Since 1984 reform efforts have shifted to the decontrol of prices. By the end of 1985, prices of most farm products had been decontrolled, with the exception of those for grain, cotton, and edible oils, which are purchased by the state under contracts. The prices of minor consumer goods have been completely decontrolled.[11] Heavy industrial goods are sold under three sets of prices: Those outside the state plan are priced by the sellers; those within the mandatory plan are sold at prices fixed by the state; and those within the guidance plan are sold at prices that can fluctuate within a certain range. In short, what we have is a multiple price system: fixed prices set by the state, floating prices controlled by the state, and market prices determined by supply and demand. In terms of sales volume, goods sold at fixed prices account for about 30 percent of the total, the rest being goods sold at state-guided or market prices.[12] All these are commodity prices. Factor prices such as wages, interest rate, and the foreign exchange rate remain under strict control of the state.

In order to pressure the enterprise managers to strive for higher efficiency and more profits, the authorities have introduced competition and penalties in the system. The structure of ownership has changed from an almost totally state-owned or collectively owned system into one that is still largely public-owned but has a limited number of private enterprises and joint ventures with foreign companies. For example, the share of retail sales by private traders in total retail sales increased from

---

[11]See Liu Guoguang, "Price Reform Essential to Growth," *Beijing Review* 29(33) (August 18, 1986), pp. 14-18; and Tian Jiyun, "Guanyu dangqian jingji xingshi he jingji tizhi gaige" (The current economic situation and problems of reforming the economic system), *Guangming ribao* (Guangming daily), January 12, 1986, pp. 1, 3.

[12]*China Daily*, September 7, 1987, p. 4.

0.7 percent in 1980 to 16.3 percent in 1986.[13] In the period 1979–86, foreign investment totaled US $8.3 billion. Over 7,000 enterprises with foreign capital have been established.[14] The revival of private and foreign business inevitably put the pressure on state-owned enterprises. Another type of pressure, a bankruptcy law, is now being investigated in Shenyang. Eventually, the state enterprises will not be able to rely on subsidies if they incur substantial losses.

To motivate workers, the former egalitarian principle in income distribution has been modified to permit the wider use of material rewards such as piece rate wages and bonuses that are linked to work performances. The centralized job placement system has been gradually replaced by a contract employment system, which in theory will remove the "iron rice bowl" and at the same time introduce some mobility of labor in the system.

With the decentralization of the decision-making power, the role of the state in managing the economy has also changed. Instead of direct economic regulation, its function is to exercise indirect control by economic means. For this purpose the government has instituted financial reforms by strengthening the banking system, by varying the interest rate to induce savings, by using bank loans instead of direct grants to finance investment and working capital of the enterprises, and by controlling the total supply of money.

To sum up, the leadership has taken some bold if small steps toward reforming the urban economy. But, as recognized by the Chinese themselves, the reform really has not made much headway, and thus far, its impact on the urban economy as a whole is not very significant.[15] According to one assessment, as of 1987, only 15 percent of the large and medium-size enterprises have been revitalized, 65 percent experienced little improvement, and 20 percent remained listless.[16]

---

[13]*Hongqi* (Red flag), no. 13 (July 1, 1987), p. 31.

[14]Ibid., no. 15 (August 1, 1987), pp. 37–38.

[15]Xue Muqiao, "Wo guo jingji tizhi gaige de huigu he zhanwang" (China's economic structural reform: prospect and retrospect), *Jingji ribao* (Economic daily), January 25, 1986, p. 3; and Zhou Shulian, "Pace of Industrial Development and Economic Structural Reform," in *Jishu jingji yu juanli yanjiu* (The study of technical economics and management), no. 5 (1985), pp. 2–7, translated in Joint Publications Research Service–China Report: Economic Affairs-86-055 (May 6, 1986), p. 53. See, however, more positive assessments by others such as Gao Shangquan, "Several Opinions on Restructuring China's Economic System," *Liaowang* (overseas edition) (Hong Kong), no. 32 (August 11, 1986), pp. 3–5.

[16]Zhou Shulian and Zhou Shaoming, "Shilun gaohuo da zhong qiye" (On revitalizing large and medium-sized enterprises), *Xinhua wenzhai* (New China digest), no. 4 (1987), p. 53.

Institutional changes other than enterprise reform are just as disappointing. In the view of a noted economist, "There have been no fundamental changes in the old system."[17]

Several factors have contributed to the sluggish development of the urban reform.

1. The first major problem is that the economic environment has not been factorable to economic reform. The marked difference in the results of rural and urban reform can be partly explained by the different initial conditions under which these reforms took place. In the countryside, most peasants were knowledgeable about farming. The infrastructure was there. What was lacking was the peasants' incentive to produce. The dismantling of the commune system, the upward adjustment of procurement prices, and opening the rural markets took care of that problem. By contrast, in the urban economy, there was a shortage of qualified personnel who could perform as entrepreneurs knowledgeable in the fields of management, operation, cost control, and marketing. The infrastructure was grossly inadequate. Energy supply was acutely short. The transportation system, originally designed for a regionally self-sufficient economy, became overloaded. The markets were hardly developed and the prices were, by and large, irrational. The enterprise director thus faced much more difficult problems than his rural counterpart.

Another major difficulty is that these structural changes had to be made under chronic and persistent inflationary pressure. There had always been repressed inflation in China, as evidenced by the higher market prices than the state-fixed prices wherever they coexisted.[18] The basic cause of inflation prior to the reform was overinvestment by the state. The decentralization of decision-making power following the reform has actually intensified the propensity to overinvest because the leaders' emphasis on growth of output remained strong and the enterprises were motivated to increase output by expanding investment. In addition, the peasants' investment in housing increased sharply as their income rose. Moreover, consumer demand surged upward as a result of wage increases, changes in the age structure of the population, urbanization, and the international and interregional diffusion of new con-

---

[17]Liu Guoguang, "Zhongguo shehuizhuyi jingji," p. 51.
[18]See, e.g., State Statistical Bureau, *Zhongguo tongji nianjian 1986* (Statistical yearbook of China 1986) (Beijing: China Statistics Publishing House, 1986), p. 632.

sumption patterns.[19] At the same time, fiscal and monetary means to control inflation have not been adequately developed. As supply bottlenecks emerged, the authorities restored direct administrative controls, thus thwarting the reform movement. A case in point is price reform. Fear of open inflation has now inhibited further decontrol of prices.

2. The decision to adopt an incremental approach to reform inevitably creates a situation in which the old and the new system coexist. The problem is that at the present stage the old system still predominates over the new. By and large, economic activities are still coordinated by administrative decrees rather than by the market mechanism.[20] Under this dual system, frictions and conflicts arose. For example, the reform provides the managers certain powers. However, the managers are still so hamstrung by myriad administrative rules and regulations that they have no choice but to keep one eye on the higher authorities and another on the market. Worse still, a number of administrative organizations are preventing the enterprises from practicing their powers.[21] In 1985, the percentage of taxes and profits retained by the state-owned enterprises was 17.5 percent. Yet out of this retained portion the enterprise had to pay other taxes and levies so that the enterprise was actually left with less than 11 percent of the total taxes and profits.[22]

The most difficult problem is that of dual prices: fixed prices set by the state and market prices outside the plan. Because of the inflationary pressures noted above, there is usually a wide gap between the official and market (or negotiated) prices. The result is that enterprises attempt to divert their resources to produce more output outside the plan, often at the expense of planned production.[23] Another consequence is that fair competition among enterprises is impossible because those who can obtain their supplies of raw materials from the state or those who can bargain for a lower output quota will be able to generate larger profits even if they are less efficient than other producers.

Quite apart from the frictions of the old and the new system, the reform movement itself has created a host of new problems. Prior to the reform the structure of output was primarily determined in accordance

---

[19]Liu Guoguang et al., "Jingji tizhi gaige yu hongguan jingji guanli" (Reform of the economic system and macro-economic control), *Jingji yanjiu* (Economic research), no. 12 (1985), p. 14.

[20]Ibid., p. 7; *Guangming ribao* (Guangming daily), October 20, 1987, p. 1; *Jiefangjun bao* (Liberation Army daily), September 15, 1987, p. 3.

[21]Song Tingming, "Review of Eight Years of Reform," *Beijing Review* 29(51) (December 22, 1986), p. 18.

[22]Zhou Shulien and Zhou Shaoming, "Shilun gaohuo da zhong qiye," p. 55.

[23]Liu Guoguang, "Zhongguo shehuizhuyi jingji," p. 52.

with the planners' preferences. Now, as a result of the reform, the farm households, managers of enterprises, and consumers share some of the decision-making power, each exercising effective demand on the market according to their own preferences. The change from planners' sovereignty to users' sovereignty generally requires a corresponding change in output structure. However, because of the rigidity of the existing system, bureaucracy, and supply bottlenecks, the structure of output often does not match the pattern of demand, resulting in excess demand for some products and unsold inventories for others.

In agriculture, the return to household farming has resulted in fragmentation of farmland. It also hinders population control because the economically independent peasants are less responsive to economic sanctions by the cadres. More serious still, rural infrastructures, particularly the water conservation facilities, that were previously maintained by the communes are now largely neglected.[24] In the urban economy, the decentralization of decision-making power gave rise to problems of suboptimization at the enterprise or local levels. For example, some managers squandered their financial resources to bonus payments or duplicated each other in building factories in order to produce products that yielded high profits in the short run. Some local authorities, in order to increase local revenue, prohibited imports from other provinces to protect the local industry.[25] Then, there is the abuse of power for personal gain by government officials. Bribery, embezzlement, extortion, smuggling, and selling information are quite common.[26] Such practices not only make it difficult for legitimate businessmen to operate, but also strengthen the position of those opposing reform who argue that economic reform inevitably breeds unhealthy trends. This brings us to the third major factor underlying the sluggish progress in the reform movement: political resistance to reform from party members and cadres.

3. Just as the political movement toward the socialist ideal under the Mao leadership bore within itself seeds of economic stagnation, economic reform disrupts the unit of the party and creates political unrest among the various groups. That there are frictions is indisputable. Apparently, some party leaders opposed the reform either on

---

[24]See *Jingji ribao* (Economic daily), September 11, 1985, p. 1; *People's Daily*, November 27, 1985, p. 5.

[25]*People's Daily*, October 8, 1986, p. 5. See also the case of Hunan government blocking the export of hogs to Guangdong to keep local prices down; *People's Daily*, October 4, 1986, p. 2.

[26]*China Daily*, January 30, 1986, p. 4; August 30, 1986, p. 4; *Jiefang ribao* (Liberation daily), December 7, 1984, p. 1.

ideological grounds or because they believe the system is not viable.[27] The political resistance by the cadres at lower levels seems a more serious matter.[28] Economic reform necessarily entails a redistribution of political power and economic benefits among these cadres. The decentralization of decision-making power and the development of markets take away some of the power of those formerly in charge of allocating resources and fixing prices. Within the enterprise, there is a shift of power, in principle at least, from the party secretary to the manager. Quite naturally cadres will resist any changes that will adversely affect their immediate political and economic interests. Cases of passive but persistent resistance to the transfer of power have been reported.[29]

With all these economic and political problems, what are the prospects of China's economic reform? The changes so far, although hesitant and limited in scale, show that the Chinese leaders are determined to push forward and that they are willing to bend on matters of ideology in order to achieve greater economic efficiency. In the Seventh Five-Year Plan period, the leaders planned to push forward with reforms that focused on the enterprises, markets, and macroeconomic control mechanisms.[30] In a report before the Thirteenth Party Congress in October 1987, Zhao Ziyang called for accelerating and intensifying the reform movement.[31] The program will center on reforming the internal mechanism of the enterprise as before, with supporting changes in the economic environment for the enterprise to operate as independent economic entities, such as reforms in the investment, financial, and market systems. But two new elements have been added. The first is the planning premise that China is still in the elementary stage of socialism, thus legitimizing policy measures that deviate from orthodox Marxist doctrines. The second is the party's intent to introduce political

---

[27] According to Hu Yaobang, there is no political opposition and no open program of resistance. Foreign Broadcast Information Service (FBIS), *Daily Report: China*, November 19, 1986, p. G2. For reports of policy disputes, see *Financial Times* (London), January 29, 1986; Zhongguo xinwen she (China news agency), October 19, 1986, reported in FBIS, *Daily Report: China*, October 20, 1986, p. K4; and Xue Muqiao, "Wo guo jingji tizhi gaige," p. 3.

[28] *People's Daily*, September 13, 1985, p. 2; FBIS, *Daily Report: China*, October 27, 1986, pp. K10–11.

[29] *People's Daily*, January 5, 1985, p. 1; *Economic Daily* (Beijing), June 2 and July 20, 1986; *Wen hui pao*, September 25, 1986, p. 10.

[30] Liu Guoguang, "Zhongguo shehuizhuyi jingji," p. 53.

[31] Zhao Ziyang, "Yanzhe you Zhongguo tese de shehuizhuyi daolu qianjin" (Advance on the road to socialism with China's characteristics), *Renmin ribao* (People's daily), November 4, 1987, pp. 1–4.

reform. The latter is crucial to the success of economic reform. This is because reforming the economic system involves not only remodeling the economic organizations and coordinating mechanisms, but also changing social and political institutions, ideology, attitudes, and habits. The sheer magnitude of the problem is overwhelming. Unless the party is solidly behind it, economic reform, which has been appropriately termed the second revolution, will fail because of political resistance to its implementation.

One can conceive of at least three different scenarios in the future. The first is that the reformists remain firmly in power and a smooth transition from the Maoist model to Deng's socialist commodity economy takes place. This scenario roughly corresponds to the Chinese leaders' goals and perceptions of the Chinese economy in the year 2000. By then China will have long succeeded in transforming a rigid, inefficient economic system into a dynamic, more efficient one. China's total GNP reached a level about one-half the size of Japan's in 1984, after growing at 7 to 8 percent per year for two decades. The economy will be characterized by much higher degrees of economic specialization, reliance on the market mechanism, and integration with the world economy than in the 1980s. After waiting patiently for economic modernization to proceed first, the military will get a substantially larger share of GNP for defense modernization. China will probably dominate the world market for certain light industrial products and will become a major exporter of oil, coal, grain, cotton, and arms. China's overall technological capability by the year 2000 will reach the levels of the 1970s or 1980s in the advanced countries.

A second scenario is that the reform movement encounters serious political and economic difficulties and the authorities are forced to move ahead gradually. The ideologues and those losing power continue to oppose and subvert the reform. The economy is persistently troubled by the many problems caused by frictions between the old and the new systems. During a prolonged transition period, only moderate economic growth is achieved. China may fail to reach its goal of quadrupling the 1980 GNP by the year 2000. But there is no stagnation; the situation is one of muddling through.

A third scenario is that the economic reform is unsuccessful due to political upheaval: The conservatives in the party, perhaps with the support of the military, come to power after a protracted struggle initiated by political reform. The new leadership abandons the reform as the economic situation worsens. A system of higher centralized, planned economy is restored. Economic growth continues, but at a much slower pace and at a much higher economic cost.

Implications for Southeast Asia

In view of the uncertainties surrounding the reform movement, one would have preferred to discuss the possible international impact of China's economic reform in terms of the alternative scenarios. However, for the present purpose, we focus only on the high-growth scenarios, not because it is the most likely but because its impact could be most significant.

Given such a scenario, what might be the economic implications for countries in Southeast Asia? First, the emergence of China as a major economic power will offer both opportunities and challenges in trade. With substantial economic growth, China could join the United States and Japan as the third major force in the Asian market. The growth of GNP and the open-door policy would mean an increase in the volume of China's trade, a small but nonnegligible portion of which would be with Southeast Asian countries. In 1985, the share of trade with ASEAN countries in China's total trade was 13 percent, not particularly large, but nonetheless significant because it represents a notable increase over 1980 during a period when China's total trade was expanding at a rapid rate of over 9 percent per year.[32] This trend is likely to continue partly because of China's growing demand for certain raw materials produced in these countries (rubber, wood and pulp, coca beans, jute and ambary hemp, and sugar) but primarily because China's trade with Singapore, by far the most important trade partner in this region, will probably continue to grow as China strives to earn more foreign exchange.

China had a trade surplus with the ASEAN countries in the last five years and the size of the surplus has been growing rapidly from US $0.5 billion in 1980 to 1.7 billion in 1985. From the standpoint of these countries, sustaining a large import surplus with China need not cause any alarm if their total exports and imports are roughly balanced. What may be of concern is possible changes in China's capability to compete with their exports in third markets. At present, China's capability is still handicapped by many unfavorable factors. Its real wage rates are not much lower than in other developing countries because the quality of labor is generally low, the incentive structure does not motivate the workers to exert their maximum efforts, and there are sizable hidden costs in the form of subsidies. Furthermore, the many shortcomings of

---

[32]For the share of ASEAN trade with China, see Jan S. Prybyla, "China's Economic Experiment: From Mao to Market," *Problems of Communism*, January–February 1986, pp. 21–38. For China's total trade, see State Statistical Bureau, *Zhongguo tongji nianjian 1981* (Statistical Yearbook of China 1981) (Hong Kong: *Jingji taopaoshe*, 1982), p. 353; and FBIS, *Daily Report: China*, April 18, 1986, pp. K1–37.

the enterprise management system noted above have resulted in manufactured products of poor design and quality, which cannot compete in
the world market except at low prices. Also, decades of isolation from
the outside world have left the Chinese totally unprepared for an
upsurge in foreign trade. The bureaucrats in charge of trade have little
marketing experience. For these reasons, China's exports at this stage
consist largely of natural resources (oil, coal), agricultural products (cotton, grain, aquatic products, raw silk), and low-priced manufactures
(cotton cloth, garments, shoes). The reform, if successful, will resolve
most of these problems, substantially increase productivity, and lower
the costs of export products. Moreover, other aspects of the economic
reform will also enhance China's competitive edge in world markets. A
rational price system will help to correct distortions in the foreign
exchange rate, making export subsidies unnecessary. The reform of the
science and technology system will stimulate technological advance and
innovation, an important element in the growth of export capacity in a
dynamic world.

The most important markets for China's exports are Japan and the
United States. These happen to be also the most important markets for
the ASEAN countries. Whether the latter countries will feel the pressure from China's competition and to what extent will depend on the
commodity structures of China's and these countries' exports. Some
commodities are more vulnerable than others, such as Thailand's rice
and corn, Indonesia's crude oil, and Malaysia's and Singapore's electronics products, textiles, and garments. But painful as it may be, China's competition will compel these countries to diversify and
restructure their exports toward technology-intensive products.

Still another major impact of the aggressive growth of China's
exports is that it could trigger the revival of protectionism in the developed countries, in which case not only China but the Southeast Asian
countries will be hurt. The difficulty that some Asian countries experienced recently in negotiating their textile agreements with the United
States is a case in point.

Apart from its emerging role as a major trading partner, China
could also affect international capital flows to other Asian countries.
One of the most important changes in the leadership's development
strategy is the decision to utilize foreign capital on a large scale. Foreign
capital is important to China's development because it alleviates the
shortage of domestic savings and foreign exchange. The need for capital
imports will probably remain a long-term problem because the demand
for resources to modernize defense and to improve the overall standard
of living will tend to depress the savings ratio even if per capita income
continues to grow. At this stage China's plan to attract foreign invest-

ment is running into difficulties. Foreign investors find it hard to make profits and even harder to remit the profits out of China. The government imposes heavy taxes on the labor and land used by the joint ventures, restricts the foreign investors' access to the domestic market, and provides no foreign exchange to convert earnings into foreign currency. More fundamentally, there is no effective legal framework to protect the investors' interests from the bureaucrats' interference. The economic reform, if successful, will greatly improve the environment for foreign investment. With a much higher per capita income, perhaps for the first time, the one-billion-people market will take on real significance.

Sustained economic growth will also greatly increase China's capacity to borrow. China will probably no longer be qualified for International Development Agency (IDA) loans but will surely be borrowing from the World Bank, Asian Development Bank, and foreign governments. China has also issued bonds abroad and will probably continue to do so. To a significant degree, China will be competing with Southeast Asian countries for foreign capital and, in some cases, for their domestic capital too because China also seeks to attract investment by the overseas Chinese. The impact could be profound because foreign capital has been quite important as a source of capital formation in the ASEAN countries.[33]

Deng Xiaoping has promised that "probably we will be able to provide more assistance to our poor friends when we make some progress by the end of this century."[34] Even if Deng's successors keep his promise, whether Southeast Asian countries will receive any significant amount of economic aid is uncertain mainly because such aid is generally influenced by political considerations. If the current pattern of Chinese economic aid is any guide, the amount will be negligible.[35]

China as a Development Model

China in the postreform era will have moved from an efficient centralized economy to a more efficient composite planned and market

---

[33]In the decade 1971–80, capital inflow as a percentage of gross domestic product in these countries ranged between 3 percent for Thailand to 10 percent for Singapore; Li-kung Ferng, *The General Situation, Foreign Trade, and Integration of ASEAN* (Taipei: Chung-hua Institution for Economic Research, 1983), pp. 6–8.

[34]*Wen hui pao*, November 5, 1986, p. 3.

[35]In 1984, Chinese economic aid to Southeast Asian countries accounted for less than 5 percent of the total, which itself was a meager US$526 billion; Central Intelligence Agency, *Handbook of Economic Statistics* (Washington, D.C.: Government Printing Office, 1985), p. 112.

economy. Together with its experience in sustaining a high rate of intensive growth, the new system may offer an attractive model for developing countries and socialist countries alike. The contribution of the market economy to rural employment is an interesting example.[36] The state used to drain resources from the agricultural sector through compulsory purchases at relatively low prices compared with industrial prices, thus depressing the peasants' income. Now, although the state continues to purchase farm products at contract prices, the prices are higher, reflecting an improvement in the terms of trade between agricultural and industrial products. More importantly, the state encourages the peasants to increase their income by producing a surplus and selling it in rural and urban free markets. The increase in agricultural income in turn generates a demand for goods and services that provides the impetus for the diversification of agriculture, the development of rural industries, and a construction boom in the villages. The outcome is a large increase in rural nonagricultural employment.

The most significant lesson to be learned from China's experience, however, is how it copes with the central issue of the cardinal economic choice that every nation, socialist or capitalist, must face: What is the appropriate role of the government and the market in the functioning of the economic system? It cannot be said that China already has found an optimal solution. Perhaps it never will. But even if the reform succeeds, in any attempt to emulate the Chinese experience, China's unique position in its development history as well as the political costs of reform must be taken into consideration. The current reforms are part of China's long and persistent struggle to transform a stagnant society into a dynamic economy. The historical events preceding the sweeping reforms of the 1980s created the pressures that made such reforms inevitable and at the same time set constraints on the effectiveness of the reforms. Frequently the reform movement has been called a second revolution quite appropriately because it requires changes of almost every aspect of one's economic and political life. Yet there is a fundamental difference between China's communist revolution and the present economic reform. The goal of the earlier movement was to seize power whereas the reform program requires not only ideological flexibility but also a cutback in the party's own political power. Any socialist country such as Vietnam that follows China's example must be ready to accept such restraint.

---

[36]In his talks with foreign visitors, Deng Xiaoping singled out this contribution as "an essential aspect of our successful experience"; *Wen hui pao*, November 5, 1986, p. 3.

Conclusion

We have sketched briefly China's reform program and explored some of the implications of a successful reform. It may be useful to recall that the high-growth scenario is based on the expectation of a continuous and stable political framework and that the leadership will pursue the current policies of reform and growth persistently during the next decade or so. Several factors could divert economic development from this projected course, among which the most important is the succession problem. It is uncertain whether the new generation of leaders will have the same political outlook and pursue the same policies as the current one. Other factors, such as the complexity of the reform itself and external events, could also affect the outcome of the reform. We have focused on the high-growth scenario simply because its impact is likely to be the most profound. But it does not mean that the other alternatives are less interesting or less plausible. In any event, from a Southeast Asian perspective, the impact of China's economic reform on the strategic environment is likely to be a mixed blessing.

4. Chinese Economic Modernization and ASEAN

REYNALDO TY Y RACAZA

When China decided to open its doors to the world, one of the immediate realities Beijing had to face was the need to improve relations with neighboring countries, including the six member states of the Association of Southeast Asian Nations (ASEAN)—Indonesia, Thailand, Malaysia, the Philippines, Singapore, and Brunei. Similarly, the ASEAN states had to deal with an emerging superpower that was, in many ways, still an underdeveloped nation. With the current modernization program in China and the changing political and economic climate in Southeast Asia, questions about the future of China's relations with ASEAN as a whole become a concern.

The People's Republic of China Today

The triumph of the socialist system in a country that holds a quarter of the world's population has drawn mixed reactions of praise and hostility. Nevertheless, it is a country closely watched by East and West alike.

In the pre-1976 period, China's accomplishments were readily attributed to Chairman Mao Zedong, who stood at the helm of the Chinese Communist Party. Under Mao the party overthrew Chiang Kaishek; destroyed feudalism, bureaucratic capitalism, and imperialism; established the socialist system; and constructed a foundation for China's future economic development. Although there was growth in urban-rural commerce, science, and public welfare and considerable progress in foreign trade, Mao's emphasis was on socioeconomic relations. He was constantly on guard against the reemergence of the new bourgeoisie.[1]

With the upheaval brought about by the Cultural Revolution and a change in party leadership after Mao's death, China turned to a somewhat new and unfamiliar road to socialist reconstruction. Some Marxists, socialists, and China-watchers abroad believe that the country is

---

The assessments and views expressed in this chapter are entirely the author's.
[1]This is widely discussed in the *Bulletin of Concerned Asian Scholars* 13(2) (April-June 1981): 3–12.

moving toward capitalism with its thrust toward modernization and for an open door policy. Some even brand as reactionary the direction of domestic and foreign trade.[2] Yet Mao himself had stated: "A serious task of economic reconstruction is ahead of us. Things in which we were well versed will soon be needed no longer, and we shall have to do things in which we are not versed. This is our trouble."[3]

After the fall of the Gang of Four, however, socialist reformation under the heading of modernization was given primary importance. As Deng Xiaoping stated in his opening speech to the Twelfth National Party Congress:

> In carrying out our modernization program, we must proceed from Chinese realities. Both in revolution and in construction, we should also learn from foreign countries and draw on their experience. But the mechanical copying and application of foreign experiences and models will get us nowhere. We have had many lessons in this respect. We must integrate the universal truth of Marxism with the concrete realities of China, blaze a path of our own, and build a socialism with Chinese characteristics—that is the basic conclusion we have reached after reviewing our long historical experience.[4]

The policy goal of the Four Modernizations was articulated by Zhou Enlai during the Fourth National People's Congress of the People's Republic of China held in 1975. Under this program, China seeks to "accomplish the comprehensive modernization of agriculture, industry, science and technology, and national defense before the end of the century."[5] Today, China is proceeding rapidly in its drive toward modernization.

Agriculture

In agriculture, economic incentives contained in a new system of farm management—the agricultural responsibility system—were started in 1979. This new policy eradicated egalitarianism, which was described as

> a product of petty production [which] is not compatible with the socialist principle of distribution according to work. The "Gang of Four"

---

[2]André Gunder Frank, "The Indochina Debate," *AMPO* (Tokyo) 13(1) (1981).
[3]From *People's Daily*, February 11, 1963, as quoted by Dick Wilson, *A Quarter of Mankind* (London: Pelican, 1968).
[4]Deng Xiaoping, opening speech, September 1, 1982, in *The Twelfth National Congress of the CPC* (Beijing: Foreign Languages Press, 1982).
[5]*Documents of the First Session of the Fourth National People's Congress of the People's Republic of China*, 1975 (Peking: Foreign Languages Press, 1979).

produced a situation in which there was no difference between working and not working, doing more or less, doing good and bad work. This attacked diligent people and encouraged lazy people and caused great harm to the development of production.[6]

The basic socialist tenet of distribution according to work was adopted. Peasants who produced more, whose households or labor power were better managed, would earn more.[7] The new policy also reduced the degree to which the peasants' work and output are determined by the state. In other words, management is now decentralized to maximize production intended to meet the assigned levels.

Combining the socialist principle of distribution according to work and the responsibility involved in self-management, the state not only allows but encourages the peasants to refine a diversified economy, which could help them raise their level of income. As a result of this policy in the management of agricultural production, the value of China's gross agricultural output reveals a steady annual increase (e.g., 7.5 percent average annual increase, 1979-82).[8]

Industrial Development

China has made it known officially that it intends to raise fourfold the gross annual value of its industrial and agricultural production by the end of this century. As the prime mover within the economy, industry must lead.

China has about 400,000 industrial and transport enterprises, which form the foundation for continued development of its industry. However, only 20 percent of these enterprises are equipped with relatively advanced technology and machinery. In another 20-25 percent the equipment is well maintained, but the technology is outdated. In the remaining 50-60 percent, not only is the technology outdated, but the equipment also needs to be replaced.[9]

Thus, in addition to building new enterprises, it is imperative to update the technology of the existing enterprises. Despite a gross annual increase of 7.2 percent in the industrial output value, with an 11.8 percent and 3.4 percent average increase per annum in light and heavy

---

[6]Wang Yengjin, Yang Zhangfu, and Wang Hongpei, "The Development of Agricultural Production and the Concern for the Peasants' Material Interest," *Jingji yanjiu*, no. 3 (1979):28.

[7]Su Wenming, ed., *China Today*, no. 6 (*Beijing Review* Special Feature Series), ch. 2, "Modernization—the Chinese Way" (Beijing: Beijing Review, 1983), pp. 17-18.

[8]*Statistical Yearbook of China, 1983* (Beijing: State Statistical Bureau, 1983).

[9]Su, *China Today*, p. 69.

industrial production, respectively,[10] technical transformation must be accelerated in order for the country to attain much larger growth. Prior to this technical transformation, two initial steps must be taken. One is the employment of Western technology that will suit the conditions and needs of present-day China. The second is the development of an administrative and economic strategy that will instill a favorable disposition on the part of Chinese scientists and technicians to participate in the technical transformation.

Science and Technology

"The key to modernizing China's science and technology lies not in whether the Chinese people have intelligence and wisdom, which they have, but in whether government policies will bring the people's intelligence and wisdom into full play."[11] The National Conference on Scientific and Technological Work, held in December 1980, disclosed that in science and technology, China would pursue a program of modernization in a socialist mode.[12] It is also evident in the guidelines that the primary impetus rests on the acceleration of economic development.[13]

Programs or statements notwithstanding, importing foreign technology is indispensable in order to develop Chinese science and technology. In the world today, production, commodity circulation, and science and technology are so highly developed that no single country has all the resources and know-how needed for expanding its economy. All countries, including the socialist ones, seek to take advantage of the growth and progress in other countries and promote their own economic growth by exchanging "what they have" for "what they lack" and soaking up the best they can find in others.[14]

Importation, however—the purpose of which is to learn from the technological development in other countries—has not led to the diminution of China's own scientific and technological investigations or progress.[15] On the contrary, it has been carried out under the watchful eye of those who value self-reliance. The importation of foreign techni-

---

[10]*Statistical Yearbook of China, 1983.*

[11]Su, *China Today,* p. 74.

[12]Yu Quangyuan, ed., *Principal Guidelines and Policies for the Development of China Science and Technology in China Socialist Modernization* (Beijing: Foreign Languages Press, 1984), pp. 633–34.

[13]Ibid., p. 634.

[14]Su, *China Today,* quoting Zheng Hongqing, p. 86.

[15]See Ch. 1 (General Provisions), Art. 1, of the Patent Law of the People's Republic of China (adopted at the Fourth Session of the Standing Committee of the Sixth National People's Congress, March 12, 1984).

cal know-how is primarily centered on those products that cannot be easily developed or mastered through self-study. The introduction of new technology must conform to the guidelines of Chinese domestic and foreign policy, notably, independence, self-reliance, equality, mutual benefit, and mutual good faith.[16]

Three mainstreams delineate China's foreign relations. When China decided to encourage the development of economic relations with the world—specifically, to allow foreign investors, to set up special economic zones (the functions of which are to boost transit trade, to attract foreign investment, to increase export trade, to expand scientific and technical exchanges, to develop tourism, and to promote the exploration of resources),[17] and to import material and nonmaterial technology as well as materials—China was at the same time establishing itself as a market. Second, when China's rank as a world exporter shifted from twenty-second to sixteenth,[18] the country became a world-class competitor. Finally, when China stands for lasting and fruitful international cooperation on the basis of complete equality and mutual benefit,[19] it becomes an unconventional friend who seeks and promotes mutual assistance.[20] Thus, China is a market, a competitor, and a friend of its Southeast Asian neighbors, with whom it shares a rich cultural heritage and economic and social ties dating back centuries. Still, tackling the question of current economic relations for these countries requires an understanding of the political climate prevailing in the region.

ASEAN: Strong Links with the West

The Association of Southeast Asian Nations is generally regarded as a regional grouping closely tied to the West. One reason is that the six ASEAN member states produce such commodities as rubber, tin, vegetable oil, sugar, and petroleum, some of which the United States, Japan, Australia, and Western Europe badly need. Second, ASEAN is a grouping of noncommunist nations, whose governments occasionally express an anticommunist ideology. Hence, the United States, Japan, Australia, and the European Economic Community have developed strong links

---

[16]"China's Economic Structure Reforms," *Chinese Documents* (Beijing: Foreign Languages Press, October 1984), pp. 28–29.
[17]Su Wenming, ed., *China Today*, no. 10 (*Beijing Review* Special Feature Series), "Interview with Gu Mu" (Beijing: Beijing Review, 1985), p. 25.
[18]Ibid., p. 5.
[19]Yu, *Principal Guidelines*, p. 670.
[20]Ibid., p. 691.

with ASEAN. In fact, when ASEAN foreign ministers meet, they are joined by their counterparts from the countries mentioned.[21]

With the triumph of socialism in the mid-1970s in the three Indochinese countries—Vietnam, Cambodia, and Laos—all six ASEAN countries banded together in fear that the socialist revolution would spread to neighboring countries. Today, in some ASEAN countries (the Philippines, Malaysia, and Thailand), people's "revolutions" exist, and their governments warn their people of the "communist threat."

Up to the present, these home-grown revolutions have not brought the ASEAN countries and China into conflict. Although the PRC has continued to proclaim support for Third World people's movements against imperialism, this support is limited to verbal declarations (except in the case of Cambodia and Afghanistan).[22]

Despite the troubled situation in Indochina and the communist insurgencies in some of the ASEAN states, China has opened its doors economically to ASEAN. China looks to ASEAN countries as a possible market for textiles, clothing, and light manufactures. In fact, China's exports to ASEAN nearly doubled during the period 1979–81, from $1 billion to $1.8 billion.[23]

China and ASEAN: Economic Prospects

For their part, before the ASEAN countries can predict a new market prospect for their commodities, they must consider the implications of the guidelines adopted by China for its importation policy. For products that can be manufactured at home in reasonable quantity to meet domestic demand, imports are to be limited. For products that can be manufactured at home, but not of a sufficiently high quality or in quantities not satisfying domestic needs, a certain number may be imported. Products that cannot be manufactured domestically but that are indispensable for certain sectors of the economy (including materials imports for joint ventures and compensation trade) will be classified as major import items. Priority will be given to imports of advanced products and technologies that can strengthen China's ability to develop independently and foster the Four Modernizations.[24]

The impact of China's modernization—as a competitor, as a market, and as a friend—could be viewed as follows: (1) Given the stringent Chinese guidelines for importation, export flow from ASEAN to China

---

[21]*Asia Yearbook* (Hong Kong: Far Eastern Economic Review, 1983), pp. 94–97.
[22]Ibid., p. 97.
[23]Ibid.
[24]Lawrence Fung, ed., *China Trade Handbook* (Hong Kong: Adsale People, 1980), p. 147.

will be limited; imbalance of trade in favor of Chinese exports to ASEAN will be the order. As the stress of the Chinese modernization drives favor the importation of technology that ASEAN lacks, China will continue looking for technology from regions other than ASEAN. (2) The entry of China into the world market can have considerable effects that could be detrimental to the ASEAN members. Competition may be sharp in the attraction of foreign investments, earning of foreign exchange, and labor export. And (3) some Chinese assistance to developing nations (a category to which the majority of the members of ASEAN belong) will continue. Also important are the implications of the Chinese modernization structures. The Chinese experience seems to prove that the adverse political, economic, and social effects that could stem from their strategies toward modernization can be controlled.

It seems likely, then, that China and the ASEAN countries may sustain relatively harmonious economic relations.

They also face common dilemmas. World recession as well as protectionist tendencies by major industrialized countries could block efforts toward progress and modernization. These protectionist tendencies have political overtones. Therefore, it is up to China and the ASEAN countries to discuss ways in which to provide mutual assistance and cooperation among themselves and against forces that may block their development and that of other similar Third World countries.

PART THREE

China's Military Policies:
Implications for Southeast Asia

5. Counter-Encirclement or Hegemonism? PRC Security Strategy in Southeast Asia

HARLAN W. JENCKS

China's military activity and strategy in Southeast Asia can be interpreted in two distinct ways. Southeast Asians tend to see the Chinese pursuing a variation on traditional Chinese hegemonism in the region, while the Chinese themselves view their efforts as defensive—intended to counter Soviet strategic encirclement of the PRC. While they may in fact be doing both, nearly everyone involved tends to see these two interpretations as mutually exclusive.

The first section of this chapter briefly summarizes the historical background and the geopolitical setting. While the historical dimension of Chinese "hegemonism" is widely recognized, the profound influence of geography on China's interactions with its southern neighbors is not widely appreciated, though it is arguably even more important. The following section examines PRC security strategy and military activity in the region, specifically in the two distinct geographical arenas of Southeast Asia: montane and maritime. Finally, future Chinese opportunities and risks are assessed, along with their implications for Southeast Asia.

Historical and Geographical Setting

Chinese military power, or the lack of it, has affected Southeast Asia for millennia. Certainly the Southeast Asian country most directly and frequently affected has been Vietnam, which suffered its first Chinese invasion and conquest by the Qin Dynasty in 218 B.C. Chinese military power has occasionally pushed into the mainland Southeast Asian massif.[1] Southeast Asia has been deeply influenced too, by the sporadic migration of peoples into the Southeast Asian massif from the north, as a result of war, conquest, and turbulence in China proper. Beyond this,

The opinions or assertions contained herein are those of the author and are not to be construed as official or reflecting the views of the Department of the Navy or any other U.S. government organization.
[1]Lim Joo-Jock, *Territorial Power Domains, Southeast Asia, and China* (Singapore: Institute of Southeast Asian Studies, 1985), pp. xi–xii.

however, only in one spectacular instance—the great voyages of the eunuch Admiral Cheng He in the early fifteenth century—has Chinese military power been felt beyond China's immediate southern border lands, by the coastal powers of Southeast Asia. Perhaps China's greatest military impact in the region was indirect: The competition and conflict among Southeast Asian maritime trading states for Chinese recognition and trade was vital.[2]

Despite its marginal military power in the region, China is, and has long been, a Southeast Asian state. The Chinese pursue their military security strategies toward Southeast Asia in the two geographical arenas which they share with their Southeast Asian neighbors.[3] The first arena is the mainland of Southeast Asia itself, where China, particularly in the interior parts of the border regions, enjoys enormous advantages vis-à-vis its neighbors. For the time being at least, China wishes to have peaceful and friendly relations with all but Vietnam, for Beijing strongly opposes creation of an "Indochina federation" dominated by Hanoi. The Chinese do not have to worry to any significant degree about military pressure from either of the superpowers in the interior mountains of Southeast Asia, where Soviet, and even American, air- and seapower are essentially irrelevant.

The second strategic arena is the maritime arena, which is a much trickier problem. Here, China's relatively inferior navy interacts not only with the two great powers, but also the formidable, if small, naval forces of the ASEAN states and the growing naval power of India. The South China Sea is the "core" or interior sea of Southeast Asia. China, with its harbor-rich southern coastline, its possession of Hainan Island and the Paracel (Xisha) Islands, and its claim to the Spratly Group, is very much part of the Southeast Asian maritime scene.

China shares with all of the mainland Southeast Asian states, except Cambodia, a share of the Southeast Asian massif, which stretches from the Himalayas in the west to the South China Sea. In this mainland Southeast Asian mountainous region, Chinese and various mountain peoples have interacted for many centuries.[4] Historically, the Southeast Asian mountains have served as a bridge, more than a barrier, between China and Southeast Asia, and they continue to do so today. For a variety of reasons, the Chinese generally have gotten along better with the residents of the mountains than have the peoples of

---

[2]Kenneth R. Hall, *Maritime Trade and State Development in Early Southeast Asia* (Hawaii: University of Hawaii Press, 1985), p. 43.
[3]Lim, *Territorial Power Domains*, passim.
[4]Ibid., pp. 37–38.

lowland Southeast Asia. Today, the Yunnan and Western Guangxi dialects of Chinese are widely spoken by the mountain peoples. Some of them, notably the H'mong and the Yao, still feel a traditional identification with their ancestral homelands to the north, in what is now the People's Republic of China (PRC). In contrast, the dominant peoples of lowland Southeast Asia tend to treat the mountain peoples with contempt. The only generic word for the mountain peoples in the Vietnamese language is *Moi* ("savage"); the only word in lowland Lao is *Kha* ("slave").

Many historians have pointed out that power in Southeast Asia has seldom been uniformly exercised throughout the territory of a lowland state. Power tends to diminish as the distance increases from the capital, and in the mountainous peripheries the power of the ruler is often weak or nonexistent. Indeed, the very concept of hard-and-fast borders is a European notion which was imposed upon Southeast Asia only in the last century. In most cases, current international borders have little reality in terms of either ethnic settlement or state administrative-political power at the peripheries. The notable exceptions, today, are the Socialist Republic of Vietnam (SRV) and the People's Republic of China, both of which effectively project their power right up to their border lines. Because of this, the Chinese and Vietnamese, by virtue of their strong administrative-political power, are at a decided advantage over the other countries of the region.[5]

One of the ironies of the pre-1949 situation, which persists to some degree in parts of montane Southeast Asia, was that internal conflict and disunity within a Southeast Asian state, which led to considerable bloodshed as the central government attempted to consolidate its power in the highlands, correlated very closely with international peace and stability. In effect, a region of intrastate conflict has served as a buffer zone, preventing the military power of two "core" lowland states from coming face to face. Since 1975, this buffer effectively has been eliminated along the Sino-Vietnamese border. Hardly surprisingly, it is there that conflict has most dramatically escalated to the point of full-scale conventional warfare. Only there are bloody battles fought over minor disagreements about the precise location of the boundary line. In most other areas of Southeast Asia, the precise location of the boundary lines is seldom of practical importance. The only other exception is in the Aranyaprathet corridor between the core homelands of the Khmer (occupied by Vietnam) and the Thai where, since 1979, there has also been significant conventional warfare.

---

[5]Ibid., pp. 53, 74, 209.

Since 1949, China has used its advantage in the mountainous regions along its southern border to apply "carrot-and-stick" measures to its Southeast Asian neighbors, to encourage them to pursue nonaligned policies, and to refuse to provide bases to maritime powers hostile to the PRC.[6] The nature of the Southeast Asian mountainous region made it easy for the Chinese to exert coercive power with little risk. It is easy to send across agents, supplies, and propaganda or simply to trade with dissidents or separatists. On the Chinese side of the border, training and logistical support also can be arranged for insurgents from the other side. Less powerful lowland states theoretically could ally themselves and unite to resist such Chinese pressure, but it really doesn't help unless they control their own peripheries. This state of affairs provided China with a stable and peaceful southern border from 1949 through 1975.

China's lopsided advantage ended when Vietnam finally managed to consolidate its own internal power and rid itself of foreign military occupation. The Vietnamese proceeded rapidly to push their administrative and political power out to their boundaries where, predictably, they came into conflict with China. That conflict has been extended westward into the mountains of Laos and, to some extent, the northern mountains of Burma and Thailand. Ironically, then, the Vietnamese victory over the United States, which was actively supported by the Chinese, gave rise to an unprecedented security threat on the PRC's southern border.

In the post-1975 period, and indeed since 1949, the perception in most of Southeast Asia of a Chinese military threat has not focused on China's ability to exploit in the montane zone, nor even on the presence of large numbers of Chinese traders and settlers in the mountainous areas of the various continental Southeast Asian states. Rather, the perceived Chinese threat to internal security has focused on the overseas Chinese (*Haw, Hoa, Huagiao*) living mainly in the cities of Southeast Asia. This urban population has been migrating to Southeast Asia for many centuries, not through the mountains, but by sea. The overseas Chinese issue is touched upon in many of the other chapters, and at length by Robert Ross and Chan Ngor Chong.

Fear of internal subversion by overseas Chinese tends to fuel fear of external aggression by the PRC. A notable proponent of this view is General L. B. Moerdani of Indonesia, who has stated on a number of occasions his belief that Vietnam poses no threat to Southeast Asia but that, on the contrary, the Vietnamese presence in Cambodia was necessitated by the Chinese threat to Vietnam. Moreover, Moerdani has

---

[6]Ibid., pp. 170–71.

urged closer ASEAN contacts with Vietnam, "to face the potential threat from a stronger China in the next century." He was quoted in 1984 as saying, "Some people are talking about a Vietnamese buffer between Southeast Asia and China—I don't want to put it that bluntly, but maybe that's what we're all thinking of."[7] Indonesian Foreign Minister Mochtar Kusumaatmadja, when asked if there was concern in Southeast Asia over Sino-American military ties, said, "Frankly, there is. We all agree that ultimately the biggest threat is China."[8]

Chinese Security Strategy

It can be argued that the Soviet threat, upon which the Americans and the Chinese are constantly harping, exists in Southeast Asia as a direct result of the Chinese threat to Vietnam. Without Sino-Vietnamese hostility, Soviet military bases in Indochina, with all their geopolitical-strategic consequences, would probably not exist.

The Chinese perception, of course, is quite different. They interpret their foreign military security problems primarily in terms of the threat from the Soviet Union, within the context of the currently primary global contradiction between the Soviet Union and the United States. The Chinese perceive the USSR to be engaged in a process of attempting to deprive the West of the critical resources and support of the non-aligned world. As an integral part of that strategy, they see the Soviets engaged in long-term efforts to encircle and dominate China. Steps in this strategy have included the conclusion of a mutual-security treaty with India in August 1971, the occupation of Afghanistan in late 1979, and, of course, the military-political relationship with Vietnam. According to the Chinese view:

> The Soviet Union moves from north to south while its proxy, Vietnam, moves from east to west to carry out Moscow's southward strategy that aims at controlling the oil-producing regions of the Middle East, North Africa, and the Gulf area, on the one hand, and Southeast Asia from the Strait of Malacca on the other, with the Gulf area being the most strategically important.[9]

---

[7]*Straits Times* (Singapore), December 17, 1984; quoted by Justus M. van der Kroef, in "'Normalizing' Relations with China: Indonesia's Policies and Perceptions," *Asian Survey* 26:8 (August 1986):919.

[8]*Asian Record*, July 1982, p. 10; quoted by van der Kroef, "'Normalizing' Relations," p. 919.

[9]Quoted from an unidentified PRC source by Yaacov Y. I. Vertzberger, *Coastal States, Regional Powers, Superpowers, and the Malacca-Singapore Straits*, Research Papers and Policy Studies no. 10 (Berkeley: Institute of East Asian Studies, University of California, 1984), p. 69.

The Chinese have been apprehensive about Soviet military encircle-ment since at least 1969, when Chairman Brezhnev first proposed his "collective security plan" for Southeast Asia, which was clearly intended to contain China. Such a security system was bound, accord-ing to the Chinese thinking of the time, to involve a strategic triangle of the Soviet Union, Japan, and India. Subsequently, Soviet relations with Japan soured while the relationship with Vietnam blossomed. The Chi-nese are now concerned that the strategic triangle of the Soviet Union, Vietnam, and India will attempt to control the sea lanes of Southeast Asia. China is, therefore, pursuing a "counter-encirclement" strategy, meaning "an indirect strategy that attacks the Soviet superpower mainly where it is deemed vulnerable and weak, in the diplomatic realm and particularly among the countries of the Third World."[10] Thus the Chinese see the Sino-Vietnamese conflict, and indeed China's rela-tionship with ASEAN, as part of the larger Sino-Soviet conflict.

The crux of the Southeast Asian problem, according to the Chinese, is the Soviet-backed Vietnamese invasion of Cambodia. The Chinese further assert that, if the Soviets and the Vietnamese succeed in destroying the Coalition Government of Democratic Kampuchea (CGDK) and legitimizing the Vietnamese occupation, then "Vietnam-ese expansion and Soviet-Vietnamese collusion would be further encouraged and more disasters would befall Southeast Asia."[11] Here we have a remarkable restatement of the "domino theory," which was pop-ular among certain American strategists in the 1960s and early 1970s.

China's "counter-encirclement" strategy explains why the PRC has tended to take the ASEAN side on a number of international issues, and to advocate strongly "Southern" views in virtually all "North-South" controversies. For example, China has supported such ASEAN initia-tives as the zone of peace, freedom, and neutrality (ZOPFAN) as a "framework for a peaceful Southeast Asia."[12] As we shall see, the PRC has also sided with the littoral states regarding control of sea frontiers and Southeast Asian straits.

Continental Strategy

With its 1975 conquest of power in the south, the Hanoi regime was able to establish Kinh-based power throughout all of Vietnam, from the

---

[10]Francis J. Romance, "Peking's Counterencirclement Strategy: The Maritime Element," *Orbis* 20:2 (Summer 1976):440–41.

[11]Ji Guoxing, "Current Security Issues in Southeast Asia," *Asian Survey* 26:9 (Sept. 1986):983.

[12]Ibid., pp. 985–86.

Tonkin lowlands to the frontiers of north Vietnam and south to the international borders in the Mekong Delta. This consolidation saw the disappearance of most areas on the state peripheries where Hanoi did not have full, effective control, but there were some exceptions. Parts of the northern border are still penetrable, particularly in the western regions where the Chinese have been able to infiltrate into Vietnamese-held areas. Further to the south, the Mekong Delta is wholly under Vietnamese control. The mountainous backbone of the Indochinese peninsula (what the Americans called "the central highlands") was, by about 1983, largely but not entirely free of insurgent activity. Today, Hanoi controls these mountains much more strongly than the Saigon regime ever did before 1975.

Nevertheless, there are still small numbers of Montagnards, anti-Vietnamese Laotians, and Khmer Rouge operating along Vietnam's western borders. Currently, none of these groups constitutes more than a nuisance within Vietnam proper, and the Vietnamese claim to have destroyed the United Front for the Liberation of the Oppressed Races (FULRO), the venerable Montagnard liberation organization.[13] Such resistance as does exist is possible only because of incomplete Vietnamese control over adjacent areas of Laos and Cambodia and the presence of Khmer Rouge forces in northern and northeastern Cambodia. All of these anti-Vietnamese elements are assisted by China.

The physical and cultural conditions of northern Vietnam and Laos make it difficult, if not impossible, to completely prevent infiltration by determined opponents operating out of China. This is apparent in Vietnamese references to troubles in "tribal" frontier areas. In 1981, *Nhan Dan* admitted that "the tribal people of the northeast border areas have experienced a number of ordeals and complicated developments in their struggle against the Chinese reactionaries in defense of our national sovereignty and the country's border security."[14] The Vietnamese accuse the Chinese of engaging in espionage, psychological warfare, and economic sabotage in these areas, sending "spies, reconnaissance agents, and henchmen across the border into our hamlets and villages in order to collect intelligence information, spread false rumors, and incite the people to riot." The Chinese are said to have "sown division among the tribal peoples and the cadres of the public security force, army, party, and administration."[15] Even deviant cadres and party

---

[13]The author was told by a Vietnamese diplomat that FULRO was "shattered" in about 1985.

[14]*Nhan Dan*, September 29, 1981, quoted by Lim, *Territorial Power Domains*, pp. 200–201.

[15]Ibid.

members are said to have been recruited by the Chinese to set up underground organizations. In a particularly telling admission, *Nhan Dan* stated that

> Chinese reactionaries have been infiltrating thousands of their hood-lums, ruffians, cadres, and solders *disguised as civilians* into our territory *where they live among our tribal people and operate clandestinely in all highland villages and hamlets of our northern border regions.*[16]

According to Lim, "That such a situation could arise, despite rather tight Vietnamese military and political control, is again an indication of the deep-rooted nature of the elements that make up the montane frontier environment and which seem to have survived Vietnamese reorganization of their borderlands."[17] In July 1983, *Nhan Dan* continued to complain that the Chinese "send spies, commandos, and secret agents to gather intelligence, carry out acts of sabotage and psychological warfare, and build bases and even armed forces to be used as an internal force in combination with an eventual second large-scale aggression."[18]

Remarkably, there is no evidence in either the Vietnamese or Chinese press, or from any other source, that the Vietnamese have successfully done anything of this nature north of the Chinese border. The Chinese have made numerous complaints of Vietnamese "commandos" (that is to say, conventional military raiders) and of the occasional infiltration of spies into Yunnan and Guangxi, but there has been no indication of any Vietnamese success in subverting or infiltrating any of the minority peoples of the PRC border region.

Since 1976, the Vietnamese have been extending their control in Laos by vigorous military action and by extensive road construction. By 1980, an estimated 20 percent of Laos's external trade was passing through Danang rather than through Bangkok, the traditional outlet.[19] Even so, the security situation in northern Laos, from the Vietnamese perspective, probably remains tenuous. The ethnic groups of northern Laos have traditional contacts with larger communities of their kinsmen in Yunnan Province rather than in Hanoi or Vientiane. Chinese cadres have been working among them for many years, and there was a fairly substantial Chinese road-building project through northern Laos right up until 1979. When Chinese construction troops withdrew in 1979, thousands of the

---

[16]Ibid. (emphasis added).

[17]Ibid.

[18]*The Age* (Melbourne), July 26, 1983; quoting *Nhan Dan*, undated.

[19]*Bangkok Post*, November 26, 1980; see Lim, *Territorial Power Domains*, pp. 181–82.

tribals reportedly returned to China with them. There have been persistent accusations by the Vietnamese that China is now running large-scale training of refugees in guerrilla warfare and subversion and reinfiltrating them into Laos.[20] Moreover, there have been reports of Khmer resistance fighters moving all the way from eastern Thailand overland through Laos to China, where they are trained and equipped and then reinfiltrated through the same areas.

There has been little military action in Laos beyond this clandestine transit. In fact, some reports reaching the outside world even tell of Chinese and Lao border commanders meeting sometimes to work out problems. This is consistent with PRC diplomatic efforts to encourage Lao independence from the Vietnamese occupiers. The potential for Chinese-sponsored guerrilla warfare remains, however.

The Chinese were attempting to "teach Vietnam a lesson" with their large-scale conventional invasion of February 1979. The "lesson" was that China must be taken seriously in Southeast Asia and its wishes considered. By taking the risk of invading Vietnam, despite the Vietnamese-Soviet treaty of November 1978, the Chinese asserted their capability and determination to prevent the Vietnamese from dominating the Indochinese peninsula by default. Moreover, they "established a clear precedent for their willingness to use force on subsequent occasions."[21]

The Chinese People's Liberation Army (PLA) maintains considerable military power along the border. In the Guangxi, Yunnan, and Hainan Island military districts there are four or five group army headquarters commanding roughly fifteen main force infantry divisions, plus five or six regional force infantry divisions and five or six border police divisions—a total of perhaps 300,000–400,000 fighting men. Ironically, the chain of air bases across southern China was constructed in the 1960s to assist Vietnam's defense against the Americans. Today, a substantial part of China's huge (over 5,000 combat aircraft) air force could operate from these bases against Vietnam.[22]

When they invaded Vietnam in 1979, the Chinese temporarily consolidated the Chengdu and Guangzhou Military Regions (MRs), which share the Vietnamese border, into a Southern Front to command the

---

[20]*Straits Times*, October 15, 1983. Also see Martin Stewart-Fox, "Laos: The Vietnamese Connection," in *Southeast Asian Affairs, 1980* (Singapore: Institute of Southeast Asian Studies, 1980).

[21]Jonathan D. Pollack, "The Evolution of Chinese Strategic Thought," in *New Directions in Strategic Thinking*, Robert O'Neill and D. M. Horner, eds. (London: George Allen & Unwin, 1981), p. 149.

[22]Author's estimates, based on *The Military Balance, 1986–87* (London: International Institute of Strategic Studies, 1986), pp. 142–45.

operation.[23] Yet the June 1985 consolidation of the MR system maintained the separation of the Chengdu and Guangzhou MRs. This was a strong indication that, despite the large forces available, no large-scale anti-Vietnamese military operations were envisioned by Beijing.

It is over the longer term that the effects of the Chinese demonstration of willingness and capacity to use force are important to PRC objectives in Southeast Asia. PLA units periodically make limited attacks, thereby compelling Vietnam to maintain large units at a high state of readiness lest the Chinese at any time launch a "second lesson." Thus, the 1979 invasion increased the price Vietnam must pay in order to assert its "special" relationship with its smaller neighbors in Indochina.[24] Hanoi has been forced to expand the size of the People's Army of Vietnam (PAVN) to the point that, in 1986, it was the third largest armed force in the world.[25] This has been necessitated not only by their need to fight in Cambodia and defend their northern border, but also by the continuing effort to push Hanoi's military control further into the peripheral areas of northern and northwestern Laos. In taking on the burden of trying to control these latter areas, the Vietnamese have tended to dissipate their power. They seem to have no choice, however, because of the danger of leaving their landward flank exposed to Chinese infiltration and subversion. All of this has made it impossible for the Vietnamese to concentrate their military and political resources on economic development at home, consolidate their control in Cambodia, and compel ASEAN to accept the "irreversibility" of Vietnamese control over Indochina. Lim Joo-Jock asserts:

> The often-repeated intention of the PRC to come to Thailand's aid in case of a Vietnamese attack on Thailand has been taken seriously by both Hanoi and Bangkok [and is] a considerable factor in the power equation in Southeast Asia. This form of support for Thailand and limited material support for the Khmer resistance, though it has not compelled the Vietnamese to evacuate Cambodia, is nevertheless a form of encirclement of Vietnam and a constriction of its present or potential ambitions.[26]

---

[23]Harlan W. Jencks, "China's 'Punitive' War on Vietnam: A Military Assessment," *Asian Survey* 19:8 (August 1979):805–6.

[24]Michael Leifer, "Post-Mortem on the Third Indochina War," *World Today* 35:6 (June 1979):253.

[25]See Douglas Pike, *PAVN: People's Army of Vietnam* (Novato, Calif.: Presidio Press, 1986), esp. pp. 60–86.

[26]Lim, *Territorial Power Domains*, pp. 201–2.

Along Vietnam's northern border, the Chinese have periodically escalated the fighting in order to keep the PAVN tied down, alert, and stressed. In February 1986 alone, according to the Vietnam News Agency (VNA), the Chinese fired about 70,000 artillery shells and rockets into the three western Vietnamese border provinces and sent "many infantry companies and battalions to attack Vi Xuyen District." There was heavy shelling and fighting, possibly up to regimental scale, in October 1986. In the heaviest fighting in at least five years, in early January 1987, the PLA claimed to have killed 500 Vietnamese, while PAVN claimed 1,500 Chinese killed or seriously wounded. Chinese reconnaissance aircraft allegedly overfly Vietnamese territory frequently. The PRC press, particularly the military press, regularly features the battles along the southern border. Indeed, to read *Liberation Army Pictorial* over the past few years, one would think that China was engaged in almost constant large-scale warfare on its southern border, particularly in the Laoshan and Fakashan areas of Guangxi (which, to the Vietnamese, are in Ha Tuyen Province).[27] Thus, while the Chinese invasion of 1979 was in many ways a military failure,[28] it, plus the subsequent Chinese military pressure, has "swung the pendulum away from total and undisputed Vietnamese hegemony in Indochina."[29]

By taking common cause with the Chinese on the matter of Cambodia, the ASEAN states, particularly Thailand, are taking a calculated risk. By facilitating the importation of Chinese arms and advisors to assist the CGDK, the Thais may be introducing weapons and agents which could be used to cause internal problems in Thailand. Under changed circumstances, or just by accident, Chinese military aid could facilitate a resurgence of the Communist Party of Thailand (CPT) and/or other insurgents, possibly including Khmer refugees on Thai territory. Nor can the Thais be terribly comforted by the fact that Khmer resistance troops seem to be travelling freely between China and the Lao-Cambodian border areas, through northern Thailand.

The Chinese loudly emphasize that they stand side-by-side with ASEAN on the Cambodian issue. In fact, they have stated on a number of recent occasions that the Vietnamese occupation of Cambodia is not only the main crux of the Sino-Vietnamese conflict, but is indeed the

---

[27]For example, see *Liberation Army Pictorial (Jiefang Jun Huabao,* hereafter *JFJHB)* no. 4 (April 1986), pp. 2–9; and no. 7 (July 1984), pp. 10–13.

[28]Harlan W. Jencks, "China-Vietnam, 1979," in *The Lessons of Recent Wars in the Third World,* vol. 1, Robert E. Harkavy and Stephanie G. Neuman, eds. (Lexington, Mass.: Lexington Books, 1985–87), pp. 148–53, 156–57.

[29]Lim, *Territorial Power Domains,* p. 195.

most serious obstacle in Sino-Soviet relations.[30] Chinese efforts to divide Vietnam from the Soviet Union are discussed in other chapters, especially by Douglas Pike and Chang Pao-min. China's key military goal is to stop or reduce the flow of Soviet military supplies, and ultimately to engineer the removal of Soviet military installations and influence from Indochina. Publicly, the Soviets maintain their steadfast backing for Vietnam. Nevertheless, the Vietnamese appear to be somewhat worried about being sacrificed on the altar of improved Sino-Soviet relations. An editorial in *Nhan Dan* on Gorbachev's Vladivostok speech of July 28, 1986, "came close to admonishing" Gorbachev for his statement that Vietnam and China were both to blame for "unnecessary suspicions and mistrust."[31]

China's effort to establish military cooperation with ASEAN has extended beyond expressions of support for Thailand and aid to the Khmer resistance. As early as March 1980, the Chinese attempted to participate in the "ADEX '80" defense equipment exhibition in Kuala Lumpur. A 21-man PRC delegation was denied visas at the last minute, ostensibly because all other communist countries had been excluded.[32] In contrast, in January 1986 PRC firms exhibited air defense and anti-ship missiles at the "Asian Aerospace '86" exhibition in Singapore[33] and a full range of military hardware at the "Defence Asia '87" exhibition in Bangkok in March 1987.[34]

In 1984–85, Thai sources reported that the Thai Air Force was considering purchase of the F-7R aircraft, the reconnaissance version of the Chinese-made MiG-21. The Thais eventually judged the F-7R inadequate for their needs, but contacts between the two countries' armed forces have developed extensively. Military delegations routinely exchange visits, and some deals have finally been made. In 1986, the Chinese provided 16–18 130mm guns as grant-in-aid to the Thai Army. In spring 1987, the Thais announced they would purchase 50–60 new Chinese Type-69 tanks and 400 armored personnel carriers at "friend-

---

[30]Xinhua Domestic Service, September 6, 1986, "Report of the Interview of Deng Xiaoping on CBS Television Program 'Sixty Minutes,' 2 Sept. 1986," trans. Foreign Broadcast Information Service (FBIS) *Daily Report, China*, no. 173 (1986), pp. B1–2.

[31]As quoted in Nayan Chanda, "Diplomacy in the Air," *Far Eastern Economic Review* (hereafter *FEER*), September 18, 1986, p. 26.

[32]*Xiandai Junshi* (Hong Kong), April 1980, pp. 26–27.

[33]*Jane's Defence Weekly* (hereafter *JDW*), January 25, 1986, p. 92.

[34]*JDW*, March 28, 1987, pp. 539, 541.

ship" prices. Also, the Thai Air Force will buy "a large number" of Chinese 37mm antiaircraft guns.[35]

The political symbolism of the PRC arms transfers to an ASEAN state is unquestionably the primary Chinese motive. However, China is also interested in extending its aggressively successful and lucrative arms export sales into the Southeast Asian market.

Maritime Strategy

The PLA Navy (PLAN) currently has about 350,000 personnel, including naval air and coastal defense units. It has 46 major surface combatants (15 destroyers and 31 frigates). Its main combat strength, however, is in its huge fleet of small coastal patrol craft and some 100 obsolete diesel-electric attack submarines. There are also three Han-class nuclear attack submarines, whose operational capability at present is subject to some doubt. The PLAN's South Sea Fleet has about twenty-five of the submarines, five missile destroyers, and perhaps 200 of the patrol craft, plus miscellaneous amphibious units. There are also several thousand naval infantrymen and 300–400 combat aircraft of the naval air force.[36]

With the United States, China shares grave concern over the growth of Soviet sea power in the Pacific. Since the early 1970s, the Soviet Pacific Fleet, headquartered at Vladivostok, has grown from the smallest to the largest of the Soviet Navy's four fleets. It currently includes two of the Soviet navy's three aircraft-carrying heavy antisubmarine cruisers (*Minsk* and *Novosibirsk*). The Chinese perceive this naval presence as an integral part of the Soviet encirclement of China, in addition to being part of the overall Soviet strategy for controlling the sea lanes of the world. It was therefore a strategic setback to the Chinese, as well as to the United States, when, as a direct result of China's 1979 invasion, the Soviet Pacific Fleet acquired the naval and air base complex at Cam Ranh Bay in Vietnam.

Soviet forces in Vietnam have expanded continuously since 1980, when only about seven Soviet vessels used Cam Ranh Bay on a continuing basis. By 1986, there were approximately 7,000 Soviet military personnel in Vietnam, most of them in the Cam Ranh Bay complex,

---

[35]"Thai Army in Chinese Tank Deal," *JDW*, March 21, 1987, p. 467; and "Thai Army to Buy 400 Chinese APCs," *JDW*, April 4, 1987, p. 575.

[36]*Military Balance, 1986–1987*, pp. 144–45. Contrary to some reports, the PLA has no "marine corps," although it is experimenting with the concept. See Gordon Jacobs's excellent analysis in "China's Interest in Amphibious Operations," *JDW*, September 27, 1986, pp. 684–86.

supporting 20–25 vessels, including 15–20 combatants and various auxiliaries.[37] Among the latter were two submarine tenders, supporting an unknown number of Soviet submarines operating in the South China Sea and the Indian Ocean. In addition, Vietnamese airfields support about 8 long-range Tu-95/Tu-10 Bear bombers and approximately 16 Tu-16 Badger bombers. These aircraft are variously configured for maritime reconnaissance, antisubmarine warfare (ASW), electronic warfare, and antishipping missions. There is also a squadron of 14 MiG-23 fighter aircraft, plus various antiaircraft units, for the defense of the Cam Ranh complex. In addition, the Soviets have extensive electronic monitoring facilities in Vietnam, and possibly in Laos.[38] This Soviet presence is oriented primarily against American forces at sea and U.S. bases at Clark Field and Subic Bay in the Philippines. It also poses a threat to the ASEAN states and China; it gives the Soviets a significant maritime reconnaissance and strike capability in the South China Sea and the eastern portions of the Indian Ocean. The Cam Ranh Bay facility reduces Soviet transit time to the Indian ocean by seven to ten days compared to basing from Vladivostok.[39] The Russians are also said to be rehabilitating deep-water ports at Kampang Sam and the former Cambodian naval base at Ream.[40] They thus threaten free movement between the Indian Ocean and the South China Sea.

The Soviet threat to the strategic sea lanes of communication (SLOCs) between the Middle East and Japan was greatly facilitated by the Chinese invasion of 1979. It is extremely unlikely that the Vietnamese would tolerate a foreign military base on their soil if they did not feel that they were faced with a grave threat from China. It has been widely assumed by outside observers that the Cam Ranh Bay facilities are provided to the Soviets as a straight quid pro quo. In this view, the Soviets provide economic and military support to the Vietnamese for their adventures in Cambodia and for defense of their land borders; in return, the Soviets are allowed to use Cam Ranh Bay for their own purposes. What is generally overlooked is the fact of the physical separation of Vietnam's two "core domains." Vietnam's geography has been likened to two baskets of rice hanging at opposite ends of a pole. Only a narrow coastal strip settled by Kinh Vietnamese connects the

---

[37]*Military Balance, 1986–1987,* p. 46.

[38]Lim, *Territorial Power Domains,* p. 182, claims there are Soviet "radar facilities in Laos, ostensibly for the surveillance of Chinese air movements and missile tests."

[39]John MacBeth, "Buildup on the Bay," *FEER,* December 29, 1983, p. 16; Gordon Jacobs, "China's Naval Program," *Navy International,* October 1985, p. 584.

[40]Ji, "Current Security Issues," pp. 982–83.

two large rice-producing areas in the Tonkin and Mekong deltas. That thin coastal strip is extremely vulnerable to attack from the sea and lies directly adjacent to major Chinese naval and air bases on Hainan Island. In 1979, a now defunct Hong Kong magazine claimed that the PLA General Staff actually had a contingency plan to strike southeast through Laos while making an amphibious landing between Ha Tinh and Than Hae, thereby cutting the SRV in half.[41] In view of China's increasing naval and aerial capacity, and its increasing naval presence in the South China Sea, the Soviet naval presence in Vietnam is more than simply a quid pro quo for economic and military aid. It is also a defensive shield against Chinese naval and amphibious attack on Vietnam's vulnerable central coast.[42] In private conversations in early 1987, Vietnamese diplomats indicated they would be loath to lose this Soviet protection, even should there be a solution to the Cambodian problem. Notwithstanding the considerable defensive importance of the Soviet presence in Cam Ranh, however, it clearly poses a naval threat to the United States, to ASEAN, and to the southern coasts of China.[43]

In addition to their own forces, the Soviets have provided between 55 and 60 combatant vessels to Vietnam and Cambodia, mostly since 1979.[44] Among the vessels provided to Vietnam have been four frigates of the Soviet Petya class which joined the two ex-U.S. frigates already in Vietnamese service. In addition, the Soviets provided 8 Osa II missile boats with STYX antiship missiles, 12–14 torpedo boats, and 26 small gunboats. The Vietnamese also have 22 gunboats of the Shanghai and Swatow classes provided by China before 1975.[45] In 1985, there were reports that the Soviets planned to provide the Vietnamese with at least one Foxtrot-class diesel-electric submarine, or already had. There have been joint Soviet-Vietnamese ASW exercises in the South China Sea, presumably directed against hypothetical Chinese submarines.[46] In the

---

[41]Huang Zhong, "Hainan Island Builds Guided Missile Bases," *Dong Xi Fang,* no. 12 (December 10, 1979):13–15.

[42]Lim, *Territorial Power Domains,* pp. 196–97, 202.

[43]On possible Soviet naval interdiction of the PRC coast, see Donald C. Daniel and Harlan Jencks, "Soviet Military Confrontation with China: Options for the USSR, the PRC, and the United States," *Conflict* 5:1 (1983):66–69.

[44]Jacobs, "China's Naval Program," p. 584.

[45]*Military Balance, 1986–87,* p. 172.

[46]Desmond Wettern, "Soviet Submarines for Vietnam," *Pacific Defense Reporter* (hereafter *PDR*), March 1985, pp. 14–15; Douglas Pike, "Vietnam: A Modern Sparta," *PDR,* April 1983, p. 35.

spring of 1984, the Soviets and Vietnamese conducted joint amphibious exercises near Cam Ranh Bay and Haiphong.[47]

Soviet-Vietnamese naval cooperation presents challenges to a number of important Chinese maritime interests. Since 1976, an extensive program of construction and purchase has made China one of the largest merchant marine powers in the world, while its fishing fleet has also expanded considerably.[48] Chinese merchant ships now regularly ply the straits of Southeast Asia. Over the past decade, China has expanded its offshore oil exploration and drilling. Because oil installations are extremely vulnerable to naval attack, the increase in Vietnamese naval power is of grave concern, particularly in the Tongkin Gulf, where there are extensive waters subject to conflicting Chinese and Vietnamese claims, and under which there are believed to be significant petroleum deposits.

Maps published in the PRC always show the South China Sea, as far south as the coasts of Kalimantan, to be Chinese territorial waters. The Chinese invaded and occupied the Paracel (Xisha) Islands in January 1974, ejecting forces of the former Saigon regime. They continue to occupy them, over the protests of Hanoi. Moreover, China maintains a claim to the far-flung Spratly (Nansha) group. Because of the rich fishing grounds and possible undersea oil and minerals around these islands, the conflicting claims involve economics as well as strategic position. Within the Spratly archipelago, there are claims by Vietnam, China, Malaysia, and the Philippines. There has been a Vietnamese garrison on Amboyna Cay and two other small islands since 1975 and a Malaysian garrison on Terembu Layang-Layang since 1983, and there are Philippine garrisons on five islands. Moreover, the Republic of China (Taiwan) maintains a garrison on Taiping Island, the largest of the group. The Philippines has been granting oil leases in the Spratlys since the early 1970s, which can only help complicate the situation. The PRC's declared position on the situation is that these territorial disputes are

> left over by history and need time to be resolved one by one and step by step, and disputes over straits' sovereignty and maritime boundaries should be approached through international consultations. . . . The disputed areas with natural resources . . . in particular require negotiated settlements. . . . In this case, common exploration and shar-

---

[47]Michael Richardson, "Watch on the Spratlys," *PDR*, September 1984, p. 9.
[48]David G. Muller, *China as a Maritime Power* (Boulder, Colo.: Westview, 1983), esp. pp. 182–87.

ing of resources, with the problem of sovereignty pushed aside for a certain period of time, is a fairly good approach.[49]

Thus far, the Chinese have not sought to assert their claims in the Spratlys militarily, since they are over 800 kilometers south of the Paracels. The Spratlys are far from Chinese naval bases and beyond the reach of Chinese airpower, while they are within range of both the Vietnamese and Philippine air forces. If they were to assert their claim and establish a strong military presence in the Spratlys, the Chinese would be in a much stronger position in any conflict involving access to the eastern end of the Malacca Strait. For the time being, however, they are just expanding their naval facilities in the Paracels.

Chinese concern with the threat posed by the Soviet fleet has led to a major modernization program in the Chinese navy over the past few years. Bases and facilities of the South Sea Fleet are being upgraded. Ships, submarines, aircraft, and coastal defense forces have been redeployed from the other two fleets to the South Sea Fleet. In particular, sizable forces have been deployed to Hainan. Some of these have already participated in training exercises in the Paracels and other offshore islands.[50]

China's naval power is still hardly threatening to anyone much beyond its own coasts. Nevertheless, the PLAN has improved considerably over the past decade. A flotilla of about thirteen ships supported the Chinese intercontinental ballistic missile test in May 1980, sailing to the impact area near the Fiji Islands in the South Pacific. During this operation, they conducted under-way replenishment, navigated through rough seas, and generally did a thoroughly professional job. Indeed, the showing of the navy, all things considered, was more remarkable than the missile test itself. Since then, the PLAN has conducted a number of long-range operations, sailing around Taiwan and the Philippines and in South Sea waters. Its most recent feat was its first ever "show the flag" voyage into the Indian Ocean, in November 1985–

---

[49]Ji, "Current Security Issues," p. 981. For detailed presentations of Chinese claims to South China Sea islands, see Shih Ti-tsu, "South China Sea Islands: Chinese Territory Since Ancient Times," *Peking Review*, December 12, 1975, pp. 10–15; "China's Indisputable Sovereignty over the Xisha and Nansha Islands," *Beijing Review*, February 18, 1980, pp. 15–24. On undersea oil in East Asia, see Selig S. Harrison, *China, Oil and Asia: Conflict Ahead?* (New York: Columbia University Press, 1977).

[50]Bradley Hahn, "China: Emerging Sea Power," *Proceedings*, March 1985, pp. 106–7; Gordon Jacobs, "Bringing China's Navy Up to Date," *JDW*, January 25, 1986, pp. 113–14; "New Chinese Anti-Ship and Air-to-Air Missiles on Show," *JDW*, September 13, 1986, p. 530; "Two New Warship Types for PLA Navy," *JDW*, August 2, 1986, p. 146; and G. Jacobs, "China's Auxiliary Ships," *JDW*, March 8, 1986, pp. 435–37.

January 1986, when a Chinese flotilla made port calls in Bangladesh, Sri Lanka, and Pakistan.[51]

The PLAN gradually has been upgrading its weapon systems and equipment, and has activated a comprehensive system of professional education and training for officers and sailors. The Chinese are also acquiring limited but significant amounts of modern naval equipment and weapons from Western Europe and the U.S.[52] These have included American gas turbine marine engines and European diesel engines, guns, electronics, missiles, and helicopters. The Chinese are co-producing the French SA-365N Dauphin II helicopter, which is suitable for shipboard ASW missions. They are also making a version of the French Exocet antishipping missile. (See Edward Ross's chapter for details on Sino-American military cooperation.)

As noted earlier, the Chinese are concerned about India's relationship with the Soviet Union. The Indo-Soviet treaty of August 1971 expanded Soviet aid to the fast-growing Indian Navy, which is now by far the most powerful navy among the Indian Ocean littoral states. The Chinese no doubt share the apprehension of several ASEAN states about the Indian naval base in the Nicobar Islands and the major airfield which has been under construction there. In September 1986, Indonesian Major General Hartas claimed that Soviet submarines were using the Nicobar base. On the 17th of September, the Indian foreign minister sidestepped General Hartas's accusation, stating that India "does not grant military base facilities to any power." Since the base is located only 400 kilometers northwest of Sumatra, it is a matter of continuing concern to the littoral states.[53]

The legal status of the Southeast Asian straits has been much debated since 1972.[54] Indonesia and the Philippines support the concept of "archipelagic sovereignty," meaning that Indonesia, for example, claims the right to control the Sunda, Makassar, Lombok, and Ombai-Wetar Straits, in order to protect the integrity of its territorial sovereignty.

Even in 1972, though its relations with Indonesia were unfriendly and its relationship with Malaysia quite cool, the PRC supported the littoral states' maritime policies. China's support was, and remains, based on its general approach to ocean policy, which has been that the

[51]"Voyage to the South Sea," *JFJHB*, no. 5 (May 1986):10–15.
[52]See Muller, *China as a Maritime Power*, sect. 3; Bruce Swanson, "Naval Forces," in *Chinese Defence Policy*, Gerald Segal and William T. Tow, eds. (London: Macmillan, 1984).
[53]Salamat Ali, "Base Statement Draws Indian Protest," *FEER*, October 2, 1986, p. 12.
[54]Vertzberger, *Coastal States*, pp. 85–86, passim.

supremacy of the coastal states in defining their maritime interests to the extent of their regulatory powers should be absolute. In this, the Chinese are taking the part of the underdeveloped coastal countries vis-à-vis the great maritime powers. China has consistently supported the Indonesian-Malaysian position that the littoral states should have power to regulate commercial and military traffic even through the Straits of Malacca. This position has supported both China's effort to contain Soviet sea power and its effort to gain friends and influence in Southeast Asia. Chinese interests here coincide with the ASEAN states' against the superpowers, so the conflict over the Malacca Straits has been an opportunity for them to demonstrate that their policy is not merely propaganda. The PRC is only too happy to stand with ASEAN against the United States, Japan, and the Soviet Union.

Even more important, of course, are China's strategic calculations. In the late 1960s, the Chinese claimed there was an anti-Chinese "unholy alliance" between the United States and the USSR. Thus, the debate over the Malacca Strait, which involved China's archrivals, facilitated Chinese efforts to gain allies in Southeast Asia and to inhibit the movements of the superpowers. In both war and peace, it is in the Chinese interest that the littoral states control, or at least observe, the movement of great-power navies through Southeast Asian waters.[55]

The Southeast Asian straits are inescapably involved in major power conflicts not only in the event of war but also in cold-war power calculations. The importance of the sea lines of communication through the straits, increased presence of the superpower navies and of the Chinese and Indian navies, plus the considerable naval power of Indonesia and Malaysia, mean that the littoral states are doomed to involvement in any major global or regional war, whether they wish it or not. In the event of a Sino-Soviet war, the PLAN probably would try at least to complicate Soviet logistics by forcing Soviet merchant ships to sail east of the Philippines.[56] This would be strategically vital to the defense of China, because the Soviet Far East is partly dependent on the Southeast Asian SLOCs. China, by contrast, could get along without them, though it becomes more dependent on seaborne commerce each year.

While the PLAN could certainly assist in interdicting the Southeast Asian straits, it could not force transit, much less keep them open, even in the absence of the U.S. and Soviet navies. Indeed, the superpowers themselves would have considerable trouble trying to force the straits against the wishes of the littoral states. The Malacca Strait, in particular,

---

[55]Ibid., pp. 6, 62, 85–86.
[56]Muller, *China as a Maritime Power*, pp. 225–26.

would be fairly easy to close if the littoral states wished to do so. Because it is fairly shallow and narrow, mines or ships scuttled in the shipping channel could stop the transit of large ships. Malaysia, Indonesia, and Singapore all have light missile boats armed with Gabriel and/or Exocet antishipping missiles. Indonesia presently has submarines, and Malaysia is planning to purchase them. Moreover, land-based air power and artillery would make it possible for the littoral states to keep the entire strait under fire.[57]

On balance, China probably would benefit if the Southeast Asian straits were closed to all navies in a crisis. Hence, again, China is happy to back the Malaysian-Indonesian position on control of the straits. The growing presence of the PLAN in Southeast Asian waters, meanwhile, serves only to complicate an already complex situation.

The Future

Vertzberger claims:

> At present, support of the coastal states' demand for more control over passage through and above international straits in general, and the Malacca Straits in particular, serves Beijing's strategic, political, and ideological interests well. . . . In the longer run, this state of affairs may undergo significant change as China's blue-water capabilities and activities extend in scope and importance. In particular, this is true in the case of China's changing nuclear strategic posture and the future role of the navy in it.[58]

Vertzberger bases his argument on his evaluation of the future of China's submarine-launched ballistic missile (SLBM) force. He foresees the Chinese deploying operational nuclear ballistic missile submarines (SSBNs) within the next few years. He believes that they can be targeted to hit European Russia provided the missiles are launched from the northwestern Indian Ocean. To do so, Chinese SSBNs would try to pass surreptitiously through the Southeast Asian straits. According to Vertzberger, the survival of the small Chinese SSBN force favors deployment in the Indian Ocean, where it could possibly be supported by surface vessels from, and repair facilities at, the port of Karachi. Thus, the deployment of SSBNs in the Indian Ocean would probably lead to considerable Chinese naval traffic through the straits. The immediate

---

[57]*Military Balance, 1986–87*, pp. 155, 162, 167; P. D. Jones and J.V.P. Goldrick, "The Far Eastern Navies," *Proceedings*, March 1987, pp. 67–69; and *JDW*, August 23, 1986, pp. 288, 291.

[58]Vertzberger, *Coastal States*, p. 90. The following discussion summarizes Vertzberger's argument on pp. 90–92.

results of this extension of Chinese naval power into the Indian Ocean, according to Vertzberger, probably would be to accentuate the fears of Indonesia, Malaysia, and even Singapore about the Chinese naval threat. These fears in turn would probably lead to two major consequences: a growing reliance on American naval presence to counterbalance both the Soviets and the Chinese, and a further emphasis on sea-denial capability in the straits.

The ideological and political dilemma that Beijing is likely to face if it does acquire a strategic need to make regular military transit into the Indian Ocean will be ameliorated by the ability of the superpowers to continue to frustrate the ASEAN states, or to disregard their efforts at controlling or monitoring traffic. Beijing, in other words, will be able to maintain a public stance of backing the ZOPFAN proposal and the claims of the littoral states, while quietly taking advantage of the fact that the great powers and Japan can frustrate Third World attempts to control their own coastlines.[59]

Vertzberger is almost certainly being overly enthusiastic about China's prospects as a naval power in the Indian Ocean. To begin with, Chinese submarines are still relatively primitive and extremely vulnerable to Soviet (or indeed Indonesian or Malaysian or Singaporean) ASW measures, especially while transiting the Southeast Asian straits. The Strait of Malacca, in particular, is so shallow that even superpower submarines cannot transit submerged without extremely high risk of detection or grounding. Moreover, the notion of a Chinese surface fleet based in Karachi is implausible for several reasons. First, it would mean a major diversion of scarce PLAN assets to the Indian Ocean and away from the coastal defense of China. Second, it would subject Chinese nuclear strategy and naval power to the vagaries of Pakistani politics. Third, as Vertzberger himself recognizes, the political costs in terms of China's relations with India and ASEAN would be very considerable.

For all these reasons, it would be far more sensible for the Chinese to attempt to develop a new class of SSBNs with a longer-range missile. Meanwhile, it is likely that the Chinese will deploy their SSBN force, such as it is, in Chinese waters, or possibly the north Pacific, and target it on the Soviet Far East.[60]

---

[59]Ibid.

[60]The first Xia class SSBN was officially declared operational in January 1987: *Beijing Review*, January 12, 1987, p. 3. *Military Balance, 1986–87* credits the PLAN with two Xia class SSBNs, with up to four more on order. These figures are probably too high. The CSS-NX-3 SLBM has a reported maximum range of 2,800 km. Each Xia SSBN has twelve launch tubes.

China's claim to the Spratlys is not likely to be pressed militarily under present politico-military circumstances. China wishes to avoid antagonizing the ASEAN states which also have claims in the archipelago. Moreover, the PLAN simply lacks the capability to project power as far south as the Spratlys, particularly in the presence of the Soviet fleet, which might assist the Vietnamese. It therefore seems far more likely that the Chinese will continue to pursue their stated policy of seeking a long-term settlement with all of the littoral states and exploiting the resources of the Spratlys on a joint basis. Even this conciliatory policy, however, if anything is to come of it, is going to call for a greater PRC civilian and military presence in the Spratlys. Therefore, we might expect to see more Chinese military, merchant, fishing, and scientific vessels in the Spratly Group.

ASEAN, the United States, the USSR, and the SRV are all concerned about the possible influence an expanded Chinese Navy might have over the coming decades. As Edward Ross makes clear in his chapter, American arms transfer policy restricts naval programs to the ASW "mission area." No such restrictions inhibit other potential suppliers of naval technology, however. The PLAN acquisition of the French Exocet missile, for example, potentially provides a major increase in antisurface warfare capability.

Even without importing foreign weapon systems, the Chinese have developed several important weapons that may increase their naval capability substantially if deployed in large numbers. The C-601 air-to-surface missile, for example, is a heavily-modified Soviet STYX which can be launched from a Chinese naval bomber. The HQ-61 air defense missile may at last provide the PLAN the seagoing air defense it needs to free itself from dependence on shore-based antiaircraft protection.

The crucial unknown in attempting to predict Chinese naval development is finance. How much are the Chinese willing to spend to deploy a really modern blue-water fleet, and how soon? In the spring of 1987, all indicators point to relatively small expenditures. Throughout the PLA (of which the navy is part), force levels are being maintained or even reduced, while technical levels are gradually being raised. The Chinese say that only once the other three "modernizations" are well advanced will they be able to manufacture and deploy significant amounts of really modern military hardware. Absolutely all available evidence indicates that the Chinese are doing exactly what they say.

Along China's southern land borders, the general strategic situation is fundamentally different from at sea, because even the superpowers are ill-equipped, and strongly disinclined, to intervene in the Southeast Asian highlands. The general strategic situation there will remain: Vietnam seeks hegemony over all of Indochina, and China is unwilling to accept it. The situation conceivably might change sometime in the future as part of a wider political settlement on Cambodia. In that context, China might accept Vietnamese hegemony in Laos and even Cambodia as a quid pro quo for Vietnamese severance of formal military ties with the Soviet Union and the removal of all Soviet forces and facilities from Indochina. Even if this were to happen, however, Vietnam and China are likely to remain at odds over various issues, and to attempt to influence events in the rest of mainland Southeast Asia, by applying their well-honed capabilities to exert low-level military-political pressures in the mountainous regions through small-unit military actions and the support of various separatist factions and groups. Given that reality, Vietnam inevitably will have to look to some outside power as an equalizer against China. That outside power is likely to continue to be the Soviet Union, although Hanoi might possibly look to ASEAN, India, or (conceivably) even the United States.

As long as the Vietnamese remain assertive beyond their own land borders, as they seem likely to do, it is difficult to imagine any end to Sino-Vietnamese hostilities in Southeast Asia, regardless of the status of Sino-Soviet relations. Because the Vietnamese therefore will seek some sort of outside support, Southeast Asia appears doomed to continue involvement in superpower politics and military activity, even if there is a solution to the current problem of Cambodia. China, as an aspiring global power, as a regional power, and as a Southeast Asian power, will therefore remain deeply involved in the political-military affairs of the region.

6. U.S.-China Military Relations

EDWARD W. ROSS

In the eleven years since the death of Mao and the end of the Cultural Revolution, China's relations with the nations of ASEAN have witnessed considerable improvement, as have China's relations with Japan, Western Europe, and the United States. China's new "open door" foreign policy is the direct result of far-reaching domestic political and economic reforms. These positive political and economic developments in China hold out the promise of further improvement in China's relationships with the noncommunist world and are viewed with great interest by China's ASEAN neighbors. While there are many positive trends, however, concerns about China's role in the region persist among China-watchers in ASEAN.

Of particular interest to the nations of ASEAN is China's military power and orientation. In this regard, ASEAN has many questions and concerns about China's military modernization and its developing military relationship with the United States. Generally, Asian friends and allies of the United States have indicated that, while they do not always agree with every detail of U.S. China policy, they understand and essentially concur with U.S. objectives. Clearly, however, for reasons rooted in history, there is not a great deal of enthusiasm in ASEAN for significant improvements in China's military capabilities. For this reason, a military relationship with the United States, the nation with the most advanced military technology on earth, is viewed with concern. This is because of the prospect that China might achieve a more rapid advancement in its military capabilities as the result of access to advanced U.S. military technology and might, for whatever reason, utilize its newfound military power in ways inimical to ASEAN interests. These concerns are further heightened because there is little accurate information available to the public on recent developments in U.S.-China military relations. This has sometimes led to an overestimation of the pace and scope of the development of the relationship and its potential impact on China's military modernization.

The opinions expressed in this chapter are solely those of the author; they do not necessarily reflect those of the Department of Defense or the U.S. government. Information contained herein was updated on September 1, 1987, in preparation for publication.

This chapter reviews the development of U.S.-China military relations and the implications for ASEAN. First, it will examine both U.S. and Chinese policy considerations with regard to the military relationship. Second, it will review significant developments in each of the three principal areas of U.S.-China military relations—high-level visits, functional military exchanges, and military technology cooperation—along with the prospects for future development of the relationship and implications for future Chinese military capabilities. Finally, it will examine the implications for China's relationships with the nations of ASEAN.

U.S. and Chinese Policy Considerations

The slow but steady growth of U.S.-China military relations over the past three years is the result of a willingness on both sides to pursue policies toward each other which satisfy each country's basic interests for both the near and long term. Neither Beijing nor Washington seeks a strategic partnership, and numerous differences continue to exist between the two countries in their approach to political, economic, and other issues. Nevertheless, there are several important issues on which we agree that provide ample incentive for both sides to engage in military interaction and technology cooperation.

As Ambassador Lord pointed out in his speech to the 1986 annual meeting of the National Council for U.S.-China Trade, we share numerous security concerns with the Chinese:[1]

1. We agree that Vietnam should get out of Cambodia.
2. We agree that the Soviet Union should get out of Afghanistan.
3. We agree that there must be global limits on intermediate-range nuclear missiles in Europe and Asia.
4. We agree that conflict on the Korean Peninsula would be a disaster and therefore we should seek ways to reduce tensions and maintain peace.
5. We agree that good relations with Japan are beneficial for all.
6. We agree, quietly, that a substantial U.S. presence in Asia serves the cause of regional peace.

Therefore, the willingness of the United States to develop a military relationship with the PRC is founded on the assessment that the United

---

[1]"Sino-American Relations: No Time for Complacency," speech by U.S. Ambassador to China Winston Lord to the National Council for U.S.-China Trade annual meeting, May 28, 1986.

States and the PRC share important parallel interests, both globally and regionally. Foremost among these is a common security concern—the growing threat posed by the Soviet Union. Thus, an objective of U.S. policy is to build an enduring military relationship with China which would support China's national development and maintain it as a force for peace and stability in the Asia-Pacific region and the world. The United States believes that a more secure, modernizing, and friendly China, with an independent foreign policy and economic system more compatible with the West, can make a significant contribution to peace and stability. A principal aim in strengthening U.S.-China military relations is to support these healthy trends.[2]

In this context, a stated U.S. goal is to play a positive role in China's military modernization—a role which not only serves U.S. and Chinese mutual interests, but also takes into account the concerns and interests of U.S. friends and allies in the region. Such a role also must take into consideration China's legitimate defense requirements and its own modernization objectives.

While Beijing articulates an independent foreign policy, China has found it in its interest to develop closer relations with the West in order to obtain the technology and trade necessary for its national development and military modernization. China also seeks reduced tensions and increased economic and cultural contacts with the Soviet Union. Nevertheless, it frequently has articulated the three obstacles to better relations with the USSR and recognizes the difficulty in finding solutions to the Afghanistan, Cambodia, or Sino-Soviet border issues.

U.S.-China Military Relations

The development of U.S.-PRC military relations began soon after the normalization of diplomatic relations between the United States and the People's Republic of China on January 1, 1979. Secretary of Defense Harold Brown's visit to Beijing in January 1980, followed by then Deputy Chief of the General Staff Liu Huaqing's visit to the United States in May 1980 and soon-to-be Minister of Defense Geng Biao's visit to the United States a month later, were the initial steps in opening a dialogue between the military establishments of the two countries. The evolution

---

[2]See testimony of Rear Admiral E. B. Baker, Jr., director, East Asia and Pacific Region, Office of the Assistant Secretary of Defense, International Security Affairs, before the Senate Foreign Relations Committee, Subcommittee on Asian and Pacific Affairs, April 29, 1986. The terms of reference used by Admiral Baker to describe U.S. policy on U.S.-China military relations have been used on numerous occasions by Secretary of Defense Weinberger, Assistant Secretary of Defense Richard L. Armitage, and others.

of U.S. policy with regard to a U.S.-China military relationship was reflected in the announcement by Secretary of State Alexander Haig in June 1981 that the United States would consider the sale, on a case-by-case basis, of defensive weapons and equipment to the PRC.

Development of the military relationship was hampered somewhat in 1981 and 1982, however, by several factors. Important among these were an internal policy debate within China over the extent to which the PRC would seek foreign participation in its defense modernization and differences between the U.S. and China over Taiwan. In August 1982, the United States and China signed the joint communiqué concerning U.S. arms sales to Taiwan. By the latter half of 1983 a growing consensus within China paved the way for further development of U.S.-China military relations.[3]

Two important events in 1983 also contributed to the advancement of the military relationship. First was the liberalization of U.S. guidelines for the sale of seven categories of dual-use items to the PRC in August following Secretary of Commerce Baldridge's visit to China. Second, was the visit of Secretary of Defense Weinberger in September. These developments came at a time of significant growth in political and economic relations between the United States and China. Moreover, they signaled an acknowledgement by both sides that it was an appropriate time for further expansion of military contacts as a natural by-product of normal relations between friendly, nonallied countries.

Secretary Weinberger's first visit was particularly significant because it established the framework for expansion of U.S.-China military-to-military contacts. The secretary's visit resumed and expanded the high-level dialogue between senior U.S. and Chinese military leaders begun by Secretary Brown in 1980. It laid the groundwork for renewed functional military exchanges between the services of the two country's armed forces. Finally, it identified and articulated to the Chinese military leadership several military mission areas, keyed to Chinese requests, which could provide the basis for future military technology cooperation between the two militaries. In addition it also energized a U.S. interagency review process designed to

---

[3]The signing of the August 17, 1982, communiqué on U.S. arms sales to China paved the way for a segment of the Chinese military leadership to argue that the time was right to open the door to a U.S.-China military relationship. This development came at a time when limited financial resources were made available to the PLA to purchase foreign military technology and equipment.

ensure consistency of U.S. policy in the military technology cooperation area.[4]

High-Level Visits

Defense Minister Zhang Aiping visited the United States in June 1984 on a reciprocal visit for Secretary Weinberger's September 1983 visit. In addition to meeting Secretary Weinberger, he had discussions with President Reagan, Secretary of State Shultz, Chairman of the Joint Chiefs of Staff General Vessey and other senior military officials. The initial exchange of visits between the two defense leaders laid the foundation for a pattern of reciprocal visits between senior defense officials and military leaders. Each visit further advanced the bilateral military relationship.

Secretary of the Navy John Lehman visited China in August 1984 as the guest of People's Liberation Army (PLA) Navy Commander Liu Huaqing, and opened the door to direct navy-to-navy contacts. Secretary Lehman's visit also established a dialogue which eventually led to the PASSEX (passing exercise) conducted between the two navies in January 1986 in the South China Sea. While such courtesy passing exercises are conducted routinely between the U.S. Navy and the navies of numerous friendly and allied nations, China's participation in such a routine activity was a small but noteworthy step in the military relationship.

General Vessey and Admiral Crowe, U.S. commander-in-chief Pacific (CINCPAC), visited China in January 1985 as the guest of Chief of the General Staff Yang Dezhi. Standing for several hours in subzero weather during a visit to the PLA training area in Shenyang, General Vessey and Admiral Crowe became the first U.S. military leaders to observe a PLA "combined service" training exercise. Like Secretary Weinberger, General Vessey carried on discussions on regional and global issues with his Chinese hosts.

Chief of Staff of the Air Force General Gabriel visited China in October 1985 as the guest of PLA Air Force Commander Wang Hai. The two air force leaders agreed to exchanges of air force training and logistics delegations and discussed ways to further the air force-to-air force relationship. Gabriel and Wang Hai got along very well and established a

---

[4]The source for the information in this chapter concerning U.S. involvement in the military relationship with China from the time of Secretary Weinberger's visit is the author's personal participation. At the time of Weinberger's 1983 visit, the author was serving as a military attaché at the Defense Attaché Office in the American Embassy Beijing. The author has held his current position as the assistant for China, OSD/ISA since February 1984.

close personal rapport. In discussing their Korean War experiences, it came to light that Wang Hai, a Chinese ace during the war, may have been shot down by General Gabriel.

PLA Navy Commander Liu Huaqing visited the United States in November as the guest of Chief of Naval Operations Admiral Watkins. Liu met with Secretary Lehman and other Navy and Defense leaders in Washington and toured U.S. Navy installations in Florida, San Diego, and Hawaii. Admiral Watkins visited China in April 1986 as Liu's guest.[5] The two navy leaders continued their discussions on ways to expand navy-to-navy interaction.

In May 1986, chief of the PLA general staff, Yang Dezhi, made his reciprocal visit to the United States and was the guest of General Vessey's successor as chairman of the Joint Chiefs, Admiral Crowe. Yang met with Secretary Weinberger and Assistant Secretary of Defense Richard Armitage. Like those who came before him, Yang visited U.S. military installations around the country and in Hawaii.

Secretary Weinberger returned to China in early October 1986, almost exactly three years after his initial visit to China. The visit came at a time when significant progress toward reaching agreement on a major cooperative Foreign Military Sales (FMS) program had been made and also resulted in the announcement that a U.S. Navy ship visit to China would take place in November. In addition, Secretary Weinberger engaged his host Zhang Aiping, and other Chinese political and military leaders, in a wide-ranging dialogue on numerous regional and global issues from China's conflict with Vietnam to U.S.-Soviet arms control discussions. Chinese leaders who received Weinberger included Deng Xiaoping, Premier Zhao Ziyang, Secretary General of the Military Commission Yang Shangkun, Yang Dezhi, and Foreign Minister Wu Xueqian. Defense Minister Zhang Aiping welcomed Secretary Weinberger as an "old friend" with the special gesture of a small private dinner on the evening of his arrival and stressed the personal relationship between himself and Secretary Weinberger on several occasions during the visit.

While the secretary of defense was in Beijing, another senior Chinese military leader, Hong Xuezhi, director of the General Logistics Department of the PLA, led a group of Chinese logisticians on a visit to the United States as the guest of Assistant Secretary of Defense for Acquisition and Logistics Dr. James Wade. Hong departed Beijing on the evening of Weinberger's arrival. The two met briefly in the Great Hall of the People along with Yang Shangkun and Yang Dezhi.

---

[5]Admiral Watkins's visit to China was cut short as a result of the U.S. bombing of Libya.

Since Secretary Weinberger's second visit to China, the exchange of high-level visits between senior U.S. and Chinese military leaders has continued apace. U.S. Army Chief of Staff General Wickham visited China in late November 1986 as the guest of PLA Deputy Chief of the General Staff Xu Xin. Marine Corps Commandant Paul X. Kelly visited China in March 1987 and PLA Air Force Commander Wang Hai visited the United States in April. Military Commission Vice Chairman Yang Shangkun, the most senior Chinese military leader next to Deng Xiaoping himself, visited the United States in May as the head of a Chinese delegation. Yang, the guest of Vice President George Bush, met with President Reagan, Secretary of State Shultz, Secretary Weinberger, and leaders of both the House and Senate. In June, Admiral Hays, commander-in-chief Pacific, visited China as the guest of Deputy Chief of the General Staff Xu Xin.

As of this writing the most recent high-level visit in the ongoing series was the visit to China in September 1987 of Secretary of the Air Force John Aldridge. Air Force Secretary Aldridge was the guest of PLA Air Force Commander Wang Hai and led the first defense delegation to visit Tibet.

In each case, visits by senior U.S. and Chinese military leaders have further improved communications and understanding between the two armed forces and have paved the way for increased contacts. The pattern of high-level exchange visits, begun by Secretary Weinberger and Minister Zhang Aiping in 1983–84, has set the overall tone for the relationship and provided a framework for functional military exchanges between the various military organizations of the two countries and for cooperative programs in the military technology field.[6]

Functional Military Exchanges

The area of functional military exchanges, as defined by the Department of Defense, encompasses the entire spectrum of military-to-military interaction beneath the level of high-level visits, exclusive of visits and exchanges associated with specific technology cooperation programs or discussions.

Although reciprocal training and logistics exchanges had been conducted in late 1980 and early 1981, the current pattern of exchanges resulted from discussions held during Secretary Weinberger's September 1983 visit to China. Representing the Joint Chiefs of Staff, General

---

[6]Although there is no precise definition of which visits are considered high-level and which visits fall into the category of functional military exchanges, the term "high-level" is usually used to describe visits by the secretary of defense, the service secretaries, the chairman of the Joint Chiefs, and the military service chiefs.

William Richardson, deputy commander of the U.S. Army Training and Doctrine Command (TRADOC), met with Zhang Tong, director of the Foreign Affairs Bureau (FAB) of the Ministry of Defense. The purpose of that meeting was to agree on a series of functional military exchanges to be conducted in 1984.

During that meeting, the two sides agreed to a new round of training and logistics exchanges. Subsequently a PLA training delegation visited the United States in April 1984 and a PLA logistics delegation visited in May. Reciprocal U.S. training and logistics delegations traveled to China in October and November 1984 respectively. Each of these delegations contained tri-service representation.

As the bilateral military relationship matured and developed throughout 1984 and 1985, functional service-to-service contacts developed. The U.S. Army TRADOC hosted a PLA training seminar in August 1985. In January, 1986 the first operational contact between U.S. and Chinese forces took place in the South China Sea, where elements of the U.S. Seventh Fleet conducted a PASSEX and met and exchanged greetings at sea with ships of the PLA Navy. Although the PASSEX was terminated early due to rough seas and bad weather, it was a significant milestone in the military relationship.

In September 1986, the PLA Air Force Song and Dance Troupe visited the United States. Beginning its tour in Washington, D.C., with a performance in the National Theater, the troupe toured various military installations giving performances at each stop for the U.S. forces stationed there and for the general public. A reciprocal visit to China by the U.S. Air Force Band took place in June 1987.

By the end of 1986, progress in the military relationship was reflected by an increase in the scope and frequency of functional interaction. On November 5, 1986, three ships of the U.S. Seventh Fleet, the USS *Reeves*, a guided missile cruiser, the destroyer USS *Oldendorf*, and the USS *Rentz*, a guided missile frigate, began a seven-day port call to the Chinese city of Qingdao. Admiral James A. Lyons, commander-in-chief, Pacific Fleet, was the senior U.S. Navy officer embarked. This historic ship visit to China was the first time U.S. and Chinese forces had the opportunity to interact face-to-face in something larger than a small group.[7] Just ten days

---

[7]Everyone who participated in the ship visit agreed that it was a most impressive event. Three thousand sailors disembarked from the three U.S. Navy ships in uniform and toured the city of Qingdao. Not since the late 1940s had the Chinese witnessed such a large uniformed U.S. military presence. Despite the fears of some that such a sight might evoke unpleasant memories, the ship visit was conducted in a superb professional manner and the Chinese themselves had much praise for the event. The last U.S. Navy ship visit to China was in May 1949 when the USS *Dixie* (AD 14) departed Qingdao and Shanghai.

following the ship visit, the first PLA Navy logistics delegation arrived in the United States and on December 1, a Department of Defense (DOD) quality assurance delegation arrived in China. Also in December were visits to the United States by a PLA medical delegation and the first PLA Air Force maintenance delegation.

Functional military visits in 1987 to date include visits to China by the Joint U.S. Mid-Level Management Team in January, the commander of the U.S. Air Force Logistics Command in February, the Joint U.S. Systems Analysis team led by Under Secretary of the Army Hollis in March, and the U.S. Navy training delegation led by Vice Admiral Thunman in April.

Military Technology Cooperation

U.S. military sales to China fall into two general categories: dual-use equipment and technology, licensed by the Department of Commerce, and those end items and technologies controlled by the International Munitions List (IML) and licensed by the Department of State. Of primary significance for the military relationship are weapons, equipment, and technologies associated with the IML.

Munitions list items can be sold to China on either a direct commercial basis by U.S. defense contractors who possess a valid munitions license or, on a government-to-government basis, through FMS channels. Equipment already purchased from the United States through commercial channels includes S-70C helicopters, LM2,500 gas turbine engines for naval ships, coastal defense radars, and communications equipment.

The United States and China reopened discussions on munitions list arms sales and technology transfer during Secretary Weinberger's visit to China in September 1983. Discussions between the Department of Defense and China's Ministry of Defense concentrated on identifying and defining military mission areas, based on Chinese defense requirements, as the basis for government-to-government sales of U.S. arms and military technology. From September 1983 onward, military technology cooperation discussions have been conducted between the Office of the Secretary of Defense, International Security Affairs (OSD/ISA) and the National Defense Science, Technology, and Industry Commission (NDSTIC).[8]

From the outset, both sides have worked to define cooperative programs which satisfied their fundamental goals and objectives. The Chi-

---

[8]NDSTIC is often referred to as COSTIND or the Commission on Science, Technology, and Industry for National Defense.

nese have sought to acquire production technologies and systems which would enable them to upgrade their own defense industries in order to be able to manufacture weapon systems and military equipment adequate to meet current and projected threats. Only in rare instances, those in which the Chinese defense industry has no capability whatsoever or in which current threats require immediate enhancement of their capability, will the Chinese procure complete end items in more than very small quantities. The United States, for its part, wants to assist China in meeting its legitimate defense requirements within existing weapons and technology transfer policies, consistent with U.S. political-military objectives in the region.

To date, four military mission areas have emerged as the basis of U.S.-China military technology cooperation. These four mission areas are antitank, artillery, air defense, and surface-ship antisubmarine warfare. Using these mission areas as the basis for discussion permitted both sides to concentrate on developing cooperative programs keyed to specific Chinese defensive requirements and to identify systems and technologies which most appropriately met those requirements. In each mission area, U.S. willingness to release specific defensive weapons or technologies to the PRC is based on a thorough analysis of their utility for enhancing Chinese defensive capabilities, while taking into consideration the political-military environment and the interests of other U.S. friends and allies in the region.

There has been a continuing series of discussions on matters related to cooperation in these mission areas and numerous visits by delegations of technical personnel from both countries. At every step, U.S. responses and proposals in military technology cooperation discussions with the Chinese have been fully coordinated and approved by appropriate officials of the departments of State and Defense, the Joint Chiefs of Staff, and the military services. In each case, appropriate representatives of these departments actively participated in the discussions. In addition to coordinating with appropriate offices and agencies of the executive branch of the government, the Department of Defense has regularly consulted with members of the Congress and their staffs on progress and developments in the U.S.-China military relationship, to include military technology cooperation and arms sales.

Reciprocal visits by Chinese and U.S. technical teams have been designed to establish a base of understanding of requirements and capabilities in order to define cooperative programs. Visits by Chinese technical teams to the United States have been to defense contractors and military installations which may be involved in implemented cooperative programs. Similar U.S. technical teams have visited China. In many cases, U.S. technical team visits to China have been funded by the Chinese under approved FMS cases related to cooperative programs for the various agreed mission areas.[9]

By late summer 1985, following two years of discussions and technical visits on the four approved mission areas, the Chinese began to submit formal Letters of Request (LORs) for specific programs. China submitted eight LORs pertaining to the artillery mission area in August 1985. The LORs were for technical data packages, plant layout designs, and technical assistance for setting up large-caliber artillery fuse and detonator plants. Formal notification of the sale was made to COCOM[10] and the U.S. Congress in September. Initial Letters of Offer and Acceptance (LOAs) for the program were signed in August 1986. The approximate value of the program is $30 million.

In December 1985, China submitted an LOR for a program to modernize the avionics for its F-8 interceptor. COCOM and Congress were notified about the program in March 1986 and an LOA signed by the Chinese on October 30. The F-8, a Chinese-developed, twin-engine, delta-wing, high-altitude interceptor, is designed to counter the Soviet bomber threat. Avionics modernization for the F-8 interceptor involves the integration of releasable avionics components into the F-8 aircraft by a U.S. prime defense contractor. The Grumman Corporation of Long Island, New York, was awarded a contract to act as the prime contractor for this program in August 1987. The U.S. Air Force will supervise this effort as an FMS program. The estimated value of the program is approximately $500 million. The integration effort will require about six years to complete and will include an airborne radar, navigation equipment, a head-up display, a mission computer, an air data computer, and a data bus. Following successful integration of the avionics package, a total of fifty F-8 aircraft will be modified by the Chinese for installation of avionics kits in China. The program is an end-item sale and does not involve co-assembly or co-production. There will be no transfer of design or production technologies. No weapons are included in the sale.[11] In order to facilitate coordination between the PLA Air Force and

---

[9]The activities referred to here are site surveys. Site surveys are routinely conducted as part of an FMS program to assist in developing price and availability data to an FMS customer prior to the issuing of an LOA.

[10]COCOM stands for Coordinating Committee, which is made up of the NATO allies, minus Iceland, plus Japan. COCOM reviews the sale of all munitions list items to communist countries.

[11]See Edward W. Ross, "U.S.-China Military Relations," in Martin L. Lasater, ed., *The Two Chinas: A Contemporary View,* Heritage Lectures no. 55 (Washington, D.C.: Heritage Foundation, 1986):83–95.

the U.S. Air Force, the Chinese have established a five-man liaison office at Wright-Patterson Air Force Base in Ohio.

In his testimony before the Senate Foreign Relations Committee, Rear Admiral E. B. Baker, Jr., explained that, prior to agreeing to pursue the F-8 avionics modernization program with the Chinese and deciding to submit the program to COCOM and Congress, the departments of State and Defense thoroughly reviewed all aspects of the program to ensure that it was consistent with both the U.S. policy objectives and releasability considerations. "This modest upgrade of Chinese air-defense capability will contribute to China's ability to protect its sovereign air space. Moreover, by enhancing China's security against external threats, this program is in the national interest of the United States."[12]

Finally, in January 1987, following the submission to COCOM in September 1986, the Reagan administration submitted to Congress a proposal for the sale of four AN-TPQ/37 Firefinder artillery-locating radars. Following COCOM and congressional approvals, the United States issued LOAs to China for sale of the system and for appropriate operations and maintenance training. Like all other weapon systems approved for sale to China by the U.S. government to date, the AN/TPQ-37 is considered a defensive system. The radar enables forces in the field to locate enemy radar batteries directing fire at their positions based on the trajectories of incoming artillery rounds. PLA students are currently undergoing training on this system at Ft. Sill, Oklahoma.

Cooperative programs in the two remaining mission areas—antitank and surface ship antisubmarine warfare (ASW)—remain under discussion. The focus of attention in the antitank area has been the co-production of the improved TOW wire-guided antitank guided missile. In the surface-ship ASW mission area, the co-production of the Mark 46 Mod-2 lightweight ASW torpedo has been the main topic of discussion. Limited financial resources available to the PLA and potential competition with indigenous development programs have contributed to Chinese indecision on these programs. Four Mark 46 Mod-2 torpedoes have been sold to China for test and evaluation, and seven Chinese students have been trained on this system at the Navy Weapons Training Center in Orlando, Florida.

Future Prospects for U.S.-China Military Relations

Prospects for continued growth and development of U.S.-China military relations appear to be very good. Developments over the past

---

[12]Baker, *Two Chinas*.

year—Secretary Weinberger's October 1986 visit to China, the continued frequent exchange of high-level military visits, the November 1986 U.S. Navy ship visit to Qingdao, and the signing of the F-8 avionics moderni-zation and AN/TPQ-37 radar LOAs—are clear indications that the mili-tary relationship is moving forward. High-level visits, functional military exchanges, and military technology cooperation will continue in 1987 and beyond. As the relationship develops, the scope and fre-quency of military exchanges can be expected to increase. Military sales and technology transfer to China also should increase, reflecting improvement in the overall political, economic, and military relation-ship.

Nevertheless, various constraints, both in China and the United States, will restrain too rapid an acceleration of the relationship. Beijing will continue to insist on maintaining a good measure of independence from the United States and therefore will proceed slowly in the military arena. Beijing will prefer functional exchanges which permit it to gain useful knowledge and experience without the appearance of strategic cooperation. On the technology front, limits on financial resources over the next several years likely will restrict both the quantity and quality of military technology and equipment China will be able to purchase from the United States or other noncommunist countries.[13] For the United States, domestic political considerations and institutional barriers to the transfer of advanced technologies serve as limiting factors. Finally, and perhaps most important, Washington must manage its relationship with China in view of its broader interests, and the interests of its friends and allies, in the Asia Pacific region.

Future Chinese Military Capabilities

It is not possible to assess adequately the implications of U.S.-China military relations without some estimate of their effects on future Chi-nese military capabilities. Since U.S. inputs to Chinese military modern-ization are by no means the sole determining factor, two questions must be answered. What is the most likely result of Chinese military modern-ization efforts through the end of the century? And how is the U.S.-China military relationship likely to affect that outcome?

---

[13]Unclassified estimates by both the Central Intelligence Agency and the Defense Intelli-gence Agency report that Chinese foreign exchange reserves have fallen from approxi-mately US$17 billion in the 1983–84 time frame to approximately US$7–9 billion in 1986. Because military modernization has the lowest priority among the Four Modernizations, the PLA will be the first to feel the effect of reduced foreign exchange reserves by a reduction in the money available to purchase foreign military weapons and technology.

Since it first articulated the Four Modernizations in 1978, the PRC has sought to improve its military capabilities through a defense modernization program which ranks fourth in national priority behind industry, agriculture, and science and technology. Nevertheless, progress is geared to the long term and is contingent upon Chinese economic modernization. Due to the limited financial resources available to the PLA in 1986 and 1987, primary emphasis in defense modernization has been placed on military education, training, and the restructuring of the military establishment. In the area of weapons and equipment modernization, Beijing's strategy is the acquisition of production technologies to modernize its own defense industries rather than the acquisition of quantities of foreign weapons and equipment. Given the present state of the PRC defense industry and the economy, it will take a considerable period of time before the PRC is capable of producing modern weapons in sufficient quantities to satisfy PLA requirements.[14]

As for Beijing's purchases of foreign military technology and equipment, there are two very serious obstacles to transforming these acquisitions into actual military capabilities. First, the reduction of China's foreign exchange reserves, coupled with the relatively low priority of defense modernization, means that China cannot afford to purchase sufficient quantities of technology and equipment to effect a near-term, across-the-board upgrade of its military capabilities. Second, because China's military industrial complex and equipment, along with its doctrine, strategy, and tactics, are with few exceptions quite outdated, China faces a major challenge in absorbing the weapons and technology that it has and will acquire in the years ahead. Most observers of the Chinese military, and the Chinese themselves, agree that modernizing the PLA is a complex and long-term undertaking.

Therefore, Chinese military modernization efforts through the end of this century and beyond are likely to result only in modest improvements to basic military capabilities. Gradual improvements in China's doctrine, strategy, and tactics, along with the limited deployment of moderately advanced weapons and equipment, should enhance the defensive capabilities of China's ground, air, and naval forces. There is nothing to suggest that China will be able to redress the serious deficiencies in logistics, mobility, and command and control which severely restrict its ability to project military power beyond its borders.

---

[14]The Chinese defense industry dates to the 1950s and was established with the assistance of the Soviet Union. Following the break with the Soviet Union and during the ten years of the Cultural Revolution (1965–75) China's defense industry deteriorated. Today, China's military industry and technology is generally accepted, with few exceptions, to be at least twenty years behind that of the United States.

In this context, U.S. arms and technology transfers to China are unlikely to alter significantly the prospects for Chinese military modernization. Commercial and FMS sales to date have been quite small when compared to China's total requirements and, therefore, are unlikely to have much impact by themselves. Barring a dramatic change in the political-military environment in the region, U.S. military sales to China should continue to support the policy of contributing to the enhancement of the PLA's defensive capabilities and should not alter the military balance in the region. In terms of China's relative military capabilities vis-à-vis its primary adversary, the Soviet Union, it can be argued that the gap has been widening in favor of the Soviet Union. Indeed, a major consideration for the United States in approving military equipment and technology sales to China is the desire to prevent further widening of the capabilities gap between China and the Soviet Union and the potential destabilization of the region.

Implications for ASEAN

ASEAN's Challenge

There remain too many uncertainties inherent in Chinese domestic politics and the dynamic political-military environment in the region to permit long-term predictions about the implications of U.S.-China relations for ASEAN with a high degree of certainty. Nevertheless, some preliminary judgments are possible, based on an understanding of China's changing political, economic, and military roles in the region and the evolving attitudes of the various ASEAN states toward China.

While there are differences in the degree of concern among ASEAN states with regard to the developing U.S.-China military relationship, there does appear to be a common denominator. To varying degrees, each country takes a somewhat pragmatic approach to near-term developments, but expresses the more traditional fear of Chinese hegemonism—the fear that some time in the future China may exercise newfound military power to extend greater influence over the countries of Southeast Asia. U.S. assurances notwithstanding, Southeast Asia's historical experience with China, along with China's size and strategic location, ensure that such concerns will persist.

For the immediate future, the reality of a gradually expanding U.S.-China military relationship is just one factor that each of the ASEAN countries must take into consideration in formulating its policies toward China and the United States. ASEAN is equally interested in China as an economic competitor and in China's current and future role in the economic development of the region. Now that Beijing no longer pursues hostile policies toward the noncommunist Southeast Asian states and has even emerged as a status quo power, the challenge for ASEAN governments is to take advantage of China's new "open door" and seek better relations with Beijing.

As for ASEAN's concern about China's military relationship with the United States, U.S. respect for the interests of its Southeast Asian friends and allies assures that ASEAN's concerns will be taken into account as Washington formulates its policy toward China and the military relationship. In the final analysis, however, ASEAN's ultimate guarantee that U.S. assistance to Chinese military modernization will not prove inimical to its interests is that ASEAN and the United States have many common goals and objectives with regard to China. Not the least of these is a desire to see China play a positive role in contributing to peace and stability in the region. Both the United States and ASEAN recognize that China will inevitably play an increasingly greater role in regional political, economic, and military affairs and should seek to help China channel its energies in positive directions. Like the nations of ASEAN, China can only pursue economic and political development if it is secure from external threats. Thus, supporting Chinese military modernization as a deterrent against Soviet and Vietnamese expansionism in Asia helps maintain peace and stability. A review of the attitudes of the individual ASEAN states suggests that, for the most part, ASEAN leaders appreciate this reality.

Conclusions

The development of U.S.-China military relations has not been a short-term phenomenon responding to ad hoc international political-military events. On the contrary, it has been, and continues to be, a fundamental element of overall United States China policy. U.S.-China military relations serve basic U.S. and Chinese strategic interests. A secure, modernizing, and friendly China has the potential to contribute significantly to peace and stability in the Asia-Pacific region and the world. The enhancement of China's defensive military capabilities plays an integral part in attaining this objective by helping to deter Soviet and Vietnamese expansionism in Asia.

Military technology cooperation—the aspect of U.S.-China military relations of greatest interest to ASEAN—has concentrated on meeting basic Chinese defensive requirements through cooperative programs within the mutually agreed mission areas of antitank, artillery, air-defense, and surface-ship ASW. Specific arms and technology sales to China by the United States, both commercial and FMS, will continue to be approved on a case-by-case basis following thorough interagency review and approval. U.S. concern for the interests of its Asian friends and allies is an important factor in the U.S. decision-making process.

The pace and nature of Chinese military modernization, in the context of current Chinese political and economic policies, suggest that it will not pose a threat to the countries of ASEAN through the end of this century and beyond. Basic Chinese military capabilities will improve only gradually and are dependent on more than the acquisition of advanced military technologies and equipment.

ASEAN, along with China's other neighbors in Asia, faces the challenge of dealing and competing with China within the new political, economic, and military environment in Asia. Differences between China and the ASEAN states will continue to exist, just as they do between the United States and China. Over the long term, however, the interests of ASEAN are best served by providing China with a positive incentive for pursuing policies in the region which contribute to regional development. Recognizing China's modernization requirement and playing an active and positive role in China's modernization process are just such incentives.

APPENDIX

U.S.-China Military Relations: Chronology of Events (1979-87)

1979

January	U.S. and China normalize diplomatic relations. U.S. Defense Attaché Office, Beijing, and PRC Defense Attaché Office, Washington, established.

1980

January	Secretary of Defense Harold Brown visits China: Brown opens dialogue with senior Chinese military officials, meets with Hua Guofeng, Huang Hua, Zhang Aiping, and others.
May	Deputy Chief of the General Staff Liu Huaqing visits U.S. Liu comes as advance party for Geng Biao.
June	Geng Biao visits U.S.: Geng named Minister of Defense after return to China.
September	Under Secretary of Defense for Research and Engineering Dr. Perry and Principal Deputy Under Secretary Dr. Dinneen visit China: First meaningful military technology cooperation discussions with PLA. Delegation visits military aircraft factory in Shenyang and sees F-8.
September	Chinese logistics delegation visits U.S.
October	PLA training delegation visits U.S.: Xiao Ke leads group from PLA Military Academy.

1980 (continued)

December   Dr. Pirie, assistant secretary of Defense for Manpower, Installations, and Logistics, leads U.S. logistics delegation visit to China.

1981

May   General William Richardson, deputy commander U.S. Army Training and Doctrine Command, leads U.S. training delegation visit to China. General Richardson is accompanied by Rear Admiral Don Jones, director, East Asia and Pacific Region OSD/ISA.

June   Secretary of State Haig visits China, announces the removal of China from the list of prohibited destinations for munitions list items and U.S. willingness to sell arms to China on a case-by-case basis.

October   PLA military medical delegation visits U.S.

1982

August 17   U.S.-PRC joint communiqué signed on U.S. arms sales to Taiwan: U.S. declares that it "does not seek to carry out a long-term policy of arms sales to Taiwan. . . . [U.S.] arms sales to Taiwan will not exceed, either in qualitative or quantitative terms, the level of those supplied in recent years since the establishment of diplomatic relations between the U.S. and China. . . . [The U.S.] intends to reduce gradually its sales of arms to Taiwan, leading over time to a final resolution."

September   U.S. military marksmanship team participates in an international competition in China.

December   U.S. military medical delegation visits China.

1983

February   Secretary of State Shultz visits China. Shultz is accompanied by Assistant Secretary of Defense ISA Richard Armitage.

September   Secretary of Commerce Malcolm Baldridge visits China and announces liberalization of controls on dual-use technology to China.

September   Department of Commerce announces "red," "yellow," and "green" line for seven categories of dual-use technology for China. China moved from category "P" to "V."

September   Secretary of Defense Caspar Weinberger visits China: Weinberger, ASD Armitage, ASD Wade, DASD Kelly, AS

1983 (continued)

State Wolfowitz, and others visit Beijing, Xian, and Shanghai. Secretary Weinberger and Minister Zhang discuss regional and global issues. Dr. Wade leads U.S. side in military technology cooperation discussions. General Richardson, deputy commander U.S. Army TRADOC, representing the Joint Chiefs of Staff, leads U.S. side in meeting with Zhang Tong, director MND, FAB, on military exchanges. Upon departing China, Weinberger announces that Zhang Aiping and Zhao Ziyang will visit the U.S. and that President Reagan will visit China.

1984

February	Work team for U.S.-China Military Technology Cooperation meets in Washington. U.S. side chaired by OSD/ISA. Chinese side chaired by NDSTIC.
March	Work team for U.S.-China Military Technology Cooperation meets in Beijing.
April	President Reagan visits China accompanied by Assistant Secretary of Defense ISA Richard Armitage.
April	PLA training delegation visits U.S.
May	PLA logistics delegation visits U.S.
June	Minister of Defense Zhang Aiping visits U.S. Zhang is accompanied by Deputy Navy Commander Nie Kuiju, Deputy Air Force Commander Wang Hai, and others. Zhang calls on President Reagan, Vice President Bush, Secretary of State Shultz, Science Advisor Keyworth, NSC advisor McFarlane. Zhang and Weinberger meet twice to discuss regional and global issues and U.S.-China military technology cooperation. Zhang meets with Joint Chiefs.
June	President Reagan certifies China eligible for FMS cash sales.
August	Secretary of the Navy Lehman visits China. Lehman opens discussions on naval technology cooperation. Talks focus on surface ship ASW (Mark 46 Mod-2 torpedo, sonars, helicopters, destroyer modernization).
October	U.S. training delegation visits China.
November	U.S. logistics delegation headed by Assistant Secretary of Defense Dr. Korb visits China.

1985

January	ASN/RES Melvin Paisley leads delegation to China to discuss U.S.-China Naval Technology Cooperation.
January	Chairman of the Joint Chiefs General Vessey visits China: Gen. Vessey is accompanied by CINCPAC Adm. Crowe.
July	PLAAF training delegation visits U.S.
August	TRADOC hosts U.S.-PLA training seminar.
September	Notice of large caliber artillery ammunition manufacturing modernization program given to Congress and COCOM.
October	CSAF General Gabriel visits China: CSAF is hosted by Wang Hai, commander PLAAF. Gabriel and Wang Hai agree to Air Force training exchanges.
October	Vice President Bush visits China, attends U.S. Navy Day reception.
November	DCGS Gen. Xu Xin makes private visit to U.S. Xu is hosted by United Nations Association of the United States. Makes courtesy call on Secretary of Defense Weinberger in Pentagon.
November	PLA Navy CDR Liu Huaqing visits U.S. CNO Admiral Watkins, Secretary of the Navy Lehman, CINCPACFLT Admiral Lyons, and CINCPAC Admiral Hays all press Liu on a U.S. ship visit to China. Liu visits Pascagoula, Key West, San Diego, and Honolulu.
December	NDSTIC Vice Min. Gen. Xie Guang visits U.S. Xie is accompanied by DCS PLAAF Zhu Yibao, Vice Min. Aviation Industry He Wenzhi, and Zhang Pin, deputy director of MND FAB. Xie and party review F-8 program statement of work at Wright-Patterson AFB. Xie meets with ASD Armitage, LTG McPeak, Under Sec. Army Ambrose. Xie signs Letter of Request for F-8 avionics program.

1986

January	U.S. Navy and PLA Navy conduct PASSEX in South China Sea.
January	DASD Jim Kelly travels to Beijing for consultations with Ambassador Winston Lord and senior Chinese military leaders. Kelly meets with Xie Guang, Wu Shaozu, and others.

1986 (continued)

February	F-8 modernization program informal notification to Congress.
March	F-8 program notice given to COCOM.
April	Congress approves F-8 avionics modernization program for PRC.
April	CNO Admiral Watkins visits China, departs early because of the bombing of Libya.
May	PLA Chief of General Staff Yang Dezhi visits the United States. Yang is guest of Chairman of the Joint Chiefs Adm. Crowe.
July	COCOM grants final approval to F-8 avionics modernization program for the PRC.
August	Initial LOAs for large-caliber artillery ammunition modernization manufacturing program signed by Chinese.
August	F-8 avionics modernization LOA briefing team visits PRC led by Brig. Gen. Delligatti.
September	PLA Air Force Song and Dance Troupe visits the U.S.
September	Visiting instructor from the National Defense University lectures at the PLA University of National Defense in Beijing.
October	Secretary of Defense Caspar Weinberger makes his second visit to the PRC as guest of Defense Minister Zhang Aiping. Secretary Weinberger meets with Hong Xuezhi, Yang Shangkun, Yang Dezhi, Deng Xiaoping, Zhao Ziyang, and Foreign Minister Wu Xueqian.
October	Hong Xuezhi, director, General Logistics Department, leads Chinese logistics delegation to the United States.
November	Three ships of the U.S. Seventh Fleet—USS *Reeves*, a guided missile cruiser, the destroyer USS *Oldendorf*, and USS *Rentz*, a guided missile frigate—make a seven-day port call to the Chinese city of Qingdao. Admiral James A. Lyons, CINPACFLT, is the senior naval officer embarked. U.S. Ambassador to China Winston Lord is in attendance. The last U.S. ship visit to China was in May 1949 when the USS *Dixie* (AD 14) departed Qingdao and Shanghai. The ship visit receives ample press coverage from both the U.S. and Chinese press.
November	Army Chief of Staff General Wickham visits China.
November	PLA Navy logistics team visits the U.S.

1986 (continued)

December	F-8 avionics modernization program liaison team arrives from China to establish an office at Wright-Patterson AFB.
December	DOD quality assurance delegation visits China.
December	PLA Air Force maintenance delegation visits the U.S.
December	PLA medical delegation visits the U.S.

1987

January	F-8 configuration conference is conducted at Wright-Patterson Air Force Base, Ohio.
January	Joint Mid-level Management Team visits China. Team of colonels and lt. colonels led by Brig. Gen. Harvey of JCS travels to China on a general orientation visit.
February	General O'Loughlin, commander Air Force Logistics Command, visits China on an informal visit hosted by the DAO. Gen. O'Loughlin meets with PLAAF Commander Wang Hai in Beijing and visits Shenyang Aircraft Factory.
March	Mark 46 Mod-2 ASW torpedo provisioning conference held in Beijing. CPT Mike Holmes of NAVOTTSA leads U.S. team.
March	CMC Gen. P. X. Kelly visits China. First visit ever of a commandant of the Marine Corps. General Kelly travels to Chinese Marine Corps Headquarters at Zhan Zhang.
March	Joint Systems Analysis Team visits China. Deputy Under Secretary of the Army Hollis leads a tri-service OR/SA delegation supported by JCS. Eden Woon accompanies the delegation.
April	USAF flight test team (F-8) visits China.
April	Air War College lecturers visit China.
April	PLAAF Commander Wang Hai visits the U.S. as the guest of Air Force Chief of Staff General Larry Welch. Wang meets with Secretary of Defense Weinberger.
April	USN training delegation visits China.
May	PLA Defense University chair, Zhang Zhen, visits the National Defense University.
May	Madame Nie, chair, Science and Technology Committee NDSTIC, visits U.S. as guest of the assistant secretary of the Navy, Research, Engineering, and Systems.
May	Yang Shangkun, permanent vice chairman of the Military Commission leads the senior PRC Government

1987 (continued)

delegation to the United States. Corps members of Yang's delegation are State Counselor Fang Yi, Vice Foreign Minister Zhu Qizhen, Deputy Chief of the General Staff Xu Xin, NDSTIC Minister Ding Henggao, Yang Side, Xiong Guangkai, Liu Huaqui, and MFA Protocol Chief Wu Minglian. Yang meets with the president, the vice president, the secretaries of State and Defense, congressional leaders, Charles Wick, and others. Yang visits Hawaii, New York, St. Louis, SAC headquarters, and Los Angeles. One highlight of the trip is Yang's speech to 850 members of the Chinese American community in Los Angeles.

June   General Skantz, commander Air Force Systems Command makes an informal visit to DAO Beijing. General Skantz meets with PLAAF Commander Wang Hai and visits the INS development center.

June   Admiral John Hayes, commander-in-chief Pacific, visits China.

June   USAF Band visits China.

September   ASD A&L Dr. Costello leads U.S. defense logistics delegation to China.

September   Secretary of the Air Force Aldridge visits China as guest of PLA Air Force Commander Wang Hai.

7. China's Military Policies

STEPHEN LEONG

China's National Security and Defense Modernization

China's military policies are primarily aimed at attaining national security vis-à-vis the Soviet Union. While the United States was China's main enemy for two decades (1949–69) after the establishment of the People's Republic of China (PRC), it was replaced by the Soviet Union in the 1970s as China's major threat. Although beginning in 1981 reassessment of China's relations with the two superpowers called for a more "independent" stance between Washington and Moscow, the latter is still viewed as the main threat to Beijing's security.[1]

Apart from the possible direct military threat to its territory, China also sees another dimension of the Soviet threat through "encirclement" of its territory by means of deployment of air and missile forces, a massive troop presence in the northern frontier, the "client-state" of Vietnam in the south providing naval facilities to Soviet vessels, and the occupation of Afghanistan. China's perception of this threat and its quest for security have caused it to embark on a policy of modernization of its armed forces. As Paul H. B. Godwin observes:

> China's defense modernization objectives are twofold. In the short term Beijing seeks to improve the combat effectiveness of its current forces through the adoption of combined arms operations as the basis for its battlefield strategy and by improving the technical and professional skills of the officer corps. The armed forces' weapons and equipment will be incrementally improved, but with only limited and selective importation of foreign weapons and equipment. The long-term goal is to build a scientific and defense industrial base capable of developing and producing weapons and equipment based upon advanced military technology. These two objectives are being sought as the nuclear weapons program continues to develop and deploy strategic systems capable of providing a more effective nuclear deterrent.[2]

---

[1]Carol Lee Hamrin, "China Reassesses the Superpowers," *Pacific Affairs* 56(2) (Summer 1983):209–31; Gerald Segal, "The Soviet 'Threat' at China's Gates," *Conflict Studies*, no. 143 (London: Institute for the Study of Conflict, 1983), passim.

[2]"Overview: China's Defense Modernization," in Selected Papers Submitted to the Joint Economic Committee Congress of the United States, *China's Economy Looks Toward the Year 2000*, 99th Congress, 2d session, May 31, 1986, vol. 2, p. 133.

Implications for Southeast Asia

While the PRC's military modernization policy aims at strengthening its defense against external threat, it has vast implications for the Asia-Pacific region, notably Southeast Asia, where China has long played a role in the politics of the region. This chapter examines the implications for communist Southeast Asia (i.e., Indochina) and noncommunist Southeast Asia (primarily the ASEAN countries).

Indochina

China's military policy concerning Indochina is to prevent the expansion of Soviet influence among the three Indochinese states, which Beijing has traditionally viewed as its sphere of influence. While the PRC sees the Soviet Union as aiming to achieve "world" hegemony, it views Vietnam as working toward "regional" hegemony among the Indochinese states. Beijing also believes that Hanoi intends to achieve its goal of setting up an Indochinese federation through the backing of Moscow.[3]

Although the PRC resorted to the use of military power in 1979 to force the withdrawal of Vietnamese forces from Kampuchea, that policy has failed in its objective. Not only has Vietnam not withdrawn from Kampuchea—much to the detriment of Chinese strategy of reducing Soviet influence in Indochina—but it has caused a greater Soviet presence in Vietnam. Soviet air and naval power in Da Nang and Cam Ranh Bay and the strengthening of the Vietnamese northern border defense are factors that militate against any Chinese military policy that may call for a second "lesson" to be inflicted on Vietnam.

Although an awareness of weaknesses in the ground forces during the Sino-Vietnamese conflict in 1979 increased the demand for modernization of the People's Liberation Army (PLA), there is general consensus among Western analysts of Chinese military affairs that China's military strategy is essentially defensive in nature, directed primarily at the Soviet threat. Consequently, reforms since 1981 have aimed largely at qualitatively improving its overall defense system. As to its defense doctrine, the present strategy—labeled a "people's war under modern conditions"—is "China's defensive strategy during its long transition from 'underdeveloped' to 'world-power' status—a transition that still has decades to go."[4] It is "a strategy combining guerrilla warfare, posi-

---

[3]King C. Chen, "The Impact of the Changing PRC-Soviet Relationship on Indochina," *Issues and Studies* 23(8) (April 1987):72–73.

[4]Harlan Jencks, "Ground Forces," in G. Segal and W. T. Tow, eds., *Chinese Defence Policy* (London: Macmillan, 1984), p. 66.

tional defense, and mobile operations principally conducted by the militia, regional forces, and main forces, respectively."[5] Since 1981, reforms in the PLA have been subsumed under the term *regularization*. As Harlan Jencks explains:

> "Regularisation" is more than improved technology and changed tactics. It entails such new (to the PLA) features as standard procedures, rationalised organisation, and tightened discipline. In particular it means curtailment of decentralised, semi-autonomous, self-sufficient "guerrilla war habits" that have long characterised the ground forces. The chain of command is to be both simplified and strengthened.[6]

Because "in the PLA, the armoured regiment is the heart of fighting power,"[7] since 1980 Beijing has undertaken efforts to improve the quality of its armored forces. Before 1980, the bulk of China's tank force consisted of Type-59s (total around 6,000). Since then, the Type-62 tank, an improved version, has been in use. It is estimated that about 1,200 Type-62 light tanks particularly suited for difficult terrain have been deployed in southern China, including areas along the Sino-Vietnamese border and the Straits of Taiwan.[8] Since 1982, the Type-59 has been superseded by the Type-69 MBT, which has a laser range finder, IR drive, spotlight, and, most probably, a new smooth-bore 105mm main gun.[9] PLA modernization also calls for further mechanization of its ground forces in order to be equipped with effective mechanized infantry combat vehicles. The YW-531 series APCs of transport and combat vehicles will continue through this decade with a newer version that is equipped with a mounted automatic cannon and an ATGM system.[10]

Despite such improvements in Chinese armored forces, compared with Western and Soviet standards, the PLA armored vehicles are still of much lower quality. According to Jencks, China's Type-69 "probably does not measure up to the Soviet T-62, let alone the newer T-64/72. There is little prospect for a really new tank before 1990, if then."[11] Moreover, from the armored personnel perspective, although armor training for officers is provided at the Shijiazhuang Amor Institute (Beijing) to promote "combined arms" warfare, a major deficiency of the

---

[5]Ibid., p. 53.
[6]Ibid., pp. 53–54.
[7]G. Jacobs, "China's Armoured Forces," *Asian Defence Journal*, April 1986, p. 5, hereafter cited as *ADJ*.
[8]Ibid., pp. 6–7.
[9]Jencks, "Ground Forces," p. 64.
[10]Jacobs, "China's Armoured Forces," p. 10.
[11]Jencks, "Ground Forces," p. 64.

PLA, "it may take the PLA a decade to begin fielding armour commanders at regimental level."[12]

Such deficiency in the armored forces and the lack of "tactical mobility and logistical supply" in the PLA in general underscore the fact that military modernization is still an arduous and long-term affair. Consequently, should China decide to invade Vietnam a second time, it will encounter once again a battle-hardened Vietnamese army, which not only has prolonged its wartime experience (since 1979) but is also equipped with comparatively superior Soviet-supplied military weapons. On troops alone, it has been reported that by 1984, Vietnam—the third largest army in the world with one million armed personnel—had deployed over 500,000 soldiers in northern Vietnam (compared with 75,000–100,000 in 1979). Huge fortifications have also been constructed along the border to meet another Chinese challenge. Consequently, it is estimated that while the PLA fielded twenty divisions in the 1979 conflict, it will now need fifty to sixty divisions to invade Vietnam's northern frontier.[13]

What are the implications of a modernized Chinese air force for Vietnam? In the 1979 conflict, China intentionally limited its objectives in battle by not resorting to air power.[14] Presently, the J-6 forms the bulk of the People's Liberation Army Air Force (PLAAF). Although the J-6 has a high rate of climb and heavy cannon firepower and is easy to maintain, nevertheless it performs rather poorly above altitudes of 20,000 feet. Moreover, it does not possess effective radar or medium-range missiles. According to Bill Sweetman, "Matched against a more modern and sophisticated aircraft such as the MiG-23 Flogger, the J-6 would be in difficult tactical predicament."[15] Even the PLAAF's Q-5 Fantan attack fighter employed for tactical support (e.g., launching air strikes against enemy ground forces) suffers from poor quality sensors, rendering it difficult to find and strike at targets. While the J-7 has a more modern design (a copy of early MiG-21s), its operational capacity is only slightly better than the J-6 while remaining deficient with limited armament and equipment.[16]

China's latest fighter aircraft is the J-8. Apparently based on the MiG-23 Flogger design, the J-8 is powered by a Chinese-built Rolls-

---

[12]Jacobs, "China's Armoured Forces," p. 11.
[13]Larry A. Niksch, "Southeast Asia," in Segal and Tow, eds., *Chinese Defence Policy*, p. 238; Jonathan D. Pollack, "China as a Military Power," in Onkar Marwah and Jonathan D. Pollack, eds., *Military Power in Asian States: China, India, Japan* (Boulder: Westview Press, 1980), p. 60.
[14]"Air Forces," in Segal and Tow, eds., *Chinese Defence Policy*, p. 80.
[15]Ibid., p. 77.
[16]Ibid., p. 78.

Royce Spey engine. Although regarded as an advance on the J-6 or J-7, "even a faithful copy of the original would not match the MiG-23 Flogger in Soviet service."[17] Moreover, production of the J-7 and especially the J-8 (estimated at only fifty in service in 1983) is far below those of the J-6 and Q-5. One reason could be that while the PRC aircraft industry is able to produce relatively modern engines, it is still unable to manufacture radar and missiles, vital features of a modern fighter.[18] Recent reports reveal that the PLAAF has sought, through a contract worth $43.5 million with GEC Avionics (UK), to update a portion of the J-7 with improved radar, head-up display, airborne communications, air date computer, and power supply. It is, however, not known how many of the PLAAF's 200 J-7s can be modernized by this effort.[19]

Compared with the PLAAF, the Vietnamese air force of 15,000 men appears to be much better equipped with Soviet aircraft. Its 400 fighter planes consist of MiG-19s, MiG-21s, SU-17s, and SU-22s. It is reported that while 170 combat planes are stationed in southern Vietnam, the remaining 230 are deployed in the north, thus underscoring Hanoi's grave concern over another Chinese invasion.[20] Its four interceptor regiments have 200 MiG-21s. Besides its own air force the Da Nang air base reveals strong Soviet protection for Vietnam with Moscow's highly sophisticated MiG-23 and SU-20 jet aircraft. The Soviet fleet of sixteen TU-16 Badger and TU-95 Bear planes also serves as a deterrent to any intended invasion of Vietnam a second time. Apart from military hardware, Moscow has stationed about 2,500 military advisers in Vietnam.[21] With its northern defense strengthened and central and southern defenses augmented by formidable Soviet air and naval power, should a Chinese invasion of the 1979 intensity recur, it is likely that Hanoi would resort to the use of air power.

Although since 1982, the Soviet threat has been judged by the PRC to be no longer a direct or imminent threat, nevertheless, Moscow's military relationship with Hanoi still represents the principal threat to Beijing and is, therefore, central to Chinese military planning for Southeast Asia now and in the foreseeable future. Because of PLA deficiencies and China's priority for economic modernization, a second Chinese invasion is very unlikely in the next decades, and the PRC military

---

[17]Ibid., p. 79.
[18]Ibid.
[19]*ADJ*, April 1986, p. 106.
[20]Ibid., p. 98.
[21]Jack Broome, "Soviet Military Expansion in the Pacific," in Ray S. Cline, ed., *U.S.-ASEAN Relations: Prospects for the 1990s* (Washington, D.C.: U.S. Global Strategic Council, 1987), p. 41.

strategy for Indochina will continue to rely on supplying weapons to anti-Vietnamese forces in that part of Southeast Asia. In Kampuchea, these forces are the National Army of Democratic Kampuchea (NADK of Khmer Rouge) with 30,000–35,000 armed personnel, the Khmer People's National Liberation Forces (KPNLF) with 14,000–15,000 soldiers plus 5,000 armed reserves, and the Armée Nationaliste Sihanoukienne (ANS) with 10,000 members.[22]

It is China's hope that the forces of the Coalition Government of Democratic Kampuchea (CGDK) will eventually wear down the occupying Vietnamese troops, causing the latter to withdraw from Kampuchea. Although Hanoi declared in 1985 that it would withdraw its troops in 1990 and despite recent changes in leadership and a new emphasis on domestic economic development, Hanoi has indicated its reluctance to do so. Trinh Xuan Lang of the Foreign Ministry stated: ''The withdrawal of Vietnamese voluntary troops from Kampuchea and the elimination of the genocidal Pol Pot clique must be carried out simultaneously.''[23]

However, given pressures from the international community, particularly ASEAN, in all probability Vietnam will undertake a partial withdrawal (perhaps one-third of its 140,000 troops) in 1990. But because Heng Samrin's People's Republic of Kampuchea Armed Forces (PRKAF) has only about 15,000 troops[24] compared with the combined CGDK forces of 60,000—the latter being almost 50 percent of the combined People's Army of Vietnam (PAVN) and PRAKF forces after the 1990 partial withdrawal—it is very doubtful that Hanoi will settle for less than a 2:1 ratio in its favor. The PRC no doubt wants a total pullout and, failing that, a substantial reduction of PAVN troops in Kampuchea after 1990. It will then feel encouraged to provide more military assistance to the CGDK (especially the Khmer Rouge) forces in order to hasten the reduction of the Vietnamese presence and influence in Kampuchea. There is a risk, however, that Vietnam will exploit this situation in the international community to rationalize its decision to redeploy its troops in Kampuchea or, at least, to retain the remaining PAVN forces there to meet increased Chinese military aid to the CGDK troops.

Apart from the Vietnamese manpower advantage in numbers and experience in Kampuchea, it appears that the Chinese military policy of assisting the CGDK forces will continue to be at a disadvantage because of the limited arms it can supply them through the Thai sanctuary. Thus

---

[22]Jacques Bekaert, "The War in Cambodia, 1979–1986," *ADJ*, August 1986, p. 17.

[23]*New Straits Times*, March 7, 1987.

[24]Bekaert, "War in Cambodia," p. 17.

far, Chinese weapons for the CGDK troops (primarily Khmer Rouge) consist of copies of Soviet arms (e.g., AK 47/Kalashnikov and SKS/ Simonov), rifles together with B-40 rocket launchers, RPGs, 12.7mm AA heavy machine guns, and mortars. The Khmer Rouge also have many trucks and jeeps. Acting on Beijing's advice, their commanders have "refined their guerrilla tactics."[25]

Weapons superiority is still enjoyed by the PAVN in Kampuchea with usage of Soviet MI-8 and MI-24 helicopters together with MiG-21 and Antonov 26 aircraft in search and destroy missions. Apart from air power, the PAVN employs standard T-54 tanks and artillery guns (105, 130, and 155mm), which were used in past assaults on resistant bases.[26]

Despite the PAVN's present tactical advantage, the PLA will continue to put pressure on Vietnam by retaining large numbers of its forces along the Sino-Vietnamese border. Beijing has learned well from Moscow what impact a border troop buildup can have on its neighboring enemy. Given a continued stalemate situation, low-intensity military engagements such as that which occurred in early January 1987 between PLA and PAVN forces in the Ha Tuyen–Yunnan border will continue to erupt from time to time in the years ahead.[27]

ASEAN

Except for Thailand, which is most affected by the Kampuchean issue, the other ASEAN states (Indonesia, Malaysia, the Philippines, Singapore, and Brunei) have not directly felt the impact of the modernization of the PLA. In Thailand's case, U.S. withdrawal since the end of the Vietnam War and fear of Vietnamese expansionism have caused Bangkok to move closer to Beijing. Their shared perception of the Vietnamese threat has in the past few years forged a close military relationship that has been labeled a "quasi-alliance"[28], even a "de facto ally."[29] While Beijing exerts military pressure on the Sino-Vietnamese border, Bangkok serves as a conduit for Chinese military aid to the Kampuchean resistance forces. Indeed, as William S. Turley observes: "The Khmer Rouge could not survive without Thai connivance in China's

[25]Ibid., pp. 16–17.
[26]Ibid.
[27]*ADJ*, February 1987, p. 104; *New Straits Times*, January 10, 1987.
[28]Michael Yahuda, "China and the Region," in *Southeast Asian Affairs 1985* (Singapore: Institute of Southeast Asian Studies, 1985), p.66.
[29]Jacques Bekaert, "The Royal Thai Army: Its Role in National Unity," *ADJ*, March 1987, p. 7.

support."[30] Sino-Thai military cooperation has benefited Thai security because China's positioning of PLA forces along the border with Vietnam has drawn some PAVN troops from the Thai-Kampuchean border.[31] The visits of Chief of Staff General Arthit Kamlang-Ek to Beijing in May 1984 and that of Chief of Staff General Yang Dezhi to Bangkok in January 1987 to discuss "matters of mutual interest, including defence and security"[32] have further enhanced the Sino-Thai military relationship. Since 1985, in its attempt to strengthen the Thai defense from the perceived Vietnamese threat, China has been supplying Bangkok with military weapons. Apart from ammunitions, a gift of sixteen 130mm artillery guns was presented to the Royal Thai Army (RTA) for use along the Kampuchean border. RTA officials were reportedly "impressed with the efficiency and effectiveness of the guns," regarding them as "more effective than the U.S.-made 155mm guns and more suitable and capable of reaching their targets with greater accuracy."[33]

The positive features of the Chinese weapons and Beijing's "friendship" prices (with a grace period of ten years before initial payment) have caused Thailand for the first time to regard the PRC as an important supplier of its military hardware. In May 1987, the main purpose of Chief of Staff General Chaovalit Yongchaiyuth's visit to Beijing was to purchase more arms from China. The weapons list included T-69 tanks, 130mm artillery guns, 37mm antiaircraft guns, and armored personnel carriers. It was reported that Beijing was willing to accommodate Bangkok with fifty to sixty T-69 tanks at about 10 percent of their market price.[34]

While the increasing use of Chinese weapons has strengthened Thai firepower along the Kampuchean border, military observers feel that problems could arise during combat if RTA units use a mixture of U.S. and Chinese weapons. It has been suggested that this problem could be avoided if certain units use weapons from only one supplier, either Chinese or American.[35] Warning of another consequence was sounded in the *Bangkok Post* in January 1987:

> Continual buying and resupplying of spare parts and ammunition at cheap prices invariably creates and increases the feeling of indebted-

---

[30]"Vietnam/Indochina: Hanoi's Challenge to Southeast Asian Regional Order," in Young Whan Kihl and Lawrence E. Grinter, *Asian-Pacific Security: Emerging Challenges and Responses* (Boulder: Lynne Rienner Publishers, 1986), p. 193.

[31]Bekaert, "Royal Thai Army," p. 7.

[32]*ADJ*, February 1987, p. 90; *New Straits Times*, May 2, 1987.

[33]*ADJ*, June 1987, p. 7.

[34]Ibid., *New Straits Times*, May 2, 1987.

[35]*ADJ*, March 1987, p. 7.

ness on the side of the receiver. Such feelings of indebtedness can put Thailand in a difficult position if our security and political interests, at some point in the future, no longer coincide with China's.[36]

China's growing military cooperation with Thailand has implications for ASEAN unity in view of Indonesia's and Malaysia's different perspectives vis-à-vis Vietnam and the PRC. While the two ASEAN states recognize that the Vietnamese occupation of Kampuchea has endangered peace and stability in Southeast Asia, Jakarta and Kuala Lumpur view the Kampuchean problem as a short-term one. The military modernization of China is regarded as the long-term threat to the region. Vietnam, it is believed, could be persuaded to cooperate with ASEAN for peace and stability in the region, and it can also serve as a buffer state to contain any future expansion of Chinese power and influence.[37]

In view of this, although no official statement has been made concerning the matter, it is widely known that Indonesia and Malaysia are concerned about the close military cooperation that Beijing's military policy has been able to achieve with ASEAN colleague Thailand. Particularly disconcerting is the fact that for the first time in ASEAN history, a member has resorted to depending on the PRC as a supplier of military weapons, thus opening ASEAN's door to an important aspect of expansion of Chinese influence in the region. Since they are not frontline states in the Kampuchean conflict and are suspicious of China's long-term goals in Southeast Asia, Indonesia and Malaysia see the close Sino-Thai military relations more as an increase in Chinese influence in the region than as a Thai security measure to preserve it from possible Vietnamese encroachment. Consequently, by allowing the PRC to have a foothold in the ASEAN region through military supplies, Indonesia and Malaysia feel that regional security may be threatened when the supplier succeeds in its military modernization program.

Although ASEAN countries like Indonesia and Malaysia are aware that it will take a few decades for a fully militarily modernized China to become a direct threat to Southeast Asia, images of that threat have already been conjured up by current PRC efforts to modernize its armed forces. This is evidenced by the fact that China had demonstrated in the 1979 Sino-Vietnamese conflict that it was willing to use armed force to attain its policy objectives. The PRC's military modernization has caused ASEAN members to register their apprehension to the United States, which is assisting Beijing in that policy. Despite attempts by

---

[36]Ibid.
[37]Yahuda, "China and the Region," pp. 62–64.

Washington to allay ASEAN fears, anxiety still persists among the non-communist countries of Southeast Asia regarding China's development as a military power in the region.

However, unlike the Indochinese states, which fear the possibility of a militarily strong PRC sending its army across the border, ASEAN states such as Indonesia, the Philippines, and Malaysia—which are not part of the mainland adjoining China—are relatively safe from any movement of PRC ground forces southward. In any case, should PLA troops move south, maritime ASEAN members would anticipate the Indochinese states as a buffer zone to prevent further advance by Chinese forces.

What the ASEAN countries are worried about is that a militarily stronger China (by the year 2000) would enhance potential armed conflict with them in the South China Sea as a result of territorial claims over the small chain of islands there. The Paracels are claimed by Vietnam and China. In 1974, conflict between the Chinese naval forces and Vietnamese troops on the islands resulted in the PRC's establishing a firm occupation over them.[38] In 1979, China claimed sovereignty over the Spratly Islands. Other states that also lay claim to these islands are the Philippines, Vietnam, Malaysia, and Nationalist China. In 1978, a few of the islands were proclaimed by Manila as part of Palawan Province to be called Kalayaan (Freedom).[39] Since 1975, Vietnam has occupied three of the islands. Malaysia's interest lies in the Terumbu Layang Layang (Swallow Reef). Taiwan, in fact, has troops on the largest of the Spratly Islands, the Taiping. Lying astride major sea lands, the islands are of geopolitical and strategic value for the PRC, whose navy has no port facilities in a Southeast Asian state (unlike the United States in Subic Bay and the Soviet Union in Cam Ranh Bay). The Paracels and Spratlys could be developed into offshore bases for China's Southern Fleet, thus not only augmenting its southern defense but also achieving some degree of naval strategic balance with the two superpowers in the region.

The strategic and economic significance of the South China Sea is well appreciated by Beijing so that it has undertaken measures to protect its interests in the region. This crucial task has been the major responsibility of the People's Liberation Navy (PLAN). The 1970s witnessed notable achievements in the development of that branch of Chi-

---

[38]Merwyn S. Samuels, *Contest for the South China Sea* (New York: Methuen, 1982), pp. 100–101.

[39]Ibid.; Estrella D. Solidum, "Philippine Perceptions of Crucial Issues Affecting Southeast Asia," *Asian Survey* 22(6) (June 1982):542.

na's armed forces. The annual allocation of about 20 percent of the defense budget contributed to the tripling of its conventional submarine force (from 35 to 100 for the period 1970–80) and an increase of missile crafts from 20 to 200 ships. In that decade, two nuclear-powered missile submarines (SSBN) and two nuclear-powered attack submarines (SSN) were launched. Additionally, guided missile frigates and various auxiliary vessels were constructed. Development continued into the 1980s, with Chinese naval vessels operating further away from the China coast. In May 1980, a Chinese navy task force of some twenty ships (including battleships and frigates) assisted in successfully launching two ICBM-type carrier rockets. Originating from western China, the missiles covered a distance of 8,000 nautical miles into the South Pacific. In October 1982, the PLAN achieved the successful firing of an underwater submarine-launched ballistic missile (SLBM) to a distance of 600–700 nautical miles.[40]

Up to 1986, the PLAN is reported to have "completed its first generation of upgraded warships, which include submarines, torpedo launches, antisubmarine escort vessels, and guided missile escort vessels." Meanwhile it has "begun work on the second generation of guided missile destroyers, light duty escort vessels, large guided missile mosquito boats, and submarines."[41]

Despite the notable achievements in the past decade, China is aware that the PLAN's weapons and electronic systems are still deficient compared with the West and the Soviet Union. The Chinese navy has yet to test-fire the SLBM from a nuclear-powered submarine. Its vessels are also poorly equipped for antisubmarine and mine warfare vital for keeping coastal sea lanes open during wartime. Moreover, Chinese naval aviation suffers from a lack of longer range surveillance and intelligence missions. Although personnel training since 1982 has greatly emphasized tactical skills instead of ideology as in the past, there is still a long way to go before training can be updated with more sophisticated computers. For the present, the conversion of the PLAN from a coastal defense to a regional capability is hampered by budgetary cuts in defense modernization that is aimed at hastening the development of the national economy.[42] Yet no one doubts that efforts are steadily under way to achieve this goal by the early twenty-first century.

---

[40]Bruce Swanson, "Naval Forces," in Segal and Tow, eds., *Chinese Defence Policy,* pp. 85–92.

[41]*Beijing Review,* no. 25 (June 23, 1986), p. 23.

[42]Swanson, "Naval Forces," pp. 92–95.

China as a Sea Power in the Twenty-First Century

A substantially modernized and militarily strong China will no doubt have greater impact on Southeast Asia than it now has. As a military power, however, the PRC will project its strength not by sending its troops across its borders into Southeast Asian countries but rather through a larger role for its modernized navy in the South China Sea.

The imperative of national defense for the southern coastal provinces and the need to protect the island territories in the South China Sea underscore the need for a stronger navy and therefore its larger role in those waters. Like the 750-vessel Eastern Fleet and the 500-vessel Northern Fleet, the main strength of the 600-ship Southern Fleet (based in Zhanjiang, Guangdong province) lies in its fast-attack gunships and submarine fleet. Its defense zone is from Xiamen (Amoy) to the Gulf of Tonkin eastward and down south to the Paracels.[43] The PLAN's tactical effectiveness and range of naval power capability is, however, seriously limited by outdated weapons (e.g., *Gordi* class destroyers and poor antisubmarine defense, which relies mainly on the MBU-1800 rocket, a weapons system that is not effective for deep or distant nuclear submarine attack). Consequently, hostile powers intent on attacking the Chinese coast can do so from distances far beyond the PLAN's defense screen. As Merwyn Samuels puts it succinctly: "Speed of maneuverability and density of numbers . . . cannot compensate for a lack of reach."[44]

China's vulnerability from long-distance attack from the sea will strongly encourage it to meet this strategic defense problem early in the next century by producing aircraft carriers and modern cruisers with up-to-date antisubmarine warfare devices. The PLAN is also pursuing its nuclear submarine program. It is believed that Beijing is constructing six SSBNs at the cost of 10 billion yuan (US$20 billion). With eighty-four 200-kiloton nuclear missiles on board the vessels when completed at the end of this decade, China will have greatly enhanced its defense capability.[45]

In order to balance the Soviet naval presence, particularly in the Gulf of Tonkin and off the coast of Da Nang, more modern Chinese warships will appear in those waters. Defense fortifications will be further strengthened on Hainan Island. For Vietnam, therefore, apart from

---

[43]Samuels, *Contest*, pp. 143–44.
[44]Ibid., pp. 144–45.
[45]Swanson, "Naval Forces," pp. 90–91.

the traditional land threat along the Chinese border, coastal cities such as Haiphong (even Hanoi), Vinh, and Quang Tri can become vulnerable targets for PLAN sea-launched missiles.

With the deployment of Chinese naval vessels in waters of immediate strategic concern during the early part of the twenty-first century, the Paracels—located significantly almost equidistant from Hainan Island to the north and Da Nang to the west but farther from Luzon Island to the east—could conceivably be developed into an operational South China Sea base (for naval vessels and naval air force) in order to achieve some degree of strategic balance with the Soviets in Da Nang and Cam Ranh Bay and the Americans in Clark and Subic Bay. South of the Paracels in the South China Sea, the disputed Spratly Islands (where national exclusive economic zones overlap) will in the next century become a contentious issue. Maintaining that ''since antiquity, *Xisha* (Paracels), *Nansha* (Spratly), *Zhongsha* (Macclesfield Bank), and *Dongsha* (Pratas Island) have been Chinese territory''[46] and that other nations have encroached on them, Beijing will no doubt make its presence felt in that area of the South China Sea. The appearance of its naval, fishing or marine resource exploration vessels will heighten the potential for conflict with Southeast Asian nations (including Taiwan) that have similar claims in the region.

As China's navy enhances its defense capability for the mainland coast in the years ahead, its vessels will also be deployed to safeguard the sea lanes of communication vital to its growing maritime trade with Southeast Asia and regions west of the Malacca Straits. Of the nineteen Chinese ports earmarked for major redevelopment to enhance the PRC's economic modernization, nine of them (e.g., Xiamen, Shantou, and Guangzhou) have trade routes in the South China Sea to Southeast Asian ports of Bangkok, Manila, Singapore, Penang, and Jakarta.[47]

Of the three branches of the Chinese armed forces, the navy, owing to its strategic defense imperative, has made the greatest strides in China's military modernization. Consequently, in all probability, by the second or third decade of the twenty-first century, China will be able to restore its image and role as a sea power, which it lost at the end of the Ming Dynasty (1368–1644). What impact the PRC, as a renewed mari-

---

[46]Su Wenming, *China's Army Ready for Modernization* (Beijing: International Book Trading Corp., 1985), p. 15. For a history of China's relations with the islands, see Samuels, *Contest*, ch. 2; and Dieter Heinzig, *Disputed Islands in the South China Sea* (Weisbaden: Otto Harrassowitz Co., 1976), pp. 21–24.

[47]Samuels, *Contest*, pp. 141–42.

time power, will have on Southeast Asia will depend on its concept of national security. As Jonathan Pollack aptly observes:

> Leaders in Peking may not have long to wait to see whether the capacity to use force beyond the nation's borders—and hence, like most great powers, pursue a more expansive conception of national security—creates inexorable pressures to move in that direction.[48]

Chinese leader Deng Xiaoping seemed to have indicated that the PRC would lean toward the "expansive conception of national security" when he announced in September 1985, "By the middle of the next century when we approach the level of the advanced countries there will be really great changes. The strength of China and its world role will be really quite different."[49]

In view of such an eventuality, the Southeast Asian nations—communist Indochina and noncommunist ASEAN—will need to find credible means to cope with China as a restored sea power in the next century.

---

[48]Pollack, "China as a Military Power," p. 89.
[49]*Far Eastern Economic Review,* March 30, 1986, p. 65.

PART FOUR

China's Policy Toward Ethnic Chinese

8. PRC Policy on the Overseas Chinese

CHAN NGOR CHONG

The overseas Chinese are a unique phenomenon that often pose problems both controversial and emotional. They have been frequently dubbed or assailed by innuendoes as the "fifth column" of the PRC dedicated to the work of infiltration, subversion, and armed insurrection to overthrow the governments of their countries of residence. They have been frequently portrayed as sentimentally and intellectually predisposed toward the PRC, ever ready at China's behest to promote Chinese interests.

The belief that the overseas Chinese are at the beck and call of the "motherland" has gained a wide currency, perhaps because of their involvement in some of the epochal events in China such as the Republican Revolution and the Sino-Japanese War in the first half of the present century. Some people are somewhat convinced that the financial resources of the overseas Chinese and their participation in the overthrow of the Manchu monarchy had been partially responsible for the triumph of the Republican Revolution in 1911. They somewhat believe that overseas Chinese patriotism demonstrated by generous financial contributions and selfless sacrifices had in some way saved China from the catastrophe of ultimate military debacle and political captivity in 1937–45. Many people in Southeast Asia also feel that the overseas Chinese involvement in the insurgency movements in the region has been inspired or supported by the PRC.

But the fact is that the triumph of republicanism in China in the early decades of the present century owed little to the efforts of the overseas Chinese. In regard to the war against Japanese aggression in 1937–45, the United States contributed immensely more to China's war efforts than did the overseas Chinese. Moreover, had there been a full-scale overseas Chinese involvement in Southeast Asian insurgency, its outcome would have been very different.[1]

The assessments and views expressed in this chapter are entirely the author's.

[1] In the case of Malaysia, involvement of the Chinese residents in the communist insurgency has been confined to a very small minority. In fact, in their various capacities, the Chinese residents in this country have played an important role in the fight against communism and in safeguarding Malaysian security interests.

125

Today people still continue to see an intimate connection that bind the PRC with the overseas Chinese, perhaps because of China's physical immensity, perhaps because of the fear of the enormous economic and military prowess that would be at its disposal should its modernization drive succeed, perhaps because of Beijing's continued efforts to enlist overseas Chinese support for its economic development, or perhaps because of the cultural and sentimental ties that bind the PRC with the overseas Chinese. Some authorities maintain that the Chinese Communist Party (CCP) did not consciously formulate any overseas Chinese policy when it came to power in 1949.[2] But from Beijing's statements on the overseas Chinese in the past three and a half decades, it is my belief that with the exception of the Cultural Revolution period the PRC has indeed consistently tried to mobilize the overseas Chinese in its national construction work.

This chapter makes no attempt to dwell on the relations that the CCP still maintains with fraternal communist parties outside China. Nor does it seek to establish a link between the PRC's overseas Chinese policy and the formula of party-to-party relations that it has ingeniously devised to avoid embarrassment in interstate relations and allay fears of states plagued with Communist insurgencies that it allegedly supports. Beijing thus far has not consciously exploited fraternal parties abroad as an instrument to promote its overseas Chinese policy, even in countries where the ethnic composition of the fraternal parties is predominantly Chinese. Such a course of action, as Beijing has foreseen, would not only thwart its attempt to mobilize overseas Chinese in support of its foreign policy and development objectives. It would further complicate the overseas Chinese issues, render the position of Chinese residents abroad more untenable, and feed intraethnic discord. Thus, in light of the problems previously encountered in the course of implementing the overseas Chinese policy and in light of the modernization needs in the coming decades, the only course consistent with Chinese interests is to stress government-to-government relations and to strive to promote peace and stability and eliminate tensions in the Asia-Pacific region. To this end the PRC has recently rejected the idea mooted by Mongolia of convening a congress of the communist parties in the Asia-Pacific region.[3] To this end the PRC has ceased to give material support to fraternal communist parties in Southeast Asia. Indeed, the restriction of Beijing's dealing with fraternal parties abroad to merely moral support and the virtual end of material support have been the most important

---

[2] A recent talk with Professor Wang Gungwu in Hong Kong gave me this impression.
[3] *Nanyang Siang Pau*, February 13, 1987, p. 24.

factors for cohorts of Thai and Malaysian communists to give up their struggle and accept the terms of amnesty offered by the Thai government.[4]

Overseas Chinese Policy, 1949–66

The overseas Chinese, although ethnically homogeneous, are often characterized by vast differences in their educational background, outlook, and perception of their rights and obligations and their connection with their ancestral homeland. The term includes Chinese nationals and stateless Chinese residents outside mainland China, foreign citizens of Chinese descent, as well as "compatriots" in Hong Kong, Macao, and Taiwan. The PRC, however, also considers as overseas Chinese those Chinese in China with overseas background or connection, that is, those overseas Chinese students who have studied and subsequently settled down in China, overseas Chinese returnees serving in China, and dependents and relatives of Chinese aboard.

Estimates of the overseas Chinese population vary with different authorities. One source puts it at 11.75 million in the early 1950s and 18.3 million in the late 1960s.[5] Another source estimates that the present figure is around 18.4 million.[6] A third source concludes that exclusive of those who do not want to be identified as overseas Chinese, the figure should be 10–12 million.[7]

The speed with which the CCP wrested control over China in 1949 from the Kuomintang (KMT) left the party hardly any time to understand the overseas Chinese and to come to grips with their problems. The domestic overseas Chinese with whom the CCP barely had any contact before it was in the saddle formed a tiny fraction of the total Chinese population. For years they had lived in peace with the local Chinese inhabitants without causing great social or political problems. The majority of the Chinese living abroad seemed to have severed links with China upon the CCP's accession. Many entertained deep-seated fears of communism, with which they preferred to have nothing to do. Many had learned with grief and helplessness of the persecutions vis-

---

[4]*Nanyang Siang Pau*, April 23, 1987, p. 24; April 28, 1987, p. 27; May 18, 1987, p. 26; June 5, 1987, p. 1; *Sin Chew Jit Poh*, April 10, 1987, p. 1.
[5]Stephen Fitzgerald, *China and the Overseas Chinese: A Study of Peking's Changing Policy, 1949–1970* (Cambridge: Cambridge University Press, 1972), p. 3.
[6]Leo Suryadinata, *China and the ASEAN States: The Ethnic Chinese Dimension* (Singapore: Singapore University Press, 1985), pp. 5–6. The PRC 1982 figure for overseas Chinese population given by Lian Guan, deputy chief of the Overseas Chinese Affairs Commission, was 22 million.
[7]Wang Gungwu, "External China as a New Policy Area," *Pacific Affairs* (Spring 1985):41.

ited upon their relatives and the fate of their landed properties into which they had injected their lifelong savings. In any case, uncertainty, ignorance of the emerging situation, and repugnance if not overt hostility toward the new regime had in the early years of the CCP's rule induced the majority of overseas Chinese to take a wait-and-see attitude before realigning themselves.

Moreover, the array of pressing problems which demanded immediate attention had compelled the new Beijing leadership to give priority to the domestic scene. In the wake of the CCP takeover, the situation in China was far from stable. Outer Mongolia had been detached from China to become a Soviet protectorate. Centrifugal tendencies were strong in Manchuria and Xinjiang while Tibet continued to maintain its sturdy independence. There was the problem of economic dislocation caused by two decades of external aggression and civil war. There was the thorny task of proletarianizing the landlords, capitalists, and bourgeois intellectuals, of acclimatizing the general populace to the new social and political order, and of organizing the broad masses for production work.

The international environment surrounding the PRC in the first years of its existence was also hardly hospitable. The United States had in some significant way contributed to the rise of Communist power in China. But Washington had consistently maintained a hostile stance toward Beijing, especially after the latter's participation in the Korean War (1950–53). There was the general foreboding that the United States might support a KMT regime effort to counterattack mainland China. Moreover, the system of alliances that the United States had erected with countries in the West Pacific coupled with economic sanctions had impressed upon Beijing that Washington's ultimate objective was to encircle and strangle China rather than to contain the expansion of communism. Apart from the U.S. threat, the continued Soviet presence in Manchuria might have suggested to Beijing that Moscow might in this initial period of uncertainty and weakness make an attempt to detach part of Manchuria from China, although by now both Moscow and Beijing had come to be the major pillars of the newly emerging global socialist fraternity.[8]

This hostile international environment had driven Beijing to concern itself primarily with threats that could compromise its integrity and independence rather than with a commitment to the salvation of Chi-

---

[8]For continuing Soviet interest in those areas of China of strategic importance, see Harry Gelman, *The Soviet-Fareast Buildup and Soviet Risk-Taking Against China* (Santa Monica, Calif.: Rand, 1982), pp. 3–8.

nese abroad. Also by now the PRC could no longer expect the overseas Chinese to be, as in the past, an unflagging source of foreign exchange. The devastations of World War II had impoverished the overseas Chinese and thus precluded the participation of the majority of them in China's reconstruction. The policy of communizing and confiscating private properties had discouraged many overseas Chinese from remitting money to China. The hostility of the United States and other Western democracies toward the PRC had also denied China access to capital not only in these countries but also in their colonies, where most overseas Chinese had congregated.

Nevertheless the PRC still somehow saw that the overseas Chinese could be mobilized to promote the United Front work, a strategy which the CCP had ingeniously exploited to build up its power base and political control before 1949 and which it now perceived could be adopted again to promote the PRC's security interests and to assist in the task of its internal political consolidation and economic reconstruction.

To this end the CCP, like the KMT before it, openly claimed the overseas Chinese to be "an extension of the Chinese population and accepted obligations and responsibilities demanded by their intimate relationship with the Chinese homeland."[9] The Overseas Chinese Affairs Commission (OCAC) was set up in 1949 with representatives from the ministries of Foreign Affairs, Commerce, Culture, Education, Foreign Trade, and Internal Affairs and from the People's Banks and Returned Overseas Chinese Associations. It also worked closely with the United Front Work Department and the Propaganda Department of the CCP. The range of representation indicates that the scope of its work was wide-ranging. This was subsequently spelled out clearly in Liao Chengzhi's statement of June 1951[10] to include the following:

1. To unite all patriotic Overseas Chinese compatriots, to educate them in patriotism and enlist their support for the PRC;
2. to expose the crimes of the Chiang Kai-shek bandits;
3. to protect the proper rights and interests of the Overseas Chinese and to oppose all crimes of persecution against them;
4. to expand Overseas Chinese educational and cultural work;

---

[9]The basic principle of KMT overseas Chinese policy is that any person of Chinese parentage is considered a Chinese citizen regardless of his place of birth. Its basic aims are to protect the rights and interests of overseas Chinese in their countries of residence, to provide education for overseas Chinese children in China, and to encourage overseas Chinese to invest in China.

[10]Liao Chengzhi's statement, issued in June 1951, was quoted in Fitzgerald, *China and the Overseas Chinese*, p. 84.

5. to propagate the thought of Mao, New Democracy, the Common Programme and all policies and laws of the People's Government;
6. to promote friendly relations between overseas Chinese and the people of the countries of residence and further their cultural exchange, their unity and mutual assistance, for the mutual preservation of world peace.

From Liao's statement it is evident that the tasks for the overseas Chinese were first, they should be politically inclined toward the PRC, be indoctrinated with the PRC's prevailing ideology and familiar with its current policies and developments; second, they should help the CCP to fight the KMT and not allow themselves to be used by the KMT to prejudice the interests of the motherland; and third, they should promote the PRC's foreign policy objectives. In return the PRC would undertake to protect their rights and look after their education and cultural interests.

Apart from OCAC the PRC had created a string of other organs to reinforce the CCP's United Front work and to help domestic overseas Chinese to revive or strengthen links with their relatives abroad. The better known among them was the All-China Returned Overseas Chinese Association (ACROCA). Through these organs the PRC hoped to augment the inflow of overseas remittances and investment funds and to expand its external trade. Through them the PRC hoped to enhance its foreign exchange earnings by attracting more overseas Chinese tourists and students to China. Through them the PRC hoped to foster the patriotic unity of the Chinese abroad whom it believed to be able to influence favorably the course of events in their countries of residence.

The objectives spelled out in the PRC's overseas Chinese policy would appear normal if they were meant to be a perfunctory propaganda exercise designed to publicize the United Front strategy. But they immediately threw into relief the PRC's limitations if they were treated seriously as goals to be realized. The most intractable issue that constantly cropped up in the course of implementing the overseas Chinese policy was the PRC's undertaking to protect the rights and interests of the Chinese abroad. Beijing soon found that overseas Chinese interests were incompatible with the PRC's security interests and contradicted its foreign policy objectives. Moreover, even if compatibility between PRC and overseas Chinese interests could be established, Beijing still lacked the political and military resources to honor this undertaking. Distrust of Southeast Asian states and the determination of the U.S. and Britain to check the southward expansion of Chinese influence made Beijing's task of protecting the overseas Chinese even less possible. It is in appreciation of this situation that Beijing as early as 1951 advised the overseas

Chinese to ensure their own survival with their own strength and to make concerted moves to defend their own rights and interests.

Beijing's prospect of success in other areas of overseas Chinese work was equally dubious. Its efforts to explain its new policies, ideology, and social system to the Chinese abroad produced no significant impact upon the overseas Chinese communities. Its influence on Chinese education was minimal and the Chinese school system abroad was either abolished or, where it was allowed to continue, placed under strict control and increasingly made to conform to the requirements of the local environment. Even the level of overseas Chinese remittances and investment was far below expectations and seemed embarrassing in comparison with the aid the PRC had given to other developing countries.[11] The campaigns among the overseas Chinese against the KMT were supererogatory. The majority of the overseas Chinese did not seem to have any link with the KMT; nor did they have any inkling of the cause for which it was supposedly fighting. Even those with KMT affiliations were gradually disassociating themselves from Taiwan, not because of PRC promptings and admonitions but because in the postwar situation, prudence dictated that they resist aligning themselves with the camps in contention for a claim to political legitimacy in China.

Moreover, the perception of an increasing number of overseas Chinese of their position vis-à-vis the PRC was changing. The majority of Chinese abroad now began to see the compelling logic of identifying their destiny with the countries of residence. These developments, coupled with some foreign policy adjustments stressing the importance of Southeast Asia, compelled the PRC to reassess its relations with the overseas Chinese. It was in this context that Beijing now saw it politic to sever political and ideological links with the overseas Chinese and to confine cultivation of the overseas Chinese to the economic sphere. It was in this context that Beijing saw the scaling down of the United Front operation among the overseas Chinese and of the overall PRC-overseas Chinese ties as vital to the improvement of Sino-Southeast Asian relations.

This perception of the necessity of change in the PRC's approach to the overseas Chinese found eloquent expression in statements made by Zhou Enlai and leading OCAC officials from 1954 to 1956.[12] To them, the

---

[11]Overseas remittances in 1949–76 did not seem to have reached an annual sum of US$100 million. But in *Towards the End of Isolation: China's Foreign Policy After Mao* (London: Macmillan, 1983), p. 100, Michael Yahuda says that China's economic aid to developing countries from 1954 to 1976 totaled about US$5 billion.

[12]Statements made by Zhou Enlai and OCAC officials are quoted in Fitzgerald, *China and the Overseas Chinese*, chs. 6, 8. Also see Suryadinata, *China and the ASEAN States*, app. 14.

crux of the overseas Chinese problem was the question of dual nationality and integration. Hence they urged as many Chinese abroad as possible to opt for the nationality of their countries of residence. They urged them to learn local languages and to acquire education that had relevance to the local environment and that would direct their patriotism and allegiance from their ancestral homeland to their adopted countries. They urged them to integrate with the local people economically and to shift their economic activities from trade to industry. With respect to the solution of the dual nationality problem, they prescribed:

1. Upon the signing of a nationality treaty between the PRC and a foreign country, those overseas Chinese who had voluntarily opted for the citizenship of their country of domicile would automatically cease to be Chinese nationals. They were no longer under the PRC's protection; nor would the PRC claim responsibility for their behavior. They must be loyal to their adopted country.
2. Those overseas Chinese who chose to retain Chinese nationality would remain as Chinese nationals. They should respect local laws and customs and should not interfere in local politics.
3. Countries with overseas Chinese should not discriminate against Chinese nationals and should respect their proper rights and interests.

But the PRC also envisaged that those Chinese abroad who chose to retain Chinese nationality would be ultimately integrated with the countries of residence, and it urged them to help forge cultural and trade links between China and their countries of residence by having their schools teach local languages and patriotism.

The conditions Beijing had spelled out for a workable solution to the overseas Chinese problem formed the cardinal principles guiding the PRC's approach to relations with countries with sizable colonies of Chinese for a decade from 1957 to 1966. But these principles did not seem to have helped the PRC project a better image to the outside world. By the time the Cultural Revolution broke out in 1966, China's relations with virtually all Southeast Asian states were strained. Indonesia, the only country in Southeast Asia which had accorded diplomatic recognition to Beijing, had suspended all ties in 1967 on suspicion of Chinese complicity in an abortive coup in 1965 that had toppled Sukarno's regime and swept the Indonesian military into power. The ferocity attendant upon the Cultural Revolution and the ensuing convulsions inspired the leftist elements in Hong Kong and some neighboring countries to acts of violence. Many Southeast Asian capitals became concerned that Beijing was about to spearhead another wave of insurgency movements in the region.

The single most important reason why Southeast Asian states were persistently hostile to the PRC and refused to normalize relations was the pervasive feeling that Beijing's attitude toward the overseas Chinese was ambivalent. Although Beijing had consistently maintained that it would not support insurgency movements outside China, especially those with massive overseas Chinese involvement, its approach to interstate relations at times yielded the impression that it had occasionally resorted to insurgency as an instrument of foreign policy. Moreover, while the PRC had since 1957 persistently jostled the Chinese abroad into acquiring the nationality of their countries of residence, it had likewise all along treated the overseas Chinese as part of China as well as part of a patriotic United Front.

The implications of this ambivalence were first that should the situation of the Chinese abroad become intolerable the PRC was under obligation to come to their assistance, and second that the overseas Chinese were under obligation to help promote the PRC's domestic and foreign policy objectives. Hence to most Southeast Asian states Beijing's apparent disinterestedness and disenchantment with the overseas Chinese did not signify that the latter had already outlived their usefulness. Nor did the PRC's disengagement from overseas Chinese affairs and preoccupation with her security interests indicate Beijing's willing acceptance of its small neighbors as equals.

In taking stock of what the PRC had achieved with its overseas Chinese policy in the one and a half decades of its existence, Beijing was found to have failed in spreading Maoist ideology to the overseas Chinese community, in drafting the Chinese abroad into a patriotic United Front, and in using them to forestall any KMT challenge to its political legitimacy. But its attempt to attract remittances and direct capital investment from the Chinese abroad had been a qualified success. Its attempt to recruit overseas Chinese scientists, engineers, and higher intellectuals into its academic institutions and research establishments had not been very fruitful when measured in terms of the number who had responded to the call of the motherland. When, however, it was judged in terms of quality, this was a brilliant achievement because some of those who did respond to its call for both short- and long-term services turned out to be the most eminent in the world of nuclear science and space technology. It is indeed still too early to assess the impact these overseas Chinese had on the PRC's science and defense capabilities and the effect of their leadership and inspiration on younger generations of PRC scientists and intellectuals.

In the domain of overseas Chinese education, Beijing could exert little influence on the orientation of the Chinese schools in the countries of residence because of the strict control wielded by their governments and because many Chinese school teachers were then in some way affiliated with the KMT. But in the provision of education for overseas Chinese within the PRC, Beijing could boast some major accomplishments. While after 1957 Beijing tended to encourage the overseas Chinese to seek education in the countries of residence, it had nevertheless absorbed some 60,000 Chinese students from abroad during this period into secondary schools and tertiary institutions specially set up to cater to their needs.[13]

Overseas Chinese Policy, 1966–76

With the outbreak of the Cultural Revolution (1966–76), the policy for the protection of domestic overseas Chinese was abandoned and the links which Beijing had built up with the Chinese abroad were cut off. The violence and accompanying scenes of lawlessness and anarchy in many parts of the country evidently showed that the PRC was engulfed in a bitter power struggle rather than in revolution. It was also in the grip of an extreme xenophobia directed partially against the overseas Chinese. From the very beginning Mao's faction with the support of the military, young students, and CCP ultra-leftists had seized the initiative. Domestic overseas Chinese became the target of persecution and the channel for venting anticapitalist antibourgeois spleen. They were dubbed "bourgeois-capitalists" and "counterrevolutionaries," and were denied career advancement and education opportunities. Schools and universities specially set up for them were closed down. Their houses and properties were unjustly confiscated. They were not allowed to communicate with their relatives abroad and often fell victim to arbitrary arrest and physical maltreatment. Even the Overseas Chinese Affairs Commission, set up to regulate overseas Chinese affairs and to look after overseas Chinese interests, was suspended.[14]

The demise of Mao and the subsequent fall of the Gang of Four in the last quarter of 1976 effected a perceptible change in the PRC's overseas Chinese policy. The policy of persecution was abandoned in favor of active cultivation. The change was mainly inspired by a fundamental shift in priorities. The PRC's dominant concern in the decade before 1976 was political etherealization which was to be achieved through the instruments of class struggle and permanent resolution. This extreme

---

[13]See Fitzgerald, *China and the Overseas Chinese*, p. 128.
[14]Wang Gungwu, "External China," p. 35; Suryadinata, *China and the ASEAN States*, pp. 64–67.

bias toward politics to the neglect of the more important task of development had depressed economic growth and destroyed the state administration and education systems.

Overseas Chinese Policy Since 1976

The revamped overseas Chinese policy was first elaborately stated
in the editorial of the *People's Daily* of January 4, 1978.[15] It gives a clear
indication that the PRC was now all the more determined to mobilize
the overseas Chinese. As before the Cultural Revolution, Beijing in its
new policy continued to encourage the Chinese abroad "to acquire the
nationality of the country of residence on a voluntary basis." As before,
they were told that Beijing would disown them politically once they had
acquired foreign nationality. As before Beijing would protect "the legitimate rights and interests" of "those overseas Chinese who wish to
retain their Chinese nationality" and consider it the duty of "the governments of those countries" to "protect the legitimate rights and interests of overseas Chinese and respect their national traditions, customs,
and habits." As before, the overseas Chinese were exhorted to "abide
by the laws and decrees of the countries in which they reside, live in
harmony with the local people, and make contributions to the development of the economy and culture of these countries." But it was disconcerting to note that in Beijing's formula for overseas Chinese nationality,
the Chinese abroad who renounced Chinese nationality were still "our
kinsfolk and friends," that is, ethnically and emotionally part of China
even though they were now foreign nationals. In a conflicting situation,
political elements would sometimes submerge in face of the assertion of
ethnic or cultural elements.

Moreover, the PRC's claimed duty to protect the rights and interests
of Chinese nationals in foreign countries theoretically endowed Beijing
with the right to intervene if the governments of these countries failed
to protect their rights and interests. The active role the PRC prescribed
for the overseas Chinese in the development of the economy and culture of the countries of residence also indicated that in Beijing's view,
the legitimacy of the Chinese presence in countries with large Chinese
settlements was indisputable and that the integration of the overseas
Chinese involved not only absorption but also sinicization of the indigenous cultures of the countries of residence.

This revamped overseas Chinese policy also paid tribute to the
domestic overseas Chinese for their previous contribution to the PRC's

---

[15]Suryadinata, *China and the ASEAN States,* app. 4.

political and economic development and intended them to be actively involved in the current modernization drive. It stated that the primary role the overseas Chinese could play in the PRC's modernization would be the introduction of new science and technology from abroad. Moreover, it asserted that the overwhelming majority of overseas Chinese could be drawn upon to form "part of the basic forces of the patriotic United Front" and would, as in the past, support "the revolutionary struggle of the motherland" because by virtue of their patriotism and proletarian background they were politically reliable. It further stated that Beijing would take measures to protect overseas remittances and continue to welcome Chinese abroad to visit, settle down, or study in China.[16]

The PRC's demands upon the overseas Chinese as spelled out in 1978 were thus essentially similar to those of the pre-Cultural Revolution period. They show that the value of the overseas Chinese to the PRC was primarily economic. Science and technology, overseas remittances, tourism, and overseas Chinese education in China would in one way or another contribute to the PRC's development or enhance foreign exchange earnings. In politics, however, the overseas Chinese as compared with PRC Chinese were far inferior in skill and sophistication and therefore could not claim to have played any conspicuous role, although it was sometimes said that some of the PRC's top leaders had overseas connections or had once lived in some Southeast Asian countries.

Desire to ensure decent progress in modernization work and to reestablish sovereignty over Taiwan and tap its abundant human and material resources had in recent years driven Beijing to stress repeatedly the importance of the overseas Chinese. On May 13, 1981, Hu Yaobang, secretary general of the CCP, said at a seminar held at Beijing on domestic overseas Chinese affairs that the guiding principle of the Party's overseas Chinese policy was to "protect and develop the enthusiasm of the compatriots' love toward the country and the motherland." He further intimated that the overseas Chinese could help speed up the modernization of China and bring about the unification of mainland China with Taiwan.[17] Again in early 1983 the CCP chief said that the good education and social contacts of overseas Chinese businessmen and industrialists could be harnessed to hasten the Four Modernizations and the reunification of China. In like manner, a People's Daily editorial of April 29, 1983, pointed out how domestic overseas Chinese intellectuals, through their continued links with friends and relatives abroad and

---

[16]Ibid.
[17]Ibid., pp. 81–82.

with foreign experts and scholars, could strengthen the PRC's external links and expedite the introduction of more advanced science and technology into China. And more recently visiting Chinese State Councillor Chen Muhua told the Chinese residents in Madagascar on March 26, 1986, that the PRC considered it important to protect the "just rights and interests" of Chinese nationals abroad and urged them to help bring about the early reunification of Taiwan and mainland China.[18] Then again, Song Hanliang, secretary of the Xinjiang CCP committee, expressed the hope at the 1986 Spring Festival gathering in Urumqi on February 3, 1986, that through returned overseas Chinese or family members of overseas Chinese in the region, Xinjiang would be able to attract funds, equipment, technology, and talented people for its development.[19]

As a step toward achieving these objectives, elaborate measures have since been devised to attract overseas Chinese investors, scientists and intellectuals, and students and settlers of means to China. Overseas Chinese have received special treatment in job placements and remunerations and their entry into the CCP, the Communist Youth League, and the People's Liberation Army (PLA) has been eased. More and more returned overseas Chinese and the family members of overseas Chinese in the provinces and municipalities have been selected for leadership posts at all levels. Moreover, miscarriages of justice involving overseas Chinese have mostly been reversed and those overseas Chinese private houses occupied or confiscated during the Cultural Revolution have mostly been returned. In Hubei, over the past few years the provincial overseas Chinese affairs departments have helped to secure foreign capital for importing technological items.[20]

Changing Nature of the Overseas Chinese Problem

This plethora of official statements has more than amply demonstrated the PRC's keen appreciation of the value of overseas Chinese to the motherland. They in no way represent a perfunctory indulgence in flattery to win over their heart and soul or to anesthetize their hostility to or rancor against Beijing. Under the circumstances, how would Beijing react if their position in the countries of residence became highly intolerable? The official statements of the PRC in the period 1954–66

---

[18]Foreign Broadcast Information Service, *Daily Report, China* (hereafter FBIS, *China*), no. 059 (1986), p. 12.
[19]FBIS, *China*-86–030, p. T8.
[20]FBIS, *China*-85–110, p. P3.

persistently intimated to foreign governments that they should protect the rights and interests of the Chinese nationals in their countries. The Chinese constitutions of 1954, 1975, and 1982 also stressed the PRC's intention to protect the legitimate rights and interests of the Chinese residents abroad.

Although the Nationality Law of the People's Republic of China (1980)[21] provides legal confirmation of the definitions of different categories of overseas Chinese as spelled out in the long succession of official statements issued since 1954, Article 13 of the law states that any person who has once been a Chinese national can seek reinstatement of his Chinese nationality. The loss of Chinese nationality is thus not permanent. The flexibility of the law enables overseas Chinese who, for one reason or another, have become disenchanted with their countries of residence and who feel that they can live more happily and meaningfully in China to regain their Chinese citizenship. Moreover, the readiness of the PRC in the three decades from 1949 to 1979 to resort repeatedly to repatriation and resettlement to lift the overseas Chinese in the countries of residence out of their plight also strongly indicates that Beijing has not deserted the overseas Chinese. Hence, the PRC's repeated assertions of its intention and duty to protect the rights and interests of Chinese residents abroad, the Nationality Law of 1980, and the resettlement scheme seem to be able to offer a new vista or perhaps a new lease on life to those disgruntled overseas Chinese who may find their prospects dismal in the countries of residence or who anticipate that in years to come they are likely to continue to chafe from inactivity and despair. But this scenario would appear disconcerting to the governments of Southeast Asian states, which fear that it would compromise the allegiance of their citizens of Chinese descent and turn them into a ready instrument for the PRC to actualize its designs in Southeast Asia, should its interest in the region revive.

Indeed, some overseas Chinese entertain the thought that a strong China, out of ethnic and cultural considerations, would get them out of their present political and economic plight. It is quite natural for people in such circumstances to entertain such thoughts. Whether this is a realistic appraisal of the situation to come or mere wishful thinking is open to question. But the certainty is that a strong China without aggressive intent is beneficial to all—to the United States, to Japan, and to Southeast Asia, although both Japan and the countries in our region are fearful of the emergence of a powerful China. The United States feels that stability in the Asia-Pacific region hinges on the ability of

---

[21]Suryadinata, *China and the ASEAN States,* app. 3.

Beijing, in active cooperation with Washington, to play an effective peacekeeping role in the region. Moreover, the Soviets now regard the whole Eurasian continent as a single strategic unit. Hence, apart from attempting to control the Northeast Atlantic and the Mediterranean, they are trying to establish dominance in the Northwest Pacific, the South China Sea, the Red Sea, and the Arabian Sea. To this end, they acquire basing facilities in North Korea and Vietnam; they invade Afghanistan; and they are covetous of Iran and Pakistan. They also try to gain control in South Yemen, Ethiopia, and Somalia. But these Soviet strategic calculations will succeed only if they can secure the PRC's benevolent neutrality.

In the recent past, great strides have been made in forging a stronger military link between the USSR and North Korea. Last year, the Soviet Pacific Fleet was for the first time granted access to the naval port of Wonsan. Soviet military aircraft were also permitted to fly over North Korea en route from Soviet bases in the Far East to Cam Ranh Bay.[22] Wonsan is of great strategic value to the Soviets, for it ensures the Soviet naval units in the Kamchatka Peninsula, Sakhalin Island, and other Far East bases a smooth passage through the Sea of Okhotsk and the Sea of Japan to the South China Sea and the Indian Ocean. In fact, in the event of conflict the first move that the Soviets are almost certain to make is to cripple the combined military strength of the United States, Japan, and South Korea in the Northwest Pacific rather than that of China. Recent generous Soviet offers of military aid in the form of MiG-23 fighter aircraft and SA3 surface-to-air missiles indeed represent no less than an attempt to induce North Korea to allow the Soviets to use Wonsan more than as an occasional port of call.

Beijing's decision to intervene in foreign countries on behalf of the overseas Chinese will be largely determined by national priorities and diplomatic alignments. Its primary concerns in the next two decades are modernization and preservation of the existing balance of forces in the West Pacific, both of which entail active economic and diplomatic cooperation with Southeast Asian states. Beijing, moreover, before deciding on intervention, has to weigh the U.S. position, which is to maintain the stability of Southeast Asia. Hence, when measured against the overwhelming importance of modernization and relations with the United States and Southeast Asia, the overseas Chinese problem tends to diminish in significance.

---

[22]*Sin Chew Jit Poh*, March 26, 1987, p. 1; May 25, 1987, p. 23; *Nanyang Siang Pau*, May 28, 1987, p. 24.

But if the PRC's present defense modernization (now concentrating on development of conventional capabilities) should in the not too distant future enable it to fight conclusive wars 1,000 miles beyond its southern border, it might be tempted to honor its pledges to protect overseas Chinese, especially when relations with Southeast Asian states have deteriorated or when, in its view, the latter have colluded with the Soviet Union to threaten China.

It may be that in due course the overseas Chinese problem in Southeast Asia will be more and more internationalized and become less of a PRC problem. The overseas Chinese have been pivotal since the past century in the development of the region. The past and present prosperity of many Southeast Asian states owes much to their presence and participation. Extraregional powers like the United States and Japan are keen to share their prosperity. These countries have extensive investments in the region and what they need most is stability that can protect their investments. They are unlikely to treat the overseas Chinese problem strictly as individual state affairs if mishandling of the Chinese residents should directly affect their interests. This is especially true of the United States, which perhaps out of a sense of decency has consistently intervened on the side of the weaker party. For example, any aggressor who plans to invade Singapore must first consider the possible U.S. reaction rather than the defense capability of the island republic.

Southeast Asia, moreover, has never been an isolated corner of the world and, as years pass by, has become more deeply ensnared in a complex web of international relations. The states in the region, being cogs in the present multipolar international system, have forfeited much of their sovereignty and the right to determine developments in their internal affairs. The Soviets seek to exploit political and interstate issues, including the overseas Chinese problem, to destabilize the region in order to expand their influence. The United States, on the other hand, is mainly preoccupied with the maintenance of stability in the region. Its recent intervention in the Philippines is a good case in point. Washington is unlikely to let events take their course freely if the treatment of Chinese in any of the Southeast Asian states compels them to make a stand and destabilizes the region or if the anti-Chinese phenomena in Southeast Asia are Soviet-inspired and likely to serve Soviet interests in the region.

The Chinese abroad need no protection from the PRC. Neither the CCP nor the KMT has ever actually shielded them when they have fallen victim to racial hysteria or unjust discrimination. The overseas Chinese indeed have never taken the PRC's pledges of protection seriously. In fact, there is no need at all for the PRC to have an overseas

Chinese policy. If China needs brains for modernization, it can buy them in all the advanced democracies in the world, especially at this moment when many of their finest scientists and engineers face unemployment. If it needs capital for modernization, export earnings and the international money market can provide. What it can obtain from tourism and from the financial institutions in Hong Kong is in fact many times greater than the overseas Chinese remittances.[23]

From the legal standpoint, the Chinese abroad should enjoy the same rights and privileges as other nationals in their country of residence so long as they are locally born or naturalized citizens of that country. They should have the right to vote and to participate in the affairs of their country. They therefore should also have the obligation to pay for the cost of governing the country and to defend its security and integrity. But more important than this legal consideration is that they are virtually indispensible to their country of residence by virtue of their skills, entrepreneurship, intellectual ability, and accumulated wealth. These assets have contributed much to the development of their country of residence, which in order to ensure continued progress and stability would not resort to a large-scale persecution or expulsion of Chinese citizens and residents. Hence, the best protection for the Chinese abroad is not the PRC's pledges of protection but their own uniqueness, their determination to survive, their ability to adapt creatively to their environment and to break new ground in the midst of adverse circumstances. The Chinese in Thailand have already integrated and partially assimilated with the native inhabitants. The Chinese in Malaysia have repeatedly insisted that they be called nonimmigrants. The Chinese in Indonesia have determined to remain despite almost insurmountable difficulties. All these developments firmly indicate their loyalty to their countries of residence and it should be clear to the PRC that dealings with the Chinese abroad cannot be based on exploitation of their sentiments.

The United States will in years to come be more involved with the overseas Chinese. While all other countries have virtually put a stop on the inflow of Chinese immigrants, it continues to accept via Hong Kong and Macao large numbers of Chinese who have disowned the PRC. The overseas Chinese problem seems to be peculiar to Southeast Asian states. Many Chinese in North America are first-generation immigrants whose ties with the motherland are still fresh and strong. They are

---

[23]A Shanghai paper reported that overseas Chinese remittances for 1985 had dropped by about 75 percent compared with those of 1979; see *Wen Wei Po* (Hong Kong), December 9, 1986, p. 1.

allowed to maintain a double identity which means they can be Chinese and North Americans at the same time. They do not seem to have generated any crisis or given rise to any problems. The Chinese in Southeast Asia, however, are mostly second-and third-generation residents. They are being subjected to a vigorous process of Southeast Asianization and educated under indigenous education systems. Their ties with the PRC tend to weaken as the generation among them born and educated in China fast disappears from the scene. Yet because of environmental challenges, their own consciousness of their identity has been rekindled or even strengthened.

The resurgence of cultural awareness among Thai Chinese has largely been brought about by improved relations between Beijing and Bangkok. In the face of the Vietnamese threat, Thailand perceives a confluence of security interests with the PRC, although such a perception is anathema to other ASEAN states. Thailand further perceives that its security and stability depend upon the PRC's willingness to project a physical presence in Southeast Asia, however elusive that may appear. In return for Beijing's security commitment, Bangkok is obliged to relax its control over the cultural freedom of the ethnic Chinese and allow them to reestablish ties with their kinsmen in China and reopen Chinese schools in Thailand. The Thai Chinese, while in large measure having accepted integration and assimilation, immediately avail themselves of the opportunities afforded by the emerging security situation in Southeast Asia to reassert their cultural rights.

The intensification of interest in Chinese culture in Singapore has been inspired by the government. While the study of English is a political and practical need, it does not enable the Chinese in Singapore to penetrate the inner sanctum of Western culture and thus fill their cultural void. They are therefore exhorted to go back to Confucianism to rehabilitate their souls and to cling to those cultural elements which they can rightly claim as their own. The Chinese in Malaysia have for decades been fighting for the preservation of their language and culture. This struggle has been intensified in recent years by their suspicion of government attempts to erode cultural rights enshrined in their state constitution.

The Chinese abroad doubtless treasure the wealth they have created and accumulated in their countries of residence. They try to keep the PRC at arm's length in order to avoid the impression that they are still politically and sentimentally alienated from their adopted countries. But the PRC seems to be attractive to some Chinese abroad who feel that their physical existence is being increasingly threatened: with continued material progress and liberalization, China may eventually create an environment that can accommodate them socially and economically. It has been recently stated in the PRC press that communism should not be the object of pursuit of the Chinese people, that their common desire is to see China transformed into a more democratic and modernized state, and that all schools of thought capable of serving the country's development and the well-being of the masses should be respected and defended.[24] It has also been pointed out in the PRC press that modernization is closely connected with westernization and that both the material civilization and spiritual culture of a modernized state are usually highly westernized.[25] Such "unorthodox" statements would not have appeared in the PRC's leading press without the endorsement of Beijing's top leadership.

The decline in the initial vigor of the Cultural Revolution by the beginning of 1969 heralded the changes that were to come. Its final collapse was a repudiation of Maoist dogmatism and with it the rigid intellectual edifice Mao had erected for China. There has been a reassertion of the traditions of rationalism and empiricism since the Third Plenum of the Eleventh CCP Central Committee in 1978. There has been the development of a new education designed to emancipate the human mind, develop individuality, and broaden mental horizons.[26] There has been a continuing attempt to revive the system of meritocracy through a systematic infusion of intellectuals into CCP ranks.[27]

Through economic reforms and rational planning, it is anticipated that by the year 2000 the PRC will be able to register marked improvement in its material circumstances.[28] All this will lead to the genesis of a more congenial environment for the maturing and articulation of intellectual ambitions. If Mao could be resurrected by the year 2000 he would be stunned to find his countrymen speaking an exotic language and dreaming a bizarre dream. Hegel's absolute is Mao's communism and it is beyond the ken of both to establish with certainty their eventual contents and forms. To both they are thus ultimately unattainable. But Mao's countrymen would explain to him that his communism is Chinese democracy which, apart from traditional values, embodies a high standard of rationality and affords ample scope for individual freedom and ingenuity and which bears some striking resemblance to Western

---

[24]The article originally appeared in *Guangming Ribao* and was quoted by a foreign news agency; see *Sin Chew Jit Poh*, November 2, 1986, p. 18.
[25]The article originally appeared in *Guangming Ribao* and was quoted by a foreign news agency; see *Nanyang Siang Pau*, November 24, 1986, p. 21.
[26]See *Beijing Review*, vol. 28, no. 46, pp. 15–16.
[27]See, e.g., FBIS, *China-85-204*, p. R1; FBIS, *China-85-139*, p. P2; FBIS, *China-85-080*, p. R1.
[28]*Beijing Review*, vol. 28, no. 44, pp. 18–20; also see FBIS, *China-85-233*, pp. K17–20.

democracy. The eventual outcome of this development will be a qualitative mutation of the PRC's body politic and will render conditions in China more acceptable to those Chinese abroad who decide to opt for a reverse migration.

Student demonstrations on 150 PRC campuses in December 1986 have threatened to obliterate the sanguine prospects recently conjured up by the reform movement. The ensuing dismissal of Fang Lizhi from the vice presidency of the University of Science and Technology in Hefei and his expulsion from the CCP in January 1987 coupled with the fall of Hu Yaobang from the pedestal of power shortly thereafter have caused a considerable stir both within and outside China. There is a widespread fear that the triumph of conservative reaction may spell the end of the reform movement.

But student demonstrations are an intrinsic part of a new development that is inexorably progressing toward some predestined end. The repressive measures that Beijing has taken against the campus demonstrations will not cause the demise of the student movement. This is eloquently testified to by the relatively mild actions that Beijing has taken against liberal intellectuals and student leaders. Despite his expulsion from the CCP, Fang Lizhi was still allowed to proceed to Italy to attend conferences and can continue to advocate democracy without fear of reprisal. That indicates that the conservative force in the party is powerless to go against the prevailing mood in the country. In due time, this student movement will be bolstered by thousands of returned students who will form a motive force for the dissemination of Western democratic liberal ideas and who will demonstrate the inseparable link between freedom and progress.

Despite the ouster of Hu Yaobang, the forces in support of reform are still formidable. Some say that reform is the only solution to the practical economic problems of the people and indeed "the common desire of the whole party and the whole nation." Some say the ultimate end of reform is to eliminate "impoverished socialism."[29] Some say that the present trend of development is irreversible.[30] Some say that reform should be accelerated and that to ensure its success the "campaign against bourgeois liberalization should not be allowed to leap beyond its boundaries and spread to the economic field."[31] Even the conservative Peng Zhen is reported to have said that it is necessary "to decentralize and delegate power to lower levels" and "to go all out for reform" and

---

[29]FBIS, *China–87–131*, pp. K2–4.
[30]FBIS, *China–87–114*, p. K2. FBIS, *China–87–066*, p. K19–23.
[31]FBIS, *China–87–115*, p. I5. FBIS, *China–87–112*, p. K6.

that it is necessary "to open up to the outside world in order to import and assimilate advanced foreign managerial experience and technology."[32] There is also widespread support for political structural reform.[33]

Judging by the prevailing trends in China, the conservative faction led by Peng Zhen, Chen Yun, Hu Qiaomu, Deng Liqun, and Wang Zhen does not have the moral authority and the support of the masses. In the decade preceding the triumph of communism in China, the KMT government and all the "isms" it advocated became targets of vilification and destruction. But after nearly four decades of communist rule, the masses are eventually told or discover themselves that the enemy of the state and people is not the KMT and all the values it stood for, but the Mao Zedong Thought and the institutions established by the man who had founded the PRC. Their antagonism should thus be directed against Maoism and the CCP. The majority of the Chinese people, especially those below the age of fifty, have either a vague memory of KMT misrule and evils or no memory whatsoever of KMT rule. What they have poignantly experienced over the years is suffering under Communist rule. Hence it will be within their understanding if they are told about the excesses of communism and the evils of abject poverty and regimentation. But they will be baffled if they are told about the evils of democracy, of freedom, and of affluence. They will be baffled if they are told that the reformist faction which is trying to make their country more democratic, free, and affluent should be condemned.

Moreover, while the power of state is presently still concentrated in the CCP, whatever policies the government implements have somehow to conform to the desires of the people. China has now entered a phase of development where the sovereignty of the masses is gradually asserting itself. The current suppression of student movements in the PRC should thus be viewed as ripples rather than tidal waves in an otherwise "pacific ocean."

The departure of Hu Yaobang from the party secretariat and the appointment of Zhao Ziyang to act on his behalf signal another heartening development on China's political scene. First, it shows that Chinese communism has now matured and mellowed. Second, the appointment of Zhao Ziyang as acting CCP general secretary indicates a fundamental change in China's power structure. It signifies that eventually important powers will be transferred from the CCP to the State Council and that eventually the CCP, no less than the NPC, will mainly endorse policy

---

[32]FBIS, *China–87–112*, p. K20.
[33]FBIS, *China–87–130*, pp. K2–8. FBIS, *China–87–090*, pp. K6–11. FBIS, *China–87–080*, pp. K11–20.

and legislative initiatives put forth by the State Council rather than play a leading role in the governance of the state.

The present development in the PRC will not be arrested or disrupted. Its pace may be temporarily decelerated. There will come a time, perhaps not too distant, when China will be governed according to the state constitution rather than party ideology and rules. There will come a time when the norm of judgment will be changed. Communism will be replaced by nationalism and the cult of efficiency. The Chinese people will no longer talk about conformity to and defense of party interests; what is uppermost in their minds will be individual and national interests. In that event, the PRC would exert a centripetal force over the overseas Chinese who hope for a more congenial environment. The overseas Chinese can tolerate a certain degree of political and intellectual conformity. After all, their acceptance of the indigenization process in their countries of residence is no less than an acceptance of a large measure of intellectual and cultural conformity.

The present overseas Chinese problem is not the creation of the PRC or the Southeast Asian states. It is true that in the past three decades the PRC has forced many of its nationals to flee mainland China. But very few of them have found their way to Southeast Asia. The Manchu monarchy was the first to "export" overseas Chinese on a massive scale and Western colonialists were the first to "import" overseas Chinese into the region on a massive scale. The KMT that succeeded the Manchus tried to help them through an inverse exploitation, which created great political and psychological problems. The ex-colonial powers, perhaps out of unconscious omissions or perhaps out of deliberate intent, failed to solve their nationality problem when they disengaged from the region. The overseas Chinese problem, as pointed out before, has now ceased to trouble Western countries with large numbers of Chinese residents but seems to be peculiar to Southeast Asian states. It will be to the benefit of the Southeast Asian governments to learn the pertinent way of handling their Chinese residents from the United States, Canada, or Australia. Failure to do so will bring complications to the region when the PRC is economically and militarily in a position to implement actively its overseas Chinese policy by spirit no less than by letter. The solution of the problem lies with the Southeast Asian states. Virtually all Chinese in the region have identified themselves with their countries of residence. Hence, it is only they who can help the PRC to wind up its Overseas Chinese policy or curtail its scope.

9. China and the Ethnic Chinese: Political Liability/Economic Asset

ROBERT S. ROSS

For the governments of Southeast Asia, the presence of the always economically influential and at times large minority of ethnic Chinese in the host societies raises many security issues. One central concern of regional leaders is Beijing's potential to affect the political and economic stability of the ASEAN countries by appealing to the Chinese communities' reputed loyalty to their "motherland" over their adopted countries. In this respect, some Southeast Asian leaders consider the ethnic Chinese an instrument of Chinese foreign policy, which Beijing wields to influence their countries' domestic and foreign policies.

It is the purpose of this chapter to address the key issue of Chinese policy toward the ethnic Chinese and to address the implications of its policy for the security of Southeast Asian states. The chapter examines the two facets of Chinese policy—its approach toward the role of overseas Chinese in the host country and toward their role inside China. The first issue concerns the implications of Beijing's relations with overseas Chinese for the domestic political stability of the host country. The second aspect concerns China's promotion of the contribution of ethnic Chinese abroad to Chinese modernization. Clearly, these two issues are fundamentally related, especially insofar as such involvement in the mainland economy on the part of Southeast Asian ethnic Chinese affects the political and economic stability of Southeast Asian countries. Therefore, after separately discussing each aspect of this problem, the conclusion will examine their interrelationship and the implications for the ASEAN states.

Implications for Domestic Political Stability

Recent Chinese efforts to rekindle the patriotism of Southeast Asia's ethnic Chinese population to expedite PRC economic development have evoked heightened concern over Beijing's ability to use the ethnic Chinese to destabilize regional governments. Beijing is acutely aware of Southeast Asian suspicions and it has attempted to allay them through various policy statements. As in the past, the centerpiece of China's diplomacy is its denial of the right of dual citizenship to ethnic Chinese abroad, implying that Beijing will not protect the interests of ethnic

Chinese who are not PRC citizens. Thus, in 1978 Liao Chengzhi, while reminding the ethnic Chinese abroad of their obligations to the motherland, also reaffirmed Chinese policy on dual nationality, insisting that "although they will no longer be Chinese citizens," Chinese leaders "encourage the overseas Chinese to choose the nationality of their countries of residence."[1] Article 3 of the 1980 Nationality Law of the People's Republic says that China "does not recognize dual nationality for any Chinese national."[2] Such statements run throughout all PRC discussions of the ethnic Chinese. This was especially the case when China retaliated against Vietnam's treatment of its ethnic Chinese community. Beijing tried to ease fears that other countries in Southeast Asia might confront similar Chinese pressures. Although it cancelled its aid program to Vietnam and escalated Sino-Vietnamese conflict, China went out of its way to assure Southeast Asian leaders that China was not responsible for the tension in relations and that the crisis did not portend a shift in Chinese policy toward the ethnic Chinese in Southeast Asia.

Nevertheless, China's own policy statements undermine Beijing's efforts to calm Southeast Asian fears of Chinese interference. While rejecting dual nationality, Liao Chengzhi nonetheless reassured Chinese that even if they adopt host country nationality, "they will still be our relatives and continue to maintain close contacts with us . . . and the spirit of the policies concerning overseas Chinese at home fully applies to them as well."[3] Even more disconcerting is Article 13 of the PRC Nationalities Law, which stipulates that ethnic Chinese "once of Chinese nationality may apply for a restoration of Chinese nationality provided that they have legitimate reasons."[4] This essentially negates China's prohibition on dual nationality insofar as it gives Chinese leaders a free hand to interfere arbitrarily in the domestic affairs of other countries on behalf of the ethnic Chinese. Indeed, since 1949 China has

---

[1]Xinhua, January 4, 1978, Foreign Broadcast Information Service, *Daily Report, People's Republic of China* (FBIS, PRC), January 4, 1978, p. E20.

[2]*Beijing Review,* October 6, 1980. Also see Gong Qiuxiang, "The Principle Basis in Handling the Citizenship Question," *Renmin ribao* (People's daily), (hereafter cited as *RMRB*), September 26, 1980, Joint Publications Research Service (JPRS), *China: Political, Social, and Military Affairs (CPSM),* no. 76825, pp. 45–46.

[3]Xinhua, June 4, 1978, FBIS, *PRC,* June 5, 1978, p. E20.

[4]*Beijing Review,* October 6, 1980, pp. 17–18. Note that this caveat will gradually lose political significance as the Southeast Asian overseas Chinese are increasingly comprised of those born in the host country of parents with host country citizenship and, thus, with host country nationality.

shown little interest in nationality issues when confronting conflict between Southeast Asian governments and their Chinese communities.

Given the ambiguity of Chinese policy statements and the futility of depending on policy statements to predict policy, a better guide to China's behavior is its actual policy toward the relations between ethnic Chinese and their host governments. An examination of Sino-Indonesian relations over the Chinese minority in Indonesia and a close look at the breakdown of Sino-Vietnamese relations in 1978 reveals a distinct pattern in Chinese policy. China has preferred that the policies of Southeast Asian governments toward their ethnic Chinese communities not become a conflictual issue in relations between China and the host government. Nevertheless, when deterioration of bilateral relations over national security issues has confluenced with a domestic crisis in a Southeast Asian country involving the overseas Chinese, Beijing has often interpreted mistreatment of the ethnic Chinese as part of a country's overall shift to an anti-China policy. It has responded by raising tension and welcoming the ethnic Chinese to China, thereby disrupting the local economy. Even so, Beijing has not been able to alter host country policy or "protect the interests" of ethnic Chinese abroad.

In May 1959 the Indonesian government promulgated a ban on alien participation in retail trade activities. Conservative Indonesian politicians used the prohibition to appease anti-Chinese indigenous businessmen, who had experienced recent commercial disappointments and feared nationalization of businesses. Social tension was further aggravated in August 1959 when a ban on alien (i.e., Chinese) residency in rural areas was announced in West Java and South Sulawesi, entailing expropriation of land and forced resettlement of Chinese. These two developments precipitated a societal crisis and violent anti-Sinicism beginning in October 1959 and extending into 1960.[5]

Since the 1955 Bandung Conference, Sino-Indonesia relations had been quite friendly, and Indonesia had been adopting an increasingly anti-Western foreign policy. Thus, China first protested the ban on alien residency in rural areas through private channels, seeking to prevent the conflict from disrupting relations. When new Indonesian legislation failed to appease Chinese demands, however, China increased the tension, reportedly threatening Indonesia with harsh reprisals, including a dock strike by ethnic Chinese. When this failed to alter Jakarta's policy, Beijing again increased the pressure. On December 12, 1959, a *Renmin*

---

[5]The best analysis of the 1960 anti-Chinese developments in Indonesia is J. A. C. Mackie, "Anti-Chinese Outbreaks in Indonesia, 1959–1968," in J. A. C. Mackie, ed., *The Chinese in Indonesia* (Honolulu: University Press of Hawaii, 1976).

ribao (People's Daily) editorial warning that it would be a "grievous mistake" if Indonesian leaders thought that the ethnic Chinese "are without any support . . . and that the Chinese government and the 650 million Chinese people would watch their compatriots be subjected to unjustified discrimination and persecution . . . without doing anything."[6] At which point, Radio Beijing attacked the Indonesian government with greater vehemence and called upon the Chinese to return to China, thereby contributing to Indonesian economic dislocation and inflation, especially as Chinese consular officials were careful to recruit the better skilled, educated, and wealthier ethnic Chinese, regardless of their citizenship. Nearly 100,000 Chinese left Indonesia for the PRC.[7]

Chinese policy was primarily motivated by the implications of Jakarta's ethnic Chinese policy for Indonesian politics and foreign policy. Indonesia's discriminatory policies were promoted by generals who likely aimed to disrupt Sino-Indonesian relations and weaken the Indonesian Communist Party (PKI), which, due to its political platform, was obliged to oppose the popular anti-Chinese policies. Chinese leaders viewed Jakarta's ethnic Chinese policy as part of this larger scheme and, thus, responded with retaliatory measures. *Renmin ribao* argued that the policies were the actions of "certain influential forces . . . hostile to Sino-Indonesian friendship."[8] By raising the tension in Sino-Indonesian relations, it may have hoped to reduce the influence or even bring about the ouster of these leaders from the Sukarno government.

Ultimately, however, China's pressure tactics failed and it had to retreat. Less than two weeks after Radio Beijing invited the ethnic Chinese to leave for the PRC, the broadcasts stopped and Chinese Foreign Minister Chen Yi adopted an increasingly conciliatory posture, no longer demanding that Indonesia revoke either the trade ban or the residency ban. *Renmin ribao* dropped its threats of retaliation and, despite "the fact that the discrimination . . . has not completely stopped," called for a joint committee to meet to promote the implementation of the dual nationality treaty and merely expressed its "hope" that Indonesia would give the ethnic Chinese the rights prom-

---

[6]Editorial, "For an Overall Settlement of the Overseas Chinese Question Existing Between China and Indonesia," *RMRB*, December 12, 1959, FBIS, *Far East*, December 14, 1959, p. AAA5.

[7]On PRC motivation and recruitment practices and the effect of the ethnic Chinese departures on the Indonesian economy, see Mackie, "Anti-Chinese Outbreaks in Indonesia," pp. 87, 92, 95; David Mozingo, *Chinese Policy Toward Indonesia, 1949–1967* (Ithaca, N.Y.: Cornell University Press, 1976), pp. 171–73.

[8]"For an Overall Settlement of the Overseas Chinese Question," p. AAA2. For a fuller discussion of this argument, see Mozingo, *Chinese Policy Toward Indonesia*, pp. 162–63.

ised them in the treaty.[9] Twenty to twenty-five thousand Chinese businesses were affected by the retail trade ban and over 15,000 Chinese had their land expropriated and were resettled to urban areas.[10] Nonetheless, Beijing salvaged good relations rather than allow the conflict to cause an irreversible shift in what was a favorable Indonesian policy toward the PRC.

China was not so understanding in 1965–66, when the ethnic Chinese in Indonesia once again suffered casualties at the hands of rioting Indonesians in the wake of the 1965 purge of the PKI from the Indonesian government. As with the previous incident, the crucial variable was elite politics in Jakarta and the implications for Indonesia's China policy. Following the PKI's unsuccessful October 1, 1965, attempt to eliminate military participation from the Indonesian government, Jakarta's new military leadership carried out violent reprisals against Indonesian communists and attacks on Chinese diplomatic grounds and personnel. For indigenous Indonesians, the military's attack on PKI members and the PKI's close political identification with the PRC amounted to a license for mass attacks on ethnic Chinese, despite the party's overwhelming indigenous Indonesian membership. Over a span of two years, mob violence took the lives of at least 2,000 ethnic Chinese.[11] Many more Chinese lost their homes and businesses.

The decimation of the PKI, China's ally in the Indonesian leadership, and the concomitant rapid accumulation of power by right-wing military leaders signalled the beginning of a dramatic about-face in Indonesian foreign policy. At the end of the month Indonesian soldiers surrounded and forcefully entered the commercial counselor's office of the Chinese Embassy, making clear that the military, not President Sukarno or Foreign Minister Subandrio, was managing foreign policy and that Indonesia would end its radical strategic alignment with the PRC. Moreover, the military formalized much of the racial anti-Sinicism by issuing decrees harmful to local Chinese interests. Thus, whereas in 1959–60 there was some ambiguity in Indonesian elite politics and policy toward China, such was not the case in 1965.

Under these circumstances, Chinese consideration for the fate of the ethnic Chinese arose in the context of its greater concern for Jakarta's anti-China acts, its anti-PKI acts, and its growing friendship with

---

[9]Editorial, "Seeking an Overall Settlement of the Question of Overseas Chinese Between China and Indonesia Through Friendly Consultation," *RMRB*, January 27, 1960, FBIS, *Far East*, January 28, 1960, pp. AAA5–8.

[10]Mackie, "Anti-Chinese Outbursts in Indonesia," p. 95.

[11]Charles Coppel, *Indonesian Chinese in Crisis* (New York: Oxford University Press, 1983), pp. 58–59.

the United States. A *Renmin ribao* editorial denounced the "full-scale fascist outrage" of Indonesia's "right-wing reactionary forces," but only briefly mentioned the "appalling brutality" inflicted on the ethnic Chinese. Beijing's ultimate concern was that a "small handful of . . . rightwing army men and reactionary politicians have all along been agents of imperialism" and that the ousting of the PKI was "engineered by U.S. imperialism." The new leaders have "openly thrown themselves in the lap of the imperialists led by the U.S. . . . and have joined their anticommunist, anti-China . . . alliance."[12]

Thus, China shaped its policy toward the ethnic Chinese to suit its larger interests. In early November, as the political crisis was only just escalating, China responded with a private note protesting that ethnic Chinese schools, residences, and businesses were being ransacked.[13] As bilateral relations and Beijing's position in elite politics further deteriorated, and as anti-ethnic Chinese violence continued unabated, Beijing publicly expressed its determined opposition to Jakarta's policy with a steady stream of protest notes. Ultimately, as in 1959–60, Beijing welcomed the ethnic Chinese to return to China, contributing to Indonesia's existing economic problems, and sent boats to Indonesia to pick up the Chinese and take them to China.[14] Beijing was making Indonesia pay a price for adopting an "anti-China" policy and realigning with the United States. Significantly, unlike in 1959, China now did not retreat. The deterioration of Sino-Indonesian political relations ensured that Beijing would maintain its pressure on Jakarta, especially in the context of the ensuing Cultural Revolution in China.

These two cases are major examples of Chinese intervention in Southeast Asia through the ethnic Chinese. Together they reveal the reactive nature of PRC policy toward the overseas Chinese. Beijing did not instigate the crises. With the exception of Chinese policy during the summer of 1967, reflecting the domestic excesses of the Cultural Revolution,[15] Beijing has responded to domestic instability, and often with great reluctance, preferring to insulate state-to-state relations from the

---

[12]Editorial, "Full-Scale Fascist Outrage," *RMRB*, April 16, 1966; U.S. Consulate General, Hong Kong, *Survey of the Chinese Mainland Press (SCMP)*, no. 3681, pp. 32–33.

[13]The November 4 protest over the treatment of ethnic Chinese was later reported in Xinhua, November 22, 1965, FBIS, *Far East*, November 23, 1965, pp. BBB2–4.

[14]Nevertheless, despite the harsh treatment suffered by the Chinese, Beijing did not broadcast appeals to the Chinese to return to the mainland. Apparently, the cost of providing for the 1959–60 immigrants was exceedingly high. Ultimately, at most 10,000 ethnic Chinese fled to China. See Mozingo, *Chinese Policy Toward Indonesia*, p. 250.

[15]See Melvin Gurtov, *China and Southeast Asia—The Politics of Survival* (Baltimore: Johns Hopkins University Press, 1971), ch. 5.

welfare of local Chinese communities. These cases also reveal Beijing's impotence, insofar as it has been unable to alter Indonesia's domestic politics, its foreign policy, or its ethnic Chinese policy. Nevertheless, when compelled by a combination of severe discrimination, absence of host government restraints on anti-Chinese acts, and bilateral conflicts of security interests, Beijing has responded with measures costly to the host country, trying both to aid the local Chinese and coerce the host government to accommodate itself to Chinese interests. This same pattern is evident in Chinese policy toward Vietnam in 1978.

Hanoi's treatment of the ethnic Chinese in Vietnam aroused Chinese attention as early as the middle of 1976, when Hanoi instituted a severe tax which was especially directed at the ethnic Chinese.[16] In early 1977, Hanoi began pushing Chinese residing on the Vietnamese side of the Sino-Vietnamese border into China. It also compelled ethnic Chinese to accept Vietnamese citizenship, apparently in accordance with a pre-1975 South Vietnamese fiat which Hanoi, along with Beijing, had denounced as illegal and which was contrary to Beijing's understanding of Vietnam's own 1955 agreement with the PRC that the Chinese in Vietnam should "voluntarily" adopt Vietnamese citizenship. Despite these "anti-Chinese" acts, China did not signal any meaningful opposition. Sino-Vietnamese political relations were satisfactory and Hanoi had yet to consolidate strategic relations with the Soviet Union. China would not look for trouble by making an issue of Vietnam's ethnic Chinese policy.

In June 1977, however, Beijing directly expressed for the first time its opposition to Vietnamese policy. In private talks with Vietnamese Premier Pham Van Dong, Vice Premier Li Xiannian charged that Hanoi "resorted to coercion" when it treated the local Chinese as Vietnamese citizens. Li warned that "every country has the duty to protect the legitimate rights of nationals in other countries" and that Chinese leaders were in an "awkward position" because Vietnam had "unilaterally taken measures to compel Chinese to adopt Vietnamese nationality without consulting us."[17] China still hoped to avoid conflict, yet it had now threatened Vietnam that continued mistreatment of Chinese would elicit a more damaging Chinese response.

This shift was not a response to the situation of the Chinese in Vietnam, which had been deteriorating since 1976, but reflected impor-

---

[16]This section draws on the author's *The Indochina Tangle: China's Vietnam Policy, 1975–1979* (New York: Columbia University Press, 1988).

[17]"Memorandum on Vice Premier Li's Talks with Premier Pham Van Dong," *Beijing Review*, March 30, 1979, p. 21.

tant changes in Vietnamese policy toward the Soviet Union. Prior to Li Xiannian's meeting with Pham Van Dong, Hanoi had moved appreciably closer to the Soviet Union. In April it joined the International Bank for Economic Cooperation, which is a COMECON bank, and the Soviet-sponsored International Investment Bank. A short time later, Hanoi consolidated bilateral economic relations with Moscow by accepting increased Soviet aid. Improved military relations ensued as General Giap led a successful visit to Moscow and the Soviet Union transferred military equipment to Vietnam. Indeed, in his talks with Pham Van Dong, Li Xiannian's foremost complaint concerned Vietnam's pro-Soviet statements suggesting that Moscow and Hanoi shared an interest in resisting Chinese influence in Indochina.[18] It was under such circumstances that Vietnam's ethnic Chinese policy first became an issue in Sino-Vietnamese relations.

Through the end of 1977 and into early 1978, Hanoi continued to step up its control over the Chinese and further consolidated Soviet-Vietnamese relations. Chinese in Vietnam endured spiraling harassment and property expropriation and Hanoi intensified its efforts to purify the border area by pushing Chinese into the PRC. In addition, Hanoi began sending many urban Chinese to the New Economic Zones. China responded by increasing the pressure on Vietnamese leaders to reconsider their policy. It sent three confidential notes to Hanoi complaining of Vietnamese "persecution" of Chinese, each note presumably expressing growing impatience with Vietnamese "intransigence."[19] In *Renmin ribao*, Liao Chengzhi wrote, without explicitly mentioning Vietnam, that it is "impermissible to compel overseas Chinese to choose one nationality over another." For those Chinese retaining PRC citizenship, it is Beijing's duty to "protect their rights and interests."[20]

China's increased concern for the Chinese in Vietnam paralleled ominous developments in Hanoi's policy toward the Soviet Union. During early 1978, Moscow and Hanoi signed additional economic agreements, thus increasing Vietnamese dependence on the Soviet Union. Moreover, Vietnam increasingly flaunted its abandonment of neutrality

---

[18]Ibid., p. 17.

[19]Vietnam News Agency (VNA), June 16, 1978, FBIS, *Asia-Pacific* (FBIS, *AP*), June 19, 1978, p. E6.

[20]Liao Chengzhi, "A Critique of the Reactionary Fallacies of the 'Gang of Four' About the So-Called 'Overseas Relations'," *RMRB*, January 4, 1978, FBIS, *PRC*, January 5, 1978, p. E14.

in the Sino-Soviet conflict, challenging Beijing to obstruct consolidated Soviet-Vietnamese economic and political relations. Yet, the controlled nature of China's response also reflected the remaining ambiguity in Vietnamese foreign policy. Hanoi had exercised some restraint in dealing with its Chinese community and it had yet to challenge directly fundamental Chinese interests, particularly in Kampuchea. Regarding the Sino-Soviet conflict, Hanoi had not burned its bridges to China nor committed itself to assisting Moscow's encirclement of the PRC.

In late March, however, Vietnam banned private trade and business in southern Vietnam. Insofar as this primarily affected the ethnic Chinese, Vietnamese military personnel surrounded Cholon, the Chinese area of Ho Chi Minh City. Overnight, hundreds of thousands of Chinese were deprived of their livelihood. Many Chinese were forcibly moved to the New Economic Zones. Then, in late April, Vietnam unified the northern and southern currencies. Because it also placed a limit on cash holdings, life savings were essentially confiscated when old currency was exchanged for new currency. Under such circumstances, it is not surprising that many Chinese fled Vietnam for the South China Sea. What was more significant, however, was the number of Chinese from northern Vietnam who crossed into China. Perhaps they were influenced by discrimination in the north, by the situation in the south, and by rumors of war, but Vietnam made no effort to stem the flow. On the contrary, Hanoi had surrendered all restraint, carrying out policies destructive to ethnic Chinese, as well as PRC interests, for the refugees imposed severe relocation costs on Beijing.

During the early phases of Vietnam's intensified anti-China policy, when the refugee flow was just beginning to increase, Beijing maintained its low profile. Subsequent to the abolition of private commerce in the South, Beijing sent its fourth secret note protesting Vietnamese policy and Liao Chengzhi, commenting on the border crossings, said that Chinese leaders are "concerned about this and we are watching developments closely." Vietnam, however, unified its currency, blamed China for the mass exodus, and incited further departures by saying that if Chinese wanted to leave Vietnam, all they had to do was ask. By mid-May, 5,000 Chinese were crossing the border each day. Then, on May 12, China secretly informed Hanoi that it would end a portion of its aid program and two weeks later it announced that it would dispatch ships to bring the Chinese to the PRC. As in each previous case of conflict between China and Southeast Asian countries over the ethnic Chinese, this decision reflected a crucial stage in the crisis—Beijing decided that the host government, in this case Vietnam, would not reverse its policy and it was time to increase the pressure. But Hanoi refused to allow the Chinese ships to enter ports on Beijing's terms.

Thus, in late May China sent a second private note advising Hanoi that it planned to withdraw almost all of its aid for the remaining projects.[21]

The Sino-Vietnamese conflict had erupted and the ethnic Chinese issue provided the catalyst. But China's primary concern was the host country's foreign policy and its implications for Chinese security. For Chinese leaders, Vietnamese policy toward the ethnic Chinese reflected Hanoi's decision to oppose China and ally itself with Moscow. How else to explain Vietnam's defiance of clear Chinese warnings? Moreover, developments in Soviet-Vietnamese relations added substance to such suspicions. Moscow's polemics encouraged Hanoi to continue this policy despite Chinese opposition, and Soviet-Vietnamese high-level military consultations and Soviet military maneuvers in Siberia and in the South China Sea all suggested that Vietnam and the Soviet Union were coordinating their policies to undermine Chinese security. Deng Xiaoping insisted that "Vietnam is leaning toward the Soviet Union, which is the archenemy of China." A *Renmin ribao* commentator observed that Moscow was the "behind-the-scenes provocateur" of Hanoi's ethnic Chinese policy, seeking a base in Vietnam to realize its plan for the domination of Asia.[22]

Thus, in Sino-Vietnamese relations, as in Sino-Indonesian relations in the 1950s and 1960s, China did not initiate the crisis in Vietnam's Chinese community. Rather, Hanoi's domestic policies, although they undoubtedly originated from fears of PRC intentions, caused great hardship and panic among its Chinese population. Only after China's private, low-level warnings went unheeded and Hanoi established security relations with the Soviet Union did China react with forceful countermeasures, making Hanoi pay a price for its Soviet policy. Also similar to its relations with Indonesia, despite its ties with the Chinese in Vietnam and its coercive tactics, Beijing was unable to alter Vietnamese foreign policy or its treatment of the ethnic Chinese.

Equally significant for understanding Chinese policy are those times when Beijing failed to respond to domestic instability in Southeast Asia involving Chinese communities. Such was the case when the Malay Communist Party (MCP), which had a primarily ethnic Chinese membership, led an armed insurgency against the British colonial authorities in Malaya in the late 1940s and early 1950s. The bulk of MCP

---

[21]Not until July did China send the final perfunctory note informing Hanoi that the entire aid program was canceled and that Chinese advisers would be withdrawn. The secret notes were released by Hanoi in VNA, June 17, 1978, FBIS, *AP,* June 19, 1978, pp. K5–8.
[22]*Nation Review* (Bangkok), June 9, 1978, FBIS, *PRC,* June 9, 1978, pp. A11–15; Commentator, "Soviet Lies Cannot Cover Up Fact," *RMRB,* June 10, 1978, FBIS, *PRC,* June 12, 1978, p. A14.

economic and political support came from rural Chinese and better-educated Chinese in Malaya, both of which believed themselves to be suffering from government and societal biases against Chinese activities.[23] The situation was presumably perfect for the new and presumably radical Chinese government to promote revolution by appealing to Malaya's ethnic Chinese. Nevertheless, although the Chinese Communists supported the insurgency and probably helped to persuade the MCP to move to guerrilla warfare in 1948,[24] the PRC recognized that it was unable to take advantage of its ties with the ethnic Chinese. Beijing's strongest statements merely exhorted the Chinese minority to ''unite together and continue the struggle for their proper rights and interests.'' By 1951, although the war continued apace, even such limited encouragement of ethnic Chinese activism was replaced by concern for innocent Chinese killed by the authorities and the growing number of refugees. China had narrowed its focus to the Chinese minority's immediate welfare, rather than its revolutionary potential.[25]

Such Chinese detachment was based on two factors. First, the Malay population interpreted the dominant role of ethnic Chinese in the MCP as proof that the party represented Beijing's interests rather than Malay interests. Active PRC encouragement of ethnic Chinese participation in the insurgency would merely have reinforced such suspicions, undermining China's ultimate objective of ousting the British from Malaya. Second, although the MCP's base of support was the Chinese community in Malaya, the insurgents often turned their brutal methods on the local Chinese. Thus, Beijing's support for ethnic Chinese participation in the insurgency would not only have damaged the popularity of the MCP, but it would have also damaged Beijing's ties with the overseas Chinese.[26] Taiwan and the British authorities would have likely been the only beneficiaries. Undoubtedly to its great disappointment,

---

[23]For a discussion of the social bases of support for the MCP, see Victor Purcell, *The Chinese in Southeast Asia*, 2d ed. (New York: Oxford University Press, 1965), ch. 34; Stanley S. Bedlington, *Malaysia and Singapore: The Building of New States* (Ithaca, N.Y.: Cornell University Press, 1978), pp. 77–81. The most comprehensive discussion of the background of MCP recruits is Lucian W. Pye, *Guerrilla Communism in Malaya: Its Social and Political Meaning* (Princeton: Princeton University Press, 1956).

[24]Bedlington, *Malaysia and Singapore*, p. 77; Jay Taylor, *China and Southeast Asia: Peking's Relations with Revolutionary Movements*, 2d ed. (New York: Praeger, 1976), pp. 257–59. Cf. Stephen Fitzgerald, *China and the Overseas Chinese: A Study of Peking's Changing Policy, 1949–1970* (Cambridge: Cambridge University Press, 1972), p. 92.

[25]Fitzgerald, *China and the Overseas Chinese*, pp. 94–97.

[26]For a discussion of the attitude of both Malays and local Chinese to the MCP insurgency, see Purcell, *Chinese in Southeast Asia*, pp. 333–36; Bedlington, *Malaysia and Singapore*, p. 76.

Beijing was unable to help the insurgency by encouraging local Chinese participation.

Malaysian Chinese once again attracted Beijing's attention in May 1969 when hundreds of Chinese were murdered during two weeks of mass violence. Nevertheless, China failed to respond. Indeed, when discussing the rioting, China usually conspicuously failed to point out that it was the ethnic Chinese who were suffering.[27] That these were clearly spontaneous riots occurring without official support or instigation must have affected Beijing's detached response. Moreover, the escalation of Sino-Soviet border hostilities in the spring and summer of 1969 undoubtedly preoccupied Chinese leaders and they were not about to look for trouble in Malaysia.

Another case of PRC detachment occurred when anti-Chinese riots broke out in Indonesia in 1963. Compared with Indonesian attacks on Chinese in 1959–60, the violence directed at ethnic Chinese in 1963 caused more casualties and greater property damage. Nevertheless, Beijing preferred to stress the excellent state of Sino-Indonesian relations, for in recent years the "Jakarta-Beijing axis" had advanced PRC policy toward both the Soviet Union and the United States. Chinese leaders were satisfied with Sino-Indonesian relations and, unlike in 1959–60, early Indonesian leadership opposition to these apparently spontaneous mass riots reassured Beijing that the riots did not portend a shift in Indonesian foreign policy. When the Chinese ambassador met with Indonesian Foreign Ministry officials, he was assured that Jakarta was firmly committed to ending the riots and to giving relief to "victimized" Chinese nationals.[28] Thus, the *Renmin ribao* observer insisted that "imperialism," rather than its domestic allies, had instigated the anti-Chinese riots and it praised Jakarta's efforts to resist the "intrigues of imperialism and the reactionaries."[29] Beijing did not permit the crisis in Indonesia's ethnic Chinese community to upset Sino-Indonesian friendship.[30]

---

[27]See, e.g., Xinhua, May 29, 1969, *SCMP*, no. 4430, p. 30; Xinhua, June 20, 1969, *SCMP*, no. 4444, pp. 22–23. The one account that accurately reported the rioting as anti-Chinese is Xinhua, May 20, 1969, FBIS, *Communist China*, May 20, 1969, pp. A1–2. For a discussion of the rioting, see Bedlington, *Malaysia and Singapore*, pp. 146–47.

[28]Xinhua, May 22, 1963, *SCMP*, no. 2987, p. 24.

[29]Observer, "Support Indonesia's Efforts to Smash Imperialist Scheme of Subversion," *RMRB*, May 30, 1963, *SCMP*, no. 2993, pp. 22–23. The origins of the riots and the government response is discussed in greater detail in Mackie, "Anti-Chinese Violence in Indonesia," pp. 97–110.

[30]China responded in a similarly detached manner to minor anti-Chinese outbursts in Indonesia in 1973, 1974, and 1980. See Leo Suryadinata, *China and the ASEAN States: The Ethnic Chinese Dimension* (Singapore: Singapore University Press, 1985), pp. 37–38.

Finally, ethnic Chinese also suffered the brutality of Kampuchea's Pol Pot government between 1975 and 1978. As many as 200,000 Chinese may have died in Kampuchea during this period.[31] Nevertheless, there was not one PRC radio broadcast which expressed sympathy for the Chinese and there is no evidence that Beijing ever discussed with Khmer Rouge leaders their treatment of the ethnic Chinese. Once again, China was prepared to forsake the welfare of the Chinese in the interest of good relations with the host country. The Khmer Rouge were China's vital and only security partner in Indochina during this period of consolidating Soviet-Vietnamese relations.

Contribution to the Four Modernizations

As China has moved from the politics of revolutionary activism to the policies of pragmatic modernization, it has taken the initiative to utilize the material and intellectual resources of the ethnic Chinese minorities around the globe, particularly those in Southeast Asia, who were once berated as bourgeois capitalists and deprived access to the promised fruits of the Chinese revolution. The Chinese media is now full of appeals to the ethnic Chinese abroad to express their patriotism for the motherland. A special overseas edition of *Renmin ribao* has been issued which uses the traditional Chinese characters more familiar to Chinese outside the mainland. Essentially, Beijing is now competing with both Taiwan and the Southeast Asian governments for the various intellectual and financial resources of Chinese worldwide.

This focus on the ethnic Chinese is one aspect of Beijing's renewed emphasis on United Front policies. Harking back to both the revolutionary period and the 1950s, Chinese leaders seek to unite with whatever groups are willing to contribute to the interests of the motherland. As in earlier periods, a central focus of the contemporary United Front policy is China's intellectuals, but other such patriotic groups include the "national bourgeoisie," many of whom are Chinese with relatives abroad, returned ethnic Chinese, and ethnic Chinese abroad, regardless of whether or not they are Chinese citizens. In the late 1970s, a major focus of the United Front was resisting Soviet hegemonism, and ethnic Chinese abroad were encouraged to do their part. Liao Chengzhi insisted that insofar as "we must exert our greatest effort to form the broadest possible United Front against hegemonism . . . how could there be any reason to exclude . . . overseas Chinese abroad and friends

---

[31]For a demographic analysis of Kampuchea under Pol Pot, see United States Central Intelligence Agency, *Kampuchea: A Demographic Disaster* (Washington, D.C.: U.S. Government Printing Office, 1980).

of foreign nationalities who are of Chinese descent?"[32] In recent years Beijing's preoccupation with the Soviet Union has receded, but Chinese leaders have retained their interest in the ethnic Chinese abroad for two other important objectives—reunification of Taiwan with the mainland and the realization of the Four Modernizations.

Regarding Taiwan, Beijing's focus on ethnic Chinese abroad reflects one aspect of its larger effort to bring about unification by persuading the Taiwan leadership of the mainland's benign features and benevolent intentions. Beijing encourages more and more Chinese to visit the mainland, particularly those from Taiwan, to witness the cleansing of radical influences and the improved standard of living of their relatives. On the one hand, this open-door policy aims to bolster Taipei's confidence in the mainland's political reliability and to break down the resistance on Taiwan to negotiating with the Chinese communists. At the same time, these same efforts aim to convince Chinese outside the mainland of Chinese pragmatism and sincerity, thus complementing Beijing's diplomatic efforts to isolate Taipei, pressuring it to open negotiations on unification.

The policy of the Four Modernizations, however, is the primary reason for Beijing's interest in the ethnic Chinese in Southeast Asia. Chinese leaders are clearly concentrating on the potential financial contribution of approximately 30 million Chinese citizens and foreign nationals of Chinese origin living abroad to accelerate Chinese development.[33] Remittances alone by individual Chinese can amount to a substantial sum. Moreover, many of the Chinese abroad, in comparison with both the indigenous population and, in particular, with the mainland population, are often well educated and wealthy. A dated estimate reports that ethnic Chinese in Southeast Asia, excluding Hong Kong, controlled well over 16 billion U.S. dollars in 1975. The value is undoubtedly far greater today. The human resources are also valuable. The percentage of students that are ethnic Chinese in Southeast Asian universities far exceeds the ethnic Chinese representation in the general population. Similarly, ethnic Chinese are over-represented in management-level positions in Southeast Asian governments and businesses.[34] Thus, there are many ways for China to benefit if it can attract ethnic Chinese participation in Chinese modernization.

---

[32] Liao, "Critique of Reactionary Fallacies," p. E15.
[33] Yang Zhengyan, "Overseas Relations Are a Good Thing," *Renmin ribao*, June 24, 1986, FBIS, *PRC*, July 1, 1986, p. K14.
[34] Yuan-li Wu and Chun-hsi Wu, *Economic Development in Southeast Asia: The Chinese Dimension* (Stanford, Calif.: Hoover Institution Press, 1980), pp. 33–37.

Chinese leaders have not been shy about their economic interest in the ethnic Chinese. It has little to do with concern for the welfare of their compatriots abroad. Just the reverse, reflecting an interest in the mainland's welfare and a clear attempt to attract ethnic Chinese money to help build China. Indeed, in 1985 Ye Fei, chairman of the Overseas Chinese Committee of the National People's Congress, encouraged returned overseas Chinese to "take the lead in becoming rich" and to "introduce more capital, recruit more gifted people, and import more advanced technologies and facilities for . . . economic construction" by "taking advantage of their extensive ties with Overseas Chinese."[35] Guangdong, with its large number of Chinese with relatives abroad, insists that the overseas Chinese "must . . . actively play the role of serving as the bridge in introducing capital and advanced technology and equipment."[36]

To promote its economic modernization plans, as well as a favorable image in Taiwan, China has developed a host of policies with the explicit purpose of restoring ties with overseas Chinese.[37] During the Cultural Revolution, overseas Chinese who had returned to the mainland, Chinese with relatives abroad, and Chinese living abroad were all vilified as class enemies. Returned overseas Chinese and Chinese with relatives abroad suffered greatly as their life chances and personal livelihood drastically deteriorated. Persecution was common and personal possessions were confiscated and destroyed. Thus, paralleling Beijing's domestic efforts to restore trust in the Chinese Communist Party, since the death of Mao it has carried out an attack on past policy toward overseas Chinese, appealing to Chinese abroad to recognize that China

---

[35]*Zhongguo Xinwen She*, January 26, 1985, FBIS, *PRC*, January 29, 1985, p. K7.

[36]Guangdong Provincial Service, March 29, 1979, FBIS, *PRC*, April 4, 1979, pp. P3-4.

[37]In the following discussion, China's overall ethnic Chinese policy is discussed, rather than its specific policies toward individual countries or toward the region. This is because China's portrayal of its policy has not differentiated the ethnic Chinese by country or by region regarding their expected role in the Four Modernizations. Similarly, there is little discussion of the specific amount of ethnic Chinese investment in China or of remittances to China originating from particular Southeast Asian countries. Neither the Southeast Asian countries nor China releases the complete data on these subjects. As a result, many of the economic figures on the overseas Chinese are skewed because they include capital transfers originating from the ethnic Chinese in Hong Kong, the leading source of ethnic Chinese capital entering China. Nevertheless, ethnic Chinese who reside in Southeast Asian countries are an important source of capital entering Hong Kong. For Southeast Asian Chinese who feel more secure when their money is abroad, Hong Kong has been the favored monetary haven. Once their financial resources reach Hong Kong, its ownership is disguised, or "laundered." See Yuan-li Wu and Chun-hsi Wu, *Economic Development in Southeast Asia: The Chinese Dimension* (Stanford, Calif.: Hoover Institution Press, 1980), pp. 43, 94–96.

is changing its ways and can once again be looked upon as the friendly motherland.

Liao Chengzhi kicked off China's new policy in early 1978 with what amounted to a searing indictment of Cultural Revolution policies and of the ideological basis for treating overseas Chinese as class enemies.[38] Lin Biao and the Gang of Four had "perpetrated serious discrimination" against returned overseas Chinese and the relatives of overseas Chinese, treated them as enemies, and made unfounded charges against them. Under the Gang of Four, contacts with overseas Chinese entailed "illicit relations" and accepting remittances meant "taking to the bourgeoisie way of life." But Liao maintained that the Cultural Revolution "has come to a victorious conclusion. . . . The situation through the country is excellent, and so is . . . the work on overseas Chinese affairs." He assured the Chinese living abroad that now no discrimination would be permitted. On the contrary, they were welcomed to participate in the United Front in building China and opposing hegemonism, and they were promised that China would give "appropriate consideration according to their special needs." *Renmin ribao* joined in on the attacks on Gang of Four policy and insisted that the interests of overseas Chinese would now be protected and that overseas Chinese were welcome to return to the motherland.[39]

The specific economic component of Beijing's policy included forthright appeals to ethnic Chinese abroad to express their patriotism for the motherland by contributing to the Four Modernizations. In his first New Year's message directed at the overseas Chinese in Southeast Asia since the Cultural Revolution, Liao Chengzhi observed that the "patriotic front of the vast number of patriotic compatriots abroad is expanding." In order to surmount great difficulties, China "must unite at home and abroad . . . so that the great motherland can advance better and faster on the road of the Four Modernizations." True patriots contribute to the mainland, Liao implied, for overseas Chinese "concern for the motherland's modernization reflects their patriotic feeling."[40] Such patriotic pressures permeate all mainland discussions of the importance of the overseas Chinese in PRC modernization. In so doing, Chinese leaders clearly hope to keep alive or rekindle overseas Chinese identification with the mainland, rather than passively permit total identification with either Taiwan or their host countries, in order to maximize their potential contribution to the Chinese economy.

---

[38]Liao, "Critique of Reactionary Fallacies," pp. E11–21.
[39]*Beijing Review*, January 20, 1978, pp. 14–16.
[40]Beijing in Mandarin to Southeast Asia, December 31, 1979, FBIS, *PRC*, January 4, 1980, pp. L1–4.

Yet, it would take more than mere words to convince the overseas Chinese that the mainland had really changed and could now be trusted and thus elicit their contribution to modernization. Most ethnic Chinese abroad have relatives in China whom they help by sending remittances. These relatives in China form a network reaching out around the world to expertise and wealth. As *Renmin ribao* put it, they are "linked to tens of thousands of compatriots throughout the world; bringing their role into play is of major importance for . . . promoting the Four Moderniza-tions."[41] For Chinese abroad, their view of the mainland is heavily col-ored by the quality of life of their relatives on the mainland. The extent that they are willing to contribute to Chinese modernization is dependent on the impact their contribution will have on their relatives. Hence, Bei-jing has gone a long way toward trying to promote the economic well-being of returned overseas Chinese and the relatives in China of overseas Chinese.

A major aspect of this policy entailed reexamining cases of unjustly accused overseas Chinese and making restitution to returned overseas Chinese whose housing had been confiscated prior to the fall of the Gang of Four. By 1986, more than 33,000 wrongly accused cases from the Cultural Revolution period had been readdressed. In Mei county, Guangdong province, alone, the class status of 2,100 relatives of over-seas Chinese had been changed by early 1979. In earlier years, overseas Chinese did not dare risk visiting their families in China for fear of bringing troubles on them. Now Beijing clearly hoped to quell such fears.[42]

China's policy regarding the return of housing arose from similar motives. Prior to the Cultural Revolution, ethnic Chinese in Southeast Asia contributed to the mainland economy by providing funds for building housing for their relatives in China. Thus, returned overseas Chinese and the relatives of Chinese abroad often had better housing primarily financed by remittances from relatives abroad. During the Cultural Revolution, however, most of this housing was confiscated, undermining the confidence of Chinese abroad that the Communist Party would protect their contributions to family members in China. Thus, Beijing placed great emphasis on returning housing to the benefi-ciaries of overseas Chinese contributions in order to restore confidence in the mainland. Party Secretary Hu Yaobang argued that it was

---

[41]Editorial, "Great Prospects for Overseas Chinese Work in the New Period," *RMRB*, January 3, 1983, FBIS, *PRC*, January 5, 1983, pp. K20–22.
[42]Xinhua, February 23, 1986, FBIS, *PRC*, February 24, 1986, pp. K20–21; Xinhua, April 26, 1979, FBIS, *PRC*, May 2, 1979, p. P4.

"imperative" to "actively solve" this issue. Guangdong considered returning confiscated homes the "key" and "most important aspect" of its overseas Chinese policy.[43] By September 1982, China reported that 72 percent of such homes had been returned. In 1984, Taishan County, Guangdong, had allocated $500,000 to the work of returning homes and since 1979 it had returned nearly 4,500 homes to their original owners. In Beijing, over 3,000 homes were returned by 1984.[44] Chinese leaders were clearly improving the climate for Chinese abroad to contribute to modernization.

An equally significant part of this effort has entailed rebuilding the various organizations in China responsible for overseas Chinese affairs. The most important of these is the Overseas Chinese Affairs Office of the State Council, but other such organizations include the Overseas Chinese Group of the Chinese People's Political Consultative Conference and the All-China Federation of Returned Overseas Chinese, one of China's six mass organizations designed to speak on behalf of the returned overseas Chinese and provide assistance to them. The Sixth National People's Congress established a new committee of Overseas Chinese Affairs in 1983. Just as important as the organizations is their leadership. Liao Chengzhi had been a leading figure in overseas Chinese affairs since the 1950s and was director of the Overseas Chinese Affairs Office under the State Council until his death in 1983. Liao had excellent nationalist credentials, not least because his father, until he was assassinated in 1925, was Sun Yat-sen's closest colleague. Liao Chengzhi was succeeded as director of the Office of Overseas Chinese Affairs by his son Liao Hui. Moreover, the office has been staffed by overseas Chinese from throughout Southeast Asia, including Deputy Director Lin Shuilong, an overseas Chinese from Indonesia who returned to China in 1952, and Vice Minister Zhuang Xiquan, a returned overseas Chinese who had lived in both the Philippines and Singapore. The Overseas Chinese Group chairman is Zhuang Mingli, a returned overseas Chinese from what is now Malaysia. The holding of important leadership positions in China by such overseas personages builds confidence among Chinese abroad that Beijing no longer considers them outcast bourgeoisie and that there is less risk in committing themselves and their resources to the mainland.

---

[43]Hu's comment is in Zhongguo Xinwen She, April 18, 1984, FBIS, PRC, April 18, 1984, pp. K1–2. On Guangdong, see Guangdong Provincial Service, March 24, 1984, FBIS, PRC, March 27, 1984, p. P1.

[44]Zhongguo Xinwen She, January 16, 1983, FBIS, PRC, January 18, 1983, pp. K5–6; China Daily, October 19, 1984, p. 1.

While improving the climate for overseas Chinese involvement in modernization, Beijing has also adopted a number of more specific policies to encourage overseas Chinese contributions to the Chinese economy. This has taken place on three levels. The first is overseas Chinese remittances to relatives and individual contributions by overseas Chinese tourists. The second is cooperative commercial projects established by overseas Chinese and their relatives in China. The third level aims to attract large-scale investment in China's major projects in industry and the services sector.

Remittances can make a great difference to the welfare of Chinese families with relatives abroad. For example, such Chinese often live in better housing and have newer bicycles and more jewelry. In the 1950s, remittances to Taishan County equalled 120 percent of the county's annual agricultural produce.[45] Remittances can also contribute to China's foreign reserve holdings as they are deposited into special accounts and redeemable only in special stores. Thus, the Chinese Communists, like their many predecessors, have focused attention on attracting remittances from overseas Chinese. Beijing has reopened the banks and the special stores for Chinese with remittances from abroad, allowing a great improvement in the standard of living of relatives of overseas Chinese on the mainland through purchases of televisions, stereos, air conditioners, and other such luxury goods, while also accumulating foreign reserves. Similarly, China encourages overseas Chinese to invest funds for the construction of public welfare works. In so doing, it is appealing to traditional Chinese values to encourage Chinese abroad to contribute to the status and well-being of their ancestral villages. As Liao Hui argued, China should assist those Chinese abroad with the "desire to enable their relatives . . . to become better off as soon as possible."[46] As a result of these efforts, remittances from abroad have increased each year since the fall of the Gang of Four. In 1979 China received $400 million in remittances, of which nearly $100 million went to Fujian, far exceeding the amount of the province's foreign investment. Other provinces besides Guangdong and Fujian, which have a disproportionately large share of Chinese with relatives abroad, have benefitted from the

---

[45]William Parish and Martin K. Whyte, *Village and Family in Contemporary China* (Chicago: University of Chicago Press, 1978), pp. 26–27. For a discussion of the contrast between villages with and without access to large amounts of remittances, see Elena S. H. Yu, "Overseas Chinese Remittances in Southeastern China," *China Quarterly,* no. 78 (June 1979), pp. 339–50.
[46]*Zhongguo Xinwen She,* March 18, 1985, FBIS, *PRC,* March 20, 1985, pp. K14–15. Also see Guangdong Provincial Service, March 24, 1986, FBIS, *PRC,* March 27, 1986, pp. P1–2.

new policy. Between 1977 and 1985, Sichuan, for example, received nearly $15 million in remittances.[47]

China's foreign reserve holdings have also benefited from increased deposits by ethnic Chinese abroad in PRC overseas banks. Although most of the deposits are in Hong Kong and Macao banks, the country of origin is impossible to determine. Of the ASEAN countries, only Singapore hosts a branch of the Bank of China. In 1980, such deposits in Chinese banks exceeded $5 billion, up 39 percent from 1979.[48]

Overseas Chinese are also being encouraged to visit China as tourists. They pay the same inexpensive rate as local Chinese for domestic transportation, they have access to special hotels, and they do not need visas to enter the country, regardless of their country of residence. Tourist agencies have been revitalized and have been organizing tours for overseas Chinese to return to their home villages. As a result of these efforts, since 1976 overseas Chinese tourists have added to China's foreign reserves. The number of such tourists, excluding those from Hong Kong and Macao, has increased by more than 225 percent between 1978 and 1982. In the five years of 1980–84, overseas Chinese tourists provided more than $2 billion to the Chinese tourist industry. Hainan Island, for example, experienced nearly an 85 percent increase in foreign exchange from overseas Chinese tourists.[49]

Clearly, the absolute amount of remittances, tourist spending, and bank deposits of foreign currencies is small compared with China's total foreign reserves. Nevertheless, the benefit of these funds should not be overlooked. In those provinces with large numbers of Chinese with relatives abroad, particularly Fujian and Guangdong, these funds can make a significant difference in modernization plans. With decentralized investment responsibility, these provinces can import a substantially greater amount of industrial equipment than if such capital were not available. Similarly, counties and villages are able to experience a meaningful improvement in their standard of living due to remittances from abroad. Moreover, this indirectly benefits the central and provin-

---

[47]Suryadinata, *China and the ASEAN States*, p. 75; *China Business Review*, September-October, 1980, p. 10; Sichuan Provincial Service, October 19, 1985, British Broadcasting System, *Survey of World Broadcasts: The Far East (SWB/FE)*, October 20, 1985, p. A17.

[48]*Ta Kung Pao* (Hong Kong), March 6, 1981, FBIS, *PRC*, March 10, 1981, p. U1. Nevertheless, most of these funds are probably deposited by mainland-owned businesses in Hong Kong and are not remitted to the PRC.

[49]State Statistical Bureau, People's Republic of China, *Zhongguo Tongji Nianjian, 1985* (Chinese Statistical Yearbook, 1985) (Beijing: State Statistical Publishing Co., 1985), p. 520; *China Daily*, September 29, 1984, p. 4; *SWB/FE*, February 15, 1984, p. A5.

cial governments, because these independent sources of local revenue ease their responsibility for maintenance of local programs.

In the cooperative sector, Beijing is encouraging the establishment of commercial enterprises established jointly by Chinese abroad and their relatives in China. A conference of provincial-level directors of Overseas Chinese Affairs offices held that "support should be given to those specialized households among the returned overseas Chinese and the dependents of overseas Chinese who are developing production with the help of their relatives abroad so that they can become well off first." Liao Hui maintained that China should "bring into full play the superiority of overseas Chinese counties . . . in running township enterprises assisted by . . . relatives abroad."[50] Beijing is thus encouraging wealthier overseas Chinese to contribute great sums of capital to develop local industry. For counties with large numbers of relatives of overseas Chinese, this has been one of the most successful aspects of Beijing's promotion of overseas Chinese contributions to the Chinese economy. Since 1979 close to 3,000 such cooperative enterprises have been established. Between 1979 and 1983, one-third of the foreign investment in Fujian was made by ethnic Chinese.[51] In 1984, in Nanhai County, Fujian, 80 percent of the cooperative enterprises were jointly run with ethnic Chinese abroad. One such cooperative is China's largest dairy farm and milk-product processing plant. Another is reported to be the largest chicken farm in Asia.[52]

The third level of overseas contribution to PRC modernization involves major investment in joint ventures for large-scale construction projects. In this area, the overseas Chinese play the same role as large Western corporations; both have the potential to make a significant difference in the pace of Chinese modernization. Nevertheless, Beijing hopes to capitalize on the crucial ethnic difference and, thus, encourages large firms owned by ethnic Chinese abroad to invest in the mainland economy. Many of the attractions that China offers to individual overseas Chinese apply to these corporate investors as well. Appeals to patriotism, restoration of Chinese credibility, and the welfare of the clan all promote a willingness to invest in China on the part of all Chinese abroad. For wealthy investors, however, Beijing has gone an extra step by giving them preferential treatment not granted to their Western coun-

---

[50]Xinhua, April 22, 1984, FBIS, *PRC*, April 23, 1984, pp. K7–8; *Zhongguo Xinwen She*, March 18, 1985, FBIS, *PRC*, March 20, 1985, pp. K14–15.

[51]Gu Mino, "Discussing the Problem of Absorbing Overseas Chinese Investment," *Fujian Luntan* (Fujian Forum), no. 6 (1983), JPRS, *China: Economic Affairs (CEA)*, May 2, 1984, p. 91.

[52]*China Daily*, January 10, 1986, p. 2; *PRC Quarterly*, July 1984, p. 214; JPRS, *CEA*, August 29, 1984, p. 112.

terparts. In this way, not only are overseas Chinese investors given a favorable investment climate, but their special treatment is a further reminder of their ethnicity and of their responsibility to their fellow Chinese on the mainland.

The most common forms of preferential treatment are tax exemptions and reductions. Normally, overseas Chinese receive three-year tax exemptions and a 50 percent reduction for the initial four years in joint ventures with state corporations. Fujian has gone even further, reportedly offering full tax exemption for the first five years and a 50 percent reduction for the next five years. It also provides a 50 percent reduction in land-use fees and permits employment priority to relatives of overseas Chinese.[53] In addition to such financial preferences, Beijing has provided other incentives, such as permitting overseas Chinese to open the first foreign law office in Beijing. The Shenzhen Special Economic Zone is offering the most ambitious program for overseas Chinese. It is planning a special area—an overseas Chinese town. Its five-year plan envisions accommodations for up to 50,000 overseas Chinese tourists and workers, with centers for the production of such goods as textiles, electronics, and precision machinery.[54]

Partially as a result of Beijing's special efforts, overseas Chinese have made large-scale investments in the mainland, often stealing the headlines from their Western counterparts. Although it is impossible to determine what percentage of overseas Chinese investment is by Hong Kong residents, the overall figures suggest that a valuable contribution is made by Chinese from throughout Southeast Asia. One of the biggest projects in China is a Fujian oil refinery. It is financed with $700 million from overseas Chinese investors. Indeed, much of China's foreign investment is made by overseas Chinese. In 1983, for example, overseas Chinese were responsible for 65 percent of joint ventures involving foreign capital. To the extent Shenzhen has been a success, it is primarily due to overseas Chinese investment. By June 1984, Shenzhen had signed 2,700 agreements valued at $1.8 billion. Ninety percent of these agreements were with overseas Chinese.[55]

China's renewed effort to mobilize foreign ethnic Chinese contributions to the Four Modernizations has not gone without domestic opposition. Similar to the problem affecting other reform policies, many cadres

---

[53]*Asian Wall Street Journal*, November 15 and 16, 1985, pp. 1, 6. *China Economic News*, November 5, 1984, p. 3; *China Economic News*, November 22, 1984, p. 7.

[54]*China Daily*, May 13, 1985, p. 3; *China Daily*, December 19, 1985, p. 2; *China Daily*, January 25, 1986, p. 1.

[55]*World Press Review*, February 1986; *China Market*, August 1983; *China Business Review*, November-December, 1984, p. 34. Also see *New York Times*, April 10, 1979, pp. 1, 9.

had been reluctant both to readdress past wrongs, particularly in regard to housing, and to grant special privileges to returned overseas Chinese and relatives of Chinese abroad. Hu Yaobang charged that cadres afflicted with lingering erroneous leftist thinking remained prejudiced and were guilty of carrying out "unequal political treatment" and excluding returned overseas Chinese from the party and from important positions for which they are qualified.[56] In 1984, at the Third National Congress for returned overseas Chinese, Ulanhu reported that "major resistance to the implementation of the policies for overseas Chinese affairs remains the pernicious remnant influence of the 'left.'" Many cadres feel the policy is "rightist deviation." Thus, the task of eliminating such "pernicious influence is very difficult."[57]

Nevertheless, despite such domestic opposition, Chinese leaders have gone a long way toward reversing past policy and attracting the support of ethnic Chinese abroad. The mere contrast of contemporary efforts with past policy is sufficient to restore much of the goodwill that China squandered over the previous ten years. The economic and tourist statistics reveal the growing role of the ethnic Chinese abroad in mainland economic development and suggest that Beijing has rekindled much of their patriotism and their interest in supporting the "motherland."

Conclusion

Two conclusions stand out in this discussion of China and the ethnic Chinese in Southeast Asia. First, the direct security relationship between China and the ethnic Chinese should be little cause for concern. Far from being a strategic asset for China, the Chinese in Southeast Asia have been a political liability. Host government concern for the loyalty of their ethnic Chinese communities has led to policies inimical to the interests of the local Chinese, precipitating Chinese involvement in domestic developments. Ultimately, such involvement has clearly been detrimental to friendly and stable bilateral relationships between China and the host government. It is no wonder that more often than not China has ignored discrimination against its citizens abroad in the interest of foreign policy objectives. Moreover, the deep suspicion on the part of regional leaders of PRC contacts with local Chinese communities has frequently blocked Beijing's efforts to compete with the Soviet Union for the friendship of host governments.

---

[56]Xinhua, July 7, 1981, FBIS, PRC, July 9, 1981, p. K2. Also see Wen Wei Po (Hong Kong), November 1, 1981, FBIS, PRC, November 5, 1981, p. 01.
[57]Xinhua, April 11, 1984, FBIS, PRC, April 16, 1984, p. K10. For a recent report, see Yang "Overseas Relations Are a Good Thing," pp. K13–16.

China's failure to take advantage of the ethnic divisions does not reflect a benevolent interest in accommodating the concerns of regional governments. There is little charity in Chinese foreign policy. Rather, China's inability to manipulate the ethnic Chinese to the disadvantage of the Southeast Asian states reflects its inherent weakness. Its distance from the region's least assimilated Chinese in Malaysia and Indonesia, its inability to project its power far beyond its borders, and the lack of appeal of the mainland's economy and political system to Southeast Asia's capitalist Chinese combine to leave Chinese leaders little choice but to make the best of the PRC's inescapable impotence. Despite their suspicions, regional leaders are well equipped to thwart any attempt by China to challenge their authority over their Chinese communities.

Should Chinese influence in Southeast Asia expand during the next twenty years, however, its policy may become less insipid. When capable, nations have shown little reluctance to aggravate their adversaries' ethnic divisions. Indeed, the PRC has had to contend with Soviet machinations among China's minorities living along the Sino-Soviet border. Similarly, as China's presence in Southeast Asia grows, it may very well develop the economic, political, and military resources required to undermine the domestic authority of Southeast Asian governments. In such circumstances, it will also be able to take advantage of, if not also aggravate, ethnic tensions to its political advantage. Thus, as in the past, for the foreseeable future, PRC relations with ethnic Chinese in Southeast Asia pose little direct political challenge to the host governments. The long-term future, however, is less certain.

Although past Chinese behavior has been ineffectual and despite the fact that most Chinese abroad view communism as inimical to their economic and political interests, host governments in Southeast Asia still have very valid security concerns regarding their Chinese communities. Regardless of the potential for international backing for domestic minorities, such as China's reputed support for rebellious activity among Southeast Asia's overseas Chinese communities, multiethnic states are particularly prone to domestic instability. Disaffection on the part of minorities, even in the absence of an historic "motherland," often leads to civil war and opportunities for meddling by adversaries, regardless of their national ethnicity. Thus, simple prudence demands that Southeast Asian governments take steps to minimize the disruptive potential of their Chinese communities.

Thus, even if China were far less powerful, far more distant, and ideologically allied with the Southeast Asian countries, the ethnic Chinese would still pose a security problem for the host governments. The issue is less one of the PRC and more an issue of ethnic minority assimilation, a policy issue faced by all multiethnic states.

That China is not the immediate source of the security threat posed by the ethnic Chinese in Southeast Asia does not mean that there are no grounds for conflict between the PRC and regional governments over the Chinese minority populations. States pursuing strictly defensive policies often elicit hostile responses from other states. Southeast Asian states, when their strategic relations with China are adversarial, can expect China to retaliate when they pursue policies detrimental to the interests of their Chinese communities. This clearly raises the risk to countries pursuing coercive policies designed to promote minority assimilation or domestic security.

Thus, the second major point is that despite the absence of any direct security threat posed by China's political relations with Chinese minorities in the region, Beijing's pursuit of the economic resources of Chinese abroad does heighten the valid domestic security concerns of the host countries. This is true not because Beijing is becoming an attractive competitor with Southeast Asian governments for the allegiance of overseas Chinese, but because participation by Chinese living abroad in the development of the mainland's economy reinforces their ethnic identity, thus undermining the assimilation policies of the host government. Indeed, Beijing contributes to this process because it offers special treatment to foreign investors of ethnic Chinese background and because in many areas it treats overseas Chinese tourists, regardless of nationality, as it does those citizens who reside in the PRC. Such policies contribute to the region's security concerns and undermine Beijing's efforts to establish cooperative relations with the ASEAN countries.

Over the long term the obstacles to assimilation of ethnic Chinese into the majority society are particularly worrisome, for should Chinese influence in the region grow while Southeast Asian Chinese remain unassimilated, the opportunities for PRC meddling will be substantially increased. Thus, the long-term prospect of Chinese growth accentuates the necessity for regional leaders to worry about ethnic Chinese participation in PRC modernization.

Ironically, China's Great Leap Forward and Cultural Revolution years best served the interests of Southeast Asian governments, when China minimized its foreign trade and vilified Chinese in capitalist countries as bourgeois enemies of the Chinese state. At that time, Beijing's policies were perfectly suited to reducing regional governments' fear of the destabilizing influence of their Chinese communities and to promoting assimilation. All that has changed, however, now that China has a "responsible" leadership that carries out "pragmatic" policies that are much better suited to the interests of Chinese both in the People's Republic and abroad.

The dilemma for host governments is clear. To cut their countries off from the potential rewards of doing business with China harms their domestic economies and merely cedes the benefit to their Southeast Asian economic competitors, as well as undermines their ability to compete with the PRC in the larger global market. On the other hand, to partake in trade with China may undermine the cohesiveness of the domestic societies, potentially creating opportunities for any of their regional adversaries, beside just the PRC, to meddle in domestic affairs for their political advantage.

The result has been a good deal of justified regional ambivalence toward expanding economic contacts with the PRC. This has been reflected in Indonesia's China policy, for example. In the past, Jakarta was reluctant to increase economic contacts with China, despite the missed opportunities of the "China market" and the benefits that accrued to Singapore, which profited from being the go-between. Eventually, the opportunities became too enticing for Indonesia to pass up, especially in the context of declining oil prices and a faltering economy. Jakarta, thus, recently opened trade relations with Beijing. Nevertheless, Indonesian ambivalence is clearly reflected in the effort to keep trade with China under strict government control, thus maintaining the prohibition on private trade relations with the PRC. Jakarta's reasoning is clear—it wants the benefit of trade with China while minimizing the ability of its Chinese community to come into contact with the mainland.

Malaysia has also been concerned with the implications of China's efforts to entice Southeast Asia's ethnic Chinese to contribute to the mainland's economic development. Like Indonesia, it watched for a long time as Singapore, as well as Thailand, reaped the benefits of trade with China. Although it demanded that China publicly renounce its support for the region's outlawed communist parties as a precondition to improved relations, in reality Kuala Lumpur was also as concerned as Jakarta with the domestic economic and political implications expanded trade with China held for PRC ties with Malaysia's ethnic Chinese. As was the case with Indonesia, the declining Malaysian economy and the apparent benefits accruing to Singapore persuaded the Malaysian prime minister to travel reluctantly to Beijing in 1985 to expand Sino-Malaysian trade ties.

The dilemma for the host countries is clear and, in the short term, apparently unresolvable. The path they have apparently chosen appears the wisest. Immediate economic dislocations resulting from temporal economic downturns are likely to exacerbate short-term ethnic tensions and domestic instability, thus undermining policies aimed at gradual assimilation of the ethnic Chinese. Such was the background to the ethnic tensions in Indonesia in 1959. On the other hand, short-term economic stability allows assimilationist policies to be effective, while promoting favorable long-term growth, which promotes further and more stable assimilation of the ethnic Chinese communities. Over the long term, the success of assimilation policies provides the best defense against domestic instability benefiting one's adversaries.[58]

Thus, insofar as enhancing current trade relations with China may actually expedite assimilation by offsetting short-term economic disloca-tions, as well as yield the other important economic benefits which promote national security, host governments are cautiously entering into new economic ties with the mainland. There is a risk insofar as Chinese ethnic identity may be enhanced because the domestic condi-tions promoting assimilation are apt to develop slowly. But rather than close their economies to the advantages of trade with China, this is a risk that Southeast Asian governments with Chinese communities have decided to take, perhaps only because of the two alternatives, it poses the least cost and offers the greatest advantage over the long term.

---

[58]For a discussion of the extent of ethnic Chinese assimilation in Southeast Asian coun-tries, see the collection of papers presented at the symposium on "Changing Identities of the Southeast Asian Chinese Since World War II," held at the Australian National Univer-sity, June 14–16, 1985.

PART FIVE

China's Role in Regional Problems in Southeast Asia

10. An Introduction to China's Role in Regional Problems

JUSUF WANANDI

The overall theme of this chapter is the nature of relations between the Southeast Asian countries and a China which has become a modern power with the dawning of the twenty-first century. The many aspects of the relationship between China and Southeast Asia today, which are discussed in depth in the other chapters of this volume, are affected—consciously or unconsciously—by perceptions of the future of that relationship.

The assumption of the present analysis is that China will be successful with its modernization program and that the change of generation and political leadership will be relatively smooth. Nonetheless, this chapter will speculate on the implications for the Southeast Asian region if China's modernization were to be unsuccessful.

An essential question underlying the theme of this chapter is the extent to which the Southeast Asian region will be within China's sphere of influence and what the implications of China's hegemony will be for the countries in the region. How far China can achieve its objectives will partly depend on the reactions and policies of the three other great powers in the region, namely, the United States, the USSR, and Japan.

A corollary question is whether cooperation between the ASEAN countries and the countries in Indochina—as well as within each of those subgroups—could lead to the creation of a stable and peaceful region, as aimed at in the idea of a zone of peace, freedom, and neutrality (ZOPFAN), so that together they could resist China's hegemony in Southeast Asia. Furthermore, it is of equal interest to examine whether individual countries in Southeast Asia would be able to structure a more "normal" relationship with China as they develop. In view of its geopolitical position in the Asia Pacific region, China should also see the development of such relationships as an important element which could influence its own international posture in the future.

Apart from the above, more general issues which may grow in relevance as the future unfolds, there are specific problems in the relationship between China and the Southeast Asian countries which remain unresolved. They include:

1. territorial disputes, in particular those involving the Spratly and Paracel islands in the South China Sea;
2. China's ambiguous policies and laws regarding Southeast Asian citizens of Chinese origin. The call for greater participation by them in the development of China has increased Southeast Asian suspicions about China's intentions;
3. competition in the economic field, in particular in the development of light manufacturing industries for international markets;
4. support by the Chinese Communist Party for communist parties in Southeast Asia, not only morally but also in the form of logistics and armaments;
5. differences in policies between China and ASEAN concerning resolution of the conflict in Kampuchea.

The Future of China-Southeast Asian Relations

An important problem that will be faced by the ASEAN countries in the future is their ability to deal with a China that has successfully modernized itself, including militarily. This problem will materialize at the beginning of the twenty-first century and then only if China succeeds with its modernization program.

The author makes two assumptions. First, that China will succeed with the modernization efforts that began in 1979, although the process will see its ups and downs. Second, that during this modernization and development period China will restrain itself and attempt to develop good relations with its neighbors, including those in Southeast Asia, thus maintaining the stable and peaceful environment it needs to catch up to the rest of the countries in the Asia-Pacific region.

The challenges facing Chinese leaders are clear. They recognize that the internal difficulties and constraints affecting the development of the huge country remain grave. This suggests the need for continuous adjustments to be made by the party leadership and the Chinese government in the country's modernization efforts. Therefore, it can be argued that this period provides a good opportunity for the countries in Southeast Asia to build a foundation for long-term relations with China.

First, the nations of Southeast Asia must sustain their national development efforts in order to better resist external pressures and intervention. This task has become more complex, for at the present stage of development, more comprehensive development efforts and greater participation by the people are necessary.

Second, it is necessary to develop a regional arrangement in Southeast Asia which could eliminate the opportunities for external forces to exert pressures on the region and could promote and strengthen regional cooperation in various fields so as to enhance regional resilience. Such a regional arrangement could consist of a strong ASEAN as its core, which would in turn develop closer cooperation with other countries in the region, namely, Indochina and Burma.

Third, it is necessary to structure an appropriate relationship with the major powers in the Asia-Pacific region, including China, to maintain a balance in their presence in Southeast Asia. It should be important for the development of such a structure to involve China in all regional and international activities as a way to encourage it to maintain openness in economic and diplomatic relations. One important regional activity to foster greater Pacific economic cooperation, as currently manifested in the Pacific Economic Cooperation Conference (PECC), has included China as an active participant since the Vancouver Conference (PECC V) in November 1986.

With regard to the relations of Southeast Asian countries with China, two observations can be made. The first observation is that China will always be seen as a possible threat to Southeast Asia. This is natural in view of size, location, and past experiences in which China considered Southeast Asia to be within its sphere of influence. However, this threat perception should be placed in its proper perspective to avoid the paranoia that tends to obstruct the development of normal relations with China.

In fact, throughout its history China has not been expansive in terms of occupying other territories or countries for an indefinite period, except for several border regions such as Inner Mongolia, Tibet, and Sinkiang. Toward other areas, including Vietnam, China has sent military expeditions which were withdrawn as soon as the respective country recognized China's superiority or hegemony in the region. Such was the case in 1979 against Vietnam, but it was unsuccessful because the Vietnamese were better prepared to deal with it. Instead, more casualties (up to 40,000 men) were incurred on the Chinese side. This episode supports the argument that the threat from China should be placed in proper perspective.

China's military capability during the coming ten to twenty years is likely to remain largely defensive in nature and thus should not pose an immediate threat to Southeast Asia. Although it is fashioning a blue-water navy, and could have some ability to project power, China's naval forces are far from adequate to compete with the Pacific Fleet of the USSR or the U.S. Seventh Fleet. China's air power is more limited in capacity and is designed for defense and interception rather than offense.

It should not be denied that the perception of a threat from China could also strongly motivate the countries in Southeast Asia to unite, develop their societies, and modernize their economies. Indeed, recent experience has shown that enhancing one's national resilience is an effective strategy for dealing with the kind of threat most frequently experienced in the region, namely, subversion and infiltration.

It appears that for the time being China has refrained from engaging in such activities via-à-vis the ASEAN countries, as suggested by the greatly reduced support and aid to local communist parties in Southeast Asia.

The second observation is that China's development and modernization lag behind those of the ASEAN countries. It will not be easy for China to accelerate development in view of the many problems created by the huge size of the country and the population, an underdeveloped economic infrastructure, highly bureaucratic organizations, and a totalitarian political system. It should also be noted that cheap labor and centralized economic management make China quite competitive in certain agricultural and manufacturing sectors. However, in view of the more dynamic and flexible nature of the ASEAN economies, one might expect a more complementary—rather than competitive—relationship to develop between China and ASEAN.

The issue, therefore, is whether indeed—as suggested by some observers—China will reassert itself as the Middle Kingdom if it succeeds in modernizing itself in twenty years time. If so, how would China's influence over Southeast Asia manifest itself?

China's attempt to exert influence on Southeast Asia will not follow the Russian model of occupation or physical expansion (such as in Siberia and Central Asia), but will be similar to the "tributary relationship" practiced in the past. This means that China will want to be recognized as having a role in the affairs of the region, and that it will influence their outcome in accordance with what it perceives as its national interest.

Some views suggest a rather extreme case of tributary relationship, namely, that China will be given a free hand—by both the United States and the Soviet Union—to exert its influence on Southeast Asia. It is hard to believe that this kind of situation will develop. First of all, Southeast Asia may be too important to be allowed to come under the influence of one major power. Furthermore, China has clearly signaled its intention to maintain an independent foreign policy posture and to adopt an equidistant policy vis-à-vis the superpowers. This means that from both the U.S. and Soviet point of view, China's interests will not always coincide with theirs. In addition, Japan's role and influence, which today are still limited to the economic field, cannot be ignored in the future. It is most likely, therefore, that all four major powers will be present in the region.

The challenge to the ASEAN countries is to preserve regional balance among the four major powers. Therefore, China should be seen as just one of the major countries with which ASEAN countries will need to structure their relations.

The so-desired structure for Southeast Asia has been formulated in the ZOPFAN idea. Implementation of this idea is still to come. It is temporarily on hold because of the outbreak of the Kampuchean conflict, since the idea will need the support and participation of the countries in Indochina.

Other views suggest that China will continue to be China and that in the long term it will attempt to regain its influence over Southeast Asia, especially since the many unresolved territorial disputes in which it is embroiled could be used as the rationale for intervention. The prescription here is to bring China into a regional or international structure which could counterbalance its urge to exert a dominating influence over Southeast Asia. China should be made to recognize that it now has a greater stake and greater responsibilities in the regional and international community, since such a posture is necessary for its modernization.

A modern and successfully developing China, which relies to some extent on regional and international relations while maintaining "Chinese-ness" or the "Middle Kingdom syndrome," is a better alternative for Southeast Asia than a radical, chaotic, and unsuccessfully developing China which feels that it has nothing to lose and therefore takes an aggressive stance.

To sum up, one could argue that the long-term relationship between the ASEAN countries and China can be seen as a relationship between a small country and a neighboring big country. Therefore, the small country will always be anxious and will feel compelled to counterbalance that presence, among other things by cooperating with other small countries or with other big countries. Apart from this geographical factor, the relationship of the ASEAN countries with China is essentially the same as that with other major powers with one exception, namely that China still has territorial disputes with Southeast Asian nations such as Vietnam, Malaysia, and the Philippines. These disputes could serve in the future as an excuse to meddle in the affairs of the Southeast Asian states.

ASEAN-China relations have become much more complex because the internal social and political problems in individual ASEAN countries magnify this geographical factor, in part because of the presence of citizens of Chinese origin in those countries.

Problems Between China and the Southeast Asian Countries

Territorial Disputes

Several countries in Southeast Asia and China have claims over the Spratly and Paracel islands in the South China Sea. These conflicting claims have not led to, but are potentially a source of, open conflict because of probable oil and gas deposits in the area. The Spratlys are claimed by China, Vietnam, Malaysia, and the Philippines, and these countries have stationed troops in the various islands: Vietnamese troops are on Amboyana Cay and two other islands; Malaysian troops are on Terembu Layang-Layang islands; and Philippine forces are on five other islands, which have been contracted to oil companies for exploration. China and Vietnam have claims over the Paracel Islands, which currently are partly occupied by Chinese forces.

These claims go back to various historical events and therefore are not easily resolved. The Chinese seem to support the idea of resolving this issue through the development of joint exploration and production schemes.

These claims have also given rise to greater mistrust on the part of Southeast Asians toward China's regional intentions, because they include claims that delineate most of the South China Sea as Chinese territory, and therefore could become in the future a major source of conflict.

The Problem of Overseas Chinese

In 1980 China issued a new law on citizenship which for the first time distinguished between Chinese citizens and citizens of Southeast Asian countries of Chinese origin. It stipulates that those who have become citizens of the country of residence automatically give up Chinese citizenship and no problems of dual nationality should emerge. Those that remain Chinese citizens, namely as overseas Chinese, are urged to observe the laws and regulations of the country of residence.

However, there is one article in the new law that remains ambiguous.[1] This article allows for non-Chinese nationals of Chinese origin to

---

[1]See text of the Nationality Law of the People's Republic of China (1980). Article 13 of the law stipulates that "aliens who were once of Chinese nationality may apply for restoration of Chinese nationality provided that they have legitimate reasons."

come back to China and automatically regain their nationality. It has been said that this article is meant to allow older people the opportunity to die in China. From the point of view of the Southeast Asian countries, such a clause greatly reduces the credibility of the loyalty of their citizens of Chinese origin. China could always use the above article to change local citizenship back to Chinese citizenship whenever deemed necessary by either side.

The distrust of China's intentions is magnified by the Chinese government's call for greater participation by non-Chinese nationals of Chinese origin, as well as Chinese nationals overseas, in the economic development of China. Ultimately, the question of loyalty not only rests with China's policies but also with those of the countries in Southeast Asia themselves. Thailand and the Philippines, for example, have successfully implemented policies for the integration of their citizens of Chinese origin. Nonetheless, the Chinese government needs to clarify this issue once and for all.

Party-to-Party Relations

It appears that the Communist Party of China no longer provides military support, that is, logistics and armaments, to local communist parties of Southeast Asia, except to the Communist Party of Burma.[2] The Chinese maintain that their support is largely moral and political and that the success of communist parties in overthrowing their governments should depend on their own capabilities.

The Chinese have also argued that the relationship between the Communist Party of China and other communist parties is of the same nature as that of Arab solidarity or solidarity among Islamic states.

The current Chinese policy of restraint in the use of party-to-party relations will continue as long as China is preoccupied with its own modernization. China needs a stable and peaceful environment. One hope is that by the time China has successfully modernized, it will have become used to attaching greater importance to state-to-state and government-to-government relations rather than to party-to-party relations.

Economic Competition Between China and the ASEAN Countries

There are worries on the part of the ASEAN countries that China will emerge as their main economic competitor in light manufacturing—

---

[2]See Bertil Lintner, "Peking's Support Continues but at a Much Reduced Rate," *Far Eastern Economic Review*, June 4, 1987, pp. 32–34.

especially textiles and garments—and in the production of a variety of minerals. The fact that China maintains considerable centralized planning increases their fears.

The prescriptions given to the ASEAN countries in this regard have been twofold: China should be introduced to and participate in the various multilateral fora, such as the IMF and the GATT, so that it will more or less adopt the international rules used by most countries; and the ASEAN countries should develop the kind of relationship with China which would open up opportunities for economic cooperation.

A certain degree of competition between China and the ASEAN countries cannot be avoided. This will manifest itself in their trade with the Western industrialized countries as well as in their relative attractiveness to investment and other financial flows.

There are many areas, however, in which the ASEAN countries and China can cooperate. Indeed, the past few years have been a steady increase in two-way trade between China and all ASEAN countries. China is also a Third World country, which could add to the leverage of the group in negotiating with the industrialized world for better concessions for the developing countries. This could also be beneficial to the ASEAN countries. More importantly, both sides contain the potential for development of greater economic complementarities in the future.[3]

The Kampuchean Conflict

The interest of ASEAN in resolving the Kampuchean conflict derives from two main concerns. First, because the continuing conflict frustrates efforts by ASEAN countries to establish a regional order for Southeast Asia which involves the participation of the countries in Indochina. Second, because of the implications of the conflict—which is essentially between Vietnam and China—for relations between China and the ASEAN countries, as well as on relations within ASEAN itself because of differing individual perceptions of the China factor.

At the meeting of ASEAN foreign ministers in Singapore in June 1987, Prime Minister Lee Kuan Yew was optimistic that a resolution to the conflict might be achieved in the next few years, citing the grave economic situation in Vietnam and greater readiness on the part of the USSR and China—as a result of gradual normalization of their relations[4]—to play a more active role in seeking such a resolution.

---

[3]See, e.g., Hadi Soesastro, "Indonesia-China Direct Trade: The First Two Years," *Indonesian Quarterly*, vol. 15, no. 3 (July 1987), pp. 323–28.

[4]See "Cambodia: Better Changes of Negotiated Settlement," *Straits Times* (Singapore), June 16, 1987, p. 1.

Drawing on this optimism, Mochtar Kusumaatmadja, the foreign minister of Indonesia, has reintroduced the possibility of sponsoring a "cocktail party" in Indonesia for the Khmer leaders of all factions, without preconditions, labels, or titles. This effort has been made partly in order to prevent a setback of the position of Coalition Government of Democratic Kampuchea (CGDK) at the 1987 United Nations General Assembly (UNGA), that could be caused by Prince Sihanouk's leave of absence for one year as president of CGDK. His reasons for doing so were the killings of Sihanoukists by the Khmer Rouge in Kampuchea.

While earlier statements by Sihanouk and Vietnam were positive about the proposal, the ASEAN foreign ministers in their meeting of August 16, 1987, differed with Vietnam over the latter's participation in the cocktail party. While Vietnam agreed to participate only in a follow-up meeting to discuss the international aspects of the conflict, the ASEAN foreign ministers have been adamant that Vietnam should attend the party immediately, and without the presence of other interested parties. They also insisted that the discussions should be based on the eight points contained in the proposal of CGDK which the Vietnamese had earlier rejected. In a meeting in Ho Chi Minh City, on July 26, 1987, the foreign ministers of Indonesia and Vietnam agreed on the idea of a cocktail party to be held in Indonesia without preconditions and titles to be followed up by a meeting of other interested parties. This agreement can still become the basis for further talks in the working group that has been set up by Indonesia and Vietnam specifically to discuss the Kampuchea issue.[5] Meanwhile Indonesia will continue to pursue its two-pronged policy of developing strong bilateral relations with Vietnam and actively promoting a political solution to the Kampuchean conflict.[6]

Vietnam still maintains that a Kampuchean government which is friendly to Vietnam is vital to its survival, since history has shown the vulnerability of Vietnam to attacks on its western flank. In Vietnam's view, China has tried to do so again by making use of the Khmer Rouge. The Vietnamese also recognize the hostility of the Khmer people toward Vietnam. It does not seem that the new leadership in Hanoi will soon modify this basic stance, since it is more than just a matter of ideology. However, the cost of maintaining its current policy, namely political and

---

[5]See, e.g., Murray Hiebert, "Mochtar Cocktail Party," *Far Eastern Economic Review,* August 13, 1987, p. 34.
[6]See also "Mochtar Threatens to Abandon Role of Interlocutor," *Jakarta Post,* August 29, 1987.

economic isolation which greatly affect development, may lead to more serious debates in Hanoi on the possibility of compromise.

China's initial position of all-out support for the Khmer Rouge (the former Pol Pot regime) was based on two considerations. First, to prevent Vietnamese domination over the countries in Indochina and to retard Vietnam's influence in Southeast Asia. Second, to punish Vietnam, which since 1975 has maintained closer relations with the Soviet Union than with China, not withstanding that China was Vietnam's main ally in its struggle against France and the United States.

China continues to exert military pressure on the Vietnamese border, following its unsuccessful military "lesson" in 1979, although at a much lower intensity now. In addition, China still provides logistic and military support to the Khmer Rouge through Thailand.

However, China recently has agreed to support the three-faction coalition government (CGDK) headed by Sihanouk. China has also realized that in the future Kampuchea need not be ruled by the Khmer Rouge forces alone, and has accepted a national, neutral, and nonaligned government—thus, not necessarily a socialist one—resulting from a compromise involving all four factions, including the Heng Samrin group. In this respect, China seems to have adopted ASEAN's policy.[7]

Initially, China was also very hostile toward Vietnam's close relations with the Soviet Union. This was seen as part of the USSR's encirclement policy. Improvement and gradual normalization of relations between China and the Soviet Union have affected China's position on this matter. She no longer even objects to the presence of Soviet military facilities in Vietnam. The Kampuchean issue has become an item in bilateral Sino-Soviet talks, but it remains unclear how far the Soviet Union will change its stance and therefore exert some pressure on Vietnam, despite the greater importance the USSR attaches to its relations with China. There were approaches made by ASEAN (Indonesia and Thailand) toward the USSR to play a more active role in the resolution of the conflict, and especially to pressure Hanoi to be more forthcoming. It remains to be seen whether the USSR would like to play the expected role. The USSR's willingness to do so will be very important in making the USSR more acceptable to ASEAN in the future.

It appears that China has become more willing to seek compromises in the Kampuchean issue for larger objectives, including normalization

---

[7]See "Deng Reaffirms Support Policy," *South China Morning Post* (Hong Kong), August 27, 1987.

of Sino-Soviet relations. Furthermore, both China and Vietnam currently are talking about normalization of their relations.

The question for ASEAN is how far it could involve China in a more positive way in resolving the conflict. ASEAN policies have been largely determined by Thailand's position as a frontline state whose security has been affected by the Vietnamese invasion of Kampuchea. The occupation of Kampuchea by Vietnam essentially removes a buffer that has long kept the balance and stability in continental Southeast Asia. Thailand therefore demanded a withdrawal of Vietnamese forces and the establishment of a government in Phnom Penh—through popular elections and not by Vietnam—which would recognize Thailand's security concerns.

As suggested elsewhere, the parties in the conflict need to undergo "structural changes" in their positions on the issue in order to reach a solution (compromise).[8] Thailand itself will be required to make some compromises. In this respect, changes in the Thai domestic political decision-making process or situation have yet to be observed.

The need to resolve the conflict remains as urgent as ever for the ASEAN countries because the longer the conflict lasts, the greater will be the strains within ASEAN. This relates to the degree in which China is perceived as a threat by individual ASEAN members. Indeed, a crucial issue here is China's continued military support of the Khmer Rouge, which in fact is a form of external intervention in the region. Another factor is the presence of the USSR at Cam Ranh and Danang which has increased superpower rivalry in the region.

In the past, there was some hope that the U.S. could play a more active role in resolving the conflict. It was suggested that the U.S. should exert pressure on China to change its hardline position on Vietnam, adopt a more flexible attitude toward Vietnam in order to provide an option to reliance on the Soviet Union, and give the necessary security guarantee to Thailand so that Thailand would not become too dependent on China. However, since this issue is of low priority to the United States, such an active role cannot be expected.

Indeed, the resolution of the conflict may well depend on the ability of the ASEAN countries to bring China and Vietnam to the negotiating table. ASEAN's ability (or inability) to do so may affect future relations between the countries in Southeast Asia themselves and their relations with China.

---

[8]See Sukhumbhand Paribatra, "Thailand: Vietnamese Neighbors Are Still Enemies," *Herald Tribune* (Singapore), December 9, 1986.

Conclusion

Relations between the Southeast Asian countries and China in the future will depend not just on the outcome of the Kampuchean conflict. The ASEAN countries, for their part, will have to continue to pursue the strengthening of national and regional resilience and the implementation of the ZOPFAN idea. ASEAN as an organization should become the core of a broader regional arrangement in Southeast Asia which manifests ZOPFAN. It is through such an arrangement that relations with the major powers can be structured in a way that their presence in Southeast Asia would be balanced and mutually beneficial. In other words, a greater confidence in their own capabilities would lead the Southeast Asian countries to have a healthier relationship with the major powers, including China.

Future relations between China and Southeast Asia will also depend on China's own development. A modern and successfully developing China would make for a more responsible member of the international community. To maintain the momentum of development China must recognize that it has a great stake in openness.

It is not improbable that China will revert to its old ambitions. But the Chinese may soon find this inconsistent with their new place in the modern world. Even if they fail to recognize this, the countries in Southeast Asia are likely to be much more prepared in the future to face this possible course of events.

11. China's Economic Relations with ASEAN Countries

CHIA SIOW-YUE

The focus of this chapter is on economic relations between China and the member states of the Association of Southeast Asian Nations (ASEAN)—Brunei, Indonesia, Malaysia, the Philippines, Singapore, and Thailand. They form the market-oriented economies of Southeast Asia. Although the focus is on economics, it is recognized that politics played a key role in the evolution of bilateral economic relationships. The first section provides an overview of the ASEAN and China economies. The second section analyzes the evolving economic relations between China and each of the ASEAN states, from early historical developments to the political constraints of the 1950s to the 1970s and the economic imperatives of the 1980s. Section three examines the bilateral trade and investment relations. The chapter concludes with a discussion of the issues and prospects facing bilateral economic relations.

Overview of ASEAN and China Economies

China is a vast country with a population of over one billion and gross domestic product (GDP) of US$266 billion in 1985, making it the most populated country and the eighth largest economy in the world. In contrast, the ASEAN countries, excepting Indonesia, are small and medium-sized in economic terms (see Table 1). The combined populations of the six ASEAN countries are only a little over one-quarter of China's, and the combined ASEAN GDP is almost four-fifths that of China.

From 1965 to 1985, China's economic performance was below the ASEAN average in 1965–80, but better than every ASEAN country in 1980–85. World Bank estimates show GDP growth in China averaging 6.4 percent a year during 1965–80 but accelerating sharply to 9.8 percent during 1980–85. For the ASEAN countries, the economic buoyancy of the 1960s and 1970s was followed by economic recession in 1980–85. The Philippines recorded the slowest and Singapore the highest growth performance in ASEAN, with a range of 5.9 percent to 10.2 percent in 1965–80 and —0.5 percent to 6.5 percent in 1980–85.

The levels of economic development and standard of living, as approximated by a comparison of per capita gross national product

189

Table 1

Indicators of ASEAN and China Economies

	Brunei	Indonesia	Malaysia	Philippines	Singapore	Thailand	China
Population mid-1985 (million)	0.2	162.2	15.6	54.7	2.6	51.7	1,040.3
Area (sq km)	6	1,919	330	300	1	514	9,561
GNP per capita (1985) (US$)	17,580	530	2,000	580	7,420	800	310
GDP 1985 (US$million)	3,940	86,470	31,270	32,590	17,470	38,240	265,530
GDP growth rate (%)							
1965–80	--	7.9	7.3	5.9	10.2	7.4	6.4
1980–85	--	3.5	5.5	-0.5	6.5	5.1	9.8
GDP sectoral distribution (%)							
Agriculture 1965	--	56	28	26	3	35	39
1985	--	24	21*	27	1	17	33
Industry 1965	--	13	25	28	24	23	38
1985	--	36	35*	32	37	30	47
Manufacturing 1965	--	8	9	20	15	14	30
1985	--	14	19*	25	24	20	37
Services 1965	--	31	47	46	73	42	23
1985	--	41	44*	41	62	53	20
Value added in agriculture (US$million, 1980 prices)							
1970	--	12,037	3,391	5,115	119	5,631	69,147
1985	--	22,011	6,274	9,104	132	10,132	139,482
Value added in manufacturing (US$million, 1980 prices)							
1970	--	2,723	1,681	4,383	1,174	2,526	46,484
1984	--	13,165	6,770	8,644	3,854	8,325	143,822

*1984.

SOURCE: World Bank, *World Development Report 1987* (Washington, D.C., 1987), pp. 202–7, 212–15. Figures for Brunei are from the World Bank, *The World Bank Atlas 1987* (Washington, D.C., 1987).

(GNP), are higher in ASEAN countries than in China. For the ASEAN states, 1985 per capita GNP ranged from a high of US$17,580 in Brunei to a low of US$530 in Indonesia. By World Bank classification, Brunei is a high-income oil exporter, Indonesia, the Philippines, and Thailand are middle-income economies, and Malaysia and Singapore are upper-middle income economies. Resource-poor Singapore capitalized on its strategic geographical location and human resources to achieve the highest per capita GNP among the nonoil Third World nation-states. The economic development of the other ASEAN countries has been heavily dependent on their wealth of natural resources. The World Bank has estimated China's 1985 per capita GNP at US$310 and classified it as a low-income economy. It should be noted, however, that the conventional GNP measure underestimates the large segment of nonmarket activities and services in a socialist economy.

The ASEAN economies are primarily capitalist and market-oriented. China operates a socialist economy based on central planning, although with the reforms of recent years, the economy is becoming more market-oriented. The ASEAN economies have also traditionally been outward-looking, with a high degree of dependence on foreign trade, technology, and investment, mainly with the advanced industrial market economies. In contrast, China's economy has been essentially inward-looking. This reflects in part the diverse resource base and large domestic market of its continental economy, but also in part its socialist economic structure. Trapped by its ideology, China became increasingly isolationist in the 1960s and a major part of the 1970s. China's total foreign trade in 1984 amounted to only US$51 billion, as compared with US$53 billion for Singapore alone; by 1985 however, China's foreign trade had grown to US$70 billion (see Table 2). Its trade dependency, as measured by the trade/GNP ratio, rose from 18 percent in 1984 to 26 percent in 1985, but remained below those of the ASEAN states, which ranged from over 30 percent for Indonesia and the Philippines to 281 percent for Singapore. Per capita trade in China was only US$67 in 1985 as compared with US$184–18,883 for the ASEAN states.

Evolving Bilateral Economic Relations

It is somewhat misleading to speak of ASEAN-China economic (or political) relations, as the six ASEAN states have no common foreign policy toward China. While there are some common political positions, such as on the security position in Indochina, there are also differences in policy approaches, representing varied national historical, political, and economic experiences, perceptions, options, and responses. The formulation of foreign economic policy toward China is essentially a

Table 2

Trade Dependence of ASEAN Countries and China

	Brunei	Indonesia	Malaysia	Philippines	Singapore	Thailand	China
Merchandise trade (US$million)							
Exports 1985	2,584	18,590	15,282	4,629	22,812	7,100	27,327
Imports 1985	749	12,069	12,302	5,459	26,285	9,231	42,526
Totals 1985	3,333	30,659	37,584	10,088	49,097	16,331	69,853
Trade dependence, 1985*							
Trade/GDP ratio (%)	85	35	120	31	281	43	26
Per capita trade (US$)	14,879	189	2,409	184	18,883	316	67
Annual growth rate (%)							
Exports 1965–80	—	9.7	4.4	4.7	4.8	8.5	5.5
1980–85	—	1.1	10.7	-2.1	5.9	8.4	8.8
Imports 1965–80	—	13.0	2.2	2.9	7.0	4.1	8.0
1980–85	—	4.9	6.4	-5.9	4.2	2.8	17.6

*Computed using population and GDP data in Table 1.

SOURCE: World Bank, *World Development Report 1987* (Washington, D.C., 1987), pp. 220–21. Trade data for Brunei from International Monetary Fund, *Direction of Trade Statistics* (Washington, D.C., 1986).

national rather than regional effort, and there is little coordination among ASEAN countries.[1]

Historical Development

China's economic relations with the countries of ASEAN and the rest of Southeast Asia have been long-standing. Early Chinese commercial involvement with Southeast Asia (or Nanyang) stemmed largely from the traditional tribute system. However, contacts were basically small in scale, unlike the later penetration of the region by European powers. Although trade between China and Southeast Asia has existed for centuries, it was only after the nineteenth century that such trade began to grow markedly, along with the steady inflow of Chinese migrants into the region. Ever since, the immigrant Chinese have played a significant role in the economic development of their host countries, at the same time becoming a key factor in the political and economic relations between these countries and China.

Economic relations between the People's Republic of China (PRC) and ASEAN countries can be distinguished by three phases. Phase 1 covers the post-1949 years up to the normalization of relations. Phase 2 covers the years of normalization of relations in 1974–76 up to 1984, with a period of cool but improving economic relations. Phase 3 starts from 1984, a period of sharp improvements in economic relations.

Foreign economic relations among nation-states based on similar political and economic systems are rarely conditioned by economic factors alone. This is even more true of the economic relationship between a capitalist market economy and a communist centrally planned economy, where economic activities of the latter are subject to a high degree of political and state intervention. In the evolving economic relations between ASEAN countries and China, it is greatly apparent that economies cannot be divorced from politics.

---

[1]For a detailed discussion of bilateral economic relations between China and the ASEAN countries, see the following papers in Chia Siow-Yue and Cheng Bifan, eds., *ASEAN—China Economic Relations: Trends and Patterns* (Singapore: Institute of World Economics and Politics [Beijing] and Institute of Southeast Asian Studies [Singapore], 1987): Dorodjatun Kuntjoro and Januar Elnathan, "Indonesia-China Trade Relations," pp. 126–49; Fu Zhengluo, "Sino-Malaysian Economic Relations," pp. 150–65; Jesus P. Estanislao, "Philippines-China Trade Relations," pp. 166–87; Gu Yuanyang, "China-Singapore Economic Relations: History and Prospects for Development," pp. 188–209; and Pang Rongqian, "Economic Relations Between China and Thailand," pp. 210–34.

Political Constraints

The formation of the PRC in 1949 changed the traditional pattern of China's relations with the ASEAN countries. The PRC pursued a prolonged period of inward-looking development and minimal international economic intercourse. There were a number of factors at play. First, there was the economic blockade imposed by the Western powers through the United Nations, following the outbreak of the Korean War in 1950. Second was the adoption of a different economic system based on central planning and the establishment of economic ties largely with the Soviet Union. In the 1960s, as relations with the Soviet Union deteriorated, China increasingly pursued a policy of self-reliance. This limited China's economic relations with other countries to a policy of mutually supplying each other's needs, rather than specialization and international exchange according to comparative advantage. The result was that only a limited variety of commodities entered foreign trade. Economic self-reliance and isolationism became even more pronounced during the Cultural Revolution.

Third, bilateral relations between China and the ASEAN states were influenced by the cold war era. China as a communist state was looked upon as a hostile country and a threat by noncommunist ASEAN countries. Close economic ties were formed by ASEAN countries with the developed market economies of Japan, the United States, Western Europe, and other countries with similar economic and political systems. When the cold war period ended, fears of China did not completely subside, partly because of the September 1965 experience in Indonesia, partly because of Chinese support for local communist insurgency groups in ASEAN countries, and partly because of the presence of a large ethnic Chinese population in the ASEAN region. These political misgivings hampered the development of economic relations with China that continued into the 1970s. Though China had some economic contacts with most of the ASEAN countries, these were merely limited to trade, which was largely restricted through such channels as the Chinese export commodities fair held in Guangzhou biannually in spring and autumn. For ethnic Chinese businessmen from some ASEAN countries, there were restrictions imposed on travel and on business transactions with China.

A change in American policy, the admission of China into the United Nations, and the 1972 Nixon visit to China heralded a new period of China–U.S. relations as well as a more favorable international environment for the development of ASEAN–China political relations. In 1974–76, visits to China were made by state leaders of Malaysia, the Philippines, Thailand, and Singapore. Diplomatic ties with China were established by Malaysia in May 1974, the Philippines in June 1975, and Thailand in July 1975, while Singapore had an exchange of commercial representative offices. It is apparent that the establishment of diplomatic ties coincided with the perception of a new configuration of power in the region following the collapse of South Vietnam and the withdrawal of the United States from Southeast Asia. In 1978 Vietnam invaded Kampuchea. The Vietnam-Kampuchea situation softened ASEAN attitudes toward China. With Vietnamese aggression on Kampuchea backed by the Soviet Union, China and the ASEAN countries had a common position. However, ASEAN countries still have doubts and fears about China's political intentions in Southeast Asia.

With the improved international political environment, efforts have been made by a number of ASEAN countries to develop political and economic relations with China through mutual visits by state leaders, and easing of restrictions on private sector contacts. China has also sought to allay ASEAN fears about its hegemonic role in Southeast Asia. It explained that the link between the Chinese Communist Party and the local communist parties in Southeast Asia is largely a moral one.

Economic Imperatives

Domestic economic reforms and the open-door policy that China pursued from the late 1970s have had profound effects on its external economic relations, including those with the ASEAN countries. Under the leadership of Deng Xiaoping, China has placed priority on economic development rather than communist ideology as a means to modernization. It has reformed the Soviet-style economic model to allow for greater economic flexibility and initiative. Centralized economic planning and administrative control have been modified in favor of greater reliance on the market mechanism and on the private sector, through the new responsibility system, use of incentives, and price reforms.[2]

China has also adopted an open-door policy to promote the inward transfer of resources to accelerate the economic modernization process. The open-door policy encourages foreign trade and investment, transfer of technology, travel, and financial and other commercial link-ups. By setting up special economic zones, and allowing access to fourteen

---

[2]For a discussion of the economic changes in China, see Cheng Bifan and Zhang Nansheng, "Institutional Factors in China-ASEAN Economic Relations", in Chia and Cheng, *ASEAN-China Economic Relations*, pp. 21–37.

coastal cities and inner parts of China, foreign capital and foreign technology are being attracted to China on an unprecedented scale. The opening up of the Chinese economy reinforced economic links with traditional trading partners and forged new ones with new trading partners.

China seems to find it strategically expedient to trade with nonsocialist economies, that is, the developed market economies (DMEs), the newly industrialized countries (NICs), and other less-developed countries (LDCs). On account of the economic and technological level so far developed and the existing economic structure in China, economic relations have been forged most strongly with the developed market economies. However, China continues to attach importance to the development of South-South cooperation. In addition, increased political and economic flexibility have made it possible for China to engage in nonideological development cooperation with its neighboring states, including increased indirect trade with Taiwan and South Korea.

Apart from political changes and economic reforms in China, economic factors in ASEAN countries also changed their perceptions toward China and heralded a new era of bilateral economic relations. After two decades of sustained growth, the ASEAN economies entered a period of economic slowdown in the 1980s. This has led to a review of the problem of overdependency on trade and investment with a few developed market economies as the engine of growth. Slow growth in the major OECD countries has contributed to the prolonged recession in international commodity markets and the rise in protectionism in major OECD markets, thus adversely affecting the exports of ASEAN primary commodities and manufactures. ASEAN countries are making serious efforts to diversify their economic relations so that export growth can be sustained and trade deficits rectified. These include the active promotion of South-South economic relations and the downplay of ideological factors to promote trade with socialist countries, including China. Economic imperatives have become more urgent because of the current severe economic recession in ASEAN.

An economically resurgent China in pursuit of an open-door policy is an important development for the world economy and more particularly for the regional economy. It is bound to alter the pattern of China-ASEAN economic relations as well as ASEAN's economic relations with third countries. China's economic transformation is viewed with mixed feelings in the ASEAN region. On the positive side, a pragmatic China in pursuit of economic development will inevitably contribute to political stability in the region, which in turn is essential for ASEAN's own economic growth. Also China's modernization program and rapidly expanding economy give some ASEAN countries hope for expanded trade and greater outlets for their investments. In consequence, the ASEAN countries have responded positively to Chinese overtures, although in varying degrees. Among the ASEAN states, the Philippines, Singapore, and Thailand have had some political and economic relations with China over the years. Even Indonesia and Malaysia, which have hitherto been very apprehensive of the potential threat posed by China, have also modified their positions. Indonesia was the last ASEAN country to reestablish direct trade with China, when a memorandum of understanding (MOU) was signed in July 1985.

However, ASEAN countries still have reservations regarding the emerging ASEAN-China relations and in general adopt a cautious approach. First, they fear that China may dominate the region politically and economically, and may use political considerations to interfere with economic relations. Some Chinese scholars have argued, however, that "it was true that historically, political reasons had led to severance of economic relations between China and some ASEAN countries, but this was not on China's initiative."[3] Second, China's development could have potentially disruptive effects on the ASEAN economies arising from intensified competition for export markets in third countries and for foreign investments. The interaction of complementarity and competitiveness will determine the extent to which the ASEAN economies will benefit from an economically resurgent China. Thirdly, the ASEAN countries remain concerned over the communist insurgency and the overseas Chinese problems in their countries.

Cheng and Zhang argue that, for its part, China finds that

> incongruous with the development of Sino-ASEAN economic relations are some restrictive measures imposed by the ASEAN countries, particularly on nongovernmental contacts between the peoples of China and the ASEAN countries. Restrictions include designated ports of call by ships from China, restricted channels for trade, rigid licensing of Chinese exports, and narrow confines for Chinese seamen after disembarking, which are contrary to China's policy of placing friendly countries on an equal footing. Though such measures have been relaxed to some extent in the last few years and enforced to varying degrees in the ASEAN countries, yet they are obstacles in the progress of Sino-ASEAN economic relations. Generally, Thailand, the Philippines, and Singapore have less restrictions.[4]

---

[3]Ibid., p. 33.
[4]Ibid.

Bilateral Relations

A review of bilateral economic relations between individual ASEAN countries and China shows the influence of historical, political, and economic factors. The focus of the economic relations is on trade. Until recently, most of the China trade with the ASEAN region had been with Malaysia and Singapore, as direct trade with the others was either banned or restricted by political factors.

Among the ASEAN countries, economic ties between Indonesia and China are the most politicized, with a close correlation between trade and political developments. Independent Indonesia established ties with China in 1953. Bilateral ties reached a peak in 1965 when China accounted for a record 11 percent of Indonesia's total trade, and provided a substantial amount of economic aid. However, the communist involvement in the Indonesian coup of September 1965 led to a severance of political and economic ties in 1967. Since then and up to July 1985, Indonesia-China trade had to be conducted via third countries, mainly Hong Kong and to a lesser extent Singapore. With indirect trade, Indonesia's imports from China fell from 14 percent of total imports in 1965 to about 2 percent in 1973. According to IMF trade statistics, Indonesia officially exported US$8 million in goods to China in 1984 and imported $224 million, largely through Hong Kong.[5] But the actual total trade for 1984 is estimated to be much larger.

Pressure from the Indonesian business sector[6] for greater flexibility in dealing with China grew. As early as 1977 the Indonesian Chamber of Industry and Commerce (KADIN) had tried to reopen direct trade. KADIN representatives visited the Chinese Commodities Fair in Guangzhou and Beijing in 1978. But there was no official Indonesian support. At the time, the Indonesian economy was enjoying an oil boom and there was no urgency in establishing direct trade with China. Moreover, memories of the September 1965 coup lingered, as did continuing concern over the problems of the overseas Chinese and China's support for the local communist movement.

However, economic circumstances changed after 1981. The recession and the need to develop alternatives to the faltering oil exports increased the pressure to develop nontraditional exports and exploit new markets. The Indonesian government eventually evolved a more

---

[5]For a discussion of the role of Hong Kong, see Hadi Soesastro, "Indonesia-China Trade Relations and the Role of Hong Kong," paper presented at Institute of Southeast Asian Studies workshop on ASEAN-China Economic Relations, Singapore, 1986.

[6]See Dorodjatun Kuntjoro and Januar Elnathan, in *ASEAN-China Economic Relations*, pp. 126–49.

"accommodating" policy toward trade with China. An MOU was signed on July 5, 1985, between KADIN and the China Council for the Promotion of International Trade (CCPIT). Presidential Instruction Inpres no. 9/1985 was issued on July 23, 1985, to endorse officially the resumption of direct trade between the two countries, eighteen years after the suspension of Indonesia-China diplomatic relations. There was no re-establishment of diplomatic ties. The MOU formulated certain regulatory guidelines for direct trade. A KADIN delegation visited China during August 1985, and a number of letters of intent were signed to purchase Indonesian primary commodities and manufactures worth over US$300 million. The resumption of direct trade appears to have boosted bilateral trade. In 1985, total bilateral trade according to the China source amounted to US$454 million, or a 60 percent growth over the preceding year; according to the Indonesian source, bilateral trade grew by 45 percent to US$337 million.

Direct trade relations between Malaysia and China have been maintained since the 1950s, but full diplomatic relations were established only in May 1974, with Malaysia the only ASEAN country to have done so at the time. Until the 1970s much of the Malaysia-China trade was actually conducted via the Hong Kong and Singapore entrepôts. More direct trade was initiated following the visit to China in 1971 by the Malaysian National Trading Corporation (Pernas). Growth of direct trade, however, has been restrained by Malaysian fears of Chinese hegemony and interference in Malaysia's domestic ethnic politics and internal security.

As with Indonesia, the severe economic recession of recent years led to the exploration of furthering Malaysia-China economic ties. In response to the rapid economic and political changes in China, the Malaysian government shifted its hitherto passive relations with China to a more positive stance. Since 1980 there has been a significant increase in the number of bilateral visits by senior officials and trade delegations. CCPIT and the Council of the Malaysian Sino-Malay Joint Chambers of Commerce also agreed to cooperate to promote direct trade between the two countries after a visit by the latter in October 1985. The largest and most important official Malaysian delegation to China was led by its prime minister in November 1985. A number of formal agreements were signed but did not affect 1985 bilateral trade, which reached US$412 million according to Malaysian trade statistics, and US$384 million according to China trade statistics. Both were below 1984 levels.

Prior to 1971 the Philippines had no direct trade with China, and Chinese goods were imported into the Philippines via Hong Kong and Singapore. In September 1971 the Philippines sent its first official trade delegation to the Chinese Commodities Fair in Guangzhou. In 1972 the Presidential Executive Order no. 384 formally legalized trade with socialist countries. Diplomatic relations with China were established in 1975. Since then, the Philippines has enjoyed cordial and stable relations with China. It has responded positively to China's open-door policy and freely allowed its nationals to trade and invest in China. To further strengthen trade, both countries signed a long-term trade agreement in July 1979 with two-way trade targeted at US$2 billion for the 1979–85 period. China agreed to export 8 million metric tons of crude oil and some refined petroleum products and to give priority to supplying the Philippines with additional amounts of crude oil and refined products if required. In return, the Philippines would export 1 million metric tons of raw sugar as well as copper concentrates and coconut oil. A further trade protocol in January 1986 provided for an exchange of products of about US$180 million each way. The growth of bilateral trade and investment has been hampered in recent years by the severe domestic economic problems in the Philippines.

Singapore has no diplomatic relations with China, and its government has openly declared that it will be the last ASEAN country to establish such relations. An exchange of trade representatives took place in July 1981. Nonetheless, among the ASEAN countries, Singapore has the most developed economic relations with China. This reflects both the city-state's pragmatic policy toward foreign economic relations and its importance as a trading nation. For a number of years the government has gradually relaxed controls on travel to China by its citizens. In more recent years, trade and investment relations have been actively promoted. The open-door policy of China and the 1985–86 economic recession in Singapore have provided additional incentives. Current economic links with China are multifaceted. They include a former senior cabinet minister acting as economic adviser to China's special economic zones, the active involvement of several government and semi-government companies in consultancy projects in China, as well as the active participation of the Singapore private sector in bilateral trade and investment projects. Singapore is an important conduit for the transfer of technology to China from the advanced countries. In addition, Singapore is playing an active role in providing various service technologies, including the development and management of major infrastructural projects such as ports, airports, and hotels. The scope for economic cooperation has been further expanded following the Singapore prime minister's visit to China in September 1985.

Singapore's systematic exploitation of economic opportunities in China is in contrast to the ambivalent stances adopted by some ASEAN countries. In part this is because the development of Singapore-China relations has not been hampered by domestic political sensitivities. Also, the institutional framework for bilateral economic relations has been better developed, including direct air links between Singapore and Beijing, minimal visa and bureaucratic controls on travel, and well-developed banking facilities. Cultural and linguistic affinities have also provided Singapore with an edge in international business competition.

Thailand banned direct trade with China in 1959 and Chinese goods reached the country only via Hong Kong and Singapore. When China was admitted into the United Nations in 1971 commercial contacts between the two countries resumed. Following the official visit to China of a Thai senior minister in December 1973, the Chinese government made a strategic move and offered 50,000 tons of light diesel oil at a "friendship price," which was below the world market price.[7] As a gesture of goodwill, in December 1974 the Thai government legalized direct trade again. Private sector trade grew and contributed to the resumption of diplomatic relations in July 1975, leading to further trade growth.

As with the Philippines, Thailand has enjoyed cordial and stable relations with China, and responded positively to China's open-door policy. Deng Xiaoping visited Thailand in 1978 and this led to the signing of a bilateral trade agreement establishing a joint committee for trade and a protocol of import commodities. The yearly protocol became the format of bilateral trade. Although such protocols are rigid, they do contribute to orderly trade between the two countries.

Bilateral Trade and Investment

Although bilateral economic relations are generally multifaceted, trade and investment are the most important avenues for such relations. In addition, the trade relation is the most readily quantifiable. The ways by which the ASEAN and China economies interact are manifested in their respective trade patterns and in their cross-investments.

ASEAN's Trade Pattern

Although Singapore is the smallest economic entity in ASEAN, it is also its largest trading nation. In 1985, Singapore alone accounted for 36.5 percent of ASEAN's total trade with the rest of the world, followed by Malaysia (20.6 percent), Indonesia (20.6 percent), Thailand (12.3 percent), the Philippines (7.4 percent), and Brunei (2.5 percent).

---

[7]See Pang Rongqian, in *ASEAN-China Economic Relations*, pp. 210–34.

ASEAN is heavily dependent on the developed market economies for capital, technology, imports of machinery and equipment and other manufactures, as well as for export markets for its primary products and growing range of labor-intensive manufactures. In 1985, 60.5 percent of ASEAN imports and 57.5 percent of its exports were with the DMEs, led by Japan and followed by the United States and the EEC. The dependence on exports to DME markets is highest for Indonesia (80 percent) and lowest for Singapore (47 percent). On the import side, the dependence on DME sourcing is highest for Indonesia (77 percent) and lowest for Brunei and Singapore (less than 50 percent). In the same year, 36.5 percent of ASEAN's exports and 39 percent of its imports were with the LDCs. However, much of this trade is intra-ASEAN, with Singapore accounting for the bulk, because of its role as regional entrepôt. Trade with Eastern Europe, including the Soviet Union, remained limited, accounting for only 1.1 percent of ASEAN's exports and 0.3 percent of its imports in 1985; this reflects a combination of weak political ties, differences in economic systems and trading practices, as well as sheer geographical distance.

The export structure of ASEAN countries, excepting Singapore, is still dominated by resource-based primary products (see Table 3). Mineral fuels form an overwhelming bulk of the exports of Brunei and Indonesia. The exports of Thailand are dominated by food and industrial raw materials, and that of Malaysia by mineral fuels and industrial raw materials. In the Philippines, primary products, mainly food and industrial raw materials, accounted for half the exports. For Singapore, exports of primary commodities reflect more its entrepôt role rather than its domestic production structure. As the most industrialized of the ASEAN countries, Singapore's non-entrepôt exports are dominated by manufactures; machinery and transport equipment accounted for 26 percent of its total exports, as compared to 6 percent for China and Thailand and less than 5 percent for Indonesia and the Philippines.

ASEAN imports show the growing importance of mineral fuels and machinery and transport equipment, and the declining importance of food and other manufacturers (Table 4). The hefty increase in petroleum prices in the 1970s meant sharply higher petroleum import bills for the Philippines, Singapore, and Thailand until recent years. Singapore imports crude petroleum for its refineries, and reexports most of it after processing. The sharp growth in imports of machinery and transport equipment reflects the high levels of investment activity in the ASEAN states. The slower growth of food imports reflects increased domestic self-sufficiency in food production as well as the lower income elasticity of demand for food products. The slower growth of "other manufactures" reflects the impact of import-substituting industrialization in

Table 3

Commodity Structure of ASEAN and China Exports, 1965 and 1985
(percentage distribution of country exports)

Country	Fuels, Minerals, Metals		Other Primary Commodities		Machinery and Transport Equipment		Other Manufactures		Textiles and Clothing	
	1965	1985	1965	1985	1965	1985	1965	1985	1965	1985
China	--	25	--	21	--	6	--	48	--	24
Indonesia	43	75	53	14	3	1	1	10	--	2
Malaysia	35	34	59	39	2	19	4	8	--	3
Philippines	11	13	84	36	--	5	6	46	1	7
Singapore	21	29	44	12	10	32	24	26	6	4
Thailand	11	5	84	60	--	7	4	28	--	13

NOTE: Categorization according to SITC Rev. 1:

Fuels, minerals, and metals = SITC 3, 27, 28, 68

Other primary commodities = SITC 0, 1, 2, 4 less 27, 28

Machinery and transport equipment = SITC 7

Other manufactures = SITC 5, 6, 8, 9 less 68

Textiles and clothing = SITC 65, 84, and are a subdivision of other manufactures.

SOURCE: World Bank, *World Development Report 1987* (Washington, D.C., 1987), pp. 222–23.

Table 4

Commodity Structure of ASEAN and China Imports, 1965 and 1985

(percentage distribution of country imports)

Country	Food		Fuels		Other Primary Commodities		Machinery and Transport Equipment		Other Manufactures	
	1965	1985	1965	1985	1965	1985	1965	1985	1965	1985
China	—	10	—	—	—	13	—	27	—	50
Indonesia	6	6	3	20	2	7	39	36	50	31
Malaysia	25	11	12	10	10	5	22	46	32	28
Philippines	20	8	10	27	7	5	33	21	30	39
Singapore	23	9	13	29	19	5	14	31	30	26
Thailand	6	5	9	23	6	8	31	29	49	34

NOTE: Categorization according to SITC Rev. 1:
   Fuels, minerals, and metals = SITC 3, 27, 28, 68
   Other primary commodities = SITC 0, 1, 2, 4 less 27, 28
   Machinery and transport equipment = SITC 7
   Other manufactures = SITC 5, 6, 8, 9 less 68.

SOURCE: World Bank, *World Development Report 1987* (Washington, D.C., 1987), pp. 224–28.

some ASEAN countries. Among the ASEAN countries, only Singapore's import structure shows a dominance of primary products, reflecting its resource poverty and its entrepôt role.

China's Trade Pattern

Like that of the ASEAN countries, China's global trade is largely with the developed market economies and developing countries, and there is only limited trade with the centrally planned socialist economies of Eastern Europe, including the Soviet Union. On the export side, its dependence on DME markets grew from 36.6 percent in 1970 to 44.7 percent in 1980, then declined but remained at over 40 percent in the first half of the 1980s. Traditionally the EEC has been its largest DME market, but in recent years it has been superseded by Japan, which accounted for half of China's exports to the DMEs. China is more dependent on DMEs as sources of supply, accounting for over two-thirds of its total imports. Japan is the leading supplier, accounting for a high of 35.7 percent of imports from all sources in 1985.

The developing world features more prominently in China's exports than in its imports, accounting in 1985 for 50.8 percent of its total exports and 24.7 percent of its total imports. Most of the trade is with Asian developing countries. For trade with Eastern Europe (including the Soviet Union), exports and imports amounted to 5.5 percent of its total trade in 1980–85.

The commodity composition of the exports and imports of China is shown in Tables 3 and 4 (as for ASEAN). China's 1985 exports consisted of 46 percent primary products, and 54 percent manufactures; its primary exports were mainly fuels, minerals and metals, and food; its manufactured exports were dominated by textiles and clothing (24 percent), with only 6 percent in machinery and transport equipment. Of China's imports in 1985, 77 percent were manufactures, and 23 percent were food and industrial raw materials. China hardly imported any mineral fuels.

ASEAN-China Bilateral Trade

Before the normalization of diplomatic relations between China and most of the ASEAN states in the mid-1970s, bilateral trade, except for Singapore, was executed largely via Hong Kong and Singapore. Because of different political systems, direct trade with China was carefully controlled by the government in most ASEAN countries. Also, since China has a different economic system, much of the bilateral trade is handled by state and quasi-state trading corporations. The ASEAN-China bilateral trade, culled from ASEAN trade data, is shown in Table 5. In abso-

Table 5

ASEAN Countries' Foreign Trade with China, Percent Distribution, 1970–85

(US$million)

	1970	1980	1981	1982	1983	1984	1985
Total Trade							
ASEAN	176.0	2,421.0	2,383.0	2,636.0	2,186.0	3,073.0	4,219.0
Percent distribution	100.0	100.0	100.0	100.0	100.0	100.0	100.0
Brunei	—	0.5	0.5	0.5	0.6	0.4	0.1
Indonesia	18.8	8.1	11.0	9.3	10.6	7.5	8.0
Malaysia	55.1	19.4	15.2	14.7	19.5	14.6	9.8
Philippines	—	11.0	12.1	12.4	4.7	9.4	8.8
Singapore	26.1	38.7	39.9	42.5	47.6	51.7	61.6
Thailand	—	22.3	21.3	20.5	17.0	16.3	11.7
Exports							
ASEAN	45.0	693.0	539.0	776.0	526.0	659.0	989.0
Percent distribution	100.0	100.0	100.0	100.0	100.0	100.0	100.0
Brunei	—	—	—	—	—	—	—
Indonesia	—	—	1.5	1.8	5.1	1.2	14.5
Malaysia	48.9	31.3	16.3	14.2	29.8	25.0	16.3
Philippines	—	6.5	14.5	13.5	4.2	9.1	8.2
Singapore	51.1	44.3	33.2	30.9	40.5	36.9	33.7
Thailand	—	17.9	34.5	39.6	20.3	27.8	27.4
Imports							
ASEAN	131.0	1,728.0	1,844.0	1,860.0	1,660.0	2,414.0	3,230.0
Percent distribution	100.0	100.0	100.0	100.0	100.0	100.0	100.0
Brunei	—	0.6	0.7	0.8	0.8	0.5	0.1
Indonesia	25.2	11.4	13.8	12.4	12.3	9.3	6.0
Malaysia	57.3	14.6	14.9	14.9	16.3	11.8	7.8
Philippines	—	12.8	11.4	12.0	4.8	9.4	9.0
Singapore	17.6	36.4	41.9	47.4	49.8	55.8	70.2
Thailand	—	24.1	17.4	12.6	16.0	13.2	6.9

Source: Derived from International Monetary Fund, *Direction of Trade Statistics Yearbook* (Washington, D.C.), various issues.

lute levels, total two-way trade with China rose rapidly from only US$0.2 billion in 1970 to US$4.2 billion in 1985, a twenty-four-fold increase, faster than either the growth of ASEAN's global trade or of China's global trade. Exports to China grew from $45 million to $989 million, or 22 times, while imports from China grew from $131 million to $3.2 billion, or 25 times.

Looking at bilateral trade from the ASEAN perspective, China remains a small trading partner of ASEAN countries, even though the share of China in ASEAN's total direct trade increased from 1.3 percent in 1970 to 3.1 percent in 1985. ASEAN is more dependent on China as a source of imports than as a market for exports, with the import share rising from 1.8 percent to 5.1 percent and the export share rising from 0.7 percent to 1.4 percent in the same period. However, the shares would be higher if the indirect trade via Hong Kong is fully taken into consideration. Also China can play a potentially larger role in helping ASEAN countries diversify the highly concentrated market structure of their foreign trade and reduce the heavy dependence on trade with the developed market economies.

Among the ASEAN countries, Singapore is China's largest trading partner, followed by Thailand, Malaysia, the Philippines, Indonesia, and Brunei. In fact, Singapore accounts for the bulk of the ASEAN-China trade. Singapore's share of the two-way trade rose from 26.1 percent in 1970 to 61.6 percent in 1985; while Singapore's export share declined from 51.1 percent in 1970 to 33.7 percent, its import share rose sharply from 17.6 percent to 70.2 percent. In value terms, Singapore's trade with China grew very rapidly in recent years, from US$0.4 billion in 1978 to US$2.6 billion by 1985. In 1985 alone, the bilateral trade grew by 64 percent over the preceding year. Singapore became China's fifth largest trade partner, and China ranked sixth in Singapore's foreign trade.

Now looking at the bilateral trade from the China side, the share of ASEAN in China's total trade is larger but shows wide fluctuations over time, ranging from 7.4 percent in 1970, falling to 4.2 percent in 1983, and recovering to 5.6 percent in 1985. Even excluding the indirect trade via Hong Kong, the direct trade alone is quite important for China, especially since the balance of this trade is invariably in China's favor. The ASEAN share of China's exports declined from 12.8 percent in 1970 to 5.2 percent in 1983, and recovered to 10.3 percent in 1985. The ASEAN share of China's total imports rose from 2.6 percent in 1970 to 4.7 percent in 1982, but declined to 2.7 percent in 1985. Thus, ASEAN is more important as a market than as a source of supply to China. The ASEAN market has always been a significant outlet for Chinese merchandise, from traditional foodstuffs to various kinds of low-priced textiles and garments, and household goods and tools. ASEAN, after Hong Kong, has been an important source of foreign exchange for China.

ASEAN-China trade shows a chronic deficit for ASEAN as a whole and for every ASEAN country, with the exception of Thailand in 1982 and 1985. The deficit has widened rapidly in recent years in spite of some attempts by China to secure balanced trade. By and large, the trade imbalance is caused by the strong demand for a wide variety of Chinese goods while China has a low demand for the limited range of commodities exported by ASEAN. The predominant imports of China from ASEAN are primary products, largely natural rubber, palm oil, copper concentrates, timber, and rice. In recent years, China has been under mounting pressure from individual ASEAN countries to balance bilateral trade. The bilateral deficit is largest for Singapore; however, Singapore to some extent balances its deficit in merchandise trade with its surplus from service exports to China.

Composition of ASEAN-China Trade

Although the volume of trade has increased, the range of ASEAN exports to China has not changed much. Traditional crude materials form the bulk of exports to China. Manufactured exports remain small, albeit growing.

Available data for 1982 shows that primary products still dominated and constituted 76.2 percent of ASEAN's total exports to China, with food alone accounting for 44.3 percent and crude materials 27.2 percent. Manufactured exports accounted for only 20.5 percent of ASEAN total exports to China, mainly chemicals and basic manufactures. As China's industrialization program gets under way, demand for ASEAN industrial raw materials should grow rapidly.

The main ASEAN suppliers of primary products to China are Thailand, Malaysia, and the Philippines; for them, primary products constituted almost their entire exports to China. For Thailand, they were mainly food products such as sugar and rice, as well as natural rubber and tobacco. For Malaysia, the bulk was mainly natural rubber and processed wood, and for the Philippines, mainly sugar, metals, and fixed vegetable oils. In addition, Indonesia's exports to China are also almost entirely of primary products, largely of coffee. Only in the case of Singapore did primary products constitute a minority share (30.0 percent) of exports to China, with rubber by far the most important commodity. In fact, Singapore accounted for most of ASEAN's exports of manufactures to China, made up largely of chemicals, machinery and equipment, veneer and plywood, nonmetallic mineral products, and iron tubes and pipes.

The composition of ASEAN imports from China has seen some significant shifts. Traditionally, food was the dominant import, not only rice and other staples, but also a wide variety of canned food and typically Chinese foodstuffs for the ethnic Chinese population. The share of food imports declined to less than 20 percent by 1982. At the same time, following the international oil crises, ASEAN increased its petroleum imports from China, so that its share in total imports rose to 25 percent by 1982 to form the largest single import item. Singapore, the Philippines, and Thailand import largely petroleum and food from China, Malaysia and Indonesia mainly crude materials and food, and Brunei mainly food. Petroleum supplies at friendship prices to the Philippines and Thailand were critical in easing the energy shortage in those two countries. At its peak, petroleum accounted for 50 percent of Thai imports from China. Thai dependence on Chinese petroleum declined following domestic production of natural gas and a return to a more balanced supply-demand relationship in the international petroleum market. For Singapore, imports of Chinese crude helped offset the slack in petroleum refining capacity caused by the falloff in Middle East crude supplies. During 1983–85 there was a dramatic rise in Singapore's imports of crude oil from China. In 1984, 3.8 million tons of crude oil was imported from China, a twenty-fold increase over the 1983 import volume. By 1985 Singapore was refining 80,000 to 90,000 barrels of crude oil from China daily, mainly for reexport to China. Underscoring the importance of the oil trade, the China National Chemicals Import and Export Corporation set up office in Singapore and has increased its direct purchase of petrochemicals from Singapore.

Manufactures constituted a little less than half of ASEAN imports from China, mostly chemicals, machinery, textiles, iron and steel, and metal manufactures. About half the manufactures were imported by Singapore.

ASEAN-China Investment Ventures

Since the 1960s, the ASEAN countries have been actively promoting the inflow of foreign investments to accelerate the pace of economic development. All the ASEAN countries have very active foreign investment promotion programs. The major sources of foreign investments are the industrial market economies of Japan, the United States, and Western Europe. However, sizable investments are originated from developing countries, particularly from the Asian NICs. Traditionally, foreign investments have moved into resource development. Since the 1960s sizable investments have moved into manufacturing activities to assist in the industrialization programs. Except for Singapore, foreign investments in the services sectors of ASEAN are still somewhat limited. There are also sizable outward investments by ASEAN countries, much of it occurring within the Asian region, with cross-investments between ASEAN countries. Thus, Singapore investments are fairly large in Malaysia and Indonesia, while Malaysia is also a significant investor in Singapore. In recent years, outward investments have also gone to China in response to the open-door policy.

For China, the promotion of inward foreign investment is a much more recent phenomenon. Opened at the first level are the special economic zones (SEZs). Foreign investors can now benefit from a much-improved infrastructure and industrial facilities, preferential taxation treatment, eased restrictions on entry of foreign personnel, and better access to foreign exchange and working capital. Export-oriented industries are foremost to be developed and complemented by import-substituting ones. Opened at the second level are fourteen coastal cities, where infrastructural facilities and preferential treatment have likewise been accorded foreign investors.

China's attraction for foreign investors lies in its vast home market and labor reservoir and its potential for growth. There are now Chinese-foreign joint ventures, as well as Chinese-foreign cooperative enterprises and wholly owned foreign enterprises in various economic productive lines. The Ministry of Foreign Economic Relations and Trade (MOFERT) statistics show that there was a total of US$16,200 million of agreed foreign investment that had been made in China in the 1979–85 period. Foreign banks have also established business operations in China. By December 1985 there were 155 branch offices of foreign banks stationed in China. China has also invested abroad since 1980. By the end of 1984, US$150 million was invested in more than 100 noncommercial cooperative undertakings in more than 30 countries. These ranged from the exploitation of natural resources, manufacturing, construction, to shipping, finance, insurance and consultancy services, as well as restaurants.[8]

Chinese data also show that ASEAN investments in China reached over US$250 million up to September 1985.[9] Most are concentrated in infrastructure and hotel construction, and in medium-technology manufacturing. ASEAN investors lack the financial and technological capability to compete with Japan and Western countries in large-scale projects. As China's investment climate improves and ASEAN businessmen develop a greater capacity for outward investments, the

---

[8]Cheng and Zhang, in *ASEAN-China Economic Relations*, p. 27.
[9]Ibid.

ASEAN countries may be expected to increase the level of their investments in China.

Among the ASEAN countries, Singapore has the largest number of investment projects in China, undertaken by both the private and public sectors in Singapore. The Singapore investments are spread thinly over a large number of projects, ranging from oil exploration to hotel management. Geographically, they are spread out over more than a dozen provinces. China has encouraged Singaporeans to negotiate investment projects directly with the provincial governments. The two countries also signed an investment protection agreement in November 1985. Businessmen from Thailand have also been quite assertive in investing in China. It is estimated that there are about twenty-five investment projects with Thai involvement. In contrast to investments from Singapore which are more diverse and technologically more sophisticated, Thai investments are in consumer durables, light machinery products, and construction.

China's investments in the ASEAN countries are still on a limited scale, and very minor when compared to the extent of foreign investments in the region. So far the investments have been mainly in Singapore and Thailand, while investments in Malaysia and Philippines are in the pipeline. China is not permitted to invest in Indonesia.

Issues and Prospects

There are a number of issues in the new phase of ASEAN-China economic relations which slow the development of bilateral economic relations. Some are long-standing and political, while others are newer economic issues.

There are two long-standing political issues. First, is the continuing support by the Chinese Communist Party of local communist parties in the ASEAN countries. The situation has reached an impasse. On the one hand, China sees such party-to-party support as distinct from government-to-government relations, and argues that such support is more token or moral than real. China cannot totally ignore these parties, for fear of creating a potential vacuum for the Soviet Union. On the other hand, the ASEAN countries, particularly Malaysia and Indonesia, see the continuing support by the Chinese Communist Party as an indication that China has not completely abandoned potential subversive intervention in the region. Second, in some ASEAN countries, notably Malaysia and Indonesia, the significant presence and conspicuous role of the ethnic Chinese has been a domestic political issue with ramifications for bilateral relations with China. It is feared that the ethnic Chinese community may undermine national security as well as benefit unduly (vis-à-vis the indigenous groups) from any extensive economic relations, because of the cultural and linguistic advantage. For these ASEAN countries, therefore, the challenge for their governments is how to forge economic ties while keeping in perspective these political issues.

On the economic front, the euphoria of ASEAN political leaders and businessmen, following the implementation of economic reforms and the open-door policy in China, has given way to a more realistic assessment of the challenge in developing economic relations with a country with a different political and economic system. China has to grapple with the political and economic problems arising from a system of partial economic liberalization. The ASEAN countries are concerned with the ability of China to maintain its present course of economic liberalization and open-door policy, the need for ASEAN countries to develop a more diversified export capacity and economic complementarity with China, and mutual solutions to problems of trade imbalance, inefficient trade practices, and the regulatory and bureaucratic controls on foreign investors in China.

ASEAN's trade with China is more subject to political influences than is its trade with other similar market-oriented economies. Any abrupt change in China's domestic political and economic scenario can affect the amount of foreign exchange allocated for foreign trade, or the reintroduction of state controls to regulate the volume of trade. Will there be a halt or reversal of China's present economic policies? In addition, will China be tempted to use foreign trade and investment as a political weapon in the future? There are no certain answers. Hence, the bilateral relations of ASEAN countries with China are in a state of flux, rather than in one of stable continuity.

China's trade with ASEAN countries has grown rapidly in recent years, but not as rapidly as trade between China and the developed market economies. The further growth of bilateral trade is somewhat restricted by the underdeveloped institutional framework supporting trade as well as by the basic lack of complementarity of the ASEAN (excepting Singapore) and Chinese economies.

The institutional support for ASEAN-China trade has to be strengthened. This would involve greater official support for the development of two-way trade, and the removal of physical, bureaucratic, and financial restrictions inhibiting the freer flow of goods and people. Trade practices (such as countertrade) and trade protocols that emphasize balanced trade are also inhibiting factors, but given the current foreign exchange problem faced by China and ASEAN countries, these practices cannot easily be replaced by more efficient trade practices.

To accelerate the pace of development of bilateral trade in goods and services between ASEAN countries and China, greater areas of economic complementarity have to be identified. Traditional complementarity arises from the differences in resource endowment between tropical and subtropical countries, giving rise to an exchange of agricultural products. But competitive elements also exist in such resource-based trade. Both China and ASEAN are major producers of rice. In addition, it is possible to grow a number of tropical crops such as rubber and palm oil in Southern China, particularly on Hainan Island. China and ASEAN also share a number of common nonrenewable energy and mineral resources, with possible competition in export markets.

Among countries at different levels of development, complementarity exists in the vertical division of labor, while among countries at advanced levels of development, complementarity exists in the horizontal division of labor. Among countries at low levels of development, there is limited complementarity. Industrialization is based on specialization not in technologies but in resource-based and labor-intensive goods. Being at similar levels of development, China and the ASEAN countries share similar trade structures, importing technology, machinery and equipment, as well as intermediate goods from the developed market economies, and exporting resource-based goods and labor-intensive goods to the markets of the advanced countries. There is limited absorptive capacity in China for ASEAN products and vice versa.

ASEAN countries are faced with the challenge to diversify the composition of their exports to China, so that the export momentum can be sustained and the bilateral trade deficits contained. They also face a potential competitive threat from China in third country markets. In particular, China is already a large producer and exporter of labor-intensive manufactures such as textiles and garments. To earn the necessary foreign exchange to support its import requirements, as well as to provide employment for its huge labor force, China will have to accelerate its exports of labor-intensive manufactures in the years to come. China has a competitive edge from an abundant labor supply and low labor costs. But ASEAN countries have the advantage of greater economic and managerial flexibility and better infrastructural support. So it is unlikely that China will have a comparative advantage over the whole spectrum of labor-intensive manufactures. The task is for ASEAN countries to find their own niches. In the final analysis, competition is the engine of growth of capitalist economies. The ASEAN countries will inevitably face competition in exports, if not from China then from other countries.

Of the six ASEAN economies, Singapore's tends to complement China the most. In the present and medium term, Singapore has a demand for China's resource-based exports, that is, foodstuffs, energy and industrial raw materials, as well as basic manufactures for which

Singapore has no comparative advantage because of land scarcity and resource poverty. China has, in turn, a demand for the high value-added and medium- and high-technology goods and services that Singapore can provide with advantage. Singapore's present phase of economic development places priority on high value-added and capital- (human and physical) and technology-intensive goods and services, which places it in a good position to supply part of China's vast needs. In addition, in view of its role as a regional entrepôt and as a transportation and financial center, its well-developed physical and human resources, and the cultural and linguistic affinity of its population with China, Singapore is well placed to act as a conduit for the movement of people, goods, services, and technology to and from China.

Like the trade relations, the ASEAN-China investment relations have complementary and competitive angles. Complementarity arises from investments in each other's economy, to take advantage of country-specific as well as industry- and firm-specific advantages. Thus, Singapore businessmen have invested in China in hotel development, shipbuilding and ship repair, and oil exploration, while both the government and private companies have set up consultancy services. Despite disenchantment with the efficiency of China's economic institutions and the associated investment risks, ASEAN businessmen cannot afford to ignore the huge potential of the China market. However, China is not only competing for ASEAN investments, but also to some extent competing with the ASEAN countries for the same pool of international investments, in particular investments from Japan, the United States, Western Europe, and the Asian NICs. The ASEAN countries will therefore have to ensure that their investment climates remain attractive.

In spite of the problems that exist in the bilateral economic relations between ASEAN countries and China, and in the potential negative spillover effects of China's open-door policy on ASEAN export and investment competitiveness, the economic benefits for ASEAN from a prosperous and economically vibrant China far outweigh the costs. As Japan has done in the last two decades, China can also become the engine of growth in the Asia-Pacific region, with beneficial direct and indirect spillover effects on the ASEAN economies. This assessment, however, is valid only to the extent that China continues to move along the path of nonideological development and contributes to the peace and security of the Asia-Pacific region.

PART SIX

China and the States of Southeast Asia

12. Indonesia-China Relations

HADI SOESASTRO

When the two major Asian countries, Indonesia and China, were close partners in the mid-1960s, they saw their collaboration as the nucleus of a world movement against "neocolonialism, colonialism, and imperialism." Their quasi-alliance was seen by many nations inside or outside the region as a destabilizing factor. Today, when these two major Asian countries remain at a distance with each other, they are told that they should feel embarrassed.

Which party should feel more embarrassed by this situation is not immediately clear. It has been suggested that Beijing's lack of success in normalizing its relations with Jakarta has meant that the Chinese are kept out of the political process of Southeast Asia whenever Indonesian interests are involved. Similarly, some have thought that Indonesia could play a bigger role in solving the Kampuchean problem if it normalizes its relations with China.

The question of normalization of relations between Indonesia and China has become one of the most interesting challenges to international relations, as well as a subject of speculation, among interested observers over the years.

The most recent official Indonesian statement on the resumption of diplomatic relations with China came from Sudharmono, the state secretary and chairman of GOLKAR (Golongan Karya, lit., Functional Group, Suharto's ruling party), when he addressed a gathering at Hasanuddin University in Ujungpandang in March 1986. He stated that diplomatic ties would not be resumed unless the Chinese Communist Party abandoned its policy of interfering in communist movements in Southeast Asia.[1] This statement suggested that Indonesia's position on the issue had not changed. Indeed, almost ten years earlier, President Suharto had clearly stated in his August 1976 Independence Day message to the parliament that the Government of Indonesia (GOI) would only normalize relations with Beijing if the latter respected Indonesia's integrity and did not meddle in its internal affairs.

This condition may indeed be "the bottom line," so to say, for Indonesian policymakers. This being the case, many observers would argue

---

[1]See *Jakarta Post*, March 25, 1986.

that it still is going to take a long time for the two countries to normalize their relations. The statement by the Chinese Foreign Minister Wu Xueqian that China maintains only "moral relations" with the communist parties and does not use such links to interfere in other countries' internal affairs is not regarded as a sufficient guarantee by the Indonesian side.

Despite this recognition, several attempts have been made in the past to produce a breakthrough. On the Indonesian side, one could refer to the two Malik initiatives, in 1977 and 1984, respectively. It is interesting to examine why those attempts failed.[2] Perhaps the more intriguing episode was the one related to Foreign Minister Wu's 1985 visit to Indonesia to participate in the commemoration of the 1955 Afro-Asia Conference in Bandung. Not a few observers hoped that the visit would lead to a breakthrough. On the one hand, there was the feeling that Indonesia was gradually readopting a higher international profile, which would require it to normalize relations with China. This was Malik's thesis all along, which was most explicitly stated at a press conference in Hong Kong on March 8, 1984. He suggested that Indonesia could not play a prominent role in Asia without first normalizing its relations with China, a powerful Asian country that no longer could be ignored by Indonesia.

On the other hand, others felt that the presence of the Chinese foreign minister at the Bandung Commemoration should be seen as a symbol, an implicit statement by the Chinese, of their intention not to interfere in the internal affairs of other countries, one of the so-called Bandung Principles. As suggested earlier, Wu's statement regarding the maintenance of moral relations, however, did not provide adequate proof. Similarly, the failure of Malik's 1977 attempt might have been related to the reported statement made in November 1978 by then Chinese Vice Premier Deng Xiaoping during his visit to Kuala Lumpur who declared that Beijing would not cease its support of communist insurgent movements in the Southeast Asian area.

Meanwhile, on many occasions, Indonesian policymakers had suggested that Indonesia would be able to cope with the imminent threat from China when it managed to solve its own internal security problems, which inter alia involved the problem of Indonesian citizens of

---

[2]On the 1977 episode, see Justus M. van der Kroef, " 'Normalizing' Relations with the People's Republic of China: Indonesia's Rituals of Ambiguity," *Contemporary Southeast Asia*, vol. 3, no. 3 (December 1981), pp. 187–218; on the 1984 episode, see Bilveer Singh, "Sino-Indonesian Relations: Problems of Normalization" in *Asian Affairs*, vol. 6, no. 4 (October-December 1984), pp. 301–15.

Chinese descent. Thus, there was this linkage which often appeared to have been used for the sake of postponing moves toward normalization, which van der Kroef described as Indonesia's rituals of ambiguity.[3]

To be sure, the Chinese also play their part in this game of ambiguity, as reflected—for example—in their citizenship law. This ambiguity, however, affects not only their relations with Indonesia, but those with some other Southeast Asian countries as well. With regard to Sino-Indonesian relations, the Chinese for their part have clearly indicated their readiness to resume diplomatic relations. Such signals have been transmitted to Jakarta either directly or through Tokyo and Canberra.[4] The Indonesian side, however, maintains that it is not in a hurry to resume diplomatic relations with China.

Attention has recently been focused on the resumption of direct trade relations between the two countries. Despite Indonesia's extremely cautious move in that direction, the Chinese side seems to consider it as possibly a first step toward normalization. The Chinese may harbor hopes that developments on the economic front—when those on the political front have failed already—could lead to the long-sought breakthrough.

This chapter reviews the development of Sino-Indonesian trade relations with the aim of examining the effect of direct trade relations on overall bilateral relations. The tentative conclusion of this chapter is a mixed assessment on its overall effect. While the resumption of direct trade could lead to increased two-way trade and more intensive interactions between the two countries, experience so far shows that a number of issues which have emerged in the conduct of trade cannot easily be solved without the development of political understanding apart from the equally important development of the necessary trade mechanisms.

This chapter briefly describes the 1985 resumption of direct trade relations between Indonesia and China. This is followed by an examination of the pattern of Sino-Indonesian trade relations. The concluding section discusses some of the policy issues which have emerged, and their implications for overall Sino-Indonesian relations.

The Resumption of Direct Trade Relations

With the issuance of Presidential Instruction (*Inpres*) no. 9/1985 on July 23, 1985, the GOI officially endorsed the resumption of direct trade between Indonesia and China negotiated by the Indonesian Chamber of

---

[3]See van der Kroef, " 'Normalizing' Relations."
[4]See, e.g., Singh, "Sino-Indonesian Relations."

Commerce and Industry (KADIN Indonesia) and the China Council for the Promotion of International Trade (CCPIT).

From the beginning, the GOI stressed the unofficial nature of the negotiations, which on the Indonesian side were carried out by a non-governmental body, KADIN. The signing of the Memorandum of Understanding (MOU) between KADIN and CCPIT took place on July 5, 1985, in a third country, Singapore, and the words Republic of Indonesia and People's Republic of China (PRC) were absent from the text of the MOU. Both provisions were meant to amplify the unofficial nature of the agreement.

The Chinese side appeared somewhat confused by Indonesia's unofficial approach. The signing of the MOU would have been further delayed had the Chinese side continued to insist that its counterpart, KADIN, produce a written mandate from the GOI.

Despite its unofficial nature, the MOU can be regarded as a breakthrough. KADIN started to explore the possibility of reopening direct trade back in 1977, involving visits by KADIN representatives to the Canton Fair and subsequently also to Beijing in 1978. That initiative failed to receive official support at home, partly due to strong objections from the parliament but most likely because the government did not see any urgency to resuming direct trade with China. KADIN's renewed efforts in 1984 found more favorable responses from the GOI, largely in connection with the decision of the government in 1982 to diversify markets for export, including the development of new markets in the socialist countries. Furthermore, public opinion no longer resented those efforts. In fact, the support of the GOI should not have been unnoticed by the Chinese, especially with the appointment of the junior minister/cabinet secretary by the president to coordinate steps toward resumption of direct trade relations. However, the deliberately unofficial, rather cautious approach was meant to affirm Indonesia's official stance, namely that the resumption of direct trade ties should not be interpreted as a concrete step toward a restoration of full diplomatic relations.[5]

The MOU stipulates six provisions to serve as guidelines for direct trade transactions. These are necessitated in part because the two countries have no diplomatic relations. The provisions relate to: (1) transaction payments; (2) procedures for visa applications; (3) berthing rights of vessels flying the respective national flags; (4) communication services; (5) exchange of trade missions; and (6) the approval by the respective governments and the termination of the MOU.

---

[5]*Jakarta Post*, July 6, 1985.

The approval by the GOI was transmitted to the Chinese side on July 29, 1985, by the KADIN trade delegation that paid a visit to China to mark the reopening of direct trade relations. Thus, Sino-Indonesian direct trade officially resumed on that day. This put an end to the necessity to conduct trade through a third country as practiced throughout the eighteen years following the break-up of diplomatic relations in October 1967.[6]

It perhaps is premature at this stage to assess the results of the reopening of direct trade in terms of "trade creation." The initial increases in trade may largely come as a result of shifts in the mode of transaction, from indirect to direct trade. In fact, on the part of Indonesia direct trade is aimed at not only increases in the level of trade but also at the reduction of the role of intermediaries.

Potentials for increased two-way trade have been identified largely on the basis of commodities already exchanged; the potentials, however, are believed to be quite large. China's modernization and Indonesia's further industrialization definitely open up new opportunities for trade. The recent purchase of Indonesia's crude petroleum by China has never been examined before, and could provide a good illustration of such development.[7] It also suggests that what traditionally is seen as an area of competition may turn into an area for cooperation. This latter aspect has not been studied sufficiently.

The development of the trade infrastructure and mechanism greatly influences the ability of the parties concerned to exploit existing and emerging potentials for trade between them. Indeed, a main challenge to the execution of direct trade between Indonesia and China today is whether it can prosper in the absence of diplomatic relations. The relatively smooth trade relations between Singapore and the PRC may not be entirely appropriate as a model in view of the different nature of their overall bilateral relations—compared with Indonesia-PRC relations—and the very developed trade infrastructure of Singapore.

Sino-Indonesian Trade Relations: Patterns and Issues

There are two distinct periods in the development of Sino-Indonesian trade. The first period began with the signing of the 1953

---

[6] For an examination of the suspension of the relationship, see Justus M. van der Kroef, "The Sino-Indonesian Rupture," *China Quarterly*, no. 33 (January-March 1968), pp. 17–46.
[7] The purchase, which took place in March 1986, was seen as a "trial" purchase with an amount of 1.5 million barrels of crude valued at US$10.40 per barrel; see *Kompas*, April 30, 1986.

Trade Agreement and ended with the suspension of formal relations tions between Indonesia and China in 1967. The second period was marked by indirect trade relations which lasted for about eighteen years until the resumption of direct trade relations in July 1985.

An excellent review of Indonesia-China trade during the first period can be found in John Wong's study.[8] A number of interesting features have been identified. The first feature was the close interaction between trade transactions and political relations. Indeed, the rise of Sino-Indonesian trade between 1955 and 1959, followed by a decline in 1960 and a recovery in 1964, very well reflected the development of political relations between the two countries. However, Wong also suggested the influence of China's economic development on Sino-Indonesian trade. The increase in bilateral trade during the second half of the 1950s might have been stimulated by China's overall Southeast Asian trade drive. Similarly, the decline in 1960 might have been caused by China's domestic economic setbacks.

As shown by Indonesian trade statistics (see Table 1), Indonesia's exports to China increased from less than US$3 million in 1954 to about US$53 million in 1959, or from an insignificant fraction of total exports in 1954 to close to 6 percent in 1959. Likewise, imports from China went up from almost nothing when the 1953 Trade Agreement was signed to over 15 percent of Indonesia's total imports in 1959. Both exports to and imports from China declined in 1960, and with the recovery in 1964 they regained the levels of 1959 for only a brief period before declining again in 1966.

Table 2 exhibits China's recorded statistics with Indonesia. It shows essentially the same developments for the period 1953–67. Imports increased from about US$5 million in 1954 to US$60 million in 1959. In terms of total imports, the rise was less dramatic than that experienced by Indonesia. In China's case it went up from 0.4 percent in 1954 to only about 3 percent in 1959. China's exports to Indonesia as a percentage of its total exports also increased from 0.3 percent in 1954 to 3.1 percent in 1959.

China's imports from Indonesia reached their height in 1964 at about 4.2 percent of its total imports; at this peak, the share of the Chinese market for Indonesia's exports was 7.2 percent. Indonesia's imports from China peaked in 1965 at around 14.2 percent of its total imports, and this peak was for China about 3.2 percent of its total

---

[8]John Wong, *The Political Economy of China's Changing Relations with Southeast Asia* (London: Macmillan, 1984).

Table 1

Indonesia's Recorded Trade with China, 1953-85

	Exports		Imports	
Year	Value, f.o.b. (US$ millions)	Percent of Total Exports	Value, c.i.f. (US$ millions)	Percent of Total Imports
1953	*	*	2.1	*
1954	2.8	*	3.5	*
1955	6.5	0.7	10.1	1.0
1956	11.7	1.3	30.2	3.7
1957	25.2	2.6	27.0	3.2
1958	43.4	5.5	41.8	8.7
1959	53.1	5.7	61.2	15.4
1960	35.4	4.2	57.0	9.9
1961	36.4	4.6	39.9	5.0
1962	34.6	5.1	34.9	5.4
1963	42.2	6.0	44.3	8.5
1964	52.2	7.2	60.9	9.0
1965	40.0	5.7	98.8	14.2
1966	9.5	1.4	40.7	7.7
1967	0.7	*	54.2	8.3
1968	*	*	38.4	5.4
1969	*	*	43.0	5.5
1970	--	--	32.8	3.3
1971	--	--	27.6	2.5
1972	--	--	39.0	2.5
1973	--	--	48.8	1.8
1974	--	--	113.9	3.0
1975	--	--	203.5	4.3
1976	--	--	131.8	2.3
1977	--	--	153.5	2.5
1978	--	--	112.2	1.7
1979	--	--	131.8	1.8
1980	--	--	197.3	1.8
1981	8.3	*	253.5	1.9
1982	14.2	*	230.9	1.4
1983	27.0	*	204.0	1.2
1984	7.7	*	224.4	1.6
1985	84.2	0.5	248.4	2.4
1986**	93.7	0.9	228.2	3.3

*Insignificant (less than US$0.5 million or less than 0.5 percent).
**January–August.

Sources: Sino-Indonesian trade figures for 1953–62 have been compiled by John Wong from U.N. and IMF statistics; see *The Political Economy of China's Changing Relations with Southeast Asia* Table 2.1; Indonesian total trade figures are taken from K. D. Thomas and J. Panglaykim, "Indonesian Exports: Performance and Prospects 1950–1970, Part I," *Bulletin of Indonesian Economic Studies*, no. 5 (October 1966). Figures for 1963–85 are based on statistics of the Indonesian Central Bureau of Statistics, various issues.

Table 2

China's Recorded Trade with Indonesia, 1953–85

Year	Exports		Imports	
	Value (US$ millions)	Percent of Total Exports	Value (US$ millions)	Percent of Total Imports
1953	*	*	--	--
1954	2.8	0.3	4.6	0.4
1955	9.0	0.7	13.3	0.8
1956	29.3	1.8	26.0	1.8
1957	21.2	1.3	27.6	1.9
1958	52.4	2.7	38.8	2.1
1959	69.1	3.1	60.0	2.9
1960	34.3	1.8	39.7	2.0
1961	46.8	3.1	36.7	2.5
1962	29.0	1.9	39.8	3.5
1963	48.9	3.1	42.6	3.6
1964	47.2	2.7	62.4	4.2
1965	65.1	3.2	43.8	2.4
1966	*	*	16.4	0.8
1967	--	--	--	--
1968	--	--	--	--
1969	--	--	--	--
1970	--	--	--	--
1971	--	--	--	--
1972	--	--	--	--
1973	--	--	--	--
1974	--	--	--	--
1975	--	--	--	--
1976	--	--	--	--
1977	*	*	*	*
1978	*	*	*	*
1979	*	*	--	--
1980	21.0	0.1	14.0	0.1
1981	54.0	0.3	63.0	0.3
1982	46.0	0.2	151.0	0.8
1983	49.0	0.2	150.0	0.7
1984	70.0	0.3	214.0	0.8
1985	124.0	0.5	330.0	0.8

*Insignificant (less than US$0.5 million or less than 0.5 percent).

Source: Sino-Indonesian trade figures for 1953–80 are taken from *The Almanac of China's Foreign Economic Relations and Trade*, 1984; China's total trade figures (1953–66) are taken from estimates reproduced in A. Doak Barnett, *China's Economy in Global Perspective* (Washington, D.C.: Brookings Institution, 1981), Table 2.1. Figures for 1981–85 are taken from IMF, *Direction of Trade Statistics*, various issues.

exports. Thus, Indonesia's external trade was more exposed to the Chinese market than vice versa.

The second feature is that bilateral trade during the period 1953–65 achieved a more or less overall balance. This was not the case with China's trade with other Southeast Asian countries. As pointed out by Wong, Sino-Indonesian balanced trade resulted from the government-to-government basis on which trade between those two countries was largely conducted, and because in accordance with Article III of the 1953 Trade Agreement, both sides agreed to maintain the trade in balance as a matter of principle.

Chinese statistics (see Table 2) showed that in cumulative terms its bilateral trade with Indonesia was in balance, with exports and imports amounting to US$455 million and US$435 million, respectively, during the period 1954–65. Indonesia's recorded trade with China showed some cumulative imbalance in China's favor, namely with imports amounting to US$510 million and exports of US$384 million, over the same period. However, no serious complaints from the Indonesian side were recorded. To the contrary, even the practice of dumping by the Chinese, which led to the adoption of countermeasures in other Southeast Asian countries, was regarded as mutually beneficial by the GOI.[9]

The maintenance of a balanced trade, however, was not without costs—at least to the Indonesian side. As recollected by a former Indonesian minister, the trade balance was artificially maintained through countertrade or barter arrangements, often to Indonesia's detriment. The example cited was a deal made in August 1965 to barter 90,000 tons of Indonesian RRS-1 rubber for fertilizers and rice from China. The deal was not implemented because the Indonesian side detected that the rubber was to be reexported—and hence, would compete with Indonesia's direct exports—and that Italy was the source of the fertilizer, which Indonesia already imported directly.[10]

The third feature was the relatively simple commodity composition of trade. During the period 1954–67, Indonesia's imports from China consisted mainly of textile goods and rice, the latter item fluctuating greatly with Indonesia's total rice imports, although China was not then the main supplier. In 1959, textile goods (cotton-weaving yarns and cotton fabrics) and rice constituted 25 percent and 38 percent, respectively, of Indonesia's total imports from China; in 1965, their shares were 51 percent and 21 percent. The commodity composition of Indonesia's

---

[9]Ibid.
[10]The story was told by the former minister of plantation, Frans Seda, to *Sinar Harapan*, August 1, 1985.

exports to China was equally very simple, and consisted almost entirely of rubber.

It is not surprising that in order for the two countries to keep an increasing and balanced trade, they had to resort to barter and counter-trade deals. This was because China's absorptive capacity for raw materials from Southeast Asia was limited and Indonesia could offer only a limited selection of export commodities. The experience of the 1954–67 period showed that increases in the level of trade between the two countries was sustainable through political will on both sides.

Sino-Indonesian trade dropped immediately after 1965. Afterward, some trade, namely, in commodities that continued to make economic sense, was handled by third countries as indirect trade. The shift in the mode of transaction may also have caused a reduction in the level of trade, but its effect may not be great.

The period since 1967 was noteworthy because trade between the two countries was conducted in an indirect manner. As a consequence, no complete picture of the total transactions is available. The incomplete statistics had rather disturbing implications for Indonesian perceptions of its bilateral trade with China. Trade imbalances, which were not an issue in the preceding period, gained considerable attention from both the general public and policymakers. This issue will be discussed later.

Indonesia's imports from China, coming mostly through Hong Kong, were relatively well recorded, in part because Hong Kong recorded its reexport trade. Some imports from China, in particular chemicals and raw materials for pharmaceutical industries, were also coming through Western Europe. China had no record of its indirect exports to Indonesia. It also had incomplete accounts of its imports from Indonesia, except for the last two or three years. Likewise, Indonesia had far from complete records of its indirect exports to China.

Indonesia's exports to China were continued mainly through Singapore rather than Hong Kong. Reexports by Singapore from Indonesia to China were believed to consist mainly of rubber, but no firm information was available. In addition to Singapore and, to a much lesser extent, Hong Kong, it was reported that some Indonesian exports to China were traded through Bangkok.[11]

Indonesia' imports from China declined from their peak of 14.2 percent of total imports in 1965 to 5.5 percent in 1969, and further to 1.8 percent in 1973. In 1974, imports from China rose to 3 percent of total imports, mainly due to large increases in Indonesia's rice imports. In

---

[11]Statement made by the Indonesian minister of trade, Rachmat Saleh; see *Kompas*, May 6, 1985.

1975, about 75 percent of Indonesia's imports from China consisted of rice. By 1979 a new pattern had emerged in Indonesia's imports from China: no longer were they dominated by rice and textiles.

The commodity composition of Indonesia's imports from China from 1980 to 1984 is shown in Table 3. Further changes in its structure took place even in that brief period. In the first half of that period, about 30 percent of total imports consisted of manufactured goods. This share was reduced to 18 percent in 1984. Instead, crude materials—mainly oil seeds and cotton fiber (see Table 4)—became the most important import items; their share rose to about 30 percent of total imports from China in 1984 from only 6 percent in 1980. Three other commodity groups, namely (a) food and live animals (mainly foodstuffs for animals and preserved vegetables); (b) chemicals; and (c) transport equipment, had a combined share of 45 percent in 1984.

The shares of major Indonesian imports from China in 1984 at the three-digit commodity level are shown in Table 4. The nine principal items had a combined share of about 55 percent of total imports, suggesting that the structure of Indonesia's imports from China has become more diversified in terms of its commodity composition. This has not happened with China's imports from Indonesia. Estimates for

Table 3

Indonesian Imports from China by Commodity Groups, 1980–84
(percentages)

SITC*	Commodity Groups	1980	1981	1982	1983	1984
0	Food and live animals	16.5	22.3	9.4	10.7	16.6
1	Beverages and tobacco	1.5	0.9	1.4	1.3	1.2
2	Crude materials, inedible	6.2	5.2	14.6	18.9	29.8
3	Mineral fuels, lubricants, etc.	1.3	1.6	2.6	2.9	1.5
4	Animal and vegetable oils and fats	0.2	0.2	0.2	0.2	0.1
5	Chemicals	20.5	18.2	17.1	21.4	15.7
6	Manufactured goods	31.0	32.5	29.8	26.1	18.3
7	Machinery and transport equipment	16.3	13.2	15.3	14.0	13.0
8	Misc. manufactured articles	6.4	5.8	10.1	5.3	3.8
9	Commodities and transactions NES	--	--	**	--	--
	Total	100.0	100.0	100.0	100.0	100.0

*Standard International Trade Classification.
**Negligible.

Source: Indonesian Central Bureau of Statistics, *Indonesian Foreign Trade Statistics, Imports*, various issues.

1984 suggested the dominance of three commodities (plywood, rubber, and coffee), which together accounted for about 90 percent of China's imports from Indonesia (Table 5). This asymmetrical development was thought to result from the absence of direct trade relations, an absence that penalized Indonesia in terms of its ability to market its nontraditional export commodities to China.

Table 4

Principal Indonesian Imports from China,* 1984
(percentages)

SITC**	Commodity	Percentage
222	Oil seeds used for extraction of soft fixed vegetables	16.8
263	Cotton	9.8
081	Food stuffs for animals	8.5
651	Textile yarn	4.0
785	Motorcycles, motor scooters, and other cycles	3.9
056	Vegetables, roots, and tubers, prepared or preserved n.e.s.†	3.7
695	Hand and/or machine tools	3.3
699	Manufactures of base metal n.e.s.†	2.9
523	Other inorganic chemicals; organic and inorganic compounds	2.4
	Other	44.8
	Total	100.0

*Above US$5 million.
**Standard International Trade Classification.
†Not elsewhere specified.

Source: Indonesian Central Bureau of Statistics, *Indonesia Foreign Trade Statistics, Imports*, various issues.

Table 5

Principal Chinese Imports from Indonesia, 1984
(percentages)

Commodity	Percentage*
Plywood	60
Rubber	25
Coffee	4
Other (palm oil, logs, fertilizers, spices, and herbs)	11
Total	100

*Rough estimates.

Source: Chinese custom's figures as cited in the *Jakarta Post*, July 30, 1985.

Trade imbalances, which became an issue during this period, were seen also as a consequence of the absence of direct trade. In fact, both sides recorded trade imbalances in favor of the other side. This was not surprising, since it was easier for both sides to identify the origin of their indirect import trade than to detect the destinations of their indirect export trade. Since 1981 some Indonesian exports to China have been recorded; they consisted almost exclusively of coffee, which must be fully recorded by destination (quota versus nonquota countries) under the International Coffee Agreement.

Table 6 is an attempt to reconstruct Indonesia's trade with China from 1980 to 1985. On the import side, three records (lines 1 to 3) are compared; they consist of: (a) Indonesia's recorded imports from China; (b) reported reexports by Hong Kong from China to Indonesia; and (c) China's recorded exports to Indonesia. The first and second sets of figures were close to each other, but have exhibited an increasing divergence since 1984, with the latter becoming lower than the former. This might suggest that imports through third countries other than Hong Kong, or indeed from China "directly"—even before the resumption of direct trade—might have increased. In fact, China's recorded exports to Indonesia showed a slight jump in 1984. The improved atmosphere in Sino-Indonesian relations since 1984 might have facilitated some "direct" trade transactions.

The records on the export side are very deficient. Reexports by Hong Kong from Indonesia to China have never been very significant, amounting to around US$40 million in the early 1980s. In later years, Chinese imports of plywood mainly came through Hong Kong. However, since 1983 reexports by Hong Kong from Indonesia to China were no longer published as a separate item, suggesting a declining importance from either Hong Kong's or China's point of view. China's records on imports from Indonesia seem to have improved in later years. In fact, the figures since 1982 might give a good indication of the magnitude of Indonesia's exports to China.

If Indonesia's recorded imports from China and China's recorded imports from Indonesia (for the later years) are to suggest the actual magnitudes of exports and imports between the two countries, it can be concluded that: (a) the trade balance appeared to be *only slightly* in favor of China; and (b) the trade imbalance tended to be reduced, and in 1985 might even have turned in favor of Indonesia.

The general belief was that Sino-Indonesian trade was very much to Indonesia's disadvantage. Two different policy suggestions followed from that belief. The first, somewhat defeatist in nature, suggested that Indonesia should limit its interactions with China because tradewise it will always be at a disadvantage. The second, a more activist position, sug-

Table 6

Indonesia's Trade Balance with China, 1980–85

(US$Million)

	1980	1981	1982	1983	1984	1985	1986*
Imports							
1. Indonesia's recorded imports from China	197	254	231	204	224	248	228
2. Reported reexports by Hong Kong, from China to Indonesia	201	228	251	224	195	164	150
3. China's recorded exports to Indonesia	21	54	46	49	70	124	—
Exports							
4. Indonesia's recorded exports to China	—	8	14	27	8	84	93
5. Reported reexports by Hong Kong, from Indonesia to China	44	33	42	(44)**	(52)**	(32)**	(21)**
6. China's recorded imports from Indonesia	14	63	151	150	214	330	—
Indonesia's Trade with China							
7. Balance (6-1)†	-183	-191	-80	-54	-10	82	—

*January–August.

**Estimates based on total Hong Kong reexports from Indonesia, assuming that proportion reexported to China is same as average for 1980–82.

†Negative sign indicates balance in favor of China.

Source: Indonesian and Chinese trade figures are based on IMF, *Direction of Trade Statistics*, various issues.

gested the need to reopen direct trade with China to rectify the imbalance, which was believed to be the consequence of indirect trade.

There were other arguments for the reopening of direct trade, first among them being the chance to have more firm data on the entire trade transactions between the two countries.[12] This may indeed be a desirable objective, but there are ways of estimating the magnitude and commodity composition of transactions, especially since there have been improvements in reporting on the Chinese side. Second, it was argued that direct trade would result in cheaper imports and higher profit margins on exports by eliminating the commission fees of intermediaries, which ranged from 5 to 12 percent in the case of Hong Kong's middlemen.[13] This suggestion also did not go unchallenged. Counter arguments pointed to the importance of the scale of transactions, which explained the efficient operations of intermediation by Hong Kong or Singapore.[14] The then-Indonesian minister of trade, Radius Prawiro, was reported to have argued that direct trade might even result in more costly transactions.[15]

A third argument for the resumption of direct trade called for lessening Indonesia's dependence on third parties, the intermediaries. It was suggested that Indonesian products traded by intermediaries cannot compete with products from countries that market their products directly—and thus, more aggressively—such as Malaysia. Therefore, it was argued, direct trade should be in Indonesia's interest if only to protect Indonesia's market share for rubber and coffee.[16]

Other arguments related to the hypothesis that direct trade would facilitate increased exports from Indonesia to China, of both traditional and new commodities, and thus, would assure a more balanced trade. Direct trade was thought to have yet another advantage, namely that it would allow greater control over the kinds of goods imported from China. There were some fears, however, that the reopening of direct trade would result in a flood of Chinese manufactured exports that would harm domestic producers.

---

[12]*Kompas*, July 8, 1985.

[13]Based on KADIN's statement in *Merdeka*, December 29, 1977; also statement by the representative of Indonesian Commodities Centre, Ltd. (ICC), *Sinar Harapan*, October 12, 1984. ICC is a private Indonesian company established in Hong Kong in 1983 to promote exports of Indonesian commodities, primarily with the Chinese market in mind.

[14]Statement by the chairman of the Association of Indonesian Importers (GINSI), Zahri Achmad, in *Tempo* (Singapore), July 13, 1985.

[15]*Kompas*, May 20, 1978.

[16]Statement by the foreign minister, Mochtar Kusumaatmadja, at a hearing in the House of Representatives; see *Kompas*, November 12, 1984.

The above concerns were expressed to the first Chinese trade delegation that paid a return visit to Indonesia on August 9–19, 1985. The chairman of CCPIT, Wang Yaoting, who headed the delegation gave assurances that China would not export goods already produced in Indonesia.[17] Other concerns have been taken into account in the drafting of the MOU; those concerns may be more political than economic in nature. Still unresolved is the issue of establishing trade representative offices in each other's country. But short of this, it was hoped that direct trade would proceed smoothly.

In spite of the reopening of direct trade, some transactions might still be undertaken by third parties, Hong Kong in particular. This may be simply for reasons of convenience, or cost considerations, or because of the greater protection—legal or otherwise—granted to transactions conducted under Hong Kong laws and regulations. These considerations may apply to both the Indonesian and the Chinese sides.

In the course of time both sides will select the kind of transactions which can be beneficially conducted through third countries. As was pointed out elsewhere, indirect trade works well so long as it is in the interest of intermediaries; exports of coffee or plywood from Indonesia to China may have benefited from the superior trade services of Hong Kong or Singapore but it is questionable how far these two countries are willing to promote those Indonesian products that compete with their own.[18]

As stated earlier, the share of the Indonesian market for Hong Kong reexports has sharply declined in the last few years, from third place (after China and the United States) in 1980 to the eighth place in 1985. However, Hong Kong's trade with Indonesia continues to be dominated by reexports. In 1984, for example, about 89 percent of Hong Kong's total exports to Indonesia consisted of reexports, and approximately 58 percent of its total imports from Indonesia were reexported.

On the origin of Hong Kong's reexports to Indonesia, until 1984 it was Japan—rather than China—that was the main source of reexports. Japan's share was about 60 percent in 1981, but that share declined to 26 percent in 1985. This decline appears to be part of—and in line with—the overall reduction in Indonesia's imports, especially from Japan, since 1983.

Hong Kong reexports from China to Indonesia remained rather stable during the past five years, but did not experience the drastic drop

---

[17]*Sinar Harapan*, August 14, 1986.
[18]Djisman Simandjuntak, "Demythologising the China-Indonesia Trade," in the *Indonesian Quarterly*, vol. 13, no. 2 (April 1985), pp. 144–49.

endured by reexports from Japan. Indonesia's share of total Hong Kong reexports from China was 5.4 percent in 1984 and declined slightly to 3.7 percent in 1985. Hong Kong's role in Sino-Indonesian trade is far more important than it is in Japan-Indonesian trade relations, since almost all Indonesian imports from China have come through Hong Kong. The commodity composition of reexports from China to Indonesia was also much more diversified than that of reexports from Japan. As shown earlier in Table 3, there had been a shift in the commodity composition of Indonesian imports from China, from manufactured goods, machinery and transport equipment toward crude materials, such as cotton and oil seeds, as well as manufactured intermediate inputs, such as textile yarn. This may explain the sustainability of Indonesia's imports from China.

It remains to be seen what role Hong Kong will play in Sino-Indonesian trade now that the two countries have resumed direct trade relations. Commodities which are imported by Indonesia in relatively large quantities—such as cotton—are now likely to be traded directly. The Chinese side has also indicated an interest in importing Indonesian plywood directly as soon as they have terminated the contract with their Hong Kong agents. However, commodities in smaller quantities, namely machinery, equipment, tools, and the like, which in total may still amount to US$100 million or so, are likely to continue to be imported through Hong Kong. All these will depend on how smoothly direct trade between Indonesia and China develops in the coming years.

Future Prospects

The KADIN delegation that visited China from July 27 to August 3, 1985, to mark the official reopening of direct trade returned with great optimism about the future of direct Sino-Indonesian trade. During the visit, the Chinese side signed letters of intent to purchase Indonesian products worth an estimated US$352.5 million. These included cement (250,000 tons), fertilizers (25,000 tons), plywood (150,000 cu m), sawn timber (75,000 cu m), rattan (5,000 tons), textile raw materials (worth US$60 million), concrete steel (5,000 tons per month for one year), natural rubber (50 to 75,000 tons), cocoa (3,000 tons), and coffee (6,000 tons).[19] In addition, it was reported that the Chinese side also indicated an interest in buying aluminum ingots and sheet glass.[20] The Indonesian side did express an interest in buying cotton fiber (50,000 tons),

---

[19]*Antara*, August 6, 1985.
[20]*Jakarta Post*, August 5, 1985.

coal, and asphalt. Beijing also sought to export silk and railway tracks to Indonesia.[21]

A return visit by China's first trade mission to Indonesia, which took place on August 9–19, 1985, immediately following KADIN's visit, was expected to finalize the above deals. The forty-three-member delegation was headed by the chairman of CCPIT and consisted of presidents, vice presidents or general managers of seventeen companies, including the Bank of China. It was a high-level delegation. However, the delegation did not leave with any signed contracts, but suggested that smaller groups would make follow-up calls.

Nonetheless, the visit was useful since it provided an opportunity for the Chinese delegation to meet with Indonesian officials and vice versa. Both the Indonesian minister of trade and the junior minister/cabinet secretary reiterated the policy of the GOI, which essentially supported direct trade activities by providing all the necessary facilities but would give no special treatment to China. Earlier, it was suggested by the chairman of CCPIT that Beijing was prepared to give special treatment to Indonesia, especially in the form of lower import duties.[22]

In late August 1985, a textile team from China indeed came to sign purchase contracts for textile raw materials. The purchase consisted of polyester fiber (5,000 tons), polyester textured yarn (8,000 tons), nylon stretch yarn (200 tons), and acrylic fiber and top (4,000 tons). However, the purchase was linked to a counterpurchase requirement for Indonesia to buy Chinese cotton.[23] A visit by a delegation from Sinochart (China's national shipping company) followed in early November 1985 to discuss shipping problems.

Throughout 1985 a number of shipments to China had been reported. Krakatau Steel—a state enterprise—was reported to have exported 5,000 tons of steel wire to China even prior to the reopening of direct trade.[24] Similarly, there were direct shipments of fertilizers (July and October), sawn timber (October), as well as rubber (November). In fact, in early January 1985 a new shipping policy had already been introduced by the GOI, allowing Indonesian vessels to go to China. However, most of the above shipments were undertaken by vessels under Chinese flags.

By the end of 1985, the realization of Indonesian exports to China as recorded by KADIN amounted to US$38 million.[25] Some of those

---

[21]Ibid.

[22]This was reported in *Kompas*, July 30, 1985.

[23]*Merdeka*, September 2, 1985.

[24]*Sinar Harapan*, January 22, 1985.

[25]*Antara*, January 6, 1986.

exports, however, did not originate with the agreements made during KADIN's mission visit to China or made through KADIN, suggesting that while KADIN has been given a coordinating function, it has no legal powers to oblige exporters to go through KADIN.

Another KADIN delegation visited Beijing on January 15–22, 1986, and during this visit the Chinese side signed another contract to buy 250,000 tons of cement, valued at US$13.5 million. The Chinese side indicated that this deal might lead to a total purchase of 1 million tons for 1986. However, the Chinese side insisted on a countertrade deal in which the Indonesian side was to purchase coal and cotton in return. The insistence on a countertrade deal by the Chinese was seen as compensation for them, since they could have imported cement from Taiwan via Hong Kong at a lower price.[26] The agreement had numerous implications. First, the deal was seen by many in Indonesia as politically motivated and therefore, not very welcome. Second, the Indonesian side found it difficult to implement the deal because KADIN cannot function as a trading house. Thus, it was left to the sellers of the cement to conduct the countertrade.

Interactions between Chinese and Indonesian traders have been quite intensive since July 1985. By July 1986, direct exports from Indonesia to China had reached US$214 million whereas direct exports from China to Indonesia amounted to US$50 million.[27] In August 1987 another countertrade deal was signed involving the exchange of 100,000 tons of cement from Indonesia with 400,000 tons of coal from China.[28] Potentials for increasing trade remain to be exploited and further identified. The absence of trade representative offices in each country will make it difficult to gather up-to-date information on market opportunities. However, this problem is not as urgent to resolve as the more serious problem of shipping, countertrade, and inspection and verification procedures for China's exports to Indonesia.

With regard to shipping, it had been agreed in principle that vessels from both countries would be given a "fair share" in the transportation of goods from Indonesia to China and vice versa. This agreement was endorsed in August 1985 between CCPIT and the Indonesian National Shipowners Association (INSA).[29] However, as later reported by KADIN, the transportation of about 5 million tons of goods throughout

---

[26]This statement was made by the head of the KADIN mission, Tony Agus Ardie, as reported in *Pelita*, January 25, 1986.

[27]*Antara*, August 22, 1986.

[28]*Sinar Harapan*, August 11, 1986.

[29]*Kompas*, February 8, 1986.

1986 between Indonesia and China—involving a freight cost of US$80 million—will be handled solely by Chinese vessels.[30] This decision was taken because KADIN believed that the freight tariffs of Indonesian vessels were 40 percent higher than those of Chinese vessels. This estimate, however, was disputed by INSA. The problem appeared to have been settled among KADIN and INSA. There was also a belief that arrangements at the ports of China tended to discriminate against foreign flag carriers.

Countertrade as practiced by the Chinese side in a number of deals with Indonesia may indeed become an obstacle to increasing direct trade. In fact, Indonesia's initiative to reopen direct trade with China may have been taken at a time when China has already started to restrict the uses of its rapidly dwindling foreign exchange (especially during 1985). Countertrade appeared to have been introduced out of necessity rather than choice. However, the Indonesian side lacks sophisticated trading services which can facilitate countertrade. Another aspect of this issue is that the high profile of Indonesian efforts to promote Sino-Indonesian trade might have aroused the attention by China's policymakers, making Indonesia a target for the imposition of certain measures, such as countertrade. This was perhaps justified by the belief in Beijing that the Sino-Indonesian trade balance was in Indonesia's favor. As a result, some suggestions have been made to take advantage of indirect trade between Indonesia and China as a way around the unwanted countertrade.

The policy implications for Indonesia are not immediately obvious. Indonesia may opt for further strengthening direct trade relations, even though countertrade is applied by China, because Indonesia may see this as a challenge to the development of a more sophisticated trading infrastructure on its part. This certainly requires a more global orientation—rather than bilateral—in the development of its trading mechanism. The coordinating function performed by KADIN is far from adequate.

The other problem relates to inspection and verification of China's exports to Indonesia. A regulation of the GOI, the Presidential Instruction (*Inpres*) no. 4, April 1985, stipulated that all imports to Indonesia must be inspected and verified by the Geneva-based Société General de

---

[30]For 1986, the following shipment was planned: (a) from Indonesia to China, one million tons of fertilizers, one million tons of cement, one million metric tons of plywood, 0.5 million tons of iron and miscellaneous goods; (b) from China to Indonesia, one million tons of coal, 0.5 million tons of finished and semifinished goods; see *Sinar Harapan*, February 1, 1986.

Surveillance (SGS) at points of loading and must be covered by SGS verification reports to be allowed into the country. The problem for China is that SGS has no subsidiaries, affiliates, or agents in China, and China does not allow foreign surveyor companies to operate in China.

Due to this problem, shipments of raw cotton fiber from China to Indonesia, which should have taken place in October, November, and December 1985 according to a signed contract, had to be postponed. CCPIT's vice chairman, Guo Dong Po, visited Indonesia in late January 1986 to resolve the problem of inspection and verification. The Chinese side proposed that the survey be undertaken by the China National Commodity Inspection Corporation (CCIC). Indonesia has not objected to this proposal so long as an agreement can be reached between SGS and CCIC. It was reported that negotiations in Beijing in March 1986 between CCIC, SGS, and P. T. Sucofindo—the Indonesian surveying company that supervises SGS's work in country—did not result in an agreement regarding the issuance of the surveyor's verification report.[31]

From April 1, 1986, SGS decided to undertake the survey in Hong Kong, which effectively meant that Sino-Indonesian trade is processed through Hong Kong. In view of this development, the Chinese side was also reported to be considering a suspension of direct trade with Indonesia—so far as its exports to Indonesia are concerned—and to let the trade be carried out through Hong Kong.[32] This problem has not been fully resolved.

The above discussion illustrates that there are a number of obstacles in the development of direct trade relations between Indonesia and China, in spite of the increases already experienced in 1985 (see Table 1).

Some of these problems originate with the lack of political relations between the two countries. However, the lack of the necessary trading mechanism also explains the difficulties faced in the relationship. As long as these problems persist, it will be difficult to expect a breakthrough in overall bilateral relations to be produced on the trade front. Where, then, should one look for a possible, new breakthrough?

As suggested elsewhere, "critical for a new breakthrough in the normalization process are not so much renewed Chinese assurances that Beijing has no subversive intent, or that there are real benefits of direct trade with China, or yet further examples of ethnic Chinese assimilation. These are important to be sure. But it is Indonesia's current regional concerns, among which the Cambodian question is para-

---

[31]*Sinar Harapan*, April 5, 1986.
[32]Ibid.

mount, that are more likely to determine the future pace of normalization."[33] However, it is not immediately obvious why at this junction the road ahead in Sino-Indonesian relations should lie through Kampuchea.

---

[33]Justus M. van der Kroef, " 'Normalizing' Relations with China—Indonesia's Policies and Perceptions," *Asian Survey*, vol. 26, no. 8 (August 1986), p. 934.

13. Malaysia-China Bilateral Relations

ZAINUDDIN A. BAHARI

China's perception of Southeast Asia and consequently its policies toward the region can only be understood in terms of its larger strategic concern with the United States and the Soviet Union. This concern is largely translated into attempts to deny control of any area within the region to any one competitive power. By the same token it also represents an attempt to preserve what is regarded as China's fundamental interests in the region. This consideration is one of the principal determinants of Chinese foreign policy objectives in Southeast Asia. Changes in the Chinese perception of threats by the superpowers, as well as their global and domestic policies, inevitably resulted in corresponding changes in China's policies toward the region. Thus, fluctuation rather than consistency was the one singular characteristic of Chinese foreign policy. The unpredictable nature of Chinese behavior in the region represented a constant source of considerable anxiety and concern to the regional states.

Any discussions of Sino-Malaysian relations have to take into account the revolutionary as well as the nonrevolutionary objectives of Chinese foreign policy. In other words, China's link with local insurgent movements represents an important dimension of its relationship with Malaysia. Equally important is the relationship—perceived or otherwise—with the Huaqiao, the overseas Chinese.

This chapter will attempt to trace the development of Sino-Malaysian bilateral relations and determine the causes and rationale behind the shifts in the foreign policies of the respective countries and how those shifts affect their bilateral relationship. It will also examine some of the current major issues in the bilateral relationship. Finally it will attempt to examine whether existing suspicions will preclude the further development of relations, especially in light of China's modernization programs and Malaysia's need to improve its economic well-being.

Historical Perspective

Political Relations

The unsettled political situation in China in the late nineteenth and early twentieth centuries resulted in a mass exodus of Chinese into Southeast Asia. Those that traveled to Malaya to work as indentured labor in the tin mines and rubber plantations provided the first modern contact between China and Malaysia. This group became the nucleus of revolutionary activities, initially fostered by Dr. Sun Yat-sen and directed against the Manchu leaders in China. As events were to unfold, the direction and thrust of revolutionary activities eventually passed into the hands of the Chinese Communist Party (CCP) working through its South Sea Branch, which later came to be known as the Malayan Communist Party (MCP). Established in 1930 the MCP began to spread its influence through the exploitation of labor unrest in 1933 and the anti-Japanese movement (among Chinese immigrants) that arose in the wake of the Japanese invasion of Manchuria. The MCP succeeded in gaining control of the anti-Japanese movements and subsequently enhanced its image as the vanguard of the struggle against Japanese imperialism.

The MCP was largely Chinese in composition.[1] Attempts to recruit from the other races failed because its principal motivating force was Chinese nationalism. Additionally, its strong anti-Japanese strain was less than appealing, particularly to the Malays.

While the party was pro-Peking in its orientation, it followed directives of the Communist International, as evidenced by its militant policy of insurrection and opposition to the British war effort after the German-Soviet Pact of 1939. This anti-British stance was dropped in 1940 upon the instruction of the CCP. Indeed with the coming into power of the latter in 1949, it asserted even greater influence over the MCP and other communist movements in Southeast Asia.

The success of the CCP led to the conviction that Mao's strategy of the Peoples' War could be readily adopted by Third World countries to free themselves from colonialist oppression.[2] Thus the CCP endorsed a policy of explicit and implicit support for the various "national liberation movements" in the region.

The consequent heightened militant activities of the MCP led to the declaration of a State of Emergency in Malaya by the British in June 1948, following which the MCP was declared illegal. The spate of terrorism perpetrated by the MCP and assisted by the CCP, however, continued unabated and climaxed in 1951 with the assassination of British High Commissioner Sir Henry Gurney.

Relations between Malaya and China deteriorated following the colonial government's adoption of measures deemed repressive to the

---

[1]Victor Purcell, *Malaya: Communist or Free* (London: Victor Gollancz, 1954), p. 135.
[2]P. Van Ness, *Revolution and Chinese Foreign Policy* (Berkeley: University of California Press, 1970), p. 11.

immigrant Chinese population. Such measures included the deportation of about 35,000 Chinese nationals suspected of complicity with the MCP and the forced resettlement of almost half a million Chinese farmers into controlled villages. Relations were further exacerbated by the embargo on Malayan rubber exports to China.

By 1953, several developments had served to cause a significant shift in China's policy from one that advocated armed revolution to one that emphasized peaceful coexistence. Foremost was the perception that the United States was organizing a collective defense arrangement among the noncommunist governments in Asia to contain the communist powers. The other was the failure of the insurrections inspired by the CCP among the Asian communist movements.

The pursuit of peaceful coexistence by China was aimed at creating a neutral Asia and establishing a collective security system with China very likely playing a major role. It would also allow local communist parties who had failed in the armed struggle to pursue their original objectives through legal and political means.

Thus, during the Asian-African Conference in Bandung in 1955, China made a major effort to promote a strategy of peaceful coexistence. It urged a negotiated settlement to the insurrection in Malaya and recognition of the MCP.[3] Following this the MCP indicated a desire to negotiate with the newly elected Alliance government in Kuala Lumpur. A meeting was subsequently held in Baling in December 1955 between Chin Peng, the MCP secretary general, and Tunku Abdul Rahman and David Marshall, the respective chief ministers of Malaya and Singapore. The meeting, however, failed to end the insurrection.

The failure of the Baling talks added further woes to the MCP, already suffering serious military setbacks due as much to its own haphazard military planning as to the unexpected ferocity of the military campaign launched by the government. The MCP was forced to retreat further into the jungle and finally withdrew across the Thai border, where it began to adopt a purely defensive posture.

There was a brief interlude in Sino-Malayan relations following the lifting of the embargo on rubber exports in 1956 and the visit to Beijing by the first trade missions from Malaya and Singapore. China welcomed Malaya's independence in 1957 but was apprehensive when it learned that Malaya intended to rely upon Britain and the Common-

---

[3]Jay Taylor, *China and Southeast Asia: Peking's Relations with Revolutionary Movements* (New York: Praeger, 1974), p. 277.

wealth for its security.[4] China was also concerned about the continued ban on the MCP.

The anticommunist policy adopted by Malaya at home and in its foreign relations further distanced Malaya from China. This policy, formulated as a result of Malaya's traumatic experience with the communist insurrection, consequently led to the proscription of all publications from the mainland and the closure of the Bank of China branch in Kuala Lumpur. Malaya also did not accord recognition to China and opposed the latter's admission into the United Nations. Malaya was one of the sponsors that condemned China's invasion of Tibet in 1959 and was equally critical of China's aggression against India in October 1962.

This period of heightened hostility indicated a hardening in Malaya's attitude toward China, which was perceived as essentially expansionist and hence a serious threat to world peace. It was against this backdrop that Malaya proposed the creation of an anticommunist Malaysia incorporating Malaya, Singapore, North Borneo, and Sarawak.

The proposal was bitterly opposed by China, which saw it as a new form of colonialism to perpetuate British imperial dominance.[5] China thus lent its support to Indonesia's confrontation policy and to North Kalimantan's separatist movement, which attempted to set up a unitary, independent state comprising Brunei, Sarawak, and North Borneo.[6]

Malaya's consent to the exchange of consulates with Taiwan in 1966, and China's continued support of the MCP through such activities as the opening of a clandestine radio station called the Voice of Malayan Revolution (VOMR) based in South China in November 1969, further exacerbated Sino-Malaysian relations.

Throughout 1967, China was in the grip of an internal power struggle brought about by the Cultural Revolution. With radicals in control of most of the important positions, including those in the Foreign Ministry, at a time of increased Sino-Soviet competition for leadership of the communist world, China was thus prompted to adopt a more forward position. Inevitably the Chinese strongly opposed the formation of ASEAN in August 1967 by Malaysia, Indonesia, Thailand, the Philippines, and Singapore. The organization, believed to have been inspired

---

[4]See Nan Chun, "On the Independence of Malaya," in Shih Shou Tse, "Current Affairs," August 1957; quoted in R. K. Jain, *China and Malaysia: 1949–83* (Atlantic Highlands, N. J.: Humanities Press, 1984), pp. 28–30.

[5]See article on "Malaysian Confederation" in Shishi Shouce (Guide to Current Affairs) June 1962 in Jain, *China and Malaysia*, pp. 53–55.

[6]For further details, see Taylor *China and Southeast Asia*, pp. 304–10.

by the United States, was perceived to be militantly oriented, to serve the U.S. policy of containing China.

Toward the end of the 1960s, with the beginning of the British military withdrawal east of Suez and the enunciation of the Guam Doctrine, doubts were beginning to emerge within the Southeast Asian leadership regarding the credibility of Western deterrence. In attempting to search for a broader balance of power, greater interest was shown in accommodating China, which was perceived as having become a credible power, especially in regional affairs. Consistent with this new perception, in October 1970, Malaysia, under the premiership of Tun Abdul Razak, voted for China's admission into the United Nations as a first step toward eventual official recognition and establishment of diplomatic relations.

This reappraisal of Malaysia-China relations should also be seen within the context of Malaysia's conception of a policy of neutralization.[7] This concept called for ending reliance on Western deterrence and placing Malaysia on equally friendly terms with all major powers. It also sought an understanding and commitment from these powers—the United States, the Soviet Union, and China—to guarantee the independence, neutrality, and integrity of Southeast Asia.

The nonofficial Malaysian trade delegation to China, led by Tengku Razaleigh Hamzah on May 6, 1971, marked the beginning of a "people-to-people" relationship between the two countries. This eventually led to the first official visit by a Malaysian premier to China on May 28, 1974. The joint communiqué signed between Tun Abdul Razak and Premier Zhou Enlai dealt with both the principles governing Sino-Malaysian relations and the question of Chinese citizens in Malaysia.[8] Both countries agreed to recognize and respect each other's independence and sovereignty and further agreed not to recognize dual nationality. Malaysia became the first ASEAN country to establish a diplomatic mission in Beijing.

It is worthy of note that the joint communiqué was silent on the question of the MCP, though Tun Razak indicated that the Chinese leadership gave an assurance of noninterference in what was considered an internal problem of Malaysia.

Establishment of Sino-Malaysian diplomatic relations was made possible also because of a change in China's foreign policy. With the end of the Cultural Revolution, the focus was no longer on competing

---

[7]For further details, see Dick Wilson, *The Neutralization of Southeast Asia* (New York: Praeger, 1975), pp. 6–8.

[8]China-Malaysia joint communiqué, May 31, 1974.

with the Soviets for leadership of the international communist movement. It was also not on opposing U.S. influence. Rather, the objective was to counter the expansion of Soviet and, to a lesser extent, Japanese influence within the Southeast Asian region.

Adding to China's strategic concern was the deterioration of relations with its former ally, Vietnam, whose relationship with the Soviet Union had been fortified by the conclusion of a treaty of peace and friendship. To counterbalance Soviet-Vietnamese influence, China had to improve relations with noncommunist Southeast Asia.

Development of Malaysia-China relations was constrained, however, by the continued Chinese involvement with the MCP—still perceived to be the primary threat to Malaysian internal security, not least because of its avowed objective of undermining the legally constituted government. While its numerical strength might have been small (slightly more than 2,000) its potential for causing internal instability was substantial. Witness the height of its armed struggle between 1948 and 1960. That a foreign power had provided support to the MCP was unforgivable. What rendered it unforgettable was that both entities had a common ethnic denominator. It is this ethnic dimension that colors the perspective on the issue of the MCP and China's involvement.

Development of Malaysia-China relations was only possible if China played down its involvement with the local insurgent movements. Yet it was just not possible for China to advocate a peaceful transition for the MCP, whose avowed objective was (and still is) the violent overthrow of the legally constituted government. And it was not possible for China to abandon the MCP without irreparably damaging Chinese ideological pretensions.

Thus, China was prompted to pursue its so-called dual-track policy of state-to-state relations that reflected recently established official ties and party-to-party relations that reflected a continued ideological link with the MCP.

It is this aspect of China's behavior that Malaysia found wanting, if not altogether unacceptable. The seeds of mutual distrust, sown much earlier in the history of China's relations with Malaysia, did not disappear with the establishment of official relations. Tun Hussein's visit to China in May 1979 contributed little toward the building of mutual trust. The shutdown of the VOMR in June 1981 also did not improve bilateral relations, for VOMR was immediately replaced by another transmitting station called the Voice of Malayan Democracy.

China was also perceived to be behind the establishment of a clandestine paper organization of the MCP called the Malay Nationalist Revolutionary Party of Malaya, headed by Abdullah C. D., a member of the MCP central committee. The organization was aimed at wooing the support of various communities, especially the Malays, and by the same token to lessen the MCP's pro-Chinese image.

Against such a background, Premier Zhao Ziyang's assurance during his official visit to Malaysia on August 9, 1981, that China had disassociated itself from the MCP was not believable. The explanation that the link between the CCP and the MCP was only "political and moral" was neither convincing nor acceptable.[9]

Aside from the MCP, China was also associated with the North Kalimantan Communist Party (NKCP). Established in 1965, the NKCP operated in Sabah and shared similar revolutionary objectives with the MCP.

Vietnam's invasion of Kampuchea in 1978 subsequently led to a strategic alignment between ASEAN and China. This alignment was predicated on the common immediate objective of forcing a Vietnamese troop withdrawal from Kampuchea. Malaysia, however, did not share China's view that Vietnam sought regional hegemony. On the contrary, Vietnam was seen as a front-line state fighting against possible long-term Chinese domination of the region.

Economic Relations

Aside from political and security considerations, economics provided a strong motive for reappraisal of relations with China. Even as early as 1970 Malaysia had become a significant trading partner of China, importing about M$228.76 million worth of Chinese products and exporting some M$66.67 million worth of Malaysian goods. By 1974 when official relations were established, Chinese exports to Malaysia had increased to M$492.9 million and Malaysian exports to China had likewise increased to M$210.6 million.[10] (Malaysia's trade with China accounted for about 3.5 percent of Malaysia's foreign trade in 1974.) Sino-Malaysian trade had always been greatly in China's favor, and this imbalance became a characteristic and major issue in Sino-Malaysian trade relations.

With the launching of China's modernization programs and the implementation of Malaysia's policy of industrialization, the expansion of trade and economic ties was seen as mutually beneficial. At the end of Tun Hussein's visit to China in May 1979, an agreement on exchanges of technical missions was signed. There was also mutual agreement to increase direct trading between the two countries. By the time Malaysia established a trade office in Beijing in 1983, the volume of

---

[9]Dr. Mahathir's press conference in Kuala Lumpur, August 10, 1981.
[10]Department of Statistics, Kuala Lumpur, 1985.

trade between the two countries had increased to M$750 million. Malaysian exports have remained unchanged over the years, with the main items being commodities such as timber, logs, rubber, palm oil, and lately, cocoa beans. Export of semimanufactured and manufactured products remained insignificant, constituting less than 20 percent of Malaysia's total exports to China. Imports from China were mainly foodstuffs like vegetables, tubers and roots, soya beans, and fruit preparations.

In 1986, the volume of Sino-Malaysian trade rose to about M$1,149.8 million with the imbalance—M$305.6 million—still heavily in China's favor.[11] What is equally significant is that this trade represented only 1.8 percent of Malaysia's total trade. Between 1974 and 1986, China had become less, not more, important as a trading partner to Malaysia.

To improve the trade climate, discussions and negotiations on investment, protection, avoidance of double taxation, maritime issues, and so on, were conducted. Pernas, a government agency, was designated official trading house for the China trade. China, however, was reluctant to engage in direct trading and refused to provide agency rights to Pernas. It also continued to conduct Sino-Malaysian trade mainly through Chinese middlemen in Hong Kong and Singapore.

Recent Significant Developments

Visit of Tan Sri Ghazali Shafie

Since he took office from Tun Hussein Onn in 1981, Dato' Sri Dr. Mahathir has endeavored to reduce Malaysia's economic dependence and traditional alignment with the West and is looking toward the East for help in the implementation of the New Economic Policy (NEP). It was felt that an enhancement of Sino-Malaysian bilateral relations would contribute significantly toward the realization of this new eastward-looking policy.

However, since the establishment of diplomatic relations in 1974, little progress had been achieved in Sino-Malaysian relations, the major impediment being China's refusal to renounce its link with the MCP. The other thorn in Sino-Malaysian relations was the special treatment being accorded by China to Malaysians of Chinese origin, including unauthorized visits to China.[12] Finally, there was the Chinese reluctance

---

[11]Ibid.

[12]Malaysian law forbids Malaysian citizens from visiting China without the express permission of the Ministry of Home Affairs. To this end, the Chinese embassy in Kuala Lumpur refrains from giving visas to Malaysians who do not possess the required permit. However, this particular limitation could be overcome by arranging for the required visas to be procured in Hong Kong and by soliciting Chinese official consent not to record the visit to China in the visitor's passport.

to provide agency rights to Pernas, Malaysia's official China trade agency, and to conduct direct trade with Malaysia.

It is against this backdrop that Tan Sri Ghazali Shafie in his capacity as Malaysian foreign minister visited China on May 29, 1984. Accompanied by a party of thirty-three senior government officials and business representatives, the visit was the most important since Tun Razak's visit to Beijing in May 1974. Tan Sri Ghazali's visit was given added significance, for it coincided with the tenth anniversary of the establishment of Sino-Malaysian diplomatic relations.

The visit provided an opportunity for very frank and candid discussions on all the major issues of Sino-Malaysian relations. On the question of security, the Chinese were told in no uncertain terms that the continued CCP-MCP link was impermissible, and that it would represent an obstacle to improvement in the people-to-people relationship.[13] Although China insisted as a matter of principle on maintaining ties with all political parties regardless of their ideological persuasions, in deference to Malaysian sensitivity, it did take steps to reduce the profile of this relationship by no longer publishing fraternal messages from the MCP to the CCP and vice versa.[14]

On the question of the overseas Chinese, China was made aware of Malaysian concern and sensitivity regarding what was perceived to be special treatment meted out to Malaysians of ethnic Chinese origin. It would appear that China treated the latter as potential returnees to China. This begs the question of China's possible motives and intentions. Given its past record of aiding local insurgents, China's actions only increased Malaysian suspicions. China's attitude was also seen as a disservice to Malaysian Chinese, whose allegiance to Malaysia was arguably suspect in view of the perceived implications carried by such special treatment. A similar concern was also expressed about unauthorized visits by Malaysian Chinese to China. (The extent of such unauthorized visits is not easily discernible.)

On economic relations, Malaysia registered dissatisfaction with China's preference to conduct trade through Chinese middlemen rather than through Pernas. It was explained that such actions were undermining Malaysia's efforts to equalize the distribution of wealth under the New Economic Policy. China assured the Malaysians that no discrimination was intended. It was pointed out that during Tan Sri Ghazali's visit, several letters of intent for a number of multimillion dollar projects

---

[13]*The Star* (Kuala Lumpur), June 2, 1984.
[14]Fraternal messages between the two communist parties have in the past been published in China's print media, and in the proscribed underground publications of the MCP.

were concluded between China and both Malay and non-Malay concerns. A contract was signed with Pernas to allow the latter to import US$700,000 worth of Chinese foodstuffs into Malaysia. Also indicated was that with the opening of special economic zones and fourteen port cities under China's development programs, there would be greater opportunities for Sino-Malaysian economic cooperation.[15]

While Tan Sri Ghazali's trip did not exactly represent a political and economic breakthrough for Sino-Malaysian relations, it did result in some significant developments. China's modernization programs, coupled with the incremental adoption of a market-oriented economic system, provided both economic and political opportunities. Malaysia could take full advantage of the opportunities presented to improve its economic links to China and by the same token enhance the realization of the objectives of the NEP. Sino-Malaysian economic relations, however, should be Malaysian in character (as opposed to only Malaysia-Chinese to the exclusion of Malays), and direct in orientation, preferably through agencies recommended by the government. Also recommended was a relaxation of restrictions on visits to China by Malaysian businessmen.

Politically, it was felt that China's modernization would lead to a more stable China, with obvious benefits to regional stability. It was also perceived that China's focus for the next thirty years or so would be on its modernization programs and that Malaysia should use this opportunity to improve its own vitality.

Prime Minister Mahathir's Visit

Mahathir's visit to China on November 20, 1985, was an affirmation of the philosophy that trade and economic cooperation should provide substance and give meaning to a political and diplomatic relationship. His nine-day tour of China accompanied by 130 leading businessmen represented the biggest trade delegation ever sent by Malaysia.

Consistent with this new philosophy, Dr. Mahathir decided to sidestep the core issue of the CCP-MCP link—which had been the major political stumbling block to better Sino-Malaysian relations—and concentrated instead on trade issues. Three agreements were signed during the visit: one on avoidance of double taxation, a memorandum of understanding on direct trade, and a joint processing venture.[16] About M$57 million worth of deals were also concluded by the Malaysians.

---

[15]*South China Morning Post*, June 13, 1984.
[16]*Far Eastern Economic Review*, December 12, 1985.

Dr. Mahathir also took the occasion to bring to the attention of his Chinese counterparts the Malaysian anxiety about the other sore point in their bilateral relations—the special treatment given to ethnic Chinese businessmen. The Chinese were said to be sympathetic to the request that all Malaysian citizens be treated equally.

China's modernization policy created more than just enthusiasm within Malaysia. It also brought anxiety. This was articulated by Dr. Mahathir during his visit to Qinghua University. Not only was Malaysia concerned in the short term about competition with China for capital and manufacturing markets, but it also worried about the long-term implications of China's military modernization.

Major Issues

Economics and Trade

Despite having established diplomatic relations with China in 1974, Malaysia still lagged behind other ASEAN countries in the China trade. Singapore, which has no diplomatic ties with Beijing, is one of Asia's largest investors in China. Since 1979, its trade volume with China has passed the billion ringgit mark and is rising. In contrast, Sino-Malaysian trade breached the billion ringgit threshold only in 1984 with an imbalance of M$281.1 in China's favor. By 1986 this trade surplus had increased to M$305.6.[17]

The Malaysian prime minister's official visit to China created the momentum for enhancement of Sino-Malaysian economic relations. Various venues for trade were explored and several letters of intent were signed. It was rather unfortunate that many of the initial explorations and most of the letters of intent—for various reasons—were not followed up. The momentum that was generated seems to have ground to a halt, at least temporarily.

This setback was certainly not due to a lack of mechanisms or instruments necessary to promote trade. There is the Sino-Malay Chamber of Commerce, established immediately after Dr. Mahathir's visit, and there is Pernas. Unfortunately, the chamber, which was supposed to provide the kind of services that JETRO does for Japanese businessmen, failed for various reasons to live up to expectations. Pernas on the other hand appeared unable or unwilling to move beyond mere collection of commission fees. There are many who believe that Pernas could

---

[17]While Malaysia's statistics indicate that the trade balance has always been in China's favor, China's trade statistics indicate otherwise. This is because Malaysian products imported from third countries are recorded by China as imports from Malaysia.

perhaps be more actively engaged, possibly in cooperation with the chamber, to promote Malaysian exports.

Most of the Malaysian businessmen who attempted to venture into the China trade appeared unprepared for the kind of difficulties encountered in China's trading climate. Many would prefer a quick profit. Very few speak Mandarin—which is essential for doing business with China—and even fewer are fully aware of the true situation and conditions in China.

There has been no shortage of Malaysian businessmen visiting China since the relaxation of visiting rules. During the 1984 commodity trade fair in Guangdong, about 400 Malaysians visited China. This figure rose to almost 500 during the autumn fair in 1985. But very few had serious business interests. Of the several letters of intent signed with China, only two actually came to fruition.

To be sure there are constraints and difficulties in trading with China, not least because of the inability of both China and Malaysia to conclude several important agreements on Sino-Malaysian economic relations. For example, negotiations on the proposed trade agreement appear to have reached an impasse on the issue of a licensing clause. The clause stipulates that all imports of Chinese goods into Malaysia require an approved permit (AP). There is also a 0.5 percent commission fee. The Malaysian rationale for this licensing clause is to allow greater control of the China trade, to encourage more direct trade, and to provide more opportunities for Malay participation. China, however, feels that such a provision, not imposed on imports from other countries, is discriminatory.[18]

There is also a lack of agreement on the currency to be used for the settlement of receipts. A shipping agreement was recently initialed but an investment guarantee agreement is still pending.

While official figures are not available, it is generally believed that indirect trade through Chinese middlemen in Hong Kong and Singapore has dropped substantially since the Chinese provision of agency rights to Malaysian businessmen and the institution of an AP for imports from China. Total direct trade between China and Malaysia for 1986 was M$1,149.8 million. Indirect trade reportedly represented about 10 percent of this amount.

China is keen on establishing a Sino-Malaysia Joint Commission that would provide a forum for top officials from both countries to discuss relevant trade matters, economic cooperation, and technical aid.

---

[18]Countries which are members of GATT (which China is not) are excluded from this provision.

However Malaysia feels that in the absence of a trade agreement—which provided the legal framework for joint commissions with other bilateral partners—a joint commission with China would be less than meaningful. Furthermore Malaysia worries that China may treat the commission as a clearinghouse to discuss issues other than economic matters.

It is generally perceived that Malaysia ranks rather low on China's trading list. Indeed China's statistics indicate that Malaysia accounted for only 0.8 percent of China's total global trade and ranked as its twenty-third largest trading partner.

In cognizance of this, perhaps Malaysia needs to reassess its economic relations with China and attempt to take advantage of some of China's predispositions, while ensuring that both Malays and non-Malays equally enjoy the accruing benefits.

Given China's present and likely future (near-term) foreign exchange and balance-of-payment problems, it is quite possible that China will reduce imports of nonproductive items like televisions, refrigerators, air conditioners, and so forth. In this event, an increase in bilateral trade between Malaysia and China could perhaps be better realized through export of Malaysia's primary commodities, rather than consumer-oriented products. Malaysia is advantageously placed to provide China with certain commodities together with their advanced supporting technologies, suitable for China's industrial development program.

Joint-venture projects and participation in tender awards, particularly in China's special economic zones, could provide further potential for increased bilateral trade.

Politics and Security

It has been argued that China's major concern in Southeast Asia is security. But the way in which China chose to respond to this concern enhances the anxiety of the regional states. It helped to nurture mistrust and apprehension of China's intentions and objectives. Within the context of Sino-Malaysian bilateral relations, the bitter experience of the communist insurgency and the implicit participation of the CCP have left an indelible if not irascible mark on Malaysia.

To be sure both Beijing and Kuala Lumpur did not let the CCP-MCP link stop the establishment of official relations between the two governments. But the dichotomy in Beijing's foreign policy did little to ease the Malaysian government's deep-rooted suspicions of China's intentions and objectives regarding Malaysia in particular and the region in general.

This suspicion is further aroused by the rather complex question of the overseas Chinese—an issue of particular sensitivity to Malaysia, where ethnic Chinese constitute almost 38 percent of the population. Although there has been no record of unauthorized visits to China by Malaysians of Chinese origin during the past three years, the Malaysian government remains wary.

Apprehensions about China's long-term intentions in the region are heightened by its conflicting claims in the South China Sea. China's claims to islands, reefs, and shoals are particularly extensive and in certain cases reach into Malaysia's exclusive economic zones. China's use of overwhelming power to assert its sovereignty over the Paracel Island Group in 1974 was a lesson not lost on the governments in the region.

While the Vietnamese invasion of Kampuchea may have given cause for a common enterprise among China, Malaysia, and the rest of the ASEAN member countries, the differences in their perceptions in the Indochina conflict only served to enhance mutual suspicions.

China's punitive war against Vietnam in 1979 was perceived as a willingness to use force as an instrument of foreign policy and did little to ease existing concerns.

Certainly there are other factors that cause apprehension toward China. Because of its sheer size, geographical proximity, and socialist ideology, China is perceived as threatening even if it has neither the intention nor the ability to seem so.

It is an indication of the intensity of distrust toward China that the members of ASEAN gave contradictory responses on the development of Sino-American relations. China's so-called alignment with the United States is welcomed, for it is perceived as a deterrent—in the short term—to any moves by China against ASEAN security interests. Yet U.S. assistance in China's modernization programs, particularly in military modernization, causes alarm because of the long-term implications to regional security.

In view of the above, Malaysia realizes that a pragmatic approach is both pertinent and necessary in defining Sino-Malaysian bilateral relations. Recognizing the need for economic opportunities and in cognizance of the imperatives of security, Sino-Malaysian bilateral relations are thus to be carefully managed and controlled. Such an approach, while not indicative of an abatement of Malaysian distrust of China, signifies a serious attempt to place bilateral relations on a more stable footing.

Conclusion

While evidence of direct material aid from the Chinese Communist Party to the Malayan Communist Party is difficult to find, there is little doubt that the MCP drew heavily from the CCP's revolutionary model and experience. The CCP offered diplomatic and moral support to the MCP and provided assistance in the regular clandestine radio broadcasts beamed from Southern China. This evidence sufficed to convince the Malaysian administration of the threatening nature of the government in Beijing. China thus looms large in the eyes of the Malaysian government as a potential subversive power intent on overthrowing the legally constituted government through insurgency.

The wisdom of history and the exigency of geopolitics would indicate that China will most likely incrementally assert its power and influence over the region. With the success of its modernization program, it is inevitable that China will become a major power to be reckoned with in global and particularly in regional affairs. Malaysia and the rest of Southeast Asia must reconcile themselves to this eventuality.

For the foreseeable future China will continue to compete with the Soviet Union for influence in Southeast Asia. To achieve this goal, China can be expected to play a positive role and to minimize actions that could be seen as attempts to either undermine existing governments or to impose a regional hegemony.

External realities and pragmatism have contributed to a significant shift in the foreign policy directions of both China and Malaysia. The hostilities identified with the Mao era have given way to peaceful coexistence. Both countries are at present concerned with building up their respective economies.

Be that as it may, there is still much wariness when talking about China. At least for the next ten years, China's military posture seems likely to be defensive rather than offensive. However, within the medium term and with continued U.S. military assistance to China consistent with current American strategic alignment, China's military capabilities are expected to be qualitatively and quantitatively improved. Unpredictability is one characteristic of Chinese history. With the emergence of China's new political leadership, their perceptions of national interests may well differ from the present and might even be inimical to the interests of other Southeast Asian countries.

This apprehension assumes greater acuity in light of the perceived economic threat posed by a modernized China. Apart from its ability to attract potential capital resources, China could potentially monopolize the markets that presently provide outlets for manufactured products from Malaysia and other ASEAN countries. China has tremendous resources and an almost infinite ability to subsidize its exports.

Malaysia is a small country. It is perhaps inevitable that it be apprehensive of the goliath that is China. Yet, it would be in Malaysia's interests to treat China more as a potential economic partner than as a major adversary. Malaysia should thus proceed with caution, but proceed positively, to engage in greater economic enterprise with China. There are areas where Malaysia can and cannot compete well with China, given certain comparative advantages. There are other areas in which the economic activities of China and Malaysia can be mutually complementary. The economic interplay between the two countries could provide a basis for the confidence that could serve as a foundation for stronger bilateral relations.

14. China and the Philippines: From Conflict to Cooperation

EDGARDO B. MARANAN

On June 9, 1975, President Ferdinand Marcos of the Philippines and Premier Zhou Enlai of the People's Republic of China (PRC) signed in Beijing the historical joint communiqué establishing formal diplomatic relations between the two countries. The Philippines became the second country of the Association of Southeast Asian Nations (ASEAN), after Malaysia, to recognize the PRC. Both the Philippines and Malaysia had had strong communist insurgency movements that were inspired by the Chinese revolution and openly supported by the Chinese Communist Party (CCP) before the onset of government-to-government relations.

The first paragraph of the joint communiqué contains an ironic reference to the two contracting parties' "desire to promote the traditional friendship between the Filipino and Chinese peoples." The relations between the PRC and the Philippines had been anything but one of "traditional friendship." After the founding of the People's Republic of China in 1949, it became the official policy of successive Philippine governments, from that of President Quirino to that of President Macapagal, to shun and politically "isolate" the huge communist neighbor in the north, while the Philippines maintained legal recognition of "Nationalist China" or the "Republic of China" on Taiwan/Formosa, as represented by the Kuomintang under Chiang Kai-shek.

In 1949, the Philippines was a three-year-old republic, having been "granted" its independence by the erstwhile colonizer United States on July 4, 1946. The conditions for independence were awesome, and in fact have had repercussions on Philippine national life to the present day. Some important conditions were the almost perpetual lease of national territory for the use of U.S. military bases, parity rights for Americans who would exploit the country's natural resources, and the unstated but foregone assumption that the young republic could not pursue a foreign policy direction different from, much less contrary to, the strategic interests of the United States in Asia and in the world.

Even during the normalization of ties with the PRC, there lingered some suspicion that the Philippine decision finally to accept the fact of the legal existence of the PRC (then already occupying the China seat in the United Nations) came only after the United States had made over-

255

tures toward the normalization of relations with the PRC. Thus, in February 1972, a joint communiqué had been signed in Shanghai between President Nixon and Premier Zhou Enlai. While formal diplomatic recognition occurred only on January 1, 1979, as a result of a long, drawn out controversy about U.S. policy toward the two Chinas, the fact that the United States had begun warming to its ideological adversary in Asia seemed to signal that the Philippines could do likewise. This line of reasoning may oversimplify matters somewhat, for a complex interplay of internal and external factors in the political environment had brought about the spectacular shift in the orientation of Philippine foreign policy away from its Cold War predictability. Certainly, the Marcos government and its policymakers would argue that the Philippine feelers to the PRC in the late 1960s and the actualization of ties with the Asian socialist power had been independent of American influence, or interests, and were premised on the imperatives of Philippine national interests. President Marcos maintained that the normalization of relations with socialist countries in general signified ''the end of the Cold War as far as the Philippines were concerned,'' which meant that the ''post-colonial pattern of Philippine foreign relations which relied almost exclusively on relations with the United States was over.''[1] He considered the opening of diplomatic relations with the People's Republic of China as possibly the most significant demonstration of the country's new orientation [under him], and the political leadership's autonomous determination to break down the ''ideological barriers in international relations.''[2]

Still, a political analyst observed that ''the China policy for the Philippines was a function of big power politics on the regional and global levels, and the Philippines [could] only rationally respond in order to optimize its otherwise minimal impact in the determination of the international order and thus insure its national viability.''[3]

The PRC, in recent years, has been expanding its ties with ASEAN, of which the Philippines is a member. The PRC's diplomatic outreach in the region—part of its far-flung Third World diplomacy—has been impelled by what it perceives to be the important role played by South-South cooperation in promoting international stability as well as in enhancing its own economic development plans by opening up new

---

[1]Ferdinand E. Marcos, *Five Years of the New Society* (Manila: Marcos Foundation, 1978), p. 142.
[2]Ibid., p. 143.
[3]Purificacion Valera-Quisumbing, *The China Policy of the Philippines and National Security* (Quezon City: National Defense College of the Philippines, 1975), p. 5.

markets and winning new trading partners. Moreover, the China-Vietnam conflict and the Kampuchean problem have compelled the PRC to seek actively the support of ASEAN in order to restore stability to the region and secure its southern border through a cessation of what it considers to be Vietnamese adventurism abetted by the Soviet Union.

Relations between China and the Philippines are important for both countries. The myths that helped maintain the chill of the cold war have not been completely dispelled. In fact, the myths have merely taken other forms and expressions and produced changed strategies in those countries that see in never-ending social unrest the indefatigable secret hand of international communist conspiracies.

Background

The cold war dictated the basic postulates of early Philippine foreign policy. The operative principle was "anticommunism." The dynamics of the confrontation between postwar capitalism and communism affected Philippine society and politics profoundly, not only in terms of diplomatic alliances, but also in the shaping of a worldview that tended toward complete rejection of the social, political, and economic systems obtaining in the emergent socialist bloc.

There were two basic reasons why the global competition between capitalism and communism impinged deeply upon Philippine reality. First, the island republic became the linchpin of American strategic defense in the Asia-Pacific area, opposite the perceived "monolith" composed of the USSR and China. Second, the Philippines had been, even before the war, in the grip of a Marxist social revolution, fueled by feudal and colonial conditions, and which drew strength and inspiration from the international communist movement.

Early Years of Marxism

The indigenous communist movement in the Philippines began in the decade before the Second World War, with the influx of Marxist ideas and programs spawned by the October Revolution in the Soviet Union. Chinese communism exerted influence only in the late 1940s, then prominently and decisively in the late 1960s. The actual armed phase of the early communist movement in the Philippines took the form of anti-Japanese resistance during the war, within the context of the antifascist United Front.

The vanguard of this movement was the Partido Komunista ng Pilipinas (PKP), or Philippine Communist Party, whose armed force, the HUKBALAHAP (Anti-Japanese People's Army), came to be regarded as a very disciplined guerilla resistance group in the country. Its radical ideology, military discipline, and deep roots among Filipino peasants in the countryside and workers in the cities would explain its effective conduct of the guerrilla war. The code of behavior of the HUKBALAHAP even bore a striking similarity to the doctrine contained in the Chinese People's Liberation Army's *Three Points of Attention* and *Eight Points of Discipline*.

> Clean the houses provided by the people . . . speak in a friendly tone . . . buy and sell things fairly . . . return the things we borrow . . . pay for the things we destroy. . . . Forcing the people to work for the army is forbidden . . . coercion, beating or insulting the people are forbidden . . . rape and robbery are forbidden. . . . These are not the actions of a revolutionary army.[4]

In 1948, the PKP entered into negotiations with the Quirino government on substantive issues such as a full and unconditional amnesty for the rebels, abrogation of the Bell Trade Act and the Military Bases Agreement, and eradication of graft and corruption, among others.[5]

The negotiations broke down. Renewed fighting erupted between government and PKP forces. The name of the PKP army was changed from HUKBALAHAP to HUKBONG MAPAGPALAYA NG BAYAN (HMB), or People's Liberation Army. By 1949, the HMB had expanded its forces throughout twenty-seven provinces nationwide, a big jump from the five central Luzon provinces where it was originally based.[6] The year was significant in mainland China. The CCP was about to achieve the biggest revolutionary success since the October Russian Revolution. The victory of the Chinese Communists in 1949 proved to be an enormous morale boost for the PKP and encouraged it to launch its own offensive for the seizure of state power.

The PKP-HMB was unable to sustain its revolutionary momentum, primarily because it had seriously underestimated the role of the United States, which could not afford a communist victory in the Philippines on the heels of the CCP's takeover in China. Indeed, the Philippines had assumed increased importance to the strategic designs of the United States. So important did the island republic figure in American military reckoning that it was described by General Douglas MacArthur as the first link in the chain of defense stretching along the coast of Asia right up to Alaska.[7] Crushing the HMB meant that Asian communism, spearheaded by the PRC, would be denied its potentially dangerous

---

[4]Luis Taruc, *Born of the People* (New York: International Publishers, 1953), pp. 52–53.
[5]Renato Constantino, *The Continuing Past* (Quezon City: Foundation for Nationalist Studies, 1978), p. 220.
[6]Ibid., p. 225.
[7]Robert C. North, *The Foreign Relations of China* (Stanford, Calif.: Stanford University Press, 1964), p. 86.

southern frontier in the Pacific and, inversely, that the Maginot Line of containment would be strengthened.

Ramon Magsaysay's appointment in 1950 as secretary of national defense signaled the start of the final offensive against the HUK insurgency in the Philippines. With the help of the Central Intelligence Agency (CIA) and the Joint U.S. Military Advisory Group (JUSMAG) in the Philippines,[8] Magsaysay was able to launch military, political, psychological, and economic warfare against the HMB that decimated its ranks and led to the surrender or capture of many of its leading cadres. By 1952, the HMB threat had been effectively defused with the once proud fighting units of the anti-Japanese guerrilla resistance wiped out, broken up, captured, or "reduced into small roving bands, some of which later degenerated into bandit units."[9]

The early Philippine communist movement, from the time it was born in the years before World War II up to its suppression in the 1950s, had always been identified with Soviet communism. From the point of view of the present-day Communist Party of the Philippines (CPP) and its military arm, the New People's Army (NPA), the old PKP-HMB collapsed because of numerous errors, not the least of these being its failure to appreciate and analyze fundamentally the "semi-colonial and semi-feudal" character of Philippine society and thus apply the principles of "protracted people's war," the type that enabled the CCP in 1949 and the Vietnamese National Liberation Front (NLF) in 1975 to seize state power after a long and arduous period of base-building and guerilla fighting in the countryside.[10]

Postwar Alignment with the United States

Even as the armed communist rebellion flared and sputtered, unable to launch a final assault to smash the state apparatus, and long before the formal start of cold war hostilities in the Asia-Pacific region

---

[8]The role of Colonel Edward Lansdale of the CIA in the counterinsurgency campaign of Magsaysay is discussed by Joseph Smith in *Portrait of a Cold Warrior* (New York: G. P. Putnam & Sons, 1976). The participation of other American officials, as well as Filipinos, in the same campaign is discussed by Constantino, *Continuing Past*.

[9]Constantino, *Continuing Past*, p. 225.

[10]The criticism of the PKP-HMB's errors, as well as the theoretical and programmatic framework of the "reestablished" CPP, form the motif of *Philippine Society and Revolution* (Manila: Pulang Tala, 1978), written by Amado Guerrero, CPP founding chairman. In 1974, a revised edition was issued, with a special section on "The Specific Characteristics of Our People's War," premised on the revaluation of the applicability of the Chinese model in Philippine revolutionary strategy.

in 1949,[11] the Philippines had already made clear the pro-West (pro-U.S.) course that its foreign policy was going to take. In his inaugural address after being elected president of the newly independent republic in 1946, Manuel Roxas had declared that the destiny of the Philippines lay "in the glittering wake of America, whose sure advance with mighty prow breaks for smaller craft the waves of fear." Again, in his state-of-the-nation message on January 27, 1947, and in another speech on February 1, 1947, the president officially inaugurated the age of "special relations" with the United States, starting off with an avowed policy of "splendid isolation" toward Asia, and announcing that the "magnetic pole of (Philippine) foreign policy will be the United States."[12]

The fact that the Philippines has never been fully accepted as a member of the nonaligned states—despite efforts of the past Marcos administration to project an image of newfound independence in its external relations—is traceable to the political mindset shaped by the postwar and postcolonial allegiance pledged by the Philippine leadership to the cause of American democracy and the "Free World."

The victory of the communist forces in China in 1949 ended virtually all political, economic, and cultural contacts between the Filipinos and the world's most populous nation. This was the beginning of the period of insulation—an apt term to use, considering the geographic location of the Philippines—that was certainly more telling than mere isolation. Insulation would mean that a country, government, or society continues to resist actively all belief systems and institutions belonging to the "enemy," with whom no economic, political, and cultural relations can be cultivated without doing violence to one's conscience and alliances.

Apart from the expression of support made by the Philippines for the Indonesian anticolonial struggle against the Dutch, the Asian reality never came quite close to being integrated into the consciousness of Philippine policymakers, let alone made part of a general educational and cultural program at large. The experience under the Japanese-sponsored Greater East Asia Co-Prosperity Sphere may have partially accounted for this distance from Asian concerns. But certainly the telling factor was the closeness with the United States, especially after the country was "liberated" from Japanese occupation. Between 1946 and

---

[11]Rogelio A. Fortez, *The China Policy of the Philippines and National Security* (Quezon City: National Defense College of the Philippines, 1975), p. 5.

[12]From *Papers, Addresses and Other Writings of President Manuel Roxas*, vol. 1, quoted by Dr. Usha Mahajani in his "The Development of Philippine Asianism," *Asian Studies*, vol. 3, no. 2 (Aug. 1965): 221.

1949, the Philippines concluded more than twenty agreements with the United States, and a number with other countries, of which China was the only Asian country. The Philippines became preoccupied with postwar rehabilitation and increasingly enmeshed in the one-track anticommunist campaign of the Free World led by the United States.

This was unfortunate. Long before the Philippines put itself in one camp of the ideological bipolarity, an intellectual fervor of "Asianism" had been present in Philippine society. Years before the war, Filipino political leaders were debating ideas such as the creation of a Pan-Asiatic Confederation that could bring together Asian countries in opposition to Western dominance. There was even a Malaya Irredenta proposed by a group of Filipino intellectuals such as Wenceslao Vinzons of the Young Philippines Party. But Asianism was limited to a few articulate groups or individuals. And even among those who had a vision of a unified Asian society, the ambivalence at once became evident with the realization that the Philippines was geographically and ethnically Asian, but its politics, bureaucracy, educational system, religion, and even customs and traditions had been influenced almost irreversibly by hundreds of years of Western colonialism.

Because the Philippines was deemed "part of the Western world," an assumption implicitly accepted by the foreign policymakers of succeeding administrations, it stood by the mightiest Western capitalist power in the latter's campaign, for the next two decades, to confront, contain, and discredit the People's Republic of China.

Directly and indirectly, Chinese and Filipinos were at war with each other in several instances during the last three decades. During the Korean War, the Philippines sent the PEFTOK (Philippine Expeditionary Force to Korea) under the auspices of the United Nations. The Filipinos saw action against both North Koreans and the Chinese People's Volunteers.

During the battle for the offshore islands of Quemoy and Matsu in 1958 between the PRC and the Kuomintang regime on Taiwan, the Philippines was the staging ground for American logistical support given to the forces of Generalissimo Chiang Kai-shek.[13]

In both French and American phases of the Indochina wars, the Philippines was again involved, first as a charter member of the Dulles-designed, post-Dien Bien Phu, anticommunist Southeast Asia Treaty Organization (SEATO), whose declaration was signed in Manila in 1954, and later as a "noncombatant" participant in the American war

---

[13]Michael Bedford, *The Strategic Role of U.S. Deployments in the Pacific and Indian Oceans,* cited in Renato Constantino, "The Deadly Connection," *Malaya,* December 15, 1986, p. 4.

effort through the PHILCAG (Philippine Civic Action Group). All the while, the Philippines continued to be the most strategic home base for U.S. naval, air, and ground forces involved in the war, apart from the bases in Guam, Okinawa, and elsewhere. In both phases of the Indochina War, the PRC was supporting the Vietnamese.

The issue of Taiwan (or Formosa) appears to have elicited the most heated controversy in postwar Philippine-Chinese relations, for two reasons: (1) the de facto alliance among the United States, the Kuomintang, and the Philippine government in opposition to the PRC, and (2) the presence in the Philippines of several hundred thousand Chinese, many of whom were already naturalized citizens, but who were assumed to be sympathizers or members of the Kuomintang Party, and therefore anticommunist.

On June 28, 1950, Premier Zhou Enlai issued a statement condemning the decision announced by the United States to come to the active defense of Taiwan in order to prevent any attempt by the PRC to liberate it. This meant that the Philippines, with its major U.S. bases, would be inexorably involved in any shooting war between the PRC and the U.S.-Kuomintang alliance. The entire decade of the fifties was a critical one for the two Chinas and the Philippines. Taiwan seemed to be on a permanent war footing, with both the Philippine government and the influential Filipino Chinese community expressing their support. A leading personality in the Philippine Chinese business community (who was also chairman of the Philippine-Chinese United Organization in Support of the Anticommunist Movement) stated in 1958 that in the entire Far East, only Nationalist China and the Philippines could be relied upon by the United States and the United Nations to fight the communist menace.[14]

In 1958, Philippine newspapers regaled their readers with stories about the aerial dogfights over the Taiwan Strait between Red MIGs and U.S.-supplied Sabrejets, the spectacular introduction of heat-seeking Sidewinder missiles, and the awesome exchange of artillery shells across the water. The way the conflict was presented by the anticommunist press, the Communists were usurpers of power in the mainland and the Nationalists were about to retake power.

It was also in 1958 that the celebrated nationalist statesman Claro M. Recto declared that the Philippines must reverse its foreign policy course for the sake of national survival, by, among other measures, "entering into relations with any country irrespective of ideologies,

---

[14]Alfonso Z. Sycip, "An Appeal to the People of Free Nations," *Fookien Times Yearbook 1953* (Manila: Fookien Yearbook Publishing Co., 1953), p. 81.

political institutions, or form of government," whenever such ties would prove beneficial to the country.[15]

The era of Macapagal, which had preceded that of Marcos, offered no indication whatsoever that the Philippines was ever going to relax its policy of nonrecognition and confrontation. The president had even banned a Yugoslav basketball team from participating in a Manila international tournament on both technical and moral grounds. In line with traditional Philippine practice—a "linear, unidirectional foreign policy anchored on the principle of total support of and identification with the foreign policy of the United States[16]—Macapagal's government spurned all political and commercial contacts with the socialist bloc. Commenting on the possibility of trade with the PRC, Macapagal had contended that "for those who are attracted by the imagined profits of trade with Communist China, our answer is that there is not a single pound of sugar, copra, coconut oil, iron or lumber for which Communist China would or could pay, or more than what our present customers now pay."[17]

The Road to Normalization

In his book *Five Years of the New Society,* former Philippine president Ferdinand Marcos set forth the reasons why his government had decided to open up relations with the socialist countries, including the PRC.[18]

1. *Independence.* For more than a quarter-century, the Philippines had "fought the wars of other nations and allowed others to fight its wars." The "special relations" with the United States had benefited only the "oligarchic elite," who wanted these relations to continue. Furthermore, excessive dependence on one country had alienated the Philippines from both the Third World developing countries and the socialist world.

2. *National interest.* The search for domestic stability and economic progress was related to the degree of success of the country's bilateral and multilateral arrangements. (The world recession and the oil crisis of the early 1970s had contributed to the Philippine decision to seek adjustments through new and cheaper sources of energy, as well as export markets.)

---

[15]Quoted in Teodoro Valencia, "New Foreign Policy Vindicates Recto, Fiery Nationalist," *Bulletin Today* (Manila), June 14, 1975, p. 6.
[16]Onofre D. Corpuz, "Realities of Philippine Foreign Policy," in *Philippine-American Relations,* Frank H. Golay, ed. (Manila: Solidaridad Publishing House, 1966), p. 55.
[17]Fortez, *China Policy,* p. 42.
[18]Marcos, *Five Years,* pp. 135–39.

3. *Decline of bipolarity*. International relations, Marcos noted, could no longer be conducted within the closed system of ideological rivalry and the cold war system of alliances, and there were new coalitions and political creeds emerging.

4. *Identification with the Third World*. The Third World movement was seeking "the establishment of a new parity in a more equitable world order," where the Philippines could get its "just share of global prosperity."

5. *Crisis in national security*. The Philippines could forestall political and material support for the resurgent local communist movement coming from nations motivated by ideological kinship by means of "diplomatic initiatives to establish friendly relations with these nations on the basis of mutual respect for national sovereignty and territorial integrity, and the principle of noninterference in each other's internal affairs."[19]

Marcos gave the first hint of wanting to alter Philippine foreign policy patterns when he declared, in his first state-of-the-nation address to the Philippine Congress in January 1966, that while the country should maintain its trade with the United States, the primary market, it would have to expand its trade horizons to include other countries, under conditions consistent with Philippine national interest. The stage was set for the end of restrictions and isolation.

From 1966 onward, a succession of events led to rapprochement with both the PRC and the USSR. In 1966, the long-standing ban on travel by Filipinos to the socialist countries was lifted. In 1967, the Philippine House of Representatives authorized an exploratory trade mission to these countries, to look into the possibility of opening both economic and cultural relations. Clearly, the initial thrust of the Philippines' opening was toward Eastern Europe. At least two reasons may account for this. One, socialism in Eastern Europe posed no immediate threat to the Philippines, unlike the Chinese communism (basically Mao Zedong Thought) that was starting to spread its influence among Filipino Marxists, who were becoming very vocal, through street demonstrations, teach-ins, and conferences, in criticizing the Philippine "neocolonial society" and U.S. imperialism. Second, despite continuing conflict and confrontation in flash points around the world during the 1960s, the international ideological environment, in general, was conducive to taking a new shift in foreign policy, where rapprochement with Western communism was concerned. The most important element in this ideological environment, for the Philippines, was the temperament of American foreign policy. Thus, in October 1965, President

---

[19]Ibid., p. 74.

Lyndon Johnson was saying that the United States desired to build "new bridges to Eastern Europe—bridges of ideas, education, culture, trade, technical cooperation, and mutual understanding for peace and prosperity." This was quoted in the Report of the Chairman of the Special Committee to Reexamine Philippine National Policy Toward Communist Countries.

In 1972, Marcos was already talking about the possible grounds for normalizing ties with the PRC. By the end of 1971, the total volume of trade with the PRC had amounted to only about $1.5 million, with the Philippines getting the shorter end of the exchange. Even if this had not been so, the extremely low volume was an acute reminder that the absence of formal relations could hamper the expansion of trade between two countries. (By 1976, a year after normalization, the PRC-RP trade had jumped to some $95 million, with the PRC still enjoying an advantage, as it has up to the present. But the point had been made; pragmatic politics could produce economic results.) In September 1974, Marcos sent his wife Imelda and brother-in-law Benjamin "Kokoy" Romualdez to visit Beijing. It was the first official step toward initiating formal ties with the PRC. At this time, the Philippine government was being influenced by several factors in the international political environment, in addition to experiencing economic difficulties at home. "Special relations" with the United States were getting a bit shaky, with the Americans failing to support the Philippines' proprietary claim over North Borneo, and refusing to accede to the Philippine government's demand for nonreciprocal preferential trade privileges for its exports. At the same time, the United States was launching its own rapprochement with Beijing, while continuing negotiations for an end to the Vietnam conflict.[20]

The following year, Marcos himself went to Beijing and talked with Chinese officials, including Chairman Mao. Out of this series of discussions came the joint communiqué of June 9, 1975, which carried the following main points:[21] (1) Mutual recognition and the establishment of diplomatic relations at the ambassadorial level; (2) adherence to the Five Principles of Peaceful Coexistence, and peaceful settlement of any dispute arising between the two countries; (3) condemnation of foreign aggression and subversion, and opposition to hegemonism and spheres of influence; (4) no dual citizenship; and (5) development of trade and economic relations, and cultural exchanges.

---

[20]Ibid., p. 49.
[21]Valera-Quisumbing, *China Policy,* p. 248.

Since 1975, exchange visits have been made by officials of both countries. Imelda Marcos traveled four more times to the PRC before the downfall of her husband's regime. Chinese officials—Li Xiannian, Zhao Ziyang, Yang Shangkun, Huang Hua, and others, made return visits.

At the end of the first ten-year period, the Chinese ambassador to the Philippines, Chen Sung Lu, made an overall assessment of PRC-RP ties, pointing out that:[22] (1) the total volume of trade between the two countries had increased more than five times since 1975; (2) more than seventy projects of scientific and technological cooperation had yielded favorable results; (3) agreements had been signed regarding civil aviation, trade, and exchanges involving science, technology, and culture; (4) sister city relations had been established between four Chinese and four Philippine cities; and (5) both countries had supported each other's policies and efforts concerning peace and security in Southeast Asia, and in striving toward a new international economic order.

The shift from a stance of nonrecognition, indeed outright hostility, to flourishing exchanges in practically every field of endeavor represents a tremendous leap for the two countries, especially for the Philippines. The Philippines, despite the political comeback of a semblance of liberal democracy, is still staggering on its feet toward the beginning of national recovery. Trade, from the point of view of Third World countries, can help the Philippines go beyond the limbo of underdevelopment. But trade is just as important to China, since it can speed up the modernizing country's socialist construction, promote South-South cooperation, and establish a new economic international order.[23]

The PRC and the Second Phase of the Philippine Communist Movement

An important issue in the development of relations between China and the Philippines has been the Communist-led, homegrown insurgency in the Philippines, considered by some as the only remaining revolutionary movement in Asia with a fair chance of seizing state power from the established government within the next decade.[24] This

---

[22]Chen Sung Lu, "A Decade in Retrospect," in *Fokien Times Yearbook 1985–1986*, Betty Go-Belmonte, ed. (Manila: Fookien Times Yearbook Publishing Co., 1986), p. 112.

[23]Chen Muhua (state councilor and minister of Foreign Economic Relations and Trade), "Developing Trade with the Third World," in *Open Policy at Work*, Beijing Review Special Features Series no. 10, 1985, p. 58.

[24]Armando Malay, Jr., "The Influence of Mao Zedong Thought on the Communist Party of the Philippines-Marxist-Leninist," in *China and Southeast Asia: Contemporary Politics and Economics* (Manila: De La Salle University Press, 1984), p. 42.

underground resistance movement, described as "Maoist" by the Philippine military establishment, is led by the National Democratic Front (NDF), whose leading organization is the Communist Party of the Philippines (CPP).

On December 26, 1968, a group of young university intellectuals and some former members of the HMB established a new Communist Party of the Philippines, "under the guidance of Marxism-Leninism Mao Zedong Thought." In China, the Great Proletarian Cultural Revolution (GPCR) was then two years old. In the Philippines, echoes of the GPCR were being heard in the youth movement, which professed deep sympathy and enthusiasm both for the reestablished CPP and the revolutionary philosophy of Chairman Mao.[25]

The "reestablishment"—which involved a thorough process of "rectification and rebuilding of the party"—was announced in the maiden issue of *Ang Bayan* (The People), the official party organ. From 1968 to 1974, *Ang Bayan* would carry regular "fraternal messages" from the CCP, particularly during the CPP's anniversary, as well as the CPP's own revolutionary greetings to the CCP on historic occasions. Radio Beijing's broadcasts contained regular news and features about the Philippine revolution, particularly battlefield reports on the victories of the New People's Army. On May 30, 1969, after the border clash between the PRC and Russian field units in Chenpao, the CPP officially accused the Soviet Union of "revisionist social-imperialism," in addition to the charge of "big-nation chauvinism" aired against the Soviets in 1968 after the invasion of Czechoslovakia.[26] *Ang Bayan* took up this criticism of the Soviet Union, even as it trained its polemics against "U.S. imperialism" and the "reactionary fascist regime of Marcos." However, this should not be interpreted as simply surrendering to the Maoist line, or as a proof of the CPP's servility to the CCP. It was inevitable that the CPP would, at this time, take a critical stand against the Soviet Union because it was in the process of "rectifying" the errors of the old pro-Moscow PKP. Relations between Moscow and the old PKP—what was left of it after the Magsaysay era and the formation of the pro-China CPP—were believed to have continued despite the "marginalization" of the pro-Moscow communists.

---

[25]The first and biggest of the youth organizations, the Kabataang Makabayan (KM), or Patriotic Youth, would later be outlawed by the Marcos government and charged with being a "front organization" for the CPP.

[26]James Chieh Hsiung, *Law and Policy in China's Foreign Relations: A Study of Attitudes and Practice* (New York: Columbia University Press, 1972), pp. 68–69.

In July 1972, a reconnaissance plane belonging to a private logging company in the northern Philippines spotted an ocean-going vessel anchored off an isolated stretch of rugged coastline in the eastern Luzon province of Isabela. Alerted, government armed forces converged on the area and discovered that the vessel, the *Karagatan*, had been unloading arms and ammunition, purportedly for the New People's Army. The crates in the shipment were reported to have Chinese markings. These weapons were later displayed during the celebrated *Karagatan* trials.

Another ocean-going vessel, the *Dona Andrea*, later alleged by the military to have sunk midway between the Philippines and China in early 1974, reportedly resumed the aborted mission of the *Karagatan*. The Philippine government failed to arrest the crew, but included their names nevertheless in the twin *Karagatan-Andrea* case. Almost 100 respondents were charged with rebellion or conspiracy to commit an act of rebellion. No prosecution was secured by the military, and all the respondents have been released, or have escaped, from detention. The *Karagatan-Andrea* episode was the last attempt at arms smuggling reported by Philippine military intelligence that implicated the PRC.

In the aftermath of the establishment of diplomatic relations between the PRC and the Philippines in 1975, the complexion of relations between the CCP and the CPP seems to have changed. Since 1975, Radio Beijing has not carried the usual battlefield reports, congratulatory messages, fraternal greetings from the CPP-NPA and its official publication. Most of the news stories and features aired on the radio and beamed to the Philippines were about development efforts of the Marcos government, such as the rice production program, Ambassador Kokoy Romualdez's experimental commune-type farm, and similar items from the official media, such as the Philippine News Agency (PNA).

China for a long time was regarded as the vanguard of the world revolutionary movement, and the leading "proletarian internationalist." But this was before rapprochement with the leading capitalist power, the United States. It has been de-emphasizing ideology as a guiding principle of international relations and has consistently stressed peaceful coexistence in the pursuit of South-South relations. Thus, it is not unexpected that this Asian power would welcome the establishment of ties with a government that was much criticized elsewhere for the corruption of its leaders and unchecked violations of human rights. Practically nothing is known about the Chinese leadership's internal assessment of the Marcos type of administration and of the "New Society" as a whole.

There was a curious anomaly to these developments. The PRC was establishing official ties with a government whose repressive policies had encouraged the growth of Asia's most significant communist insurgency. The Philippine guerillas were patterned in many ways after the Chinese People's Liberation Army. The letter and spirit of the Five Principles of Peaceful Coexistence could, of course, justify the course that the PRC had decided to take as far as the Philippines was concerned, for after all, "the affairs of any country should be governed by its own people," and "the developing countries have the right to independently choose which social and economic systems they will have."[27]

The difficulty, undoubtedly, was greater on the part of the CPP. As early as 1971, the party recognized that it would not be too long before diplomatic relations would be established between the PRC and the Marcos government. When that happened, material assistance would not likely be forthcoming from the Chinese.[28] *Ang Bayan* commented on this matter in its issue of August 1, 1971:

> The absence of war between a socialist country and a non-socialist country does not require the proletariat and people in the latter country to stop from making revolution. In the Philippines, the people's democratic revolution will continue to be waged even if diplomatic relations between the Chinese government and the Philippine reactionary government are established.

At present, the National Democratic Front, whose leading and most influential member is the CPP-NPA, is waging armed struggle against the Philippine government, although armed hostilities were temporarily halted by a sixty-day cease-fire which lasted from December 10, 1986 until February 7, 1987. The Philippine insurgency is still the most relatively successful in the region. Despite the end of substantial material support—and moral encouragement—from the PRC, it has managed to preserve a reputation for self-reliance, resiliency, and expansion capabilities. What worries the present Philippine administration is the possibility that the communists could turn to sources of logistics, funds, and political support other than the PRC.

This does not mean that the NDF-CPP-NPA has written off China as a source of material assistance. In the wake of recent announcements by the Aquino and the American governments that "total war" shall be unleashed against the communist movement primarily through improved weaponry in the hands of the AFP, the party has declared that it, too, shall actively solicit support from socialist countries and "frater-

---

[27]Zheng Weishi, "Independence Is the Basic Canon," in *China and the World*, Beijing Review Foreign Affairs Series no. 7, 1986, p. 15.
[28]Ibid.

nal parties." The fact that a number of "traditionalist" or "Maoist" elements remain in the Chinese Communist Party may prove to be a boon for the Philippine communist movement in the more critical days ahead.

The Aquino government inherited not only a financially strapped system but also the challenge of a full-blown communist revolution. Jose Ma. Sison, allegedly the founding chairman of the "re-established" CPP, commented during a lecture series at the University of the Philippines in May 1986, and in recent speeches delivered during an international speaking tour, that the NDF-CPP has more than even chances of wresting political power within the next five to ten years even assuming direct American intervention, Vietnam-style. The projection may sound too optimistic, but the potential of the Philippine Left can no longer be ignored. Should the NDF come close to achieving stalemate and even approach the offensive phase, an interesting issue will present itself. How would the PRC react? By that time, China may be near its modernization goal of quadrupling income. It may then be less interested in urging or even propelling a nearby "war of national liberation" to victory, than in continuing to emphasize modernization. There is no way to gauge the likely Chinese ideological inclination by the 1990s, although the words of Deng Xiaoping may provide some guidance about future Chinese views.

> Conditions vary greatly from people to people, and the class relations and the alignment of class forces in one country are vastly different from those in another. . . . The Chinese revolution was carried out not by adopting the model of the Russian October Revolution but by proceeding from the realities of China, by using the rural areas to encircle the cities and seize power with armed force. . . . The correctness of the domestic principles and line of a Party in a given country should be judged by the people of that country.[29]

Conclusion

The relations between the PRC and the Philippines have gone through the stages of hostility and harmony: isolation, normalization, and regional cooperation. At the moment, the Philippine government does not have the same fears that past administrations experienced, as far as the Chinese role in the Philippine communist movement is concerned.

---

[29]Deng Xiaoping, "An Important Principle for Handling Relations Between Fraternal Parties," in *Selected Works (1975–1982)* (Beijing: Foreign Languages Press, 1984).

The normalization of relations between the PRC and the Philippines has been proceeding smoothly. No matter whether the initiation of ties with the PRC was a genuinely independent act of the Philippine government under Marcos or was deeply influenced by the strategic and tactical shifts in American foreign policy which, critics argue, has historically tended to drag along in its wake Philippine foreign policy, the fact remains that political realism has finally appeared in the domain of Philippine diplomacy.

Since the signing of the joint communiqué in 1975, the PRC and the Philippines have concluded numerous economic, trade, scientific and technological agreements, and have conducted joint venture projects as well as cultural exchange programs. Despite liberal arrangements, the balance of trade has been consistently in China's favor. When Vice-President Laurel visited the PRC in June of 1986—three months after the February Revolution that swept the Aquino government into power—the Chinese government made a commitment to help reduce the imbalance through increased imports of Philippine products.[30] This will no doubt prove beneficial to the Philippines, long plagued by overdependence on a single special market (the United States) through a few agricultural cash crops (such as sugar) which could at any time fall victim to the vagaries of that traditional market. Instructive is the recent U.S. decision to cut down by 40 percent the import quota for Philippine sugar in favor of American manufacturers of sweeteners.

China and the Philippines face similar challenges common to countries of the developing world. But the two are tremendously disparate in economic resources, in technological level of development, in social and material infrastructure, in international political clout, and even in political stability.

The PRC, precisely, has arrived at its level of spiritual and material civilization by means of a social and political revolution. Despite the continuing controversy between economic reformers and old-school revolutionaries, the PRC's modernization program seems to have considerable momentum.

On the other hand, the Philippines has only begun—under the leadership of President Corazon Aquino—to raise itself up from the most disastrous twenty-year period in its history, a period dominated by crony capitalism and corruption, to the extent that during the last two years of the Marcos rule, national economic growth plunged to negative 5 percent, the lowest in ASEAN. This dangerous contraction has only recently been checked but then only so slightly, with a fourth-quarter

---

[30]*Beijing Review*, no. 26, June 30, 1986, pp. 8–9.

gain in 1986 of 0.13 percent. In short, while China is dramatically modernizing, the Philippines is enthusiastically trying to recover. Light-years could mark the distance between "modernization" and "economic recovery."

Both Maoist and non-Maoist can agree that, given the economic backwardness of a country plagued by the remnants of feudalism and warlordism, a huge foreign debt, and a predominantly agrarian economic base, the proper route for the Philippines to take ought to be "revolution, construction, modernization." Of course they can disagree on methods. Not everybody wants to go through a bloody civil war, as the Chinese did. At any rate, there is no gainsaying the fact that countries like the Philippines can learn from China with respect to land reform, industrialization, diversification of products and markets, and dealing with foreign investments and joint venture projects with outside capital.

As the optimistically named Pacific Century nears, with the countries around the Pacific Lake drawing closer together in a commonality of interests centered on the ideal of all-around economic development, cessation of conflicts in the region, and the absence of the nuclear threat (being aptly summed up in the zone of peace, freedom, and neutrality, or ZOPFAN), the People's Republic of China and the Philippines are likely to find an increasing mutuality of interests and a complementarity of objectives.

But this will come to pass only if (1) the old-fashioned fear of communism as a godless, anticapital ideology disappears, and if (2) the PRC can maintain its avowed policy of building itself up into an economic power but not at the expense of its partners. A veteran Filipino China analyst interprets Chinese policy in the most positive light:

> Precisely because the Chinese leaders perceive that most developing countries are not free from economic bondage from the capitalist and hegemonist powers of the world, they have included a new element in their foreign policy which is the pursuit of mutual economic cooperation among developing countries, commonly known as the encouragement of South-South cooperation. Such cooperation, in the eyes of the Chinese, is of great strategic significance as it helps to change the existing unequal relations in the international order.[31]

At this point, it would be foolhardy to conclude that the Philippines' multifarious problems can be solved by the simple expedient of

---

[31]Benito C. Lim, "China's Foreign Policy and ASEAN," in *China and Southeast Asia: Contemporary Politics & Economics* (Manila: De La Salle University Press, 1984), p. 27.

relying on expanded contacts (and contracts) with its neighbors, such as the PRC. The economic dimension of the national crisis goes beyond trade imbalances. Externally, it means having to come up with a level of productivity that can help pay for the enormous foreign debt ($26.5 billion) incurred by the Marcos government, as well as having the debt service rescheduled, and possibly finding new sources of soft loans. Internally, it means having to face squarely the age-old problem of the landlessness of millions of peasants—the original cause of the Philippine insurgency, which bears a striking similarity to the characteristics of the agrarian unrest and social revolution in pre-1949 China.

Relations between the PRC and the Philippines are, on the whole, assured smooth sailing given the premises of China's policy of economic cooperation with developing (South) countries, and the Philippines' urgent need for economic recovery. As Deng Xiaoping has put it, relations between the countries have been, so far, almost "problem-free."

15. A New Phase in Singapore's Relations with China

CHIN KIN WAH

In its twenty-two years of existence as an independent state, Singapore has had relations with the People's Republic of China that can be likened to two streams or flows, one overlaying the other. The lower layer of economic/commercial relations has been comparatively steady and consistent while the upper layer of political relations has registered greater volatility although it, too, in recent years, has become more settled and mature without being officially "normalized."

Singapore's commercial relations with China have a long history that goes back before the establishment of the PRC. A branch of the Bank of China has operated in Singapore since 1936. It survived the transition of political orders in both countries and, in the absence of official diplomatic representation in Singapore, served as a semiofficial representative of Beijing. Even while Singapore was a quasi colony, David Marshall (the island's first locally elected chief minister) paid a visit to China between August and October 1956. He was joined by a trade delegation made up of Singapore Chinese businessmen. Although by then he had resigned from high office, he was accorded official treatment throughout the trip, which marked the first major contact with the PRC.

While Sino-Singaporean commercial and trading relations were on the whole reasonably pragmatic (despite lapses during the Cultural Revolution and the prosecution in the late 1960s of the Bank of China in Singapore for its failure to observe local banking regulations), the same could not be said for the political relationship, which was punctuated by certain vicissitudes and "abnormalities." In the early years of Singapore's independence, when the political leadership grappled with a local Beijing-inspired communist movement, the challenge of left-wing politics, and Chinese chauvinism, the PRC withheld diplomatic recognition of the island republic, often labeling its government the "Lee Kuan Yew clique." With the onset of the Cultural Revolution, Singapore found itself the target of Maoist polemics and attempts at promoting the Cultural Revolution abroad. However with the petering out of that revolution and the advent of "ping-pong" diplomacy and Sino-American rapprochement, the context for an improvement of Sino-Singaporean relations was set. Following the normalization of Malaysia's relations with China, Singapore's foreign minister, S. Rajaratnam, led the first official visit to China in March 1975 to clear up any existing misunderstandings between the two countries. The way was cleared for Singapore's Prime Minister Lee Kuan Yew to undertake his first visit to China in May 1976. In subsequent years, the level, variety, and extent of contacts between the two sides have been steadily built up.

Since 1985, observers of Singapore's relations with China could hardly have missed noticing the steady increase in the number and level of contacts between the two countries. Barely a week passes without some report of a visiting Chinese mission (from ministers and officials to cooks and hairdressers) to Singapore. The Chinese Trade Mission in Singapore estimates that the number of official missions from China to Singapore has averaged about 400 a year over the past three years. The flow in the opposite direction is equally impressive and varied. Yet this improvement has taken place in a situation where formal diplomatic relations are nonexistent.

The intensification of these interactions is attributable as much to China's "open-door" policy, designed to facilitate its economic modernization, as it is to Singapore's economic recession, which hit a nadir in 1985 and has led Singapore on a relentless search for overseas economic and commercial opportunities. Without doubt, new ground is being broken in Singapore's relations with China. One local Singapore journal has even featured the euphoric headline, "End of the Rainbow Shifts to the Middle Kingdom."[1]

Precisely because of such expectations, it has become necessary to view these developments in the perspective they deserve. What is the nature of the so-called new ground that is being broken? What sort of foundations are being laid? What is being built up and with what degree of durability? Above all, what kind of political implications in regional and Singaporean terms may be drawn from these growing linkages? What follows is an attempt to address some of these questions.

Foreign Policy Context

Singapore's relations with China are circumscribed by a number of factors, the most obvious of which is the great disparity in their respective sizes. Sino-Singaporean relations are those between a (largely agrarian) regional big power and an industrializing city-state, geographically the smallest in ASEAN. Although Singapore does not share the fate, and hence the vulnerabilities, of the smaller states contiguous to

---

[1]*Singapore Business*, September 1985, p. 11.

China, it is nevertheless captive to the great power environment in the Asian-Pacific region, which is invariably affected by any redefinition of China's interests or any exertion of its influence. Indeed the changes in the international environment of the early 1970s, marked by the launching of China's "ping-pong diplomacy" and rapprochement with the United States, followed in the late seventies by China's active courting of the ASEAN states as the Sino-Vietnamese conflict unfolded, had been the milestones for Singapore's own adjustment to a more normal relationship with China. Also, the abatement of the Cultural Revolution and China's resolve to embark on a modernization drive since 1979 created a new basis for a more concrete relationship with China.

Such disparity in their sizes also feeds into their perceptions of each other and their respective perceptions of regional issues, of which the Cambodia problem remains the most prominent. The contrasting perspectives were graphically depicted by Singapore's prime minister, Lee Kuan Yew, who commented that China and Singapore were looking at the same world through different lenses: a wide-angle fisheye lens for China, a zoom lens for Singapore. Hence, for China, any settlement of the conflict with Vietnam (over Cambodia), however important in itself, was only a partial removal of the overall Soviet threat. For Singapore, as with the rest of ASEAN, the occupation of Cambodia by Vietnam was the major concern. If the conflict could be resolved politically, a major threat to regional peace would be removed, and an involvement in great power conflict avoided, at least in Southeast Asia.[2]

The size factor is just as important when we consider the new linkages that are being cultivated between Singapore and China. The invocation of such images as "dynamo," "interface," and "gateway" in public discussions of Singapore's contribution to China's modernization drive (whether it relates to economic development, industrial expansion, investment, or the tourist industry) reflects both the underlying constraint on Singapore's part and its attempt nevertheless to exploit its smallness. Lee Kuan Yew himself has acknowledged that to move a nation of China's size, every project that Singapore undertook would have to be multiplied five hundred times.[3] It may be said, of course, that Singapore expects to help itself in the very process of helping China—there is at least the expectation that the spin-off for Singapore's own economy would be proportionately higher.

---

[2]Text of interview with Lee Kuan Yew by David Bonavia of *The Far Eastern Economic Review* (hereafter *FEER*), in Beijing, November 13, 1980, Singapore government press release, Ministry of Culture, No. 02–1–80–11–20, p. 3.

[3]*Business Times* (Singapore), September 26, 1985.

While the size factor does influence perceptions, there is a unique feature in Singapore's demographic structure that complicates not only Singapore's perceptions of China but also others' perceptions of Singapore. Small as Singapore's population may be, over three-quarters of it is ethnic Chinese (making the republic the only Chinese-majority state in ASEAN) and nearly 40 percent of that community have ancestral ties that are traceable to just one province in China. Singapore is both stronger yet more vulnerable as a result of this racial arithmetic. Lee Kuan Yew has often enough reminded Chinese Singaporeans that they are part of an ancient civilization with an unbroken history of over 5,000 years. He sees this as "a deep and strong psychic force, one that gives confidence to a people to face up to and overcome great changes and challenges."[4] For these and other reasons Singapore has exhorted its Chinese population to speak Mandarin and inculcated Confucianist ethics as a part of moral education. In the case of the former campaign, some dividends are being reaped by Singapore's entry into China's modernization program. These elements of cultural and psychological ballast must nevertheless be kept in balance lest they run over into "Chinese chauvinism"—a term synonymous with the spread of pro-China sentiments among the local ethnic Chinese. Although in recent years the Singapore government has become more confident about the emergence of a Singaporean identity among the local Chinese, it remains vulnerable to being perceived in a negative light by others in Singapore's immediate regional environment. As Lee himself puts it, "We have our own separate identity as Singaporeans. But there is always that lurking doubt, suspicion, uncertainty in the minds of ASEAN members that because Singapore is 75 percent ethnic Chinese, therefore Singapore will be easily manipulated by China, and will side with China."[5] In this regard, the tendency on China's part from time to time to play up kith-and-kin ties with the overseas Chinese, whether for remittances, investments, commercial gain, or even psychological "patronage" is viewed with unease in Singapore.

The decision, therefore, not to establish diplomatic relations with China until Indonesia does so is an acknowledgement of and concession to neighborly sensitivity.[6] It is also a decision that suits Singapore's

---

[4]*Straits Times* (Singapore), September 22, 1984.
[5]Text of interview with Lee Kuan Yew by Amir Daud and Zulkifly Lubis in the Prime Minister's Office, *Tempo* (Singapore), June 27, 1980, p. 13.
[6]Singapore recognizes the PRC government as the legitimate representative of China in the United Nations and had even voted for the Albanian resolution in 1971 on the seating of China in the United Nations.

national interest. Singapore has repeatedly stood by its own terms on this issue as a means of demonstrating both to its ASEAN neighbors and to China that the latter could not go over the head of the Singapore government to the local Chinese community to get them to pressure the government to reverse its position. This is seen as a point worth making.

For Singapore, the need to be in tune with the sensitivities of its neighbors (a need that remains as important as ever) has to be balanced by the prime consideration that Singapore's foreign policy must be made and seen to be made in Singapore. Therefore, it is possible that Singapore may not immediately establish diplomatic relations with China even after Indonesia has done so, if the costs of the status quo continue to be eminently bearable.

Some commentators have pointed to, among other things, a domestic security consideration behind Singapore's reluctance to countenance a Chinese embassy on its soil in view of the past connections between the essentially Chinese-led Malayan Communist Party (MCP) and local political agitation.[7] It may be said in counterpoint that the China trade mission in Singapore established since 1981 is a *de facto* Chinese embassy and that the loyalty of the local Chinese community is more dependable than in the past. Yet the so-called security argument does reflect historical baggage that does count in this discussion of the context of Singapore's relations with China.

One unresolved problem "left over by history" (as the Chinese are wont to say) is China's unrelinquished party-to-party support for affiliated communist movements in the region. The issue was sufficiently thorny to result in aborting the planned banquet speeches during Lee Kuan Yew's second visit to China in November 1980. The advance copy of Lee's speech was known to have touched on this matter, which the Chinese considered sensitive. As Lee himself revealed, "They told us that if I made my speech . . . their people would be upset and Premier Zhao (Ziyang) would have to reply to it publicly. They said it might lead to unnecessary strain in our relationship."[8] Rather than leave out a portion of his speech, Lee chose to have no speech at all. But he did make his points at the highest levels in discussions with all three Chinese leaders, that is, the then chairman Hua Guofeng, Deng Xiaoping (then vice chairman), and Premier Zhao.

---

[7]See, e.g., Lee Lai To, "Singapore and East Asia," in Peter S. J. Chen, ed., *Singapore: Development Policies and Trends* (Singapore: Oxford University Press, 1983), p. 350.

[8]Text of interview with Lee Kuan Yew by Singapore journalists, in Xiamen, November 23, 1980, Singapore government press release, Ministry of Culture, No. 02-1-80-11-25, p. 14.

The point of the Chinese Communist Party's right to party-to-party relations with insurgent groups was raised by Lee to illustrate how any ASEAN position toward Vietnam and the Soviet Union was bedeviled by the suspicion that ASEAN might be sacrificing its own longer-term interests "by helping the restoration of Chinese influence through a Khmer Rouge regime in (Cambodia), besides weakening Vietnam as another Southeast Asian counterweight to any Chinese push southwards."[9]

Although Singapore does not have an insurgency problem, the internal communist threat in Malaysia is a threat to Singapore since the MCP makes no tactical or political distinction between the two countries. More importantly the communist movements present political challenges to the local regimes. In this respect the issue of the PRC's party-to-party support for these movements is joined (albeit somewhat tenuously) to Singapore's cautious approach toward the establishment of diplomatic relations with China. This cautiousness in a sense puts a question mark over China's long-term intent as much as the communist movements pose a question mark over the political legitimacy of the local regimes.

If it is possible at all to speak of a Singaporean perception of the threat from China, such perception relates to the long-term rather than the immediate future. There is little to suggest that the views expressed by Lee back in 1980 on the question of the China threat have changed substantially. Lee saw that if China developed industrially in twenty to thirty years, it might possess the potential to become a major threat to Southeast Asia; even then, he doubted whether China would have the power to be the main threat. (China, as Lee has observed elsewhere, is simply not in the same league as the Soviet Union.) For the short term, having been devastated by twelve years of the Cultural Revolution, China would not have the industrial and military capacity to threaten Southeast Asia other than by aiding guerrilla insurgencies.[10]

It may be asked whether China's modernization program has affected the shaping of Singapore's threat perceptions. Here, the views of Singapore's prime minister suggest two possibilities. With respect to military modernization, if American weapons technology does enable China to build up an amphibious capacity, it would complicate the regional balance in the long run. There is the further apprehension that

---

[9]Interview with Lee Kuan Yew by David Bonavia, p. 6.
[10]Interview with Lee Kuan Yew by Derek Davies of FEER, September 22, 1980, Singapore government press release, Ministry of Culture, unnumbered, p. 7.

the transfer of American arms technology may go toward providing an additional role for the PRC, that is, the containment of the Soviet threat in Southeast Asia.[11] On the other hand, the economic dimension of China's modernization may moderate the threat perception because a "more prosperous China means a better trading partner and a more peaceful China."[12] This assumes that China would really enter the mainstream of the global economy instead of opting for greater economic nationalism. It is indeed with such hopes (besides expectations of pure economic gain) that the new phase in Singapore's relations with China is being defined.[13]

The discussion so far has drawn heavily upon the comments of Lee Kuan Yew, who is principally responsible for setting the tone of Singapore's relations with China. Besides the prime minister, two others who have contributed major inputs into foreign policy for a sustained period are S. Rajaratnam and Goh Keng Swee. The former (who remains the senior minister in the prime minister's office) marked the normalization of relations with China by leading, in his capacity as foreign minister, the first official Singapore delegation in the postindependence period to China in March 1975 shortly after Malaysia had established its embassy in Beijing. Although Dr. Goh has retired from active politics, he remains an important influence in Singapore's economic relations with China, besides being retained by the PRC government as an adviser on the development of the new economic zones and tourism. While a second generation is being groomed for political leadership in Singapore, Lee Kuan Yew remains the paramount influence in the charting of Singapore's foreign policy.

Developing Pragmatic Linkages

Despite the absence of formal diplomatic ties, Singapore has been able to develop and, in recent years, expand its economic and other linkages with China. This has in some ways made the absence of such diplomatic ties bearable to both sides. But more than that, as one study of China's changing relations with Southeast Asia has shown, the dura-

---

[11]Text of interview with Lee Kuan Yew by Derek Davies and Susumu Awanohara of *FEER*, Singapore, October 16, 1981, Singapore government press release, Ministry of Culture, No. 02-1-81-10-22, p. 8. The concern is that the United States on its own may not match the increasing Soviet influence in Southeast Asia and must therefore bring China into the balance.

[12]Transcript of interview with Lee Kuan Yew by Louis Kraar of *Fortune* magazine in Singapore, November 23, 1984, Prime Minister's office, December 9, 1984, p. 4.

[13]John Wong, *The Political Economy of China's Changing Relations with Southeast Asia* (London: Macmillan, 1984), pp. 100–101.

bility of China's trade with Singapore is ''reflected not only in its ability to survive political intervention in the form of trade bans . . . but also in its potential to continue expanding even under adverse conditions, as during the Cultural Revolution.''[14] Other indicators of social and commercial interactions (such as the number of telex and telephone calls, telegram messages, and the number of mail items) support the impression of a general rise in these flows between the PRC and Singapore, especially since the mid-seventies.

Prior to 1981, the Bank of China in Singapore had acted as a quasi-official representative of Beijing, facilitating commercial, trade, and other contacts between the two countries. Short of issuing visas, its nonbanking services extended to acting as a channel for Chinese nationals seeking to locate relatives in Singapore and vice versa. On the Singapore side the partly government-owned trading corporation Intraco Ltd. initially coordinated and supervised Singapore's trade with China. Later it involved itself more actively in trade promotion and more recently in investments in China. There are over 400 companies in Singapore holding agencies or dealing in Chinese goods. About 80 percent of these companies are members of the Singapore Chinese Merchandise Importers and Exporters Association, formed in 1970 to cater to the interests of companies trading with China.

The institutionalization of commercial linkages was furthered by a trade agreement signed in Beijing between Singapore's finance minister, the late Hon Sui Sen, and the then Senior Vice Premier Deng Xiaoping, in December 1979. The pact provided a broad framework for increased trade and economic cooperation and was followed by an agreement in June 1980 that paved the way for the establishment of permanent trade missions in each other's capitals the following year. The Singapore mission subsequently opened a branch in Shanghai in May 1986.

Besides handling trade matters, the missions also process visa applications. Before that, the nearest offices for Singaporeans to apply for a visa to visit China were the Chinese Embassy in Kuala Lumpur and the China Travel Service in Hong Kong. Although the PRC's mission in Singapore is headed by a senior official from the Ministry of Foreign Economic Relations and Trade, it is known to be staffed also by Foreign Ministry personnel. Indeed, Hon Sui Sen had described the 1979 agreement as ''an establishment of some formal relations and obviously the ultimate situation will be diplomatic relations.''[15] For his part,

---

[14]These data are presented and interpreted in Lee Lai To, ''Singapore and East Asia,'' pp. 351–52. These data cover the period 1967 to 1979.
[15]*Straits Times*, January 6, 1980.

S. Rajaratnam admits that Singapore has "all the benefits of diplomatic relations except for the official presence of an embassy or an ambassador."[16]

The nonrealization of that "ultimate situation" has in no way inhibited contacts at the highest political level between the two sides. To date, Singapore's prime minister has led three official missions to China (1976, 1981, and 1985), while PRC leaders who have visited Singapore include Deng Xiaoping (1978), Zhao Ziyang (1981), and Foreign Minister Wu Xueqian (1985). Within a year of the signing of the trade agreement, at least twelve Chinese trade and study missions (not including those invited by the private sector) had visited Singapore.[17]

A measure of the pragmatism reflected in the evolving Singapore-China relations can be gauged from Singapore's ability to keep the channels open to Taiwan. S. Rajaratnam freely admits to pressures that had previously been exerted upon Singapore by the United States and Taiwan to "join with them to exclude China." Singapore, which was neither anti- nor pro-Taiwan, had to devise its own policy: "We decided to have good relations discreetly with the Taiwanese and with the People's Republic of China, without antagonizing either. Today, our troops are being trained in Taiwan, but we maintain good relations with the People's Republic of China."[18]

Indeed these relations are borne out, among other indicators, by the steady growth in the volume of trade between Singapore and Taiwan, which kept pace with the volume of Singapore-PRC trade until around 1980 when the later began to rise far more sharply (see Table 1). Nevertheless, the volume of Singapore-Taiwan trade has risen steadily from 1975 to 1985 while Singapore's domestic exports to Taiwan (see Table 2) have been consistently much higher than those to the PRC over the same period. Furthermore, Singapore plays a role in the indirect trade between China and Taiwan. In 1984, Singapore was Taiwan's fourth largest buyer. In March of that year, Singapore placed orders totalling S$128 million—an increase of 184 percent compared with the same period in 1983. Most of the orders, with 40.6 percent in textiles and 27.3 percent nonferrous metals, were destined for transshipment to China.[19]

The prime minister of Singapore is, according to a journalist from *Asahi Shimbun*, the only national leader with access to top leaders on

---

[16]Chan Heng Chee and Obaid ul Haq, eds., *The Prophetic and the Political: Selected Speeches and Writings of S. Rajaratnam* (Singapore: Graham Brash; New York: St. Martin's Press, 1987), p. 489.

[17]*Business Times,* February 10, 1981.

[18]Chan and Haq, *The Prophetic and the Political,* p. 488.

[19]*Straits Times* and *Business Times,* April 24, 1985.

Table 1

Singapore: Trade with PRC and Taiwan
(in million S$)

Year	Exports		Imports		Totals		Deficits	
	PRC	Taiwan	PRC	Taiwan	PRC	Taiwan	PRC	Taiwan
1965	22.4	11.5	224.5	33.8	246.9	45.3	202.1	22.2
1975	98.5	131.1	682.0	383.6	780.5	514.7	583.5	252.5
1976	95.4	166.7	659.0	536.9	754.4	703.6	563.6	370.2
1977	144.7	292.3	670.4	583.8	815.1	876.1	525.7	291.5
1978	130.7	349.2	775.5	732.6	906.2	1,081.8	644.8	383.4
1979	369.6	450.6	894.1	984.2	1,263.7	1,434.8	624.5	533.6
1980	657.9	702.0	1,332.1	1,216.3	1,990.0	1,918.3	674.2	514.3
1981	377.3	606.6	1,628.8	1,275.1	2,007.1	1,881.7	1,251.5	668.5
1982	516.7	575.8	1,881.0	1,309.9	2,397.7	1,885.7	1,364.3	734.1
1983	449.8	687.5	1,747.2	1,601.5	2,197.0	2,289.0	1,297.4	914.0
1984	519.3	829.6	2,881.1	1,997.8	3,400.4	2,827.4	2,361.8	1,168.2
1985	730.2	855.2	4,971.7	1,922.1	5,701.8	2,777.3	4,241.5	1,066.9
1986	1,243.8	1,097.2	3,109.6	2,244.1	4,353.4	3,341.4	1,865.8	1,146.9

SOURCE: Department of Statistics, Singapore, *Yearbook of Statistics, Singapore,* 1971–72, pp. 80, 81; 1985–86, pp. 156, 158, 160; and 1986, pp. 157, 159, 161.

Table 2

Singapore: Domestic Exports to PRC and Taiwan
(in million S$)

Year	PRC	Taiwan
1975	22.1	56.1
1976	49.7	53.1
1977	53.8	139.6
1978	35.9	171.0
1979	151.4	179.0
1980	238.2	387.2
1981	114.1	324.2
1982	117.6	293.6
1983	117.6	330.5
1984	194.4	462.6
1985	398.8	513.4
1986	858.4	655.6

SOURCE: Department of Statistics, Singapore, *Yearbook of Statistics, Singapore*, 1985–86, p. 162; and 1986, p. 163.

both sides of the Taiwan Strait. Lee Kuan Yew has been a frequent visitor to Taiwan (where he is described among official circles as "an old friend" of the late President Chiang Ching-kuo) although his visits were never officially announced in Singapore until his seventh visit in 1985.[20] In the opinion of one Hong Kong newspaper, the public announcement served to put on notice to Chiang Ching-kuo that Lee's recent visit to China did no harm to the good relations between Singapore and Taipei.[21] A Singapore-based Japanese correspondent has even raised with Lee the possibility of talks between China and Taiwan involving Singapore. While the prime minister discounted himself as a mediator, he was nevertheless quick to say that Singapore was open to all who wanted to come and use it as a venue.[22]

Widening the Relationship with China

Traditionally, Singapore's economic relations with China have been forged through trade which, since 1979, has witnessed dramatic

---

[20]*Straits Times*, November 6, 1985. Since then Lee has made three other trips to Taiwan, the most recent being in January 1988 to attend Chiang's funeral.

[21]Ibid., November 13, 1985.

[22]Ibid., October 15, 1986.

increases both in exports and imports so that total trade with China rose from about S$1.3 billion in 1979 to S$5.7 billion in 1985—a 438 percent increase. One recurring feature of this trade is the imbalance in favor of China. (A recurring deficit is also a feature in Singapore's trade with Taiwan.) This, however, does not pose too great a concern to Singapore since a great proportion of the imports from China are reexported to Malaysia and Indonesia. In the Indonesian case, that reexport trade is not officially reported. Moreover, in its traditional entrepôt role, Singapore compensates for its trade deficits through the export of services and other invisible earnings.[23]

The new phase in Singapore's economic relations with China (since 1979) is signified by changes not only in the volume of trade, but also in the pattern of Singapore's exports, which had been traditionally marked by the reexport of rubber. Now the pattern features more nontraditional items including those produced by Singapore-based multinational corporations (MNCs). Between 1979 and 1985 Singapore's domestic exports to China (these include industrial machinery and transport equipment and parts, industrial and domestic electronic and electrical equipments and components, rubber products and processed wood, chemicals and petrochemicals, pharmaceuticals and fine chemicals, medical and scientific instruments) rose by 286 percent.

The second feature of the new phase is the increasing Singaporean participation in China's internal economic development. An example is Singapore's involvement in large-scale Chinese offshore oil exploration activities. Intraco leads nine Singapore companies in a joint venture (struck in August 1983) with the Chinese to establish and manage the Chiwan offshore oil service base. One possible spinoff from such activities is the revitalization of Singapore's refining and support industry, which is experiencing excess capacity as a result of new refineries coming into operation elsewhere in the region.[24]

Since 1983 there has been a sharp rise in the level of Singaporean investments in China. Among the ASEAN countries, Singapore is the most active in economic cooperation with China. One conservative estimate given by the Chinese trade mission in Singapore puts the level of Singapore's investments in China between 1979 and 1984 at around S$900 million. Most of the money went into joint ventures or partner-

---

[23]Wong, *The Political Economy*, p. 117. In 1986, Singapore's domestic exports to the PRC registered a sharp increase of nearly 115.2 percent over the previous year. The overall trade deficit was reduced to S$1.866 billion from S$4.24 billion in 1985.

[24]See Lam Lai Sing, "Singapore's Role in China's Offshore Oil Venture," *Asia Pacific Community*, no. 31 (1986), pp. 118–42.

ships in hotels, warehouses, labor-intensive light industries, and oil-based servicing projects.[25] By 1985, Singapore was reported to have entered into 150 projects in various fields.[26] The investments of Singapore firms are spread over fifteen Chinese inland and coastal cities and on Hainan—the highest concentration in Guangdong and Fujian provinces partially reflecting the close business and family ties with those areas.[27]

Singapore's construction industry, badly affected by the recession, has been looking for new opportunities in China. The partly government-owned Keppel Group has contracted to build a block of flats in Beijing for the use of expatriates while another group of Singaporean real estate and construction representatives has signed letters of intent to invest S$290 million in four development projects in Shanghai.[28]

The growth of economic cooperation with China has also resulted in a greater role for Singapore's financial institutions. The "Big Four" of Singapore's banks, that is, the Development Bank of Singapore (DBS), United Overseas Bank, Overseas Chinese Banking Corporation, and Overseas Union Bank, already have some foothold in China, either through branches or representative offices. China has agreed to make greater use of their facilities, in particular for countertrade. In February 1986, the first financial joint venture between Singapore and China was launched with the establishment of Central China International Leasing—the only leasing joint venture so far between a Chinese company and an Asian country other than Japan. This joint venture between the Overseas Chinese Banking Corporation and Wearne Brothers on the Singapore side and the Hankow branch of the Bank of China and Wuhan Leasing Company on the China side will initially service the financial needs of four provinces, engaging in the leasing, subleasing, credit purchase, and sale of industrial, transportation, building, and scientific equipment and acting as a conduit for overseas credit directly related to the importation of capital equipment.[29]

China's need for intermediate technology has led it to cooperate with several major Singapore statutory boards such as the Housing and Development Board (HDB), the Jurong Town Corporation, the Singa-

---

[25]*Business Times*, February 6, 1985.
[26]Ibid., September 20, 1985.
[27]For a profile of these firms see Pang Eng Fong and Rajah V. Komaran, "Singapore Firms in China," *Singapore Business*, September 1985, pp. 12–15.
[28]*Straits Times*, July 4, 1986.
[29]*Business Times* and *Straits Times*, February 22, 1986.

pore Tourist Promotion Board, Telecommunications Authority of Singapore, National Computer Board, and the Port of Singapore Authority. The last named is involved in developing the port of Rianjin near Beijing while the Civil Aviation Authority of Singapore may yet have a bigger role (beyond the airport management already in the cards) in the development of Shanghai's Hong Qiao Airport.[30]

The so-called technology transfers from Singapore extend to skills development and consultancy services. Prominent among those who are providing consultancy services to China are three former ministers. In May 1985, Goh Keng Swee, the former first deputy prime minister, was officially appointed as an economic adviser to China's coastal areas and four economic zones. He was also China's tourism adviser. He reported directly to then State Councillor Gu Mu, who in turn answered to Premier Zhao Ziyang. In his consultancy work Goh has tapped the expertise of Lim Kim San, another former cabinet minister who had held portfolios in National Development, Finance, Interior and Defense, Education, Environment, and Communications. A former minister of state for culture, Fong Sip Chee (who is still a member of parliament), is an adviser for economic and industrial development of Tianjin. From the private business sector, a prominent local businessman and council member of the Singapore Chamber of Commerce and Industry, Lau Ing Woon, has been appointed the Southeast Asian agent of the Guangdong provincial government. His task is to promote certain joint ventures and technology transfers.[31]

One effect of the various skills development programs has been the steady increase in the level and extent of people-to-people contacts between China and Singapore. Chinese trainees started coming to Singapore in 1982 on programs that varied between two weeks and three months. The programs have included hotel catering and even hairdressing. In 1985 China sent thirty teachers to Singapore for the Institute of Education's Diploma of Education course lasting eleven months. In 1986 Telecoms began a training program for 200 Chinese trainees on the Fetex-150 digital telephone switching system for a Japanese supplier, Fijitsu Ltd. China is expected to send middle managers to Singapore for training and observation with Singapore's Ministry of Trade and Industry acting as the contact point. Interestingly, certain skilled workers from China are also being recruited to work in Singapore. The four HDB core contractors are known to have recruited about

---

[30]The CAAS was part of a Singapore consortium that failed to clinch the contract to design and undertake the expansion of the airport.
[31]*Straits Times*, October 16, 1986.

300 skilled construction workers for public housing projects in Singapore.

Singaporeans have also gone to China to facilitate the skills transfers. They include Singapore Airlines flight instructors; retirees who have taken up teaching, management, and advisory posts; and senior managers and lecturers involved in the transfer of managerial expertise. In all these exchanges, Singapore has had the advantage and benefit of a bilingual population, many of whom have acquired proficiency in Mandarin.

The exposure of Singaporeans to China's domestic scene has also increased with the rise in the number of visitors to China. The number of Singaporeans visiting China increased from 18,000 in 1982 to 32,000 in 1984 and will rise further with the establishment of direct air services between the two countries. Nowadays, Singapore's prime minister takes a rather sanguine view of such exposures. As he puts it, "My personal experience, and that of my own observations of Chinese Singaporeans in China, lead me to believe that the best reminder of a Chinese Singaporean that he is Singaporean, not Chinese, is a longish stay in China."[32]

So far, official contacts between Singapore and China on furthering economic cooperation have resulted in three bilateral agreements: on investment protection, tourism, and double taxation avoidance. The fifteen-year investment protection agreement that came into force in February 1986 provides for protection of investments against expropriation or nationalization (unless done by law and with proper compensation), the repatriation of capital and profits, and international arbitration.[33] The five-year agreement to promote tourism was signed during the visit of State Councillor Gu Mu. Under the agreement, a joint committee on tourism cooperation will be set up to look into specific projects such as tourism promotion and training and the exhibition of Chinese historical relics in Singapore. The idea underlying the tourism joint venture is to encourage tourists visiting Singapore to also visit China, thereby making Singapore a gateway to China.[34]

Under the taxation agreement initialed in April 1984 Singapore fully recognized any tax exemption or reduction granted by China on income derived by local entrepreneurs from their investments. It means that

---

[32]Text of interview with Lee Kuan Yew by Kensaku Shirai and Teruo Kunugi of *Asahi Shimbun*, Singapore, January 5, 1981, Singapore government press release, Ministry of Culture, No. 02–1–81–07, p. 26.
[33]*Straits Times*, June 27, 1986.
[34]Ibid., February 15, 1986.

Singapore will give tax credit for any reduction or exemption of Chinese tax under various incentive schemes and in the agreement.[35]

Quite evidently there is now a much wider range of cooperation (from trade, joint ventures, provision of services, transfer of medium technology, and skills development) in the economic relations between Singapore and China. Also, the institutional and taxation framework necessary to promote such cooperation is being created. Nevertheless it is necessary to put in perspective the opportunities and benefits that Singapore is said to derive from the opening up of China, lest there be excessive or unrealistic expectations from those hoping for quick returns.

Viewing China in Perspective

The role envisaged for Singapore in China's modernization has been vividly portrayed by Zhao Ziyang, who told Lee Kuan Yew that ''China can be compared as the stomach and Singapore as the eyes and mouth. While China had a lot of capacity to digest, Singapore could be an open channel for technology.''[36] Lee himself has put the role of Singapore in sharper perspective. He saw the English-educated Chinese Singaporeans (say, those working in China for the MNCs) as the cultural and linguistic ''interface'' between China's workers and foreign engineers and managers to pass on knowledge and know-how. Industrial co-production with a third partner is part of Singapore's own efforts to bring high technology industries to Singapore. In fact it is the Western industrialized nations, and not Singapore, which will provide the technology and managerial skills for China's modernization.[37]

One may choose to view the indicators presented so far of Singapore's ''entry'' into China as the mere beginning of the long haul necessary before China can become an important factor in Singapore's economy. Lee Kuan Yew has noted that even after ten to fifteen years, Singapore's economic links with China will be less important than its links with America, Japan, or Europe, all of whom possess high technology and a much larger GNP than China.[38] There should be no expec-

---

[35]*Business Times*, April 4, 1986.

[36]Text of interview with Lee Kuan Yew by Takuhiko Tsuruta of *Nihon Keizai Shimbun*, Singapore, November 25, 1981, Singapore government press release, Ministry of Culture, No. 02-1-81-11-27, p. 15.

[37]Interview with Lee Kuan Yew by Kensaku Shirai and Teruo Kunugi of *Asahi Shimbun*, Singapore, January 5, 1981, Singapore government press release, Ministry of Culture, No. 02-1-81-01-07, p. 26.

[38]*Business Times*, March 3, 1986.

tations that a heavier reliance on trade and economic ties with China will pull Singapore out of its economic recession.

Admittedly Singapore's trade with China has grown tremendously—in the six years since 1979, it grew twice as fast as Singapore's trade with the rest of the world. Yet by 1985 China still accounted for only 5 percent of Singapore's total trade. As a trading partner Singapore ranked fourth after the United States, Japan, and peninsular Malaysia. But as an export market, China ranked thirteenth—not counting Indonesia, for which official trade figures were unavailable. It has been estimated that a 7 percent increase in exports to the United States is all it would take to produce the same effect as a doubling of exports to China.[39] In the view of Trade and Industry Minister Lee Hsien Loong, the potential for Singapore lies more with selling services than goods to China.[40]

But even in the service sector, certain limitations are evident. So far, Singaporean companies in China have been able to exploit their expertise in financing, marketing, and management to compete against firms from other countries. Such skills have enabled them to extend their intermediary role. However, it can be expected that the Chinese, too, will learn quickly and develop the skills themselves, thus reducing the competitive advantages enjoyed by Singaporean firms, which will then have to discover new strengths.[41]

But even economic relations can never quite be divorced from their political context or political undertones. Lingering ethnic sentiments might intrude into dealings with China. Lee Kuan Yew chose significantly to raise a word of caution in Xiamen, the business center of Fujian province (which has strong cultural and emotional appeal to at least the older generation of the major Chinese dialect group in Singapore) during his 1985 visit to China. On that occasion, he urged the Chinese not to bank on sentiment when doing business with Chinese Singaporeans—the bottom line would be defined by profitability of the venture.

Furthermore, given the economic recession faced by every ASEAN country, the need to diversify markets could lead to greater competition and even conflict among those who seek commercial opportunities in China. On the one hand Singapore's merchants are concerned about the establishment of direct trade links between China and the countries in Southeast Asia that would undercut their traditional intermediary

---

[39]Ibid., March 1, 1986.

[40]Ibid., April 18, 1986.

[41]See Fong and Komaran, "Singapore Firms in China," p. 15.

role. On the other hand, they could stir up regional resentment if they were treated as "favored sons" by the Chinese. Lee himself feels that cause for complaint will depend on "whether we are the only people doing business or whether we are all doing business and the business is done with whoever offers the best terms."[42]

The danger exists that as economic cooperation with China expands, Singapore would be (or would seem to be) "too dependent" upon China, an undesirable condition especially since China, despite its open-door policy, remains a communist state.

The development of tomorrow's relations with China will continue to be affected by domestic political change in China, just as recent changes have created today's new opportunities. Should there be a political upheaval in China (Just how irreversible is the open-door policy? How much further down the "capitalist road" can China go without setting off a domestic political reaction?) no investment agreement can provide watertight protection for Singapore's interests.

Finally, although the sense of long-term economic threat posed by a modernized, more export-oriented China is less acutely felt in Singapore than elsewhere in the region, what will always remain is the question of how much longer Singapore can keep one step ahead and continue playing "mouth and eyes" to China.

Given the above considerations, Singapore will need to tread carefully in defining a course toward China, even though, or shall we say especially since, all Singapore may really want at the end of the day is a "friendly business relationship."

---

[42]*Business Times*, September 26, 1985.

16. Dictates of Security: Thailand's Relations with the PRC Since the Vietnam War

SUKHUMBHAND PARIBATRA

Over the last two decades the relationship between the People's Republic of China (PRC) and the noncommunist states of neighboring Southeast Asia has undergone a significant transformation. In the mid-1960s, the combination of the *Gestapu* incident in Indonesia, the U.S. intervention in Vietnam, the outbreak of a Chinese-supported communist insurgency in Thailand; and the Great Proletarian Cultural Revolution in the PRC meant that mutual suspicions and hostilities were the dominant features of their relations. Indeed, when the Association of Southeast Asian Nations was formed in 1967, China was predisposed to seeing its noncommunist states—Indonesia, Malaysia, the Philippines, Singapore, and Thailand—as a "counterrevolutionary alliance," a "twin brother of SEATO" (Southeast Asia Treaty Organization), an "instrument of U.S. imperialism," and a part of "U.S. imperialism's ring of encirclement around China."[1]

But by the mid-1970s, with the end of the U.S. military presence in mainland Southeast Asia and the emergence of a victorious, unified Vietnam under Hanoi's leadership, mutual suspicions and hostilities were considerably toned down, and most of the ASEAN states moved toward some sort of normalization with Beijing. By the end of the decade and the early 1980s, in the aftermath of Vietnam's invasion of Cambodia, the two sides engaged not only in a common endeavor to contain the expansion of Hanoi's power but also in rapidly increasing economic exchanges.[2]

---

[1]See Khaw Guat Hoon, *An Analysis of China's Attitudes Toward ASEAN, 1967–76* (Singapore: Institute of Southeast Asian Studies, Occasional Paper no. 48, 1977), pp. 5–6.

[2]For a brief survey of the transformation of the relations between ASEAN and the PRC, see Lucian W. Pye, "China and Southeast Asia," in Robert A. Scalapino and Jusuf Wanandi, eds., *Economic, Political, and Security Issues in Southeast Asia in the 1980s* (Berkeley: Institute of East Asian Studies, University of California, 1982), pp. 156–76. The present economic relationship is well analyzed in a number of recent works, e.g., John Wong, *The Political Economy of China's Changing Relations with Southeast Asia* (London: Macmillan, 1984); Zakaria Haji Ahmad and Paul Chan, *Riding the Chinese Dragon: The Politics and Economics of ASEAN's Relations with the People's Republic of China* (Tokyo: Japan Center for International Exchange, forthcoming); and Chia Siow-Yue, "China's Economic Relations with ASEAN Countries," in Joyce K. Kallgren, Noordin Sopiee, and Soedjati

Increasing cooperation with the PRC, however, does not mean that the ASEAN countries feel entirely reassured about the intentions of their northern neighbor. On the contrary, there is a great deal of ambivalence toward China. On one hand, as a result of the decline of the United States' security role in juxtaposition with Soviet expansion of power and influence in the region and of Vietnam's reunification and resurgence, as manifested in its domination over Laos and Cambodia, the PRC is looked upon as a valuable countervailing force against Soviet and Vietnamese threats. Furthermore, the PRC's apparent lack of revolutionary fervor, its emphasis on promoting state-to-state relations rather than "people-to-people" or party-to-party ties, and its growing preoccupation with domestic economic development at this junction also serve to reinforce the view that China has become a power oriented to the status quo, a force for moderation and stability where Southeast Asia is concerned. On the other hand, because of its geographic contiguity, demographic weight, and continued adherence to a totalitarian ideology, as well as the presence in the region of a large number of its "kith and kin," the PRC is also regarded by many in ASEAN, particularly in Indonesia and Malaysia, as the greatest long-term danger to the region.[3]

One crucial player in the evolving cooperative relationship between noncommunist Southeast Asia and China is Thailand. The kingdom's position as a "frontline state"—a country directly threatened by Vietnam's Soviet-supported occupation of Cambodia—makes it perceive Beijing's role as being indispensible for containing Hanoi and safeguarding Thai security. Accordingly, the Thai have striven to develop a close security relationship with the PRC. Because the other ASEAN countries regard Thailand's security concerns as paramount in importance where the Cambodia conflict is concerned, Sino-Thai cooperation has been "allowed" to develop and in many ways has served as a cata-

Djiwandono, eds., *ASEAN and China: An Evolving Relationship* (Berkeley: Institute of East Asian Studies, University of California, 1988).

[3]ASEAN's ambivalence vis-à-vis China is well expressed in Jusuf Wanandi, "China's Role in Regional Problems," in Kallgren, Sopiee, and Djiwandono, *ASEAN and China*. Individual ASEAN countries' views of the PRC, including perceptions of the latter as a threat, are systematically analyzed in Robert O. Tilman, *The Enemy Beyond: External Threat Perceptions in the ASEAN Region* (Singapore: Institute of Southeast Asian Nations, Research Notes and Discussions Paper no. 42, 1984), passim. The reality of China's threat to Southeast Asia is examined in Sukhumbhand Paribatra, "Power, Ideology and Ethnicity: China's Environmental Possibilism and the Security of Southeast Asia," paper prepared for the Thirteenth World Congress of the International Political Science Association, Paris, July 15–20, 1985; see also Michael Yahuda, *The China Threat* (Kuala Lumpur: Institute of Strategic and International Studies, 1986).

lyst of wider Sino-ASEAN cooperation. Yet, as in the cases of other ASEAN countries, Thailand also feels uncertain about the intentions of the PRC, and it is this ambivalence, when allied with Indonesia's and Malaysia's openly articulated fears of their northern neighbor, that is likely to set a limit on future cooperation with China.

This chapter examines in some detail Thailand's evolving relationship with China. The core of this relationship is bilateral security cooperation, which limits the present work in its ability to be a comprehensive treatise on the subject. To put it simply, Thailand's security cooperation with the PRC is a subject concerning which "hard" data are difficult to find. The reason is clear: While China, unlike the United States for example, is still a relatively closed society and general access to information on certain political and security questions remains limited, Thailand's security cooperation with Beijing is considered by the Royal Thai Government to be an extremely sensitive issue. For most Thai officials, when in doubt, silence on this matter seems to be the golden rule. Nevertheless, it is hoped that, with the information available, to a certain degree one can accurately portray and analyze Thailand's relations with the PRC and thus stimulate further understanding of and interest in the subject.

From Conflict to Convergence

> Dear Listeners, the Voice of the People of Thailand will temporarily suspend its broadcasts beginning 11 July onward. . . . The last song will be "Proceed to Expand Operational Areas," and I take this occasion to bid farewell to listeners. May you enjoy good health and success in your work.[4]

Journalists, academics, and politicians love dramatic turning points, and if one has to seek one in Thailand's relations with China over the last decade, it is the broadcast of these simple but poignant words over the clandestine radio Voice of the People of Thailand (VOPT) in July 1979. This message signaled the end of the era of enmity, which had begun immediately after the Chinese Communist Party (CCP) took power on the mainland in 1949 and persisted—though in a latent form—after the opening of diplomatic relations in 1975 and the beginning of the area of cooperation, which continues to this day.

From Thailand's point of view, since it began broadcasting from southern China in 1962, the VOPT symbolized the PRC'S implacably aggressive intents toward the kingdom. For it was this radio that in

---

[4]*Foreign Broadcasts Information Service,* Asia and the Pacific (hereafter cited as *FBIS,* APA), July 10, 1979, p. J1.

January and February 1965 had announced what Bangkok had long feared—the beginning of a communist-led armed struggle in Thailand[5]—and which throughout the rest of the turbulent 1960s and most of the even more turbulent 1970s had helped to keep burning the fire of revolution.[6]

Between 1949 and 1979 Thailand's foremost security threat was perceived to take the form of communist-inspired and communist-led internal armed dissent. This concern was reflected in a series of laws against communism, ranging from the Anti-Communist Activities Acts of 1952 and 1969 to the still effective Order of the National Reform Council of 1976, which over the long run have collectively served to identify in legal terms communism as the main threat to the nation's security and to give the Royal Thai Government a wide scope for interpreting what constitute communist-inspired activities and a wide range of powers for mobilizing resources to deal with them. The concern with communism also led Thailand to forge a close alliance with the United States, and it was no coincidence that where the Thais were concerned, the focal point of the day-to-day activities of this alliance was the development of what amounted to a joint counterinsurgency program. Furthermore, the degree of Thai preoccupation with the threat of a communist insurgency can be gauged from the fact that efforts to suppress it were begun well before the actual outbreak of violence in August 1965 (the so-called "day gunfire erupted") and became both conceptually and operationally integrated into the structure and functioning of the Thai state apparatus, involving as the efforts did a large variety of key government agencies, civilian organizations, and security-oriented development programs. Indeed, during this period, with the exception of the years between 1973 and 1976, anticommunism—or, more specifically, promises to protect the institutions of the nation, religion, and monarchy from the threat of communism—became the main instrument of legitimation for both the military regime and individual military leaders.[7]

---

[5]See Jay Taylor, *China and Southeast Asia: Peking's Relations with Revolutionary Movements* (New York: Praeger, 1976), pp. 288–91.

[6]For surveys and analyses of the CPT armed insurgency movement, see Kanok Wongtrangan, "The Revolutionary Strategy of the Communist Party of Thailand: Change and Persistence," in Lim Joo-Jock and Vani S., eds., *Armed Communist Movements in Southeast Asia* (Aldershot, England: Gower Publishing Co., 1984), pp. 133–82; and Kusuma Snitwongse, "Thai Government Responses to Armed Communist and Separatist Movements," in Chandran Jeshurun, ed., *Governments and Rebellions in Southeast Asia* (Singapore: Institute of Southeast Asian Studies, 1985), pp. 247–72.

[7]For a fuller discussion of the foregoing points, see Snitwongse, "Thai Government Responses;" also see Chai-Anan Samudavanija and Sukhumbhand Paribatra, "In Search of Balance: Prospects for Stability in Thailand During the Post-CPT Era," in Kusuma

For the Thais, a root cause of internal armed communism was seen to be the PRC. Thai perceptions of the latter were well expressed by a high-ranking official in 1968:

> Since its establishment, mainland China has relentlessly and conscientiously sought to impose its hegemony on neighboring countries by various means, including naked armed aggression, insidious aggression under the label of "wars of liberation," subversion and infiltration. Its major export is revolution. It is single-mindedly dedicated to the overthrow of legitimate authorities of neighboring states without exception. . . . Chinese communist leadership has in effect declared a guerrilla war on Thailand.[8]

One reason for perceiving the PRC in this way was the underlying belief, held as an unquestioned and unquestionable article of faith by many of the Thai elite especially in the military, that communism and communist activities were alien to Thailand, phenomena externally influenced rather than internally generated.[9] Another reason was that the Chinese were instrumental in the founding of the Communist Party of Thailand (CPT),[10] which to this day continues to be led by Thais of Chinese origins,[11] thus enhancing the racial dimension of the threat perceptions of those Thais already concerned with the economic dominance of the Sino-Thai business and financial community.[12]

The third reason was geography. The shape of the kingdom was a factor that traditionally impeded the central government's access to and control of the north, the northeast, and the deep south. Moreover, the length, the topography, and the sociocultural features of its boundaries were, and indeed continue to be, perceived as factors making the coun-

---

Snitwongse and Sukhumbhand Paribatra, eds., *Durable Stability in Southeast Asia* (Singapore: Institute of Southeast Asian Studies, 1987), pp. 188–99. The most comprehensive treatment of Thai-American cooperation in counterinsurgency planning and operations, of course, is provided in George K. Tanham, *Trial in Thailand* (New York: Crane, Russak and Co., 1974).

[8]Thailand's representative to the United Nations, Ambassador Anand Panyarachun, at the U.N. General Assembly, November 19, 1968; text of the speech in R. K. Jain, ed., *China and Thailand, 1949–1983* (New Delhi: Radiant Publishers, 1984), pp. 145–46.

[9]See Tanham, *Trial in Thailand*, p. 90; see also Snitwongse, "Thai Government Responses," p. 250.

[10]For a good discussion of the CPT's early development, see David A. Wilson, "Communism in Thailand," in Frank N. Trager, ed., *Marxism in Southeast Asia* (Stanford, Ca.: Stanford University Press, 1959), pp. 58–101.

[11]Wongtrangan, "Revolutionary Strategy," pp. 179–80.

[12]The second Pibulsongkram regime (1948–57) was particularly concerned with this issue. See, e.g., Donald E. Neuchtertein, *Thailand and the Struggle for Southeast Asia* (Ithaca: Cornell University Press, 1965), pp. 100–5.

try vulnerable to subversion and infiltration. The geographical proximity of China, Chinese road-building and other activities in Laos, and the persistence of the Chinese-influenced Communist Party of Malaya's (CPM) insurgency in areas in and adjacent to southern Thailand all combined to make the Thai see the PRC and the pro-Chinese CPT as feared rivals to the Royal Thai Government (RTG) for the control of the peripheral areas of the country as well as for the hearts and minds of the Thai living there. The RTG's sensitivity on this score was reflected in the ferocious nature of the military campaigns conducted against the hilltribe insurgency that broke out in the north in 1967.[13]

The American failure in Vietnam led to a readjustment of Thailand's foreign policies. During this process the Thai policy of nonrecognition and containment of the PRC was discarded, and in 1975 diplomatic relations were opened with the latter, with peaceful coexistence affirmed as the principle for the conduct of their bilateral relations.[14] The focus of Thailand's security concern clearly shifted toward Vietnam, and greater attention was paid to domestic political and socioeconomic conditions as causes of armed dissent. But suspicions of the PRC remained, as the CPT insurgency increased to new peaks between 1975 and 1978, with the party able to field 12,000 to 14,000 armed guerrillas, to control directly more than 400 villages and to exert some degree of influence over 6,000 more villages with a combined population of nearly 4 million, and to conduct combat operations in well over half of the kingdom's seventy-one provinces.[15] The RTG's grave concern with the continuing links between the increasingly strong CPT and the CCP was one of the key factors to prompt the then Thai premier, General Kriangsak Chomanan, to visit the PRC in March 1978.[16]

---

[13]The protracted nature of the northern insurgency problem prompted the RTG to move the elite First Infantry Division from Bangkok to the north to engage in counterinsurgency operations, but it was soon withdrawn. However, by that time, the damage had been done: There were many casualties, not only among insurgents and government troops, but also among innocent civilians. See Saiyud Kerdphol, *The Struggle for Thailand: Counter-Insurgency, 1965–1985* (Bangkok: S. Research Center Co., 1986), pp. 116–17. The author is a former Supreme Commander of the Royal Thai Armed Forces and throughout his military career had been closely involved in the RTG's counterinsurgency policy planning and implementation. This volume is an excellent source of information and ideas concerning Thailand's insurgency experiences.

[14]The best work on Thai diplomacy in the early 1970s is Sarasin Viraphol, *Directions in Thai Foreign Policy* (Singapore: Institute of Southeast Asian Studies, Occasional Paper no. 40, 1976); esp. pp. 19–25 for Sino-Thai relations.

[15]Snitwongse, "Thai Government Responses," pp. 259–60; and Wongtrangan, "Revolutionary Strategy," pp. 134–36.

[16]General Kriangsak Chomanan's interview with the author in Bangkok, February 10, 1987.

In 1978–79 the situation was transformed, and in Thailand's relations with the PRC, conflict gave way to a convergence of security interests. The key development was the Vietnamese invasion of Cambodia. From Thailand's point of view, the fall of Saigon in April 1975 was a cause of grave concern. For not only did it reconfirm beyond any shadow of doubt that the American alliance could no longer be relied upon for protection as before, but it also meant that for the first time in almost a century and a half, the kingdom had to face an independent, unified Vietnam, which had once been its most bitter rival for power and influence in mainland Southeast Asia and which now also championed a hostile, revolutionary ideology. At that point, however, with Cambodia under the rule of the Khmer Rouge, the Vietnamese threat to Thailand was still largely putative and long term rather than actualized and immediate, and, consequently, opportunities for achieving some sort of modus vivendi were always present, as evident from the joint communiqués issued during Vietnamese Premier Pham Van Dong's tour of the region in September–October 1978.[17]

However, Hanoi's invasion of Cambodia at the end of 1978 not only shattered the prospect of this modus vivendi developing into a durable structure of peace, but it also presented a "clear and present danger" to Thailand at the very time that the latter was no longer assured of direct military assistance from the United States. The stationing in Cambodia and Laos of between 200,000 to 250,000 Vietnamese troops, well supplied with Soviet military hardware and backed by the growing Soviet naval presence in the region, was and to this day remains perceived by Thais as a threat in a number of ways, ranging from psychological intimidation, subversion, and incursion to invasion and outright colonization.[18]

---

[17]For a detailed account of the conduct of diplomacy between Vietnam and the ASEAN countries in 1978, see K. K. Nair, *ASEAN-Indochina Relations Since 1975: The Politics of Accommodation* (Canberra: Australian National University, 1984), pp. 92–107.

[18]For example, a senior Thai officer stated:

> The concept or plan of integrating Laos and Cambodia under Vietnam's control has been Vietnam's long-term objective throughout history and has not changed with the times. . . . In the last two to three years Vietnam has succeeded and is able to exert its influence completely in Laos and Cambodia. . . .
> The next target is Thailand. Vietnam tries to bring this about by both open and covert means. Covertly, Vietnam is using the Vietnamese refugees, who had fled to Thailand during the wars in Indochina and after 1975 number more than 100,000, by setting up networks under Hanoi's command to carry out sabotage and support insurgency in Thailand. Openly, Vietnam, by using hot pursuits and pacification campaigns against the Cambodian resistance groups as justifications, has constantly committed acts of aggression against Thailand. . . . Vietnam's aggression and psychological campaign put the Thai government in an unstable position because of internal pressures for retaliation and external

Thai threat perceptions in turn led them to take a firm stand against Vietnam's occupation of Cambodia, and their policy was and to this day remains aimed at removing the Vietnamese military presence from that country by using all possible means, short of a direct military confrontation. These means also included the use of Cambodian resistance groups, particularly the Khmer Rouge, as proxies to exert military pressure on Hanoi.[19]

For the PRC the danger from the Vietnamese invasion of Cambodia was, of course, less "clear and present." China's fears of Soviet encirclement on its peripheries, its self-image as a power with the right to exercise influence on the affairs of Southeast Asia, and its commitments to the Khmer Rouge, factors which had originally helped to precipitate the Sino-Vietnamese conflict after 1975, now moved Beijing to take a hard-line stand against Hanoi, to the point of attempting to teach the latter a lesson through the use of military force in February-March 1979. By extension, these factors also induced the PRC to perceive that it had concrete interests in common with Thailand, which by virtue of its geographical location became indispensable for the channeling of Chinese arms, ammunitions, and other supplies to the Khmer Rouge fighting the Vietnamese occupation forces.[20] The convergence of China's and

---

pressures [for moderation?]. So long as this problem remains unresolved, the country's national security will be exposed to the greatest dangers. (General Arthit Kamlang-ek, "Indochina and Thai National Security," paper presented at a seminar on "National Security Problems in Thai Leaders' Perspectives," organized by the Institute of Security and International Studies, Chulalongkorn University, Bangkok, March 29–30, 1982, pp. 9, 12.)

General Arthit was at that time an assistant commander-in-chief of the Royal Thai Army. The original text was in Thai and was translated by the author.

[19]Thailand's views of the Vietnamese threat and the Cambodia conflict are more extensively discussed in Sukhumbhand Paribatra, "Strategic Implications of the Indochina Conflict: Thai Perspectives," *Asian Affairs: An American Review* 11(3) (Fall 1984): 28–46.

[20]The subject of the PRC's security interests in Southeast Asia and relations with Vietnam has been extensively treated in many publications. See, e.g., Lucian W. Pye, "The China Factor in Southeast Asia," in Richard H. Solomon, ed., *The China Factor: Sino-American Relations and the Global Scene* (Englewood Cliffs, N.J.: Prentice-Hall, 1981), pp. 216–56; Wilfred Burchett, *The China-Cambodia-Vietnam Triangle* (London: Vanguard Books and Zed Press, 1981); Robert G. Sutter, "China's Strategy Toward Vietnam and Its Implications for the United States," and Banning Garrett, "The Strategic Triangle and the Indochina Crisis," in David W. P. Elliott, ed., *The Third Indochina Conflict* (Boulder, Col.: Westview Press, 1981), pp. 163–92, 193–242, respectively; Steven I. Levine, "China in Asia: The PRC as a Regional Power," in Harry Harding, ed., *China's Foreign Relations in the 1980s* (New Haven: Yale University Press, 1984), pp. 107–45; Chang Pao-Min, *Kampuchea Between China and Vietnam* (Singapore: Singapore University Press, 1985); and John F. Copper, "China and Southeast Asia," in Donald E. Weatherbee, ed., *Southeast Asia Divided: The ASEAN-Indochina Crisis* (Boulder, Col.: Westview Press, 1985), pp. 47–64.

Thailand's security interests was first indicated in a series of statements made in mid-1979 by the CPT-led Committee for Coordinating Patriotic and Democratic Forces (CCPDF) condemning Vietnam and in the July 10, 1979, closing broadcast of the VOPT, which was widely interpreted as a directive for the CPT and its followers and allies to take a common stand with the RTG against "the aggressor enemy," for "it is like seeing the fire which is burning neighboring houses lapping at our own roof. What should we choose—uniting to extinguish the fire or letting it burn our house? . . . It is better to die a Thai than to live as a slave.[21]"

This convergence of the two countries' security interests still endures, and indeed where Thailand is concerned, the Vietnamese threat has been "institutionalized" in a number of ways, just as the Chinese threat had been in the 1950s and 1960s. During the drafting of both the Fifth (1982–86) and Sixth (1987–91) National Economic and Social Development Plans, a great deal of attention was paid to (1) identifying in concrete terms the threat coming from Vietnam, (2) assessing the resources needed to deal with it, and (3) analyzing the ways and means of organizing such resources in the most cost-effective manner. Procurements of major weapons systems, most notably the F-16A fighter aircraft, have been made, and paramilitary and civil defense organizations developed, on the assumption that Vietnam is, and is likely to remain for the foreseeable future, the foremost external security threat.[22] Moreover, where domestic armed communism is concerned, Vietnam has clearly replaced the PRC as the chief instigator, as evident from the oft-repeated charges that Vietnam, with the assistance of the Soviet Union, is actively promoting a new insurgency movement under the nominal leadership of the so-called "Pak Mai" ("New Party") group; indeed, the incumbent army chief, General Chavalit Yongchaiyuth, has even argued that if the CPT were free of Chinese influence, it would pose a greater security threat to the country.[23]

Security Cooperation

The convergence of Thailand's and China's interests after the Vietnamese invasion of Cambodia has brought about close security coopera-

---

[21]Voice of the People of Thailand, "The Thai People Must Totally Destroy the Aggressor Enemy," July 10, 1979, in *Summary of World Broadcasts*, Far East (hereafter cited as *SWB*, FE) /6165, July 12, 1979, p. A3/7.

[22]See Sukhumbhand Paribatra, "Thailand: Defence Spending and Threat Perception," in Chin Kin Wah, ed., *Defence Spending in Southeast Asia* (Singapore: Institute of Southeast Asian Studies, 1987), pp. 84–90.

[23]Reported in *Bangkok Post*, November 27, 1986, p. 3.

tion between the two. This in turn has formed the basis for a relation-ship that has evolved in a number of other directions and has given rise to speculation and fears that a full-fledged Sino-Thai alliance may soon transpire. After first examining the nature and extent of the bilateral security cooperation, I will discuss this evolving relationship, as well as its scope and limitations.

It is an impossible task to portray and document fully and accu-rately the shadowy world of the Sino-Thai security relationship. Never-theless, on the basis of the information available, including numerous formal and informal interviews with military and civilian officials con-ducted by the author between 1980 and 1987, it is possible to piece together the general outlines of this relationship.

Thailand's security cooperation with the PRC takes place in two interrelated areas. The first is an informal exchange of quid pro quo concerning the CPT and Chinese supplies to the Khmer Rouge. The second is China's role, both direct and indirect, in the strengthening of Thai military capabilities. These will be discussed in turn.

CPT-Khmer Rouge Exchange

There was little doubt as a result of the communist Pathet Lao's takeover of power in Vientiane in December 1975, the Lao People's Democratic Republic (LPDR) became an increasingly valuable logistical asset for the CPT insurgency movement. Supplies of arms, ammuni-tions, food, and clothing from not only the PRC but also Vietnam were greatly facilitated. More importantly, in addition to training schools that had been set up in the 1960s, new facilities were also rapidly made available, including supply depots and hospitals, especially in key bor-der areas opposite the Thai provinces of Nan and Ubon Rachathani. Laos, in other words, became a place where CPT insurgents could find sanctuary, live, train, as well as heal, arm, and feed themselves in readi-ness for the fray across the border.

However, during the period of growing Sino-Vietnamese conflict in late 1977 and 1978, the pro-Hanoi LPDR began to put pressure on the CPT to support Vietnam's stand. Although wishing to preserve good relations with both Vietnam and the LPDR, the staunchly pro-Beijing CPT leadership refused to do so.[24] In November 1978, after Pham

---

[24]According to a CPT insider, Therdphum Chaidee:

> The main point of contention among party members was whether to be friends with the Indochina countries or not. There was never any discussion of cutting or reducing ties with China. There was pressure from the Vietnamese and the Laotians to reduce attacks on the Soviet Union and Vietnam. They knew they had a lot to lose if they did not become

Van Dong's visit to Thailand in September, the CPT was given an ulti-
matum by Vientiane: It had either to endorse Vietnam's position vis-à-
vis the PRC and the Khmer Rouge or withdraw from the bases in Laos
within one month. Inevitable delays took place, and the dateline,
though extended, was not met. Accordingly, after Vietnam's invasion of
Cambodia in December 1978–January 1979, the Lao authorities began to
evict forcefully the remaining CPT insurgents and their dependents and
shut down the bases.[25] This development, together with astute diplomacy on the part of Thai premier Kriangsak Chaomanan, who reinforced the schism between the LPDR and the CPT by offering the
prospect of much improved Thai-Lao relations,[26] put the Thai insurgency movement in considerable disarray.[27]

It was in this context that, despite initial reluctance on the part of
the Thai,[28] probably sometime before June 1979, when the CCPDF
stepped up its public condemnations of Vietnam, an informal deal was
struck between the RTG and the PRC leadership. In return for the former's assistance in channeling Chinese supplies to the Khmer Rouge, the
latter promised to end its support of the CPT and to ensure that the

---

friendlier. But the vote of the (seven-member politburo) *krom Kanmuang* came out four to
three in favor of staying on the same course and refusing to give in to the pressure. Once
the vote was taken, they did not discuss the issue again. They all accepted the majority
decision and tried to explain it to the others. (Quoted by the interviewer, Yuangrat Wedel, in
her monograph, *The Thai Radicals and the Communist Party* [Singapore: Maruzen Asia, 1983],
p. 19.)

[25]See ibid., pp. 19–21; also Nopporn Suwannapanich and Kraisak Choonhavan, "The
Communist Party of Thailand and Conflict in Indochina," paper prepared for the confer-
ence on "Vietnam, Indochina, and Southeast Asia: Into the 1980s," organized by the
Institute of Social Studies, the Hague, September 29–October 3, 1980.

[26]Kriangsak's interview with the author.

[27]The immediate impact was on the movement in the northern provinces of Tak and
Chiang-rai and in the northern part of the northeastern region of Thailand, which had
relied heavy on the Lao sanctuaries; see Wongtrangan, "Revolutionary Strategy," p. 136.

[28]On January 16, 1979, Geng Biao, CCP Politburo member and secretary general of the
Military Commission, reported that Deng Xiaoping had requested the Thai deputy pre-
mier, Sunthorn Hongladarom, who had just visited China, "to tell" Premier Kriangsak
Chaomanan that

the Government of China wishes that the Government of Thailand will permit China to
send material aid to Cambodia via Thailand. As regards this request, the Thai government
still has not expressed its opinion. The Thais of course have their own problem for they are
unwilling to get into conflict with Vietnam. We know this well. However, we must explain
the fact very clearly. ... The relationship between Cambodia and Thailand or between
Cambodia and Southeast Asia is one of mutual dependence. If one falls, the other will be in
danger. Therefore, it is impossible for Thailand to stay aloof. Quoted in Jain, *China and
Thailand*, p. 234.

communist movement did not impede the RTG's efforts to cope with the Vietnamese threat.[29]

The available evidence tends to suggest that, when first struck, the deal was intended to be only a limited stopgap measure, one "instinctive" move among many on the part of the Thai to keep the Vietnamese forces away from the Thai border areas. From Kriangsak's point of view, with the Khmer Rouge still in disarray and memories of their atrocities against Thai villagers still fresh, the effort to shore up the Cambodian resistance was certainly not designed to be a fully committed, large-scale undertaking, and the real emphasis was on maintaining direct contacts with the Hanoi leadership aimed at securing an agreement not to threaten Thailand's territory.[30]

However, as time went on, the deal began to take on a life of its own. The "Sino-Thai partnership," whereby the PRC provides weapons and other supplies to the Cambodian resistance and the RTG unloads them off ships and trucks and convoys them to various supply points, has now become a permanent, large-scale operation, with some 300–500 tons of material being sent to the Khmer Rouge every month, according to one estimate.[31] One reason was the departure from office of Premier Kriangsak, who was much more ambivalent than his successor, General Prem Tinsulanonda, about the wisdom of being too close to Beijing and of maintaining an implacably hard-line posture vis-à-vis Hanoi.[32] More importantly, another reason was that the deal had a number of consequences which in turn served to strengthen the commitment of both sides to it. Or, to put it differently, the process of implementing the deal had the effect of sustaining and reinforcing it so that

---

[29]"Hard" facts are impossible to find. The only Thai public figure who has publicly alluded to the existence of such a deal was former Supreme Commander General Saiyud Kerdphol, who wrote:

> The Cambodian conflict made Peking suddenly more dependent on Thai goodwill in order to pursue its goals in the region. Most specifically, this shift saw the need to channel munitions and logistics support to pro-Chinese Khmer Rouge guerrillas along the Thai border in order to provide continued resistance to Vietnamese occupation forces. Bangkok found itself in a position to appeal to Peking to end its support for the CPT. (Kerdphol, *Struggle for Thailand*, pp. 166–67.)

[30]In his interview with the author, General Kriangsak related how he tried to create some sort of understanding with Pham Van Dong concerning how far Vietnamese forces should go. At first the Thai premier tried to make them stop at the Mekong's left bank. When that failed, he asked them to stop at a line 30 kilometers from the Thai border. And when that also failed, he successfully gained Hanoi's promise that Vietnamese troops would not cross into Thai territory, which of course was later broken.

[31]Paul Quinn-Judge, "Hollow Victory," *Far Eastern Economic Review* (hereafter cited as *FEER*), June 14, 1984, p. 30. Major weapons are small artillery pieces, grenade launchers, mortars, rifles, and mines.

[32]Kriangsak's interview with the author.

now in a way it has become an "institutionalized" mechanism for close Sino-Thai security cooperation.

In the first place, the "Sino-Thai partnership" has contributed toward the strengthening of the Cambodian resistance forces, and the latter's growing strength inevitably reinforces the rationale for sustaining and indeed increasing assistance to them. Despite much talk about the lack of unity within the anti-Vietnamese movement, the fact is that the Cambodian resistance has become a viable enterprise. Between 1979 and 1986, the total number of armed Cambodians fighting the Vietnamese occupation troops increased nearly threefold, from some 22,000 to over 60,000, with the Khmer Rouge now being able to field up to 40,000. The latter in particular are capable of operating deep inside Cambodian territory and often close to main urban centers.[33]

Moreover, despite the fact that it was a "shotgun" union, forged from disparate groups with disparate and conflicting aims and ideologies,[34] the Coalition Government of Democratic Kampuchea (CGDK), the "united front" of the Cambodian resistance forces, has survived for nearly five years, and its legitimacy as the rightful government of Cambodia continues to be accepted by an overwhelming majority of the international community.[35] From the Thai point of view, the ability of the CGDK to sustain military and political pressures on Vietnam is a crucial factor, confirming the correctness of Thai policy toward the conflict over Cambodia and the utility of the Sino-Thai security collaboration. It also lends credence to the off-repeated claim that time is on the side of those opposing Hanoi's occupation of that troubled land.[36]

Second, the deal contributed to the decline of the communist insurgency problem in Thailand. China's promise to cease all but moral sup-

---

[33]One of the earliest published works verifying the Cambodian resistance forces' effective penetration of the interior and raids on urban centers was John McBeth, "Jumping the Gun," *FEER*, February 16, 1984, p. 22.

[34]See, e.g., Jacques Bekaert, "Year of the Nationalists?" in Pushpa Thambipillai, ed., *Southeast Asian Affairs, 1983* (Singapore: Institute of Southeast Asian Studies, 1983), pp. 164–72, 176–78; Carlyle Thayer, prepared statement for a hearing on "Cambodia After Five Years of Vietnamese Occupation," before the Subcommittee on Asian and Pacific Affairs, Committee on Foreign Affairs, House of Representatives, 98th Congress, First Session on H. Con. Res. 176, September 15 and October 6 and 8, 1983 (Washington, D.C.: U.S. Government Printing Office, 1983), p. 40; and Steve Heder, "KPNLF's Guerrilla Strategy Yields Mixed Results," *Indochina Issues*, April 1984, pp. 1–7.

[35]Since the formation of the CGDK in June 1982, ASEAN's resolutions on Cambodia have been approved by 105 votes for, 23 votes against in 1982; 105–23 in 1983; 110–22 in 1984; 114–21 in 1985; 115–21 in 1986; and 117–21 in 1987.

[36]Sarasin Viraphol, "Thailand's Perspectives on Its Rivalry with Vietnam," in William S. Turley, ed., *Confrontation or Coexistence: The Future of ASEAN-Vietnam Relations* (Bangkok: Institute of Security and International Studies, Chulalongkorn University, 1985), pp. 28–31.

port for the CPT, its insistence that the party stand by Beijing in its conflict with Hanoi, and its alignment with the RTG in the Cambodia conflict generated dilemmas and divisive ideological debates within the CPT-led Thai radical movement concerning the movement's appropriate leadership, objectives, roles, and external affiliations. These dilemmas and debates in turn exacerbated the already existing tension between the staunchly "conservative" pro-Chinese Politburo and many of the party's more progressive, nationalistic and youthful rank and file, who wished to see the CPT adopt an independent revolutionary strategy based upon consideration of Thai interests.[37]

The combination of these developments—the loss of Lao sanctuaries, the RTG's more balanced and sometimes also more sophisticated approach for dealing with armed communism (including an amnesty program),[38] and growing disillusionment with the insurgents' way of life among many who had joined the movement after the October 6, 1976, coup—had a dramatic effect on the CPT. In 1979 defections went up three times the previous rate. In 1980 and early 1981 prominent radical leaders, including Seksan Prasertgul and his wife, Therdphoum Chaidee, Khaisaeng Suksai and Thirayuth Boonmee surrendered to the authorities. By mid-1981 the main communist united front organization, the CCPDGF, already strained since its founding in 1977 by tensions between the dominant CPT and its other member groups, for all intents and purposes ceased to function. At the same time the CPT in fact began to sue—unsuccessfully, as it turned out—for a ceasefire with the RTG. In the middle of 1982, after the CPT's Fourth National Congress ended, the intraparty split became public knowledge,[39] and the first mass exodus of guerrillas and sympathizers from the CPT began. By the mid-1980s, the number of armed insurgents dropped to somewhere between 2,000 and 400–500[40] and the number of incidents of violence

---

[37]See Suwannapanich and Choonhavan, "Communist Party of Thailand"; and Wedel, *Thai Radicals.*

[38]This includes greater stress on political and socioeconomic measures, one of which was the much heralded order of the prime minister's office No. 66/2523, promulgated in April 1980; see Paribatra, "Thailand: Defense Spending and Threat Perception," pp. 84–90.

[39]One of the best accounts of the debates during the Fourth Congress was provided by a defected CPT Central Committee member, Dr.Wang Tochirakarn, himself one of the younger and more progressive party cadres, in his article "The Truth About the Fourth Congress of the Communist Party of Thailand," for *Matichon Sud-Supda* in 1983; the English translation can be found in *ISIS Bulletin* 2(3) (July 1983): 8–15.

[40]The higher figure was given in Kerdphol, *Struggle for Thailand*, p. 173; the lower one by the present commander-in-chief of the Royal Thai Army, General Chavalit Yongchaiyuth, reported in *The Nation*, July 23, 1986, p. 3.

involving the party and RTG personnel decreased rapidly from the peak of 4,144 in 1978 to 2,772 and 1,891 in 1979 and 1980, respectively, and reached an all-time low of 353 in 1983.[41] For the post-1979 CPT, although funds are sometimes made available by a number of Sino-Thai trade associations, self-reliance has become an absolute necessity.[42] These developments have prompted at least one senior army officer to assert on the record that the present party had lost its capacity to take military initiative and hence no longer posed a serious military threat.[43]

The decline of the CPT insurgency movement in turn created the psychological basis for the development of close cooperation between the PRC and members of Thailand's conservative security establishment. Before 1979, with the communist insurgency in full swing, the Thai military, the National Security Council (NSC), and other RTG agencies responsible for safeguarding the nation's security had not relinquished their fears of China. Indeed, for a long time during the so-called "Democratic Period" between 1973 and 1976, the NSC successfully blocked any move on the part of civilian governments to open up diplomatic relations with the PRC.[44]

After 1979, however, although suspicions remained, Thai apprehensions were considerably reduced, as the domestic insurgency movement dramatically declined, with the Chinese keeping their promise not to support the CPT and turning their attention increasingly inward to economic reforms. The trust that has grown in Thailand's conduct of relations with the PRC since 1979 is indicated by the frequency of visits by high-ranking Thais to the PRC since 1979, a list which includes not only the incumbent holders of all the most important security or security-related offices, but also Crown Princess Sirindhorn in 1981 and the Crown Prince in 1987. Indeed, the transformation of ACM Siddhi Savetsila, from being the secretary general of the NSC, which had been fervently Sinophobic in the mid-1970s, to being the minister of Foreign Affairs, who stresses the importance of collaboration with Beijing in the 1980s, epitomizes this new psychological climate in Thai dealings with the PRC.[45]

---

[41]See the table in Kerdphol, *Struggle for Thailand*, p. 204.

[42]Kerdphol, *Struggle for Thailand*, p. 172.

[43]The remark of the then assistant chief-of-staff of the Royal Thai Army, Lt. Gen. Chavalit Yongchaiyuth, reported in the *Nation Review*, October 18, 1984, p. 1. General Chavalit, however, has subsequently modified his view.

[44]For the NSC's standpoint concerning normalization with the PRC, see Viraphol, *Directions in Thai Foreign Policy*, pp. 20–21.

[45]See ACM Siddhi's interviews in *The Nation*, November 19, 1986, p. 4, and January 7, 1987, p. 4.

Third, the Sino-Thai deal also created a concrete operational basis for closer cooperation. In channeling supplies to the Cambodian resistance and overseeing its activities on Thai territory, Thai military officers have found it necessary to coordinate their actions with the Chinese, who continue to have direct access to the Khmer Rouge leadership. The dealings are impossible for outsiders to document, but from the evidence available there has developed in recent years an extremely close working relationship between some members of the PRC embassy staff on one hand and a group of RTA officers under the direct command of the present army chief, General Chavalit Yongchaiyuth, on the other. This relationship not only creates a good deal of familiarity among all officials concerned, but also helps to forge common vested interests, bureaucratic and otherwise, which in turn form the basis for further cooperation.[46]

Strengthening of Thailand's Military Capabilities

The second area of Sino-Thai security cooperation is the strengthening of Thailand's military capabilities. Again it is difficult, if not impossible, for outsiders to assess with any degree of confidence and accuracy the nature and extent of this relationship. But the available evidence suggests that Sino-Thai security cooperation in this area takes two forms and has rapidly increased since 1979, in the same manner as the operation of supplying the Cambodian resistance.

One is some sort of informal understanding that the PRC would contribute to Thailand's deterrence posture and help ensure that major incursions or invasions by Vietnam are prevented. This understanding probably evolved in the first year of the Cambodia conflict when the Thais were highly apprehensive about the border situation and the Chinese were eager to secure Thailand's assistance in facilitating supplies to the Cambodian resistance and its participation in the "united front" against Hanoi.[47] In October 1979 the first public indication of such understanding appeared when Deng Xiaoping told the visiting Thai National Assembly speaker that China "will stand on the side of Thai-

---

[46]Indeed, informed sources are of the opinion that the meteoric rise of General Chavalit from an obscure Signals Corps staff officer to the position of army chief within the space of seven years was due not only to his personal relationship with Premier Prem Tinsulanonda, but also to his control of the Thai-Cambodian border policy. This allowed him to demonstrate deft touches in handling political, diplomatic, and security problems that arose, to make himself known to the foreign diplomatic and security community, and to utilize whatever resources that might be available to an officer in charge of a sensitive border in pursuit of political gains.

[47]See, e.g., Geng Biao's comments quoted in n. 28 above.

land if Vietnam attacks it."[48] Indeed, by 1987, the PRC might have even privately promised to retaliate against Vietnamese attacks on Thailand within a specified period of time.[49]

The credibility of China's contribution is based upon the demonstration in February–March 1979 that alone among the great powers involved in the affairs of Southeast Asia it is prepared to use force, and suffer great losses, to contain Vietnam's expansion. It is also based upon the continued stationing of a large number of troops on the Sino-Vietnamese border, who keep preoccupied up to twenty-five of Vietnam's fifty-six frontline infantry divisions and thus make it difficult for any of them to be redeployed in Cambodia or on the Thai-Cambodian border.[50]

The PRC's commitment to Thailand's security is signaled to Hanoi in a number of ways. One is a series of statements of commitment by high-ranking Chinese officials issued to coincide with major incidents on the Thai-Cambodian border or after all major rounds of meetings with Thai officials. In this respect one significant statement was that announced by the Chinese Foreign Ministry in the aftermath of the Vietnamese incursion into Thai territory at Non Mark Moon in June 1980. The Chinese delivered a stern warning, demanding the Vietnamese to "stop their aggression in Thailand at once" and calling the attention of the Vietnamese to the "grave danger involved" if they persisted in "military adventures."[51] Another significant statement was the one issued in Bangkok by the visiting Chinese army chief-of-staff Yang Dezhi in February 1983, warning that "if Vietnam dares to make an armed incursion into Thailand, the Chinese army will not stay idle; we will give support to the Thai people to defend their country."[52] As John McBeth pointed out, this was the first time a Chinese military leader had delivered a warning to Hanoi while in Thailand.[53]

---

[48]Quoted in Jain, China and Thailand, p. 248.

[49]An "Intelligence" item, headlined "Kunming Hotline," in FEER, reported: "In a bid to assure Thailand of its firm commitment to Thai security, China recently established a radio-telephone link between its Kunming Military Region Headquarters and the Thai Supreme Command in Bangkok. Under the arrangement the Thais can report Vietnamese shellings or attacks on their border and expect that within six hours the Chinese army stationed along Vietnam's northern border will repay the Vietnamese in kind" (January 2, 1986, p. 9).

[50]See William S. Turley, "Vietnam/Indochina: Hanoi's Challenge to Southeast Asian Regional Order," in Young Whan Kihl and Lawrence E. Grinter, eds., Asian-Pacific Security: Emerging Challenges and Responses (Boulder, Col.: Lynne Rienner Publishers, 1986), pp. 190–91.

[51]SWB, FE/6456, June 27, 1980, p. A3/1–2.

[52]Bangkok World, February 5, 1983, p. 1.

[53]John McBeth, "Close Ties for Comfort," FEER, March 17, 1983, p. 19.

Another way through which the PRC's commitment to Thailand's security is signaled to Hanoi is Chinese troop movements and/or the shelling of Vietnamese positions during periods when incidents on the Thai-Cambodian border occur or are in prospect, or when doubts are expressed concerning the extent of Chinese commitment to Thai security.[54] Recently, certain procedures may have been worked out by Thai and Chinese officials for coordinating their action in the event of an incident on the Thai-Cambodian border.[55]

The third way is frequent exchanges of visits by high-ranking military officials and consultations on security issues during these visits, which have increased rapidly since Chinese air force chief Zhang Tingfa went to Thailand in March 1981. The list of Thai visitors to the PRC includes the incumbent holders of all the majority security portfolios, with many of them being invited to inspect the Sino-Vietnamese border. The most recent visit was Yang Dezhi's second to Bangkok in mid-January 1987, during which not only did the Chinese army chief-of-staff go to the Thai-Cambodian border, but the RTA also did not hide the fact that discussions were held to find ways and means of significantly increasing Sino-Thai security cooperation, including military grant aid, exchange of training, and more arms transfers.[56]

The other form of security cooperation in this area is more direct. It involves transfers of Chinese weapons. According to some reports, in 1982 the Thais tried to acquire some arms from the PRC, but the latter expressed its preference for, and did propose, a joint arms production project.[57] Apparently the subject was too sensitive to pursue at that time, but in 1985, either during or after Hanoi's dry season offensive, the Chinese began to provide, free of charge, 130mm artillery pieces and shells for use on the Cambodian border.[58]

After many unconfirmed reports since 1985 that Thailand has acquired from China a number of T-69 tanks, a modified version of the Soviet-built T-54 and T-55,[59] the RTA finally confirmed in March 1987, a

---

[54]The most recent example is probably China's armed clashes with Vietnam on January 5–7, 1987, which by all accounts were the most serious since the 1979 war. Analysts believed that this was caused by Beijing's concern with a Vietnamese troop buildup in strategic areas in Cambodia, as well as the perceived need to reassure Thailand and the Cambodian resistance of its continuing commitment; see Murray Hiebert, "A Border Flare-up," *FEER*, January 22, 1987, p. 26.

[55]*FEER*, January 2, 1986, p. 9.

[56]*The Nation*, January 15, 1987, p. 1; also Kavi Chongkittavorn, "Sino-Thai Defense Relations Firming Up," *The Nation*, February 5, 1987, p. 5.

[57]*Nation Review*, October 31, 1982, pp. 1–2.

[58]Chongkittavorn, "Sino-Thai Defense Relations," p. 5.

[59]*Nation Review*, November 19, 1985, pp. 1–2; and *The Nation*, January 26, 1987, p. 1.

few weeks after Yang Dezhi's second visit, that it planned to buy fifty to sixty T-69s "at only a token price of 10 percent of the market price and with a grace period."[60] This was followed by the announcements that the Royal Thai Air Force (RTAF) would buy a number of P-74 37mm Chinese antiaircraft guns and that, in addition to the T-69s, the RTA would purchase some 400 armored personnel carriers (APC) from Beijing in 1987.[61] Discussions are under way to find venues for promoting cooperation in this regard. The Chinese have offered to sell a range of weapons, from more artillery pieces to F-7 aircraft and conventional "Romeo"-class submarines,[62] but the Thai so far have not responded by making further purchases, preferring to talk about direct military assistance (free 130mm shells and credit for arms procurements)[63] and exchanges of military training.[64] But after incumbent Thai army chief General Chavalit's visit to Beijing in May 1987, further purchases of Chinese weapons are indicated.[65]

The PRC's contribution to Thailand's deterrence posture has not proved to be completely effective, as demonstrated by the Vietnamese dry season offensives in 1984–85, which led to a number of incursions into Thai territory and armed clashes with Thai security forces.[66] Moreover, Thai acquisition of heavier Chinese weapons has been limited: only sixteen or eighteen 130mm artillery pieces have been provided so far,[67] and the core of the RTA's armored strength will continue to consist of U.S.-made M-48 tanks, which now number 190[68] and will soon increase to 230, with the addition of 40 more M48-A5.[69] But China's direct and indirect contribution toward the strengthening of Thailand's military capabilities has conferred a number of "benefits" on the latter, which in turn have served to enhance Sino-Thai cooperation over time.

First, it gives Thailand a great deal of psychological assurance. The Vietnamese invasion of Cambodia came at the time when the kingdom's security was perceived to be at the lowest ebb. At home, 1978

---

[60]*Bangkok Post*, March 7, 1987, p. 1. A number of these tanks have arrived and have been publicly tested; see *The Nation*, December 25, 1987, p. 1.

[61]*The Nation*, March 22, 1987, pp. 1–2, and April 12, 1987, pp. 1, 3.

[62]*The Nation*, January 8, 1987, pp. 1–2.

[63]*The Nation*, January 15, 1987, pp. 1–2, and January 16, 1987, p. 4.

[64]Chongkittavorn, "Sino-Thai Defense Relations," p. 5.

[65]*Bangkok Post*, May 12, 1987, pp. 1, 3.

[66]Sukhumbhand Paribatra, *Kampuchea Without Delusion* (Kuala Lumpur: Institute of Strategic and International Studies, 1986), pp. 1–3.

[67]*Bangkok Post*, March 7, 1987, p. 1.

[68]See *The Military Balance, 1985–1986* (London: International Institute for Strategic Studies, 1985), p. 135.

[69]*Bangkok Post*, March 7, 1987, p. 1.

was the peak year for the number of violent incidents involving CPT insurgents and for the number of government casualties.[70] Abroad, Thailand's future seemed to be dependent only on its adversaries' goodwill.[71] Thus, when Vietnam invaded Cambodia, neither the accelerated armament program of 1977–78 nor words of assurance from the American ally could alter the fact and the perception that the kingdom had to stand alone with an inadequately prepared defense system.[72]

Security cooperation with the PRC, which demonstrated in February-March 1979 in particular that at present it is the only great power involved in the affairs of Southeast Asia both able and willing to use force in pursuit of its goals, helped to alleviate Thai fears and restore their self-confidence. As one Thai Foreign Ministry official observed:

> The Thai perception of Indochina has been transformed since 1975 from one of loss of confidence to one characterized by the restoration of a considerable degree of confidence. This has been brought about by the ability of Thailand to subsequently adapt itself to the new environment: finding new strength in ASEAN unity and solidarity, making peace with China and working out a meaningful symbiosis, and rediscovering the viability of Thailand's own institutions.[73]

Moreover, security cooperation with the PRC in this area has engendered a good deal of trust and faith in the latter's ability and willingness to support Thailand against Vietnam. A survey of the Thai elite conducted in 1982 found that over 80 percent of the respondents believed China could be depended upon for assistance if Vietnam attacked Thailand directly and that nearly half of this number believed assistance would come in a military form.[74] The restoration of Thai self-confidence and the faith in the PRC's commitment to Thai security have helped to convince the Thais of the correctness of their policy toward the Cambodia conflict, to make them less willing to compromise with Vietnam, and to generate the belief that over the long run the correlation of forces is decisively against Hanoi and that in time the latter will be forced to capitulate.

The "hardening" of the Thai perspective, together with the close Sino-Thai alignment, has made the structure of the Cambodia conflict

---

[70]Kerdphol, *Struggle for Thailand*, pp. 186–87.
[71]Viraphol, "Thailand's Perspectives," p. 21.
[72]Kriangsak's interview with the author.
[73]Viraphol, "Thailand's Perspectives," p. 26.
[74]Kramol Tongdhammachart, Kusuma Snitwongse, Sarasin Viraphol, Arong Suthasasna, Wiwat Mungkandi, and Sukhumbhand Paribatra, *The Thai Elite's National Security Perspectives: Implications for Southeast Asia*, (Research Report in 1983).

less amenable to resolution through compromise. The reduced likelihood of settlement in turn means that the Thais continue to attach value to psychological assurances arising from their security cooperation with the PRC and to seek to increase it over time, thus further diminishing the possibility of compromise. Such is the "vicious cycle" of the conflict over Cambodia.[75] Furthermore, as in the case of the deal concerning the CPT and supplies to the Cambodian resistance, Sino-Thai cooperation to enhance indirectly and directly Thailand's military capabilities has created a concrete operational basis for yet closer cooperation.

For one thing, although the day-to-day working relationship between Thai and Chinese security officials is impossible for outsiders to document, the available evidence seems to suggest that a good deal of familiarity and mutual trust seems to have developed out of the extensive exchanges between the two sides. Indeed, it is significant that PRC officials have been allowed to attend Thai-U.S. military exercises, code-named *Cobra Gold*, which have taken place annually since 1982,[76] or that Yang Dezhi during his second visit was taken to inspect the Kanchanaburi-based Ninth Infantry Division, which along with the First Division is considered to be the RTA's "pride and joy" and which is to be used as a prototype for the present Thai army chief's modernization program.[77]

For another, arms transfer from the PRC fit well with the RTA's overall development plans. Since the withdrawal of the United States from mainland Southeast Asia in the mid-1970s, the Thai military have striven, first, to make the Thai armed forces more independent or, at the very least, far less dependent on the United States than before; and, second, to equip them with modern weapons for conventional rather than counterinsurgency warfare purposes within the constraints imposed by budgetary and general economic considerations.[78]

Acquisition of arms from the PRC is becoming increasingly an integral part of the process of diversifying suppliers. Furthermore, Chinese 130mm artillery pieces and T-69 tanks are considered to be excellent weapons, obtainable at far cheaper prices and in a shorter time than

---

[75]A more extensive discussion of the foregoing is provided in Sukhumbhand Paribatra, "Irreversible History? ASEAN, Vietnam, and the Polarization of Southeast Asia," in Karl D. Jackson, Sukhumbhand Paribatra, and J. Soedjati Djiwandono, eds., *ASEAN in Regional and Global Context* (Berkeley: Institute of East Asian Studies, University of California, 1986), pp. 221-37.

[76]See "Cobra Gold '84: U.S. and Thai Military Forces Working Together," *Asia-Pacific Defence Forum*, Winter 1984-85, p. 32.

[77]*Bangkok Post*, January 15, 1987, p. 3.

[78]Paribatra, "Thailand: Defense Spending and Threat Perception," passim.

American weapons, attributes which are highly attractive at a time when budgetary constraints are being felt more, border security needs rapid reinforcement,[79] and the United States has cut its Foreign Military Sales (FMS) program to Thailand. In other words, procurement of Chinese weapons at this juncture is perceived to be highly appropriate for the Thai military's present professional requirements and thus is likely to increase over time.

This process may be self-sustaining, for arms transfers inevitably help to forge common vested interests, bureaucratic or otherwise, between sellers and those empowered to make purchases. As the PRC has more weapons to sell rather than to give away to Thailand, the likelihood is that more will be bought. Such is the "virtuous cycle" of the arms bazaar.

The Evolving Relationship

As a result of the convergence of Sino-Thai security interests and the cooperation in security matters that this process has engendered, there has evolved a great degree of coordination in the overall conduct of diplomacy, with the focus inevitably being on the Cambodia conflict.

As demonstrated by what took place in the International Conference on Kampuchea (ICK) in 1981 and by many other diplomatic developments since the Vietnamese invasion of Cambodia, the PRC wields the power of veto in all major questions pertaining to the Cambodia conflict, adamantly refusing to abandon both the policy of attrition of Hanoi and the policy of support for the Khmer Rouge.[80] This power of veto, together with the growing security relationship between Beijing and Bangkok, has given much anxiety to Indonesia and Malaysia, which continue to entertain great distrust of the PRC.[81] Paradoxically, the development of a close working relationship between China and Thailand has been one of the main factors helping to prevent polarization and to preserve a level of cohesion in the Sino-ASEAN anti-Hanoi alignment *in the short run*. As indicated most recently by Indonesia's

---

[79]Chongkittavorn, "Sino-Thai Defense Relations," p. 5; and Chinwanno, p. 7. See also Pichai Chuensuksawasdi and Banyat Tasaneeyavej, "New Angle in Ties with China," *Bangkok Post*, February 14, 1987, p. 4.

[80]For analyses of China's policy and role in the conflict, see, e.g., Copper, "China and Southeast Asia," pp. 47–64; and Sheldon W. Simon, "The People's Republic of China and Southeast Asia: Protector or Predator," in Jackson, Paribatra, and Djiwandono, *ASEAN in Regional and Global Context*, pp. 342–46.

[81]See, e.g., Michael Leifer, "ASEAN Under Stress over Cambodia," *FEER*, June 14, 1984, pp. 34–36; and Bernard K. Gordon, "The Third Indochina Conflict," *Foreign Affairs*, Fall 1986, pp. 78–80. See also Paribatra, "Irreversible History?"

revival of the "cocktail party" proposal, Thailand's role as some sort of "interlocutor" between China and ASEAN has helped to ensure that intramural differences are kept largely intramural and that the exertion of Chinese veto power, when it is put into effect, takes place behind the scene, not in the glare of international publicity.[82]

Furthermore, the development of a close working relationship between Thailand and China on the issue of Cambodia has served as a starting point for cooperation and coordination in a number of international forums. These include, not only the U.N. General Assembly (UNGA), where ASEAN submits its proposals on Cambodia every year, but also the Security Council—where Thailand was elected as a nonpermanent member in 1985—North-South dialogues, the Group of 77, and GATT meetings.[83] A survey of UNGA voting patterns undertaken by the author clearly indicates concurrence between the two in most international issues (see Table 1).

The convergence of Sino-Thai security interests and the bilateral security cooperation were also crucial stimuli for the expanded economic relationship between the two countries since 1979. China's modernization programs begun in 1978 certainly created the ideal psychological climate for such expansion, as evident from the signing of the bilateral trade agreement in March 1978. But it was only in November 1978, at the time of growing tension in Indochina, that a protocol on import and export was signed during Deng Xiaoping's visit to Bangkok, translating the generalities concerning trade expansion based on "mutual advantages" and "equality of status," as contained in the March 1978 agreement, into concrete details concerning the items and

---

[82]During his visit to Hanoi in July 1987, Indonesian foreign minister Mochtar Kusumaatmadja agreed with his Vietnamese counterpart, Nguyen Co Thach, that there should be a meeting among all the warring Cambodian factions on an "equal footing, without preconditions and with no political label," and only at a later stage would Indonesia invite others, including Vietnam, to participate. This agreement was not endorsed by Thailand and Singapore and thus was later amended at the ASEAN foreign ministers meeting, held in Bangkok on August 16, 1987, to make Vietnam participate immediately after the initial meeting among Cambodians, thus making clear Hanoi is a party to the conflict and also to include as agenda elements of the CGDK's eight-point peace plan, which Vietnam had already rejected; see Paisal Sricharatchanya, "New Mix to Old Cocktail," FEER, September 3, 1987, pp. 8–9. The PRC opposed these initiatives, but after a discussion between Thai foreign minister Siddhi and Chinese foreign minister Wu Xueqian, it voiced limited support, thus avoiding an open breach with ASEAN; see Bangkok Post, August 21, 1987, p. 2.

[83]Prachyadavi Tavedikul, "China-Thailand Links Making Good Progress," Bangkok Post, October 1, 1986, p. 4. The author was until recently a high-ranking Thai Foreign Ministry official.

Table 1

Pattern of Thailand's and China's Voting in the
U.N. General Assembly

Year	No. of Times Votes Taken	No. of Times Voting the Same	Percentages of Voting the Same
1979	125	105	84
1980	116	85	73
1981	133	107	80
1982	156	124	79
1983	146	115	79
1984	151	129	85
1985	157	130	83
1986	171	130	76

SOURCE: Department of International Organizations, Ministry of Foreign Affairs, Thailand.

the volumes of such items to be traded. Since then, annual trade protocols have been signed, stipulating what was to be imported and exported by the two countries each year. Furthermore, in November 1979, another agreement was made, establishing a joint Sino-Thai committee for trade, which subsequently came to meet annually, alternating between Beijing and Bangkok, to keep track of all bilateral trade matters.

As Ahmad and Chan pointed out, although the use of annual protocols as the format for the conduct of bilateral trade is a rather inflexible approach, it seems to work.[84] Total exchanges between Thailand and the PRC increased 103 percent between 1978 and 1979 and a further 70 percent between 1979 and 1980, and at the end of 1985 they stood at baht 13,440.4 million (see Table 2). Along with this expansion a process of diversification has also taken place, and Thailand's importation of Chinese oil is no longer as dominant an item as before. Whereas in 1980 trade in nonoil products formed only 55 percent of the total bilateral trade, in 1985 the proportion rose to 83 percent. Thailand's nonoil imports from the PRC now cover a wide range of goods, including chemical products, soya bean cake, industrial and agricultural machinery, cotton, raw silk, medicinal plants, and various medicines. The PRC has also expanded its range of imports from Thailand. Apart from such "traditional" products as rice, maize, green beans, smoked rubber sheets, tobacco leaf, tapioca, building material, and synthetic fibers, in

---

[84]Admad and Chan, *Riding the Chinese Dragon.*

Table 2

Thailand's Trade with the PRC 1972–85
(baht millions)*

Year	Exports	Imports	Total Trade	Trade Balance
1972	0.0	0.3	0.3	−0.3
1973	0.0	0.0	0.0	+0.0
1974	2.3	91.9	94.2	−89.6
1975	391.3	343.9	735.2	+47.4
1976	1,266.0	1,462.5	2,728.5	−196.5
1977	2,081.6	1,370.6	3,452.2	+711.0
1978	1,497.6	1,703.7	3,201.3	−206.1
1979	1,571.9	4,939.5	6,511.4	−3,367.6
1980	2,530.7	8,535.1	11,065.8	−6,004.4
1981	4,063.5	6,982.9	11,046.4	−2,919.4
1982	7,053.0	5,374.5	12,427.5	+1,678.5
1983	2,467.5	6,099.2	8,566.7	−3,339.1
1984	4,295.1	7,448.8	11,743.9	−3,153.7
1985	7,367.2	6,073.2	13,440.4	+1,293.9

*Before 1980, the official exchange rate of the baht to the U.S. dollar was 20, between
1980 and 1984 about 23, and between November 1984 and early 1987 about 25-26.

SOURCE: Department of Business Economics, Ministry of Commerce, Thailand.

the trade protocols of 1986 and 1987 it has agreed to buy coconut oil, gem stones, fruits, fish meal, leather, and pulp.[85]

The security-stimulated nature of this trade expansion is further indicated by the fact that recently the PRC has agreed to purchase a number of commodities, which it obviously does not need but for which Thailand could not find markets elsewhere. Examples are US$43 million-worth of rice and maize in early 1986, 30,000 tons of Thai glutinous rice and 20,000 tons of green mung beans in November 1986,[86] and between 100,000 and 200,000 tons of raw sugar in December 1986.[87]

Similar trends can be discerned in investment, although the exact figures may be very difficult to identify because a number of Chinese investments in Thailand and Thai investments in the PRC may have "originated" in Hong Kong. While in 1980 the value of registered capital investment by the PRC in Thailand amounted only to baht 200,000, by 1985 the total has gone up to nearly baht 100 million. Now there are over twenty Sino-Thai joint ventures in Thailand, the largest number in

---

[85]According to information provided by Department of Business Economics, Ministry of Commerce, Thailand (hereafter cited as Department of Business Economics).
[86]Paisal Sricharatchanya, "Staying Just Friends," *FEER*, December 11, 1986, p. 34.
[87]*The Nation*, November 29, 1986, p. 17.

an ASEAN country with the exception of Singapore, with the focus of investment being on construction, travel agencies, transportation, shopping centers, housing estates, and factories for manufacturing salt, processing timber, and producing farm machineries.[88] As Ahmad and Chan pointed out, the PRC's investments in Thailand have been facilitated by the fact that Indonesia and Malaysia, two other resource-rich ASEAN countries, are unwilling to accept Chinese investments. Indeed, among the ASEAN countries Thailand is unique in allowing Chinese labor to be used in Thailand for construction projects, the value of which was estimated to be over baht 1 billion in 1984.[89]

Since 1980 Thai investments in China have also been on the increase. A total of twenty-five investment agreements have been made,[90] and some US$23.3 million invested in a number of enterprises ranging from animal feeds, glass, consumer durables to golf courses and hotels.[91] Again with the exception of Singapore, among the ASEAN countries Thailand's investors have been the most active in the PRC.[92]

Because the investment relationship is new, there is still some uncertainty, especially on the part of Thai investors who find the PRC's case-by-case approach in the structuring of Sino-Thai joint ventures there somewhat disconcerting.[93] But the two governments at present seem to have the political will to smooth things over. Since 1980, a number of investment promotion agreements have been signed; they have served to eliminate many legal impediments and shortcomings. These include one on investment-capital protection in March 1985 and another on double taxation avoidance in October 1986.[94]

Concurrent with this expansion of economic relationship there have also been greater social exchanges. According to Thai foreign minister ACM Siddhi Savetsila, while ''formal and semiformal'' visits by high-ranking Thais numbered only sixty-one in 1979, by 1985 they had increased to 722.[95] Although those who are neither Thai nor Chinese are included in the figures, the growth of the number of passengers flown on the Thai national carrier, Thai Airways International, between desti-

---

[88]According to information provided by the Economic Relations Promotion Division, Department of Economics, Ministry of Foreign Affairs, Thailand (hereafter cited as Economic Relations Promotion Division).

[89]Ahmad and Chan, *Riding the Chinese Dragon*.

[90]Ibid.

[91]Economic Relations Promotion Division.

[92]Ahmad and Chan, *Riding the Chinese Dragon*.

[93]Ibid.

[94]Economic Relations Promotion Division.

[95]Interview in *The Nation*, November 19, 1986, p. 4.

nations in Thailand and China is also indicative of the prevailing trend. Between 1981 and 1985 the annual total increased three and a half times, from 12,953 to 47,232[96] with significant proportions being those living in one country traveling to the other to visit relatives.[97]

"Maturing" is often used to describe both the quality of and the trend in the evolution of Thailand's relations with China,[98] and given the expansion of economic and social exchanges, as well as the development of close working ties in political and security issues, between the two countries since 1978–79, this word is accurate. Indeed, present good relations are symbolized by discussions under way to make Bangkok and Beijing "Twin Cities."[99] However, the relationship is still not without difficulties and constraints.

The first is that the present close relationship between Thailand and the PRC ultimately is based on one thing, and one thing only, namely, a common interest in preventing a Vietnamese military *diktat* in Indochina. This is the relationship's strength, as well as its weakness. As long as Vietnam maintains a significant military presence in Cambodia, Sino-Thai security cooperation is likely to endure, but there is little scope for expanding bilateral ties in other directions. As Table 2 indicates, the level of trade did not increase significantly from 1980 to 1985 and may now be in the process of decline. The December 1986 protocol envisages a trade target ceiling for 1987 of only US$500 million, which at current exchange rates is equivalent to less than baht 13,000 million, a lower figure than in 1985.[100]

The limited scope for expanding bilateral trade in the future is due to two reasons. One is that given the present trends in the world oil market and the development of its own energy resources, Thailand no longer needs as much Chinese oil as before. According to the latest figures published by the Ministry of Commerce, only baht 570 million worth of oil products was purchased in the first seven months of 1986.[101]

The second reason is that Thailand and the PRC on the whole are at a similar stage of development, producing and exporting primary commodities and low-level technology, and importing higher level technol-

---

[96]According to information provided by Market Research Division, Thai Airways International.

[97]According to the Thai Ministry of Foreign Affairs, in 1985 there were 2,000 applications for visas by PRC residents to visit relatives in Thailand.

[98]For example, by Foreign Minister Siddhi in his interview in *The Nation*, November 19, 1986, p. 4.

[99]According to information provided by the Thai Ministry of Foreign Affairs.

[100]Department of Business Economics.

[101]Department of Business Economics.

ogy and other capital goods.[102] There is not much that China needs to buy from Thailand, and in several cases, as mentioned previously, it has agreed to buy only for political reasons, or more specifically, to satisfy Thai concerns with the continuing trade imbalance with the PRC and with overproduction of certain commodities. Indeed, Beijing sometimes has to reexport certain items, for example, mung beans, of which it is already producing a surplus.[103] Indications are that China is increasingly reluctant to keep its end of the bargain where these "goodwill" import items from Thailand are concerned.[104] Moreover, the two countries are competitors in many markets, most noticeably in primary commodities, textiles, handicraft and leather goods, and price-cutting has emerged as a bilateral problem.[105] The lack of complementarity is likely to persist, and this means that for both Thailand and China trading ties with third countries are, and will continue to be, much more important than bilateral ones.

The scope for expanding investments is similarly constrained. Partly because of the dominance of Japanese and Western investments and partly because of China's own financial and technological limitations, Chinese investments in Thailand take the form of "bits and pieces," distributed over a wide range of enterprises, which are by no means central to Thailand's pattern of development and are unlikely to pose a serious challenge to the established foreign capital in the near future.[106] Thailand's entrepreneurs in general are quick to respond to economic incentives, and at least two Bangkok-based corporations have invested substantially in China, namely, the Charoen Pokphand argoindustrial group and the Srifuengfung manufacturing group, but the overall response of Thailand's entrepreneurship to China's offers of investment opportunities has been so sluggish that it is difficult to foresee substantive changes in this area in the near future. As many have pointed out, in the longer term, conflict may arise because the PRC may increasingly compete with the ASEAN countries, including Thailand, for international investments from Japan, the United States, Western Europe, as well as the Asian "newly industrializing countries" or NICs.[107]

---

[102]Ahmad and Chin, *Riding the Chinese Dragon.*

[103]Ibid. In fact, China has been selling significant quantities of mung beans to India and Japan; see Sricharatchanya, "Staying Just Friends," p. 34.

[104]*The Nation*, November 29, 1986, p. 17.

[105]*The Nation*, December 23, 1986, pp. 1–2.

[106]According to information provided by the Board of Investment, Thailand. China ranks fourteenth in the list of foreign investors in Thailand, with only baht 99.6 million registered capital, compared with Japan's baht 2,835 million, the U.S. baht 1,820 million, Taiwan's baht 987 million, and Britain's baht 730 million.

[107]Chia, "China's Economic Relations."

Indeed, the limited scope of the economic relationship between Thailand and the PRC is demonstrated further by the strong ties between Thailand and Taiwan in trade and investment, despite the fact that the latter two ended their diplomatic relations in 1975 when Bangkok recognized the PRC. Trade has in fact grown rapidly since 1975, from baht 2,679.4 million in that year to baht 10,923.2 million in 1985, and at present Taiwan ranks fifteenth as a market for Thai products and eighth—four places above the PRC—as a source of Thai imports.[108]

More significant, however, is the investment relationship. Taiwan ranks third as a source of foreign investment in Thailand. At present, 116 Taiwan-based companies have invested in the kingdom under the Thai Board of Investment's (BoI) promotion schemes. The nature of the enterprises ranges from agroindustries, metallurgical industries, ceramics, chemicals, and electrical appliances to construction and services, all of which can be considered part and parcel of the "core" of Thailand's development drive.[109]

The second constraint is that even though Thailand and China share a common interest in preventing a Vietnamese military *diktat* in Indochina, their goals are not necessarily identical, and the differences between them may have an adverse impact on their future relationship. Although Thai leaders have opted to use the Khmer Rouge as one of the kingdom's quiver of arrows against Vietnam in Cambodia and see the former's involvement in the task of governance therein as a part of the solution of the conflict itself, they have not indicated in any way that they would like to see the Khmer Rouge replace the Heng Samrin group as *the* ruling party in Phnom Penh or that they would prefer Chinese to Vietnamese rule in Cambodia. In fact, continued Chinese insistence on preserving the Khmer Rouge as the predominant military force in the CGDK and on maintaining influence over the Cambodian resistance movement is likely to remain a potential source of friction between Thailand and the PRC in the future. Indeed, ironically, should the present Sino-ASEAN alignment succeed in driving Vietnam from Cambodia and the Khmer Rouge return to rule in Phnom Penh, a conflict is likely to develop between China and Thailand.

First, even though Thai leaders realize ASEAN's limitations and acknowledge that the organization lacks the wherewithal to guarantee

---

[108]Department of Business Economics. Major Thai exports to Taiwan are tapioca, green mung beans, rubber, fish products, sesame seeds, maize, electrical circuits, gypsum, and fluorite. Major Thai imports from Taiwan are iron scrap, steel, yarn, electrical appliances, machinery, bicycle parts, and motorcycle parts.

[109]Economic Relations Promotion Division and Board of Investment.

Thailand's security, they still attach a great deal of importance to ASEAN and what has been achieved through regional cooperation over the last decade.[110] Because Indonesia and Malaysia still harbor suspicions of China, the Thais are unlikely to endorse any political arrangement in Cambodia, planned or actualized, that allows Beijing substantially to increase its power and influence in Southeast Asia.

Second, there is no love lost between the Thais and the Khmer Rouge. Even though there is some sort of working relationship between the two, the Thai military has a long institutional memory, and past violence committed against Thais by the Khmer Rouge while in power in Cambodia still generates distrust and even hatred. For this reason the Khmer Rouge's triumphant return to Phnom Penh as the ruling party is likely to be perceived by Thailand with grave concern.

Third, and most important, the Thais still consider the PRC a dangerous subversive power. This is indicated by the survey of the Thai elite conducted in 1982.[111] It is also reflected in the RTG's continuing concern with the CPT despite the fact that the armed insurgency has declined to a very low level.[112] Indeed, it is significant that the Thais have adamantly refused to conclude a cultural agreement with the PRC because such an agreement is seen to offer opportunities for subversion by Beijing, and in July 1986 when restrictions were placed by the RTG on movements of diplomats from a number of countries for reasons of "security" and "reciprocity," China was included in the list.[113] The PRC may have developed a powerful "constituency" in Thailand, comprising the RTA officers, who have worked closely with Chinese officials, and the members of the financial and business community, who have benefited from the Sino-Thai economic relations, but this "constituency" is neither all-powerful nor coherent nor invulnerable to charges of being too pro-Beijing and hence "pro-communist." It is significant that the present army chief, General Chavalit Yongchaiyuth, who has been instrumental on the Thai side in forging close cooperation with the Chinese, is one of the very few RTA officers who have said on record that "China is still supplying arms to the guerrillas of the Communist

---

[110]The attitudes of the Thai elite toward ASEAN are discussed in Tongdhammachart et al.
[111]Ibid.
[112]Report of commander-in-chief of the Royal Thai Army General Chavalit Yongchaiyuth to the Internal Security Operations Command (ISOC) Conference on "Assessing the Fight to Win over Communism," Bangkok, October 29, 1986; text reproduced in *Siam Rath Subda-Vijarn*, November 2, 1986 pp. 2, 4.
[113]See Kavi Chongkittavorn, "Much Remains to Be Accomplished Since That Historic Handshake in Peking," *The Nation*, November 19, 1986, p. 4. The PRC was later omitted after its representatives lodged a complaint with the Thai Foreign Ministry.

Party of Thailand (CPT), despite claims that only moral support was being extended."[114] Indeed, if General Chavalit comes under attack from critics and enemies for espousing ideas thought to be influenced by communism,[115] most likely he will be forced to preserve a "decent" distance between himself and the PRC; if so, this in turn is bound to have a negative impact on future bilateral security cooperation.

The last constraint is the PRC's relative lack of disposable power. As discussed above, China's willingness to maintain a hardline posture toward Vietnam and to contribute toward the strengthening of Thailand's military capabilities has given the latter a good deal of psychological and physical security, and the Thai security establishment in particular is highly appreciative of the value of the evolving ties with Beijing. The recent arms transfers announcements and Deng's insistence that "the main obstacle in Sino-Soviet relations is Vietnamese aggression against Cambodia"[116] indicate that in the immediate future Thailand's relationship with the PRC, particularly in the area of security, will continue to be close.

But in the longer run the credibility of China as a deterrent force is likely to be strained by the simple fact that ultimately it can do very little to prevent an escalation of violence on the Thai-Cambodian border. The PRC is unlikely to attempt to give its recalcitrant Vietnamese "pupil" a second "lesson." One reason is that the first "lesson" was a mutual learning process, during which Beijing suffered a great many casualties and was made painfully aware of its military shortcomings.[117] Another is that Vietnam has substantially reinforced its military capabilities since 1979, particularly its northern defenses, albeit at a great cost to itself, and a second Chinese "lesson" is likely to involve an even greater commitment of resources on the part of China.[118] The third reason is that the Chinese leadership, like its Soviet counterpart, seems to be committed to the task of reducing the conflict and normalizing relations between the two countries, and hence is unlikely to undertake a military opera-

---

[114]*Nation Review,* July 24, 1983, p. 1.

[115]See, e.g., former Prime Minister M. R. Kukrit Pramoj's remarks at the seminar on "Thai Politics at the Cross-Roads?" organized by the Institute of Security and International Studies, Chulalongkorn University, Bangkok, April 1, 1987; report in the *Bangkok Post,* April 2, 1987, pp. 1–2.

[116]Interview on *Sixty Minutes,* broadcast by the Columbia Broadcasting System, September 2, 1986.

[117]Larry A. Niksch, "Southeast Asia," in Gerald Segal and William T. Tow, eds., *Chinese Defence Policy* (London: Macmillan, 1984), pp. 238–39.

[118]Ibid., pp. 238–39.

tion against Hanoi, which will greatly hamper or even end the present process of rapprochement.[119]

Moreover, although the *quantities* of arms bought from China may increase over time, the range of arms that the RTG has already indicated its willingness to *buy* from the PRC—namely, 130mm artillery pieces, T-69 tanks, APCs, and antiaircraft guns—may be just about all that the RTG wishes to *buy* from China in the long run. Given the level of its technological development, China may not be able to offer the type of relatively sophisticated yet reliable weapon systems that the Thai military require for their modernization programs, such as an integrated early warning radar system, various types of missiles, missile-armed attack ships, and submarines. Indeed, significantly, when the Thai navy showed its interest in Chinese submarines, it was stressed that Thailand would be willing to acquire them only if they were provided free of charge.[120]

Throughout history, one thing has been abundantly clear: Thais understand, respect, and appreciate power and what power can achieve, especially in terms of survival and progress. This is reflected in their propensity toward finding a powerful protector and patron for their cause, both in domestic affairs and in foreign relations. After the end of Pax Americana in Southeast Asia, China's ability and willingness to offer Thailand protection has been one of the bases for the development of close bilateral ties especially in the security arena. But the scope and extent of this evolving relationship will partly be determined by what Beijing can offer to the kingdom. Since it is likely that over the long run the PRC's ability to contribute to Thai security will be, and will be seen to be, circumscribed, the Thais will not be anxious to upgrade their security cooperation with China and, indeed, will not hesitate to downgrade it if the utility of the Chinese connection diminishes.

Alignment Without Alliance?

In what may be termed the post-CPT era, Thailand's policy toward China has been transformed, from containment generated by fears and suspicions, to cooperation based upon a convergence of security inter-

---

[119]For discussions of the recent developments in Sino-Soviet relations, see Robert A. Scalapino, "U.S.-USSR-PRC Relations," in Kallgren, Sopiee, and Djiwandono, *ASEAN and China*; and Donald S. Zagoria, "The Sino-Soviet Conflict," paper prepared for the First Asia Pacific Roundtable, Kuala Lumpur, January 10–11, 1987.

[120]*The Nation*, January 8, 1987, p. 1.

ests. What has evolved is an alignment[121] between the two countries in the Cambodia issue. To one degree or another, Thailand and China have committed their military power and diplomatic support to each other's purposes. The former facilitates and protects the latter's supplies to the Cambodian resistance and works closely with it in the international diplomatic arena, while China contributes to Thailand's deterrence posture and war-fighting capabilities. With the CPT insurgency showing no real signs of revival and with large Vietnamese forces still being deployed in Cambodia, it is clear that bilateral relations continue to flourish. Indeed, the alignment between Thailand and the PRC may prove to be self-perpetuating, for close Sino-Thai cooperation serves to sustain Vietnam's fear of encirclement and hence its reluctance to abandon its present course, which in turn helps to ensure the continuation and enhancement of the alignment.

It is not inconceivable that this alignment may eventually be transformed into a full-fledged military alliance.[122] A number of factors, singly or in combination with one another, may bring about this transformation. One is the CPT's takeover of the Thai state. Another is a general war between Thailand and Vietnam, during which it becomes evident that China, and China alone, is prepared to lend Bangkok significant military assistance. The third possible factor is the termination of the United States' security commitments to Thailand. The fourth is the Philippines' decision not to renew the bases agreement with the United States in 1991.

The first three developments seem unlikely. The CPT is weak. There is no reason to believe that either Vietnam or Thailand will be willing to risk the costs inherent in the conduct of a general war or to allow the situation to deteriorate to a point where a general war becomes inevitable. And the Democrats' recent upsurge notwithstanding, there is no reason to think that a future U.S. administration would or could fundamentally revise its policy toward Thailand in the absence of major changes in the kingdom's domestic politics and external affiliations. And if the public position vis-à-vis the bases of the present Philippines

---

[121]For a discussion of the concept of "alignment," or rather "nonalignment," see K. J. Holsti, *International Politics: A Framework for Analysis* (Englewood Cliffs, N.J.: Prentice-Hall, 1972), p. 106.

[122]For a discussion of the concept of "alliance," see ibid., pp. 113–21.

foreign minister, Raul Manglapus, can be taken as an indication,[123] the fourth may yet be avoided.

As things stand, it is clear that the relationship between Thailand and the PRC still falls far short of being a full-fledged alliance. Security cooperation is based upon informal understanding, not signed agreements. To be sure, there is some sort of *casus foederis,* or the definition of the situation in which certain military commitments are to become operational, whereby China publicly promises "not to stay idle," "if Vietnam dares to make an armed incursion into Thailand," and privately may have undertaken to retaliate against Vietnamese attacks on Thailand within a specified period.[124] But both the *casus foederis* and the pledged commitments are by no means clear-cut, interpretations of which are likely to depend on the exigencies of the situation concerned in each instance. Bilateral military cooperation remains largely ad hoc and limited, in no way involving joint planning, exercises, and deployment or large-scale military assistance and arms transfers. The geographical focus of the various security commitments undertaken by the two sides is generally confined to the Thai-Cambodian border.

Moreover, there are a number of difficulties and constraints in the relationship between China and Thailand, which are likely to persist, if not increase, and which would continue to hamper the development of their bilateral ties over the long run. The most important problem is Thailand's age-old concern with domestic armed dissent. Given the existence of these difficulties and constraints, fears that Sino-Thai security cooperation would develop much further, perhaps even into a full-fledged military alliance, are likely to be misplaced. In the long run, hopefully in what may be termed the post-Cambodia conflict era, the ties that will prove to be most binding for Thailand will be with ideologically compatible or economically complementary states, in particular the United States, Japan, and the ASEAN countries.

---

[123]Immediately before being appointed foreign minister, Manglapus voiced very strong criticisms of the bases and argued for American withdrawal. But after his appointment, he toned down his criticisms and emphasized the necessity for ASEAN collectively to declare support for the American presence and to share "moral responsibility" for the bases; see, e.g., *The Nation,* November 5, 1987, p. 4.

[124]See n. 49.

17. Vietnam and China

DOUGLAS PIKE

This chapter seeks briefly to examine Sino-Vietnamese relations in the context of ASEAN security interests, that is, the meaning and significance of the Sino-Vietnamese relationship for Southeast Asia. The chapter is divided into eight sections successively examining: the long historical reach of the relationship; its breakup after the Vietnam War; the basic principles of Vietnamese foreign policy in dealing with China; the effects of the Sino-Soviet dispute; the present Sino-Vietnamese cold war; the major contentious issues between the two; the subliminal level of the relationship; and the future prospects.[1]

Long Historical Reach

Vietnam's association with China is complex and stretches far back into history. According to the Vietnamese version, it began about 500 B.C. when there were living in China south of the Yangtze River a "hundred tribes" that, one by one, were assimilated by the Chinese (Han), all save the Nam (South) Viets who fled southward to the Red River delta, determined to resist the pressures of Han-hwa or Sinoization. The durability of this racial memory is found in this story told by Hoang Van Chi:

---

[1]This chapter is based on source materials drawn from the Indochina Archive at the University of California, Berkeley. The file, SRV/For. Rels/China, contains an estimated 65,000 pages of documentation, most of it primary source materials such as official statements and documents. There are few full-length studies on the subject. Most notable perhaps are William J. Duiker's China and Vietnam: The Roots of Conflict, Indochina Research Monograph no. 1 (Berkeley: Institute of East Asian Studies, University of California, 1986); King C. Chen's Vietnam and China, 1938–1954 (Princeton: Princeton University Press, 1969); and Eugene K. Lawson's The Sino-Vietnamese Conflict (New York: Praeger, 1984). The works of Chang Pao Min, Dennis Duncanson, Donald Zagoria, and Robert A. Scalapino also contain much useful material. Douglas Pike has produced "Reader: Vietnam and China" (1986), a collection of articles and conference papers on Sino-Vietnamese relations, including his "Vietnam and China: Past, Present, and Future Relations" (1975), "New Look at Asian Foreign Policies: China and Vietnam" (1977), "Notes on the Sino-Vietnamese Border War" (April 1979), "Southeast Asia on the Superpowers: The Dust Settles" (1983), "Vietnam and Its Neighbors: Internal Influences on External Relations" (1984), "An American View of Vietnam's Relationship with China" (1985), and "Vietnam and China" (1986).

During a banquet for Sun Yat-sen in Tokyo in 1911, his host, the Japanese statesman Ki Tsuyoshi Inukai, asked him unexpectedly, seeking to trap him: "What do you think of the Vietnamese?" Caught off guard, Sun replied: "The Vietnamese are slaves by nature. They have been ruled by us and now they are ruled by the French. They can't have a very brilliant future." Inukai said: "I don't agree with you on that point. Though not independent at present, they are the only one of the 'Hundred Yueh' (Viet tribes) successfully to resist the process of Han-hwa (Sinoization). Such a people must sooner or later gain their political independence." Sun, it is said, blushed but made no reply, realizing that Inukai knew he was a Cantonese, one of a people regarded as inferior by the Vietnamese because they became so completely Sinified that they lost all their Yueh cultural identity, considering themselves wholly Chinese.[2]

The Nam Viets fled southward, but the sons of Han pursued them and by 258 B.C. the Red River delta had come under Chinese suzerainty. By most accounts Chinese rule was not particularly oppressive and in the long run proved far more beneficial for the Nam Viets than for their overlords, for it permitted the Vietnamese to appropriate virtually in toto an entire civilization: culture, architecture, art, literature, religion, and educational and legal systems.

What the Chinese got for their trouble was constant low-grade resistance punctuated by rebellions and village-level disturbances requiring "pacification" efforts. Vietnamese history and legend are filled with accounts of heroic anti-Chinese *beaux gestes*—the famed Trung sisters (Hai Ba Trung), for instance, who went forth on battle elephants leading an army against an infinitely superior Chinese force. When defeated, they drowned themselves in a lake in Hanoi that even today is venerated by a mystic cult. The tradition was that every Vietnamese was a soldier, and when the call came, he would drop his hoe and march off to battle the Chinese.

The book *Annam Chi Luoc* records the fact that "all the people fought the enemy" during the Tran Dynasty. The historian Phan Huy Chu wrote in his work, "Everyone was a soldier during the Tran Dynasty," which is why they were able to defeat the savage enemy. . . . This is the general experience throughout our people's entire history.[3]

The Vietnamese see themselves in history as defensive while their reputation among their neighbors is more martial, if not aggressive.

---

[2]Hoang Van Chi, *From Colonialism to Communism: A Case Study of North Vietnam* (New York: Praeger, 1964), p. 5.
[3]Nguyen Khac Vien, *Vietnam 1978* (Hanoi: Foreign Languages Publishing House, 1978).

Looking back on the history of their relations with the Chinese, the Vietnamese see their martial spirit of the past as simply a manifestation of exemplary behavior in responding to cruel aggression. It is the spirit of *chinh nghia*, "just cause," connoting a highly moral act, rooted in rationality, compassion, and responsibility. The heritage of these early experiences became what might be called a spirit of virtuous militancy, the Vietnamese regarding themselves as peaceful people, never offensive-minded, seeking only to defend their legitimate interests, but forever destined to deal with less honorable outsiders. Others may regard their behavior as hypocritical moral posturing, but not the Vietnamese.

Vietnam's thousand years as a Chinese province ended in the tenth century, but something of an intimate master-pupil relationship lingered on. As late as the 1880s, Vietnam was still according symbolic deference to China—the Court of Annam in Hue occasionally sending a token tribute to the Emperor of China: a single coin in a silk-lined lacquered box.

Such cultural attitudes as these were regarded by true Marxists, Chinese and Vietnamese alike, as mere "feudalist-bourgeois sentimentality." And for a time in the first half of the twentieth century, it did seem that they had given way to a new spirit of red brotherhood, one that linked Chinese and Vietnamese communists together in a common destiny. Ho Chi Minh and other early Vietnamese communists, working out of Canton in the 1920s, owed much to Mao Zedong, who supported the Vietnamese revolutionary movement more energetically than did Moscow. It was the Chinese who largely funded the Vietnamese in the Viet Minh War. When the Vietnam War began, China again opened its military warehouses to the Democratic Republic of Vietnam (DRV) and sent railway transport units and antiaircraft battalions to serve in Vietnam. There developed what was called at the time "a lip-and-teeth relationship."

From what the Chinese said later[4] we now know that relations between the two were never as warm or as harmonious as believed at the time, in the late 1950s. We also have learned that the breakup began earlier.[5] The Vietnamese fix the turning point as the Chinese Cultural Revolution, when China refused to address itself to the problem Vietnam was encountering in getting military hardware from the USSR

---

[4]For a good detailed account of the slow deterioration of Sino-Vietnamese relations, including details of their many wartime contretemps, see Lawson, *Sino-Vietnamese Conflict*.
[5]Mao Zedong in a number of interviews with foreign journalists, including Edgar Snow, indicated that serious trouble with the Vietnamese began as early as 1949.

through China.[6] The Chinese attitude began to change in the late 1960s, initially because China was moving from regional to world power, a shift that brought an attendant change in national interest. Later, in putting the blame for the final 1978 breach of relations on Hanoi, the Chinese said the decline began with the death of Ho Chi Minh (September 3, 1969) when Vietnamese foreign policy began tilting toward Moscow. As evidence, Beijing cited discrimination against ethnic Chinese members of the Vietnamese Communist Party—purging them, refusing cadre promotions, and generally treating them like "bees up one's sleeve." It interpreted Hanoi's quick unification of North and South Vietnam in 1976 as a move to keep a Chinese presence out of southern Vietnam. Other grievances of the mid-1970s included what the Chinese considered excessive Vietnamese intrusiveness into the affairs of Kampuchea, usually at China's expense; assertive claims to the offshore Spratly and Paracel archipelagoes; blocking efforts by Cholon Chinese seeking, after the fall of Saigon, repatriation to China; other actions the Chinese considered racist, such as confiscating and nationalizing ethnic Chinese property in South Vietnam, weeding "pro-Chinese" officials out of the Vietnamese government, and making Cholon Chinese the scapegoat for Vietnamese economic ills; and finally, provocative gestures involving flags and published maps (symbols so important in Asia) along with constant belittling rhetoric toward China in the Hanoi press.[7]

The Breach of Relations

The breakup of the previous close Sino-Vietnamese relationship was engendered—some might say made inevitable—by several overlapping factors.

---

[6]Hanoi's retrospective view (in the 1980s) of the Vietnam War is that Chinese behavior throughout the war amounted to collusion with the United States to defeat the Vietnamese communists. General Vo Nguyen Giap told a Cuban journalist:

"The Chinese government told the U.S. that if the latter did not threaten or touch China, then China would do nothing to prevent the attacks [on Vietnam]. It was really like telling the United States that it could bomb Vietnam at will, as long as there was no threat to the Chinese border. . . . We Vietnamese leaders felt that we had been stabbed in the back. . . . When we recount all these events and link them to the war in the southwest (i.e., Kampuchea), we can see the treachery of the Chinese leaders."

This was said to Miguel Rivero of the *Verge Olivo* (Havana) in an interview published February 10, 1980. For what might be called an official account of Chinese perfidy, see the Socialist Republic of Vietnam Foreign Ministry, *White Paper* (Hanoi), October 1979.

[7]For a detailed tracing of 1975–78 events leading up to the breach of Sino-Vietnamese relations, see Duiker, *China and Vietnam*. See also the SRV Ministry of Foreign Affairs, *China's War: Escalation and Aggravation of Tension Along the Vietnam China Border* (Hanoi, 1984).

The first factor was the end of the Vietnam War. This was a development that was doubly difficult for Beijing to handle because it came largely unanticipated. The Chinese assessment, it became clear later, was that with the signing of the 1973 Paris Agreements, the war in Vietnam would devolve into a more or less permanent standoff, one in which neither the North nor the South Vietnamese would be able to prevail in any decisive manner, an ending much like the Korean War two decades earlier. Probably Beijing anticipated that gradually the Saigon government would move to the left, the Thieu government being replaced by a series of governments and eventually by some sort of neutralist/third-force rule, much like that in Cambodia under Sihanouk. And they expected that both Cambodia and Laos would remain essentially independent from Hanoi. These calculations were based on the assumption that the United States would stay the course in Vietnam, and thus would perpetuate the stalemate. This is a hard thesis to document, that China in effect holds the United States to blame for the outcome of the war. Mao Zedong observed to a West German ambassador[8] that "the Americans were never serious about the Vietnam War, otherwise they would never have left after only 50,000 casualties." From Mao's view, and the Chinese sense of magnitude being what it is, this is a plausible conclusion (although the ambassador thought Mao was being sardonic). If "only" 50,000 casualties changed a U.S. policy, this meant that Washington was not serious about the war in the first place. Mao had depended on the United States to forestall a Hanoi-dominated Federation of Indochina and the Unites States had disappointed him.

The expectation that the United States would persevere, or perhaps it was only a hope in Beijing, proved faulty and left China in the immediate post–Vietnam War era in a distinctly untenable position with respect to Hanoi. More importantly the USSR, because of luck or greater perspicacity, was left by the victory in a highly favorable position in Hanoi.

The postwar Vietnamese leadership in general handled the Chinese badly, taking a "high posture" (as the Japanese would express it) rather than seeking to placate them, as Ho Chi Minh probably would have been able to do had he been on hand. Probably the initial "lip-and-teeth" relationship was doomed in any case. During the course of fifteen years of the Vietnam War, China had moved from a regional to world power and its foreign policy interests had changed accordingly. Where once it had been in China's interest that the United States be

---

[8]This story was told to the author by the ambassador, who prefers not to be quoted by name.

expelled from the region, now it better served her interests if the United States remained as a counterweight to the USSR.

The second factor was the new strategic order that emerged in Southeast Asia as a result of the outcome of the war. Vietnam was a major regional power; it had the third largest army in the world, was strategically located, and was moving into close alliance with the USSR. Inevitably this meant it (and its Cambodian and Laotian associates) was pitted against the ASEAN states. Contributing greatly to the changed balance of power was the rise of ASEAN as an institution, the steadily improving economic conditions of the individual ASEAN states, and the general individual and collective resilience they had begun to demonstrate. U.S. withdrawal from the region, even if only in a psychological sense, was such as to create a political vacuum that irresistibly drew in the USSR. China became alarmed by the sudden quantum jump in Hanoi's geopolitical strength and influence, doubly so when it began to tilt toward Moscow, and moved to create a "united front" in Asia to help redress the strategic imbalance.

The third factor was the resurgence of indigenous nationalism in Indochina. Vietnam with respect to China, and Cambodia with respect to Vietnam, were strongly gripped by what might be termed the spirit of neo-nationalism. This spirit sustains the Khmer against the Vietnamese, and the Vietnamese against the Chinese, and while it may be rooted in ancient ethnic antipathies and racial animosities, it is authentically twentieth-century nationalism.

Finally contributing to the breakup of the alliance were various finite issues: Hanoi's growing intimacy with the USSR; its intrusiveness into Cambodia; the failure of China to recognize the need for a new definition of Sino-Vietnamese relations; quarrels over borders and islands; mistreatment of ethnic Chinese in Vietnam; Beijing's efforts to tie strings to its economic aid programs in Vietnam; and what Hanoi considered China's generally abusive behavior toward Vietnam.

Hanoi's China Policy

The Vietnamese leadership since 1975 has employed a series of policies in dealing with the world, and China in particular, that has proved to be generally unsuccessful, in part because the policies have been so ineptly managed.[9] The result is that Vietnam finds itself isolated in the region, surrounded by hostility. In fact, it has only two truly reliable allies worldwide, the USSR and Cuba, and only one nominally close

---

[9]See Duiker, *China and Vietnam*.

noncommunist associate in Asia, India. This is a condition neither acci-
dental nor deliberate, but rather the product of contemporary events
coupled to Hanoi's singular mismanagement of external relations. It is a
bad situation that China has made worse.

What gave an enduring quality to the Sino-Vietnamese breach was
Hanoi's strongly held ideological position which might be described as
philosophic fundamentalism. Throughout the long Sino-Soviet dispute,
the Vietnamese consistently insisted that the world was divided into
two contradictory systems which were locked in a struggle from which
ultimately there can emerge only one winner. The capitalist world must
be ruined and this was possible only with a return by China and the
USSR to proletarian monolithism dedicated to world revolution. The
great sin of the Chinese (also, to a considerable extent, the Soviets) was
to abandon the earlier Marxist-Leninist "offensive strategy for revolution" in favor of "negative strategy" (peaceful coexistence), "compromise strategy" (détente), or "passive strategy" (wave-of-the-future
notion that events can be left to take their course and eventually communism will triumph).[10] What was involved here was not simply a
metaphysical argument over time and change, but the very practical
issue of risk-taking in global geopolitical competition. From the earliest
days of the Sino-Soviet dispute, Ho Chi Minh led a campaign to get the
two disputants back on what he considered the right path, but in vain.
Now, with the rise of Nguyen Van Linh and the demise of the "ideologues" in Hanoi this attitude, which might be called Hanoi's ideological hostility for Beijing, is fading and all evidence suggests it will
continue to do so.[11]

In conducting its foreign policy with China (and others), Hanoi's
diplomats treat the conduct of foreign relations in the manner of strategically oriented military campaigns. Tactics are chosen to manipulate
influential elements in the opposing camp, and to mobilize support for
the Hanoi position both within the ranks of the opposition and among
onlookers around the world. Hanoi leaders pursue their objectives with
respect to China as a militant campaign to be conducted over an
extended period of time—years, even decades. They bring von Clause-
witz full circle: diplomacy is warfare conducted by other means. The
diplomats sent to Beijing and elsewhere—this is the testimony of almost

---

[10]This ideological dispute is traced in some detail in Pike, "Reader: Vietnam and China."
[11]This is discussed in detail in Douglas Pike, *Vietnam and the USSR: Anatomy of an Alliance*
(Boulder: Westview, 1987). For possible relevance, see the text of Mikhail Gorbachev's
speech in Vladivostok in Foreign Broadcast Information Service (FBIS), *USSR Daily Report*,
July 29, 1986.

everyone who has dealt with them (including the Soviets)—are belligerent, militant, implacable, humorless. They use the protracted conflict device to draw negotiations out in time. They assume successive policy positions as if defending a barricade, seldom in the spirit of give-and-take or horse-trading negotiations. They tend to regard opposition offers of compromise not as gestures of conciliation but as proof that their strategy of diplomacy is succeeding. Hanoi-style diplomacy thus is strong because it is determined and has confidently fixed intentions. It is weak because it is rigid and virtually unable to adjust to opportunity or need.

The Chinese, perhaps understandably, return this treatment in kind. Possibly a Sinologue would say many Vietnamese practices and techniques were learned from the Chinese. In any event, relations between the two tend to resemble an immovable object meeting an irresistible force.

The Sino-Soviet Factor

The central element—or the great contradiction, as they would say in Hanoi—in Vietnamese-Chinese relations is the USSR and by association the Sino-Soviet dispute.

Earlier the Sino-Soviet dispute was seen by Hanoi as an ideological and geopolitical competition. It took on new meaning after the end of the Vietnam War, but continued to condition both Chinese and Soviet behavior toward Vietnam. As far as Hanoi is concerned, the dispute has lost all of its original meaning along with most of its utility for Vietnam. When Hanoi leaders in 1978 chose to ally themselves with the USSR they were forced to define the dispute anew, and now characterize it as merely a manifestation of China's Asia-wide hegemonism.

Vietnam and the USSR do not—and cannot—share identical interests with respect to China. Vietnam faces China with its own objective, to fend off Chinese hegemonism, but ultimately to achieve a viable relationship. The USSR must protect the long porous border it shares with China, must compete for influence and leadership within the communist world, and must relate China to its complicated bilateral relationship with the United States. Vietnam must forestall military attack by China, either through improving relations or by invoking Soviet protection. It must improve relations with the ASEAN countries at the expense of China, and must achieve a preeminent position within Indochina in the face of Chinese opposition. Soviet-Vietnamese interests may coincide but they can never be anything as simple as Moscow and Hanoi joined against Beijing.

China seems to recognize this and in both word and deed distinguishes between Vietnam and the USSR in policy expectations, as in

Cambodia. While China may be hostile to both, its hostility toward the USSR has an unremitting quality; the hostility toward Vietnam is more in the nature of feelings toward a misguided junior who has fallen into bad company. The implication is that there is hope for Vietnam given a new, more enlightened leadership.

Hanoi leaders are (or profess to be) in constant anxiety about the possibility of a Sino-Soviet rapprochement. Continually, they demand assurances that their interests will not be negotiated away and dutifully, Soviet officials make them after every ministerial meeting with the Chinese. China lists Moscow's backing of Hanoi's policies in Cambodia as one of the "three obstacles" to improved Sino-Soviet relations (the other two are the Soviet occupation of Afghanistan and the large numbers of Soviet troops along the China-Mongolia border). China gives every indication of holding the line here, which means markedly improved relations with the USSR are unlikely in the foreseeable future.

Hanoi's assumptions on the Sino-Soviet dispute today appear to be that it will continue essentially on a straight-line course, neither seriously worsening nor vastly improving; that both China and the USSR will continue to place their respective national interests over those of Vietnam (meaning that in the long run Moscow is no more to be trusted than Beijing); and that whatever form the Sino-Soviet relationship ultimately takes, it will remain the central fact of life for Vietnamese external relations.

If the dispute lessens in hostility, a new Sino-Vietnamese condition could emerge, although it would remain in the context of a power struggle. An improved Sino-Soviet relationship might not diminish Moscow's interest in Vietnam but probably would alter Moscow's outlook.[12]

The "Multifaceted War"

For nearly a decade now there has been fought in the rugged mountainous border region separating Vietnam and China a most peculiar semi-secret war. It is more than a series of border incidents, as it is commonly described by the press abroad, for it has strategic intent, continuity, and involves massive allocation of resources by both sides.

The Vietnamese call it a "multifaceted war of sabotage"—a term that seems appropriate. They describe it as a steady campaign of mili-

---

[12]For a full description of the Sino-Vietnamese "multifaceted war of sabotage," including specific tactics and Hanoi publication citations, see Douglas Pike, "Vietnam's Relationship with China," in Robert A. Scalapino and Chen Qimao, eds., *Pacific-Asian Issues: American and Chinese Views*, Research and Policy Studies no. 17 (Berkeley: Institute of East Asian Studies, University of California, 1986).

tary harassment by artillery fire, infantry patrol intrusions on land and naval intrusions and naval mine planting at sea and in the riverways, and (the "sabotage" aspect) clandestine activity employing for the most part the ethnic minority highland people of the border region. According to the Hanoi press, teams of Chinese agents systematically sabotage agricultural production centers and port, transportation, and communication facilities. Psychological warfare operations such as systematic rumor-mongering are an integral part of the campaign, as is what the Vietnamese call "economic warfare," for example, encouraging the Vietnamese villagers along the border to engage in smuggling, currency speculation, and hoarding of goods in short supply.

For their part, the Vietnamese have responded by turning the districts along the China border into "iron fortresses" manned by well-equipped and well-trained "paramilitary." In all, the Vietnamese have in the region an estimated 600,000 troops assigned the mission of countering these Chinese operations and standing ready for another Chinese invasion.

This "multifaceted war of sabotage," it is clear, is more than a cold war or war of nerves but less than a limited small-scale war. Exactly what are its dimensions is difficult to determine, but its monetary cost to Vietnam obviously is considerable as is indicated in this description.

> The Chinese expansionists and hegemonists pursue a multifaceted war of sabotage, which they hope to "win without fighting," that is exhausting Vietnam's resources, crippling its economy, creating political chaos and internal disorder so, without firing a shot, we are forced to become their vassals. . . . In this multifaceted war of sabotage, the enemy attacks us in many fields: economically, politically, ideologically, and culturally. They do everything possible to undermine our national defense system and our military potential. They use dangerous means and malicious tricks to foment rebellion and a coup d'état when the time is ripe. Militarily they routinely send armed forces across our northern border along with espionage agents, commandos, aircraft, and so forth. They seek to exert pressure, harass, provoke and engage, and thereby create a state of constant tension. They look for methods to distort our military draft system. They cause a longing for peace and encourage our troops to desert, and youth to evade the draft. . . . The most deadly form of this multifaceted war of sabotage is economic. In sabotaging us economically they use lackeys to sabotage machinery, set warehouses afire, sabotage production discipline and the managerial mechanism, so as to stagnate production. They encourage smuggling, speculation and hoarding, and cause a gold "hemorrhage" to undermine our monetary system. . . . China undermines our economic policies, sows skepticism to cause our people to lose faith in the Party's economic leadership. They distort our relationship with other coun-

tries and our practice of international economic cooperation. China frantically fixes embargoes, pressures private capitalist individuals and companies not to sign contracts with us, or to cancel, postpone, or reduce them. The Chinese sabotage our warehouses, seaports, industrial installations. They organize gangs of smugglers to bring in contraband and take out gold and gems. They also introduce chemical poisons, insects, and microorganisms to injure food production. . . . They conduct intense psychological war to distort Party and State policies. They secretly send reactionary and decadent cultural products into our country to sow the seeds of a decadent lifestyle especially among youth. They provoke dissatisfaction and political opposition. They bribe or exert pressure on corrupt elements in the State apparatus to get them to serve as their lackeys. All these schemes are designed to erode the confidence of the people, confuse our friends, paralyze our revolutionary will, undermine the solidarity of PAVN and the Party, the special solidarity among Vietnam, Laos, and Kampuchea, and the solidarity and cooperation between Vietnam and the USSR.[13]

The meaning of this shadowy struggle along the long mountainous border must be read in the broader strategic terms of the cold and sometimes hot war that has been going on between China and Vietnam since 1979. Vietnam is now a strategic force—with a 2.9 million-man army and an alliance with the USSR—that China must respect. Further, Vietnam can now challenge China regionally, hence is more than simply a surrogate of Moscow, a condition that quite probably will continue regardless of any change of status in Sino-Soviet relations or other geopolitical developments. At its roots, however, this "multifaceted war of sabotage" is not so much a war as an integral part of the ongoing process by the two to delineate their new relationship.

Contentions and Issues

Examination of Hanoi's behavior in the region during the past decade, both with respect to China and Southeast Asia, suggests it has four major regional foreign policy objectives:

---

[13]Drawn from Nhuan Vu, "Concerning Chinese Military Strategy" and Thien Nhan, "Fighting the Enemy's War of Economic Sabotage," in *Tap Chi Cong San,* August 1982. For additional discussion of the PAVN high command's view of Chinese purposes and intentions, see Major General Dang Kinh, "Building District Military Fortresses Along the Northern Border"; Central Committee agit-prop expert Nam Huy's article, "Fighting the War of Sabotage on the Ideological Front in the Northern Border Provinces," in *"Tap Chi Quan Doi Nhan Dan,* January 1983; and an editorial in the same publication titled "Determined to Win the War of Sabotage."

1. To secure a cooperative, nonthreatening Indochina (i.e., Kampuchea and Laos), eventually perhaps achieving a federated or confederated arrangement. This is Hanoi's overriding concern because it is security-based.
2. To increase its political and diplomatic influence among ASEAN countries. In part this would be for its own sake, and in part to forestall any sort of common anti-Vietnam front from being formed, as the Chinese urge. This could be a regional, that is ASEAN—Indochina Federation, relationship.
3. To limit superpower activity in the region where possible, particularly the U.S. but also China and (in a sense) the USSR.
4. To nudge its Southeast Asian neighbors to the left, hopefully to the point that ASEAN countries become a string of people's republics. Certainly for the time being this is more a wish than an active Hanoi policy.

Some of these directly challenge Chinese national interests; none can be said to be entirely compatible with them. Thus competition for influence in Southeast Asia is the first of the contending issues between Vietnam and China. To some extent the Hanoi-ASEAN relationship that emerged after the end of the war was inadvertent. In 1975 Hanoi seemed to have a strong sense of identification with the Third World, including even the capitalist nations of Southeast Asia. It said at the time that it wanted to maintain equidistance between the socialist and nonsocialist world. It was forced off this policy by internal difficulties that tilted it toward the USSR. Then it said it sought flexible external relations in Southeast Asia. Confrontation with ASEAN over Cambodia ruined this intention. Competition between Vietnam and China in the region—with the exception of the Kampuchea issue—remains amorphous and ill defined at the present.[14]

The second specific issue is the future political configuration of Indochina, centering on the notion of a Federation of Indochina that

---

[14]Regional meanings of Vietnam-China relations are discussed by Sarasin Viraphol in his chapter, "The People's Republic of China and Southeast Asia: A Security Consideration for the 1980s," in Robert A. Scalapino and Jusuf Wanandi, eds., *Economic, Political, and Security Issues in the 1980s*, Research and Papers Policy Studies no. 7 (Berkeley: Institute of East Asian Studies, University of California, 1982). See also Lucian Pye's "China and Southeast Asia" in the same volume. Policy issues are explored in some detail in "China and the Southeast" by John Franklin Copper (Rhodes College) in *Current History*, December 1984.

would incorporate Vietnam, Laos, and Cambodia. China opposes such a development while the Vietnamese consider it not only desirable, but inevitable. China's feelings on the matter are obvious from its actions in Cambodia, the fundamental meaning of which is to prevent federation if it can.

Resistance in Cambodia represents the third contending issue. The battle line there is now clearly drawn as a surrogate war, one that at this writing neither side appears able to win. Possibly the future governing structure of Cambodia can be separated as an issue from the issue of federation of Indochina. China and Vietnam agree that the central issue in Cambodia is the excessive influence the other is attempting to establish in that country. Theoretically at least, this means a possible acceptable settlement would be one in which neither has such influence. A new governing arrangement in which both Vietnamese and Chinese influences were diminished, but in which each had a Khmer faction on which it could base its future presence, could end the present suffering.

Laos is a fourth specific issue and essentially resembles Cambodia, that is, excessive Vietnamese intrusiveness in China's view. Laos also represents a potential security threat for Vietnam. The Chinese have close ties with the ethnic minorities in the Laotian hills through their cousins in China and could mount a troublesome anti-Vietnam resistance. Such a campaign would also, of necessity, alienate the Lao. China apparently regards the Lao as unwilling collaborators with Vietnam and considers that a hostile move would permanently throw Laos into the Hanoi camp. Thus, to date, the Chinese have restrained themselves in Laos, foregoing anti-Vietnamese opportunism.

The fifth specific issue—discussed above—is Vietnam's intimacy with the USSR, which has resulted in an extensive Soviet naval presence in Indochina and an association that is an alliance in all but name. Here China faces a genuine problem in strategy: how to force distance between the Vietnamese and the Soviets. Its basic approach is what might be called the technique of protracted intimidation, that is, sustained pressure of various sorts on both Vietnam and the USSR— military, diplomatic, psychological—in the expectation that eventually the USSR will see it as in its interest to distance itself somewhat from Vietnam and the Vietnamese will seek a modus vivendi.[15]

Finally there is a clutch of lesser issues between Vietnam and China. Mistreatment of ethnic Chinese in Vietnam has been particularly embarrassing for China in terms of its image among overseas Chinese in

---

[15]Soviet-Vietnamese relations are a subject of a full-length study in Douglas Pike, *Vietnam and the USSR: Anatomy of an Alliance* (Boulder: Westview, 1987).

Southeast Asia. Extraordinary intransigence has surfaced between the two over the various small dots in the South China Sea that Chinese sailors traditionally call the Isles of Dangerous Places. China considers her claims to the Spratly and Paracel groups to be clear and just; the Vietnamese act in a more opportunistic than righteous manner. The matter is more than nominally important because the islands are believed to be rich in oil.

Subliminal Level

The issues discussed above concern the Sino-Vietnamese relationship at the surface level. Beneath them lies a subliminal relationship which perhaps is more important and of greater "reality" than any specific issue.[16]

Vietnam's enhanced status that resulted from victory in war convinced Hanoi leaders at the time they must alter their pupil-*sensei* relationship with China, replacing this centuries-old pattern of deference by pupil to master with a new one, defined by equality. The Chinese view was that conditions had not changed that much, that the original association based on mutual obligation still obtained and that the overriding principle that must prevail was harmony of relations.

While this may strike outsiders, especially those from the United States or Europe, as an obscure exercise in Oriental metaphysics, the fact is that it represents a reality that already has had grave meaning for millions. Much of Vietnam's behavior in Cambodia is traceable to this subliminal struggle with China. The Chinese "lesson" in the 1979 border war was part of the redefinition effort. The Soviet presence in Vietnam most certainly is a contribution, although probably an unwitting one on Moscow's part. Hence, this is no metaphysical exercise, but a psychological condition with profound meaning for the future.

Future Relations

The present poor state of relations between Hanoi and Beijing came about as much through error or blunder on the part of both parties as for any other reason. That there would be postwar difficulties between them, that there would be competition between them in Southeast

---

[16]The subliminal level of Sino-Vietnamese relations was explored in some detail in Douglas Pike, "Vietnam and Its Neighbors: Internal Influences on External Relations," in Karl D. Jackson, Sukhumbhand Paribatra, and J. Soedjati Djiwandono, eds., *ASEAN in Regional and Global Context*, Research Papers and Policy Studies no. 18 (Berkeley: Institute of East Asian Studies, University of California, 1986).

Asia, that there would be no turning back to the simpler "lip-and-teeth" years, seemed inevitable. But relations need not have deteriorated as badly as they did. The Hanoi Politburo acted ineptly. It could have handled China more skillfully. Had Ho Chi Minh been alive he probably would have been able to avoid a breach. The Chinese were clumsy in their efforts to force distance between Vietnam and the USSR. A more carefully designed policy, one built around economic aid, could have preserved some Chinese influence in Hanoi.

Studies conducted by the author over a decade and based on interviews with Vietnamese on attitudes toward China (and the USSR) strongly indicate that most Vietnamese—probably including future policymakers—believe that in the long run the two must get along. China is simply too vast, and too close, to allow Vietnam to treat it as a permanent enemy. That is a fact of a thousand years standing. A viable Vietnam requires peace with China. Deep down every Vietnamese, even the most rabid China-hater, accepts this final truth. However, this does not and cannot mean "eating Chinese dung" as the Vietnamese express it. Rather it requires the proper mix of Vietnamese assertiveness and deference to China, difficult to achieve because of the premium Asia places on face. Sooner or later a workable relationship will be established. Arriving at that point is Hanoi's overriding foreign policy problem.

The generational transfer of political power now under way in Hanoi, marked by the advent of a new Party secretary, Nguyen Van Linh, and a new Central Committee and a new National Assembly (both with at least 50 percent first-time members) has altered the substance/issues of the ever-present factionalism. It appears that Hanoi doctrinal infighting in the future will be restructured, the former "pragmatists" becoming "reformers," the former "ideologues" becoming "conservatives." With respect to relations with China, probably there is a consensus between the two sides that an improved relationship with China is both necessary and desirable. If there is a quarrel here it has to do with the pace of change, not with the fact of it. Also however, probably there is the assessment by both that Vietnam is largely locked into a cold war that China means to continue, and therefore realistically there is little Vietnam can do to change Chinese policy. Thus the "renovationist" or *glasnost* spirit in Hanoi will probably have less effect on policy making with respect to China than on other decision making such as on the economy, relations with ASEAN, and relations with the United States.

Future Vietnamese-Chinese relations will be subjected to the constant pull and haul that results from the obvious geographic fact that Vietnam shares the same region with China while the USSR does not.

From this follows the equally obvious geopolitical fact that Vietnam cannot deal with China in the same manner and using the same policies, as can the USSR. Moscow may be able to afford a permanent cold war with Beijing, but because of China's proximity and size, Hanoi cannot. When improved relations are established by Vietnam and China, the essential geopolitical condition of Southeast Asia will not be appreciably changed. There always will be a certain degree of struggle for power among China, Vietnam, and the ASEAN countries. This will not be necessarily destructive. Competitiveness, within bounds, is normal and generally beneficial, since it tends to keep excesses in check. Much worse would be Southeast Asia dominated by a single power.

In any event, it seems the density of the region is to be an arena for two struggles for power—one from within and one from without.

PART SEVEN

U.S.-USSR-PRC Relationships: Implications for Southeast Asia

18. U.S.-USSR-PRC Relations

ROBERT A. SCALAPINO

Not since World War II have relations between major states exhibited the fluidity of today. This condition is testimony to a complex medley of economic, political, and strategic challenges facing each nation, none susceptible to easy answers. Socialism, at least in its traditional Leninist form, has faltered, and its troubles have spawned a wide range of remedial measures, from the effort to make the system work better to more fundamental alterations that place a greater premium upon incentives and the market. Traditional capitalism, meanwhile, disappeared without fanfare some time ago and, in its place, the regulated economy—in many forms—has come into being. Yet "guided capitalism" faces its own problems. We stand on the threshold of a new phase of the industrial revolution—more global, more swift, more intensive in its implications than any economic transformation mankind has witnessed. Already, the international financial marketplace defies the regulation of any nation, and vast economic transformations are taking place outside any plan or program. Where is there not nervousness about the economic future?

Politics generally takes second place to economics at present, and is guided by it. It was not always so, especially in Asia. First-generation revolutionaries like Nehru, Sukarno, and Mao reveled in politics and made their mark as mobilizers and nation-builders. They paid lip service to economic development, but their hearts—and minds—were elsewhere. With few exceptions, however (Burmese leaders remain mired in the past despite the revolutionary labels they appropriate), current leaders are placing the highest premium upon economic growth—rapid, sustained, and encompassing both the agrarian and industrial sectors.

Recent decades have amply demonstrated that both failures and successes in economic development can be productive of political problems. Crises, especially a downward cycle after a period of growth, can quickly generate political instability. It must be admitted that stagnation combined with coercion is one strategy for stability that a few elites have adopted with temporary success. Yet as the Philippines graphically illustrated recently, sustained mismanagement of the economy, especially when accompanied by other ills, is sooner or later translated into unrest not merely at the mass level but, more important politically, within the all-important middle and upper classes. Indeed, a number of Asian developing societies were recently in an economic trough, strain-

345

ing the still fragile political institutions under which these societies operate.[1]

Economic success, however, can have at least equally volatile political repercussions. Witness current trends in Japan and the Newly Industrializing Countries (NICs). Japanese politics is undergoing a gradual but significant shift from being a polity in which the bureaucracy reigned supreme within a parliamentary framework to a polity in which the private sector, represented by interest groups and professional politicians, is moving to play a more prominent role in the political process. Thus, policy debates are being advanced into the public arena more forcefully, with the potential for less stability in the years ahead.

The political trends within the NICs—and especially in South Korea and Taiwan—are more dramatic. Sustained economic development produced a widening gap between a political system heavily traditional and a revolutionary socioeconomic environment. Newly literate, relatively affluent elements within the society, influenced by international currents, demand greater representation in the political system. Thus, we are currently witnessing major efforts to alter the political system in the direction of democratization, efforts supported or at least tolerated by the government in power. But this development must surmount not only the opposition or ambivalence of some portions of the elite but more importantly, the continuing cultural impediments to the democratic system that lie imbedded in the society, including those within the very forces demanding change. Adaptation, not mechanistic borrowing, is required.[2]

---

[1]A current discussion of the issues and problems of political institutionalization in Asia is to be found in Robert A. Scalapino, Seizaburo Sato, and Jusuf Wanandi, eds., *Asian Political Institutionalization*, Research Papers and Policy Studies no. 15 (Berkeley: Institute of East Asian Studies, University of California, 1986).

[2]The literature on Asian economic systems and developmental issues is voluminous. For recent works, see James Abegglen, *The Strategy of Japanese Business* (Cambridge, Mass.: Ballinger, 1984); Roger Benjamin and Robert T. Kudrie, *The Industrial Future of the Pacific Basin* (Boulder: Westview Press, 1984); James W. Morley, ed., *The Pacific Basin: New Challenges to the United States* (New York: Academy of Political Science, 1986); Robert A. Scalapino, Seizaburo Sato, and Jusuf Wanandi, eds., *Asian Economic Development—Present and Future*, Research Papers and Policy Studies no. 14 (Berkeley: Institute of East Asian Studies, University of California, 1985); *China: Long-Term Development Issues and Options*, World Bank Country Economic Report (Baltimore: Johns Hopkins University Press, 1985); John J. Stephan and V. P. Chichkanov, *Soviet-American Horizons on the Pacific* (Honolulu: University of Hawaii Press, 1986); Chalmers A. Johnson, *MITI and the Japanese Miracle* (Stanford: Stanford University Press, 1982).

Basic systemic changes in Asian governance are likely to be rare in the years immediately ahead. The democratic, Leninist, and authoritarian-pluralist systems now existing will be modified but rarely toppled. The age of political revolution is largely over for Asia, but that of accelerating political evolution is at hand. That evolution does not exclude the existing democracies. They must wrestle with problems of stability, coherence, and legitimacy at a time when extra-state forces such as the media, private interest groups, ethnic-religious divisions, and international events make governance ever more difficult.[3]

On the surface, Leninist systems seem most capable of preserving order even under conditions of strain because of the organizational and coercive mechanisms available to them as well as the much greater control exercised over the information and mobility available to their citizens. Yet the classic defenses of the Leninist state are weakening under the impact of the global scientific-technological revolution now unfolding. Ideology has been reduced to dogma, with self-interest—individual and national—rising to the fore. Knowledge is leaping across state boundaries, producing cleavages particularly within the elites. China currently leads the way in experimenting with changes which if sustained may lead to an authoritarian-pluralist system. Other Leninist states including the USSR are likely to be influenced if the Chinese reforms—and those in East Europe—are on balance successful. In sum, for Leninism, the past is no gauge of the future.

It is the authoritarian-pluralist states of Asia, however, that are currently undergoing the greatest political trauma. Increased political openness—greater freedom and enhanced political competition—seem en route, although flat predictions or sweeping generalizations are hazardous. Linear progression toward an open society cannot be expected. Retreats as well as advances are very likely. Moreover, as has been suggested, homage to the unique political inheritance of each society will be necessary. Many if not all of these states will adopt some type of dominant party system, at least initially, rather than accept the risks of a frequent transference of power through elections. Yet if there is any general political trend in Asia today, it is toward broadened participation and greater civil liberties for the citizen.

This is the context in which relations between and among the major Pacific-Asian states are unfolding. And those states no less than the smaller nations are being affected by the trends outlined above. The major, rapid changes in the global economy taking place raise one pro-

---

[3]For a discussion of this and related issues, see Robert A. Scalapino, "Asia's Future," *Foreign Affairs* 66(1) (Fall 1987):77–108.

found issue for the advanced industrial societies: can economic institutions and policies—national, regional, and international—be created and amplified to keep pace with the revolution now under way? Given the surge of interdependence, the answer to this question is of universal significance. That answer is also very unclear, and the uncertainties surrounding economic issues at home and abroad contribute mightily to the fluidity in major state relations.

Politics makes its own contribution to the complexities of current international relations. Whereas ideology—or, put more broadly, common political values—provided the central bonds cementing alliances in the immediate post–1945 era, current alignments are based on a pragmatic assessment of national interests with the paramount issues being security and economic growth. Hence, on the one hand, ties are fashioned across ideological-political lines and, on the other hand, relations between states politically similar are rendered fragile or hostile because of differences over vital security or economic interests.

Meanwhile, security issues have recently been subject to awesome changes no less than have economic issues. As our globe contracts and our universe expands, it is more and more difficult to separate national or regional security concerns from those that are global in nature. Science and politics combine to march forward with respect to the art of war as well as on other fronts, leaving the adequacy or soundness of past policies in ever greater doubt. Moreover, the central security issue that is global in character—U.S.-USSR policies—has been intensely politicized, being played out on a global stage before a world audience. At the other end of the continuum, security for the individual citizen begins at home. If one's immediate neighborhood is not safe, that concern takes precedence over all else. At another level, however, if one's society is in general disarray, that represents a potential threat going beyond national boundaries. Thus, societies in turmoil constitute convenient targets for external intervention. The most common type of war in our times is the combined civil-international conflict, and many such conflicts involve the major states directly or indirectly. As a consequence, security issues for the latter have become vastly more complex, especially since the mix of factors going into civil-international conflicts can rarely be met with massive military power alone. Yet military interventions continue, adding further complications to major state relations.[4]

---

[4]Recent discussions of Asian security issues include Claude A. Buss, *National Security Interests in the Pacific Basin* (Stanford: Hoover Institution, 1985); Richard H. Solomon and Masataka Kosaka, eds., *The Soviet Far Eeast Military Buildup* (Dover, Mass.: Auburn House

The Sino-Soviet Relation

Against this background, let me first examine developments in the Sino-Soviet relationship, with special reference to its implications for Southeast Asia. The background of these relations has been so extensively treated as to require only the briefest mention.[5] Various factors combined to bring China and Russia together shortly after the end of World War II. With the advent of the Chinese Communists to power, ideological union and a common set of political institutions underwrote the new alliance. The Chinese Communist elite thought of themselves as good Marxist-Leninists, with an obligation to the international socialist movement. To learn from the Soviet Union was morally as well as politically correct. Even in this period of maximum idealism, however, nationalist undercurrents formed a powerful part of the attitudes and policies of those who founded the People's Republic of China. The one cause that could bring internationalist and nationalist sentiments together was the sense of a common enemy in the United States, and this above all bound Moscow and Beijing to each other in the early 1950s.

The imprint of Soviet institutions, economic and political, upon the New China was deeply set during these years, and remains to the present in many respects. The initial Sino-Soviet cleavage, however, was due in part to growing doubts on the part of certain Chinese leaders, including Mao, that the Soviet economic model was fully serviceable for China with its massive, depressed agrarian population that threatened to overrun the urban centers. China could not afford to ignore or exploit the peasant in the same manner as the Soviets, nor was it in the character of the Chinese peasant-military leaders to do so, although in searching for some solution compatible with socialist tenets, they were to make massive mistakes. While the divergence in economic program undertaken by 1957 irritated Khrushchev, however, the more fundamental reasons for the split lay in nationalist rivalries and rapidly expanding differences relating to perceptions of security needs. Highly nationalistic Chinese resented Soviet overlordship. The personal idiosyncrasies of

---

Publishing Co., 1986); Robert A. Scalapino, Seizaburo Sato, and Jusuf Wanandi, eds., *Internal and External Security Issues in Asia*, Research Papers and Policy Studies no. 16 (Berkeley: Institute of East Asian Studies, University of California, 1986); and Young W. Kihl and Lawrence Grinter, eds., *Asian-Pacific Security—Emerging Challenges and Responses* (Boulder: Lynne Rienner, 1986).
[5]See the works of A. Doak Barnett, Harold Hinton, William Griffith, and Donald S. Zagoria along with the Russian works of Borisov, Kapitsa, and Sladkovsky, and the voluminous Chinese materials, most of which are official documents or collectively written.

Khrushchev and Mao contributed to the tension. But the most basic issue was impersonal: at this point in time, the USSR and the PRC conceived of their security interests in different terms. The Soviets wanted to pursue détente with the United States and "united front" policies with developing nations like India so as to concentrate upon domestic problems. It was a policy virtually identical to that which China was to adopt in the post-Mao era, but the China of earlier times wanted an ally prepared to take risks in assisting China to complete its nation-building process and to confront "the imperialist world." When in these terms, the USSR proved to be an unreliable ally in Chinese eyes, the raison d'être for the alliance ceased.

Nations, like people, behave irrationally on occasion. The historic xenophobia implanted within Chinese culture combined with the paranoia of an aged, frustrated but unchallengeable leader to bring about the inanities of the Cultural Revolution. The willingness to treat both superpowers as enemies and to proclaim identity with the so-called Third World (while in fact alienating many nations, particularly Asian states) could not serve Chinese interests. Even if it had been more rationally cultivated, the Third World could not guarantee China's security or advance its economic growth. The shock of a threatened conflict with the USSR brought Chinese leaders including Mao to this realization. The turn outward got under way, with overtures to the United States—a logical tactic since the U.S. was a central key to the internationalization of Chinese foreign policy at the end of the 1960s.

Pragmatism ruled as both parties compromised with their political principles and set the Taiwan issue aside to undertake a process leading to diplomatic normalization. Indeed, at the close of the 1970s, Deng Xiaoping and others were calling for a global entente against Soviet hegemonism in which the United States and China were to play prominent roles. Chinese leaders were genuinely worried about what they perceived to be American weakness in the aftermath of Vietnam, and the steady rise of Soviet military power, especially in Asia.

Chinese calls for a united front against the USSR were short-lived, as is well known. By the early 1980s, Chinese foreign policy was undergoing an important shift, with the new theme being nonalignment. Once again, Beijing's leaders proclaimed identification with the Third World and publicly rebuked both superpowers for various transgressions. But the policies of the 1980s were by no means identical to those of the 1960s. China now consciously pursues a low-risk, low-cost foreign policy so as to concentrate upon its modernization objectives. Thus, a sustained effort has been under way to reduce tension with the USSR. The ideological quarrel has been set aside. The Soviet Union has been proclaimed a socialist state, and care is taken in strictly limiting criticism of Soviet domestic policies. Economic and cultural relations are advancing; a dialogue at ever higher levels has been undertaken. While Chinese leaders insist that normalization cannot take place until the three obstacles are satisfactorily resolved, if one considers normalization a process, it is under way.

In this process, the Soviet leaders beginning with Leonid Brezhnev have played their role. The Soviet Union has long been torn between its West-oriented policies epitomized by Andrei Gromyko and its deep concerns about a massive, hostile China stretched some 4,800 kilometers along its vulnerable central Asian-Siberian frontier. The renewed hostility between the USSR and the United States, combined with the fear of a strategic tie between the U.S. and the PRC, increased Soviet desires to reach an accommodation with China and provided the basis for the Gorbachev initiatives set forth in his Vladivostok speech of July 28, 1986. That speech, reflective of the increased influence of a younger, able generation of Soviet specialists on Asia, broke new ground.[6]

In addition to the time-honored and almost universally rejected call for an Asian collective security initiative (this time dressed in Helsinki clothing, with Hiroshima advanced as a possible site in a ploy that was too crude to be effective), Gorbachev indicated for the first time publicly that the USSR was prepared to address some of China's specific grievances, advancing certain proposals relating to border and economic issues.

The Chinese have responded cautiously, and in subsequent high-level discussions, progress on strategic matters appears to be slight thus far. Deng has clearly indicated that the one concession that matters most to the Chinese is that Moscow put pressure on Hanoi to end its occupation of Cambodia. Nevertheless, additional economic agreements have been signed and cultural relations are gradually being extended. Soviet motion pictures, literature, and ballet are being reintroduced into the PRC. China, moreover, is reestablishing party-to-party relations with such Soviet allies as East Germany.[7]

---

[6]For studies of Soviet Asian policies, see Gerald Segal, ed., *The Soviet Union in East Asia—Predicaments of Power* (Boulder: Westview Press, 1983); Herbert R. Ellison, ed., *The Sino-Soviet Conflict: A Global Perspective* (Seattle: University of Washington Press, 1982); and Donald S. Zagoria, ed., *Soviet Policy in East Asia* (New Haven: Yale University Press, 1982). See also Allen S. Whiting, *Siberian Development and East Asia—Threat or Promise?* (Stanford: Stanford University Press, 1981). For recent articles on the same subject, see the essays by Paul Dibb, Harry Gelman, and Robert Scalapino in *Adelphi Papers* 217, pt. 2 (London: Institute of International and Strategic Studies, Spring 1987).

[7]A recent authoritative exposition of China's current foreign policy is by Xue Mouhong, "A New Situation in China's Foreign Relations," *Chinese People's Institute of Foreign Affairs Journal* (Beijing), no. 2, (June 1986):26–37.

In conversations with Americans, however, PRC spokesmen insist that the Soviet Union continues to constitute the principal threat, and that there has been no significant Soviet movement on the critical issues. On all fronts, moreover, PRC "nonalignment" is tilted, and the tilt is perceptibly toward Japan and the West, notably the United States, as will be underlined later. The immediate issues from a Chinese perspective are Vietnam and Afghanistan in the security realm, and practical barriers to greatly expanded Sino-Soviet trade. The broader issues are the Soviet strategic encirclement of China and the limited capacity of the USSR to assist China in its quest for rapid modernization.

From a Soviet perspective, are current developments and future prospects vis-á-vis China hopeful? In private discourse with Americans, Soviet specialists express satisfaction with the general course of developments, noting that the trend is from hostility toward normalcy, despite the limited strategic concessions thus far advanced by Moscow. It is acknowledged that there will be no return to the days of alliance, but the Russians believe that they have friends in China, some of whom occupy or are moving into positions of prominence, individuals who will work for a steady improvement in relations. They assert that Gorbachev's overtures at Vladivostok represent the beginning of a progress that will be serious and sustained. On the strategic front, it is argued, the Soviet Union represents no threat to China, and in strategic arms limitations agreements, Asia as well as Europe will be included. Sino-Soviet economic interaction, including the training of personnel, it is asserted, can be less disruptive of the socialist system than assistance from the West, and it is assumed that China will remain socialist, thereby providing an ideological-systemic linkage with the USSR.[8]

One is thus confronted at present with an interesting juxtaposition of Soviet and Chinese views of the future, private and public. Knowledgeable Soviets profess optimism privately, caution publicly, whereas their Chinese counterparts are pessimistic privately, "hopeful" publicly. Naturally, one must assume that private comments are often packaged for American consumption by both parties. Apart from this, however, it is essential to understand the basic objectives of the two parties, both the goals that are congruent and those that are divergent.

The USSR and the PRC each has a vital interest in a reduction of tension enabling the redirection of key resources to pressing domestic

---

[8]Soviet views on China can be found in *Far Eastern Affairs*, a journal of the Institute of the Far East, USSR Academy of Sciences. See, e.g., M. Ukraintsev, "The Soviet Union's Growing Cooperation with Asian Socialist Nations and Kampuchea," *Far Eastern Affairs*, no. 1 (1986):51–63.

concerns. Further, such a reduction would provide greater flexibility in dealing with others, and notably with the United States. However much Moscow and Beijing may insist that there is no China or Russia card, to have a credible option in any negotiatory situation is of great advantage. The Soviet Union clearly wants to inhibit any U.S.-PRC alignment, especially one involving security. Its concern about a "Northeast Asian NATO" has repeatedly been made manifest, and if to the perceived threat of an American-Japanese-South Korean entente were added China—either directly or indirectly—a truly formidable constellation of forces would be arrayed against the Soviet Union in the East. In China, latent fear of ultimate American-Soviet rapprochement exists, a vision of the type of détente that paves the way for a global condominium with ensuing restraints upon the PRC. Beyond this, China naturally sees political advantages in the flexibility that enables it to criticize both superpowers and side rhetorically with the Third World at a time when it can provide little concrete assistance to other developing nations. And such a stance is in line with Chinese nationalism which today stands virtually alone as the ideological force shaping attitudes as well as policies.

It would probably be unwise to predict a certain course for Sino-Soviet relations over the coming years. The variables are numerous and complex. Internal developments in both countries constitute one key to the future. The course of events at regional and global levels is equally important. There are, however, certain constants that make possible the construction of a table of probability. First, let us outline several possible scenarios. The first we may label that of maximum accommodation. Briefly sketched, such a scenario envisages first the minimization of security issues between the two parties through the achievement of political solutions regarding the two current hot wars, Cambodia and Afghanistan, satisfactory to China. Such solutions would require a realignment of Vietnam from a position of challenge to perceived Chinese interests to some degree of accommodation with those interests, and the reduction of Soviet pressure upon Pakistan in conjunction with the withdrawal of Soviet forces from Afghanistan and a Kabul government that had at least a semblance of independence. These developments would be accompanied by a drawdown of Soviet and Chinese border forces, and the elimination or substantial reduction of Soviet strategic weapons in Asia as a part of a global strategic arms limitation agreement.

Maximum accommodation would also require or be greatly facilitated by a similarity of economic strategies. A promising development would be the type of Soviet economic reforms that would be compatible with those of China, also enabling the Soviet Union to interact more extensively with the emerging Pacific economic community. This would not only require policies aimed at turning outward, but ones enhancing the role of the market, albeit, without departing from an essentially state-controlled/guided economy. Under such developments, Sino-Soviet compatibilities with respect to trade and technology transfer would be enhanced.

Finally, under this scenario, further impetus for close relations might come from one or more of the following factors: a crisis with the United States over Taiwan, deteriorating U.S.-PRC economic relations or some combination of concerns that increased the desirability or need of Soviet support; the complete elimination of ideological issues between Beijing and Moscow, and the reestablishment of party-to-party relations; the rise to power in the PRC of leaders personally favorable to closer Sino-Soviet relations.

A second scenario might be labeled "normalcy without warmth." This scenario could be considered a continuation of current trends. Under it, economic and cultural relations would continue to evolve, without reaching either in volume or intensity those with Japan and the West. Compromises would ultimately be reached with respect to the three obstacles but neither side—and particularly China—would lose its apprehensions of the other in matters relating to security. Soviet military encirclement of China would continue, and from a Soviet perspective, the image of China as an emerging twenty-first-century power would serve to sustain concerns. Indeed, these concerns would grow rather than diminish as China's modernization program in all of its aspects unfolded. Nonetheless, it would remain in the interests of both parties to keep tensions as low as possible, and work out specific problems without expecting a resolution of the basic issues. Above all, heightened nationalism in both societies, with a sizable quotient of racial prejudice, would serve to make each party wary of the other, causing adjustments to be tactical rather than strategic.

A third general scenario is that of minimal accommodation. Such a scenario envisages a resurgence of hostility short of conflict, and would be based primarily upon heightened tensions over security issues: a sustained or even strengthened Soviet military presence around China's borders together with a network of alliances that prevented the PRC from obtaining an adequate buffer state system. Thus, to the close Soviet ties with Mongolia, Vietnam, and Afghanistan would be added a heightened competition over North Korea. Border incidents, or a broader array of problems with one or more of the states beholden to the USSR, would translate into intractable problems with Moscow itself. Economic and cultural relations would be affected, with recent gains cancelled or held at minimal levels. Ideological issues would again project themselves into the scene, with mutual criticisms voiced in rising crescendo, and renewed competition for legitimacy in the "socialist world" and among developing nations.

The present array of factors bearing upon these alternate scenarios favors "normalcy without warmth," accompanied by a continued tilt toward Japan and the West, albeit, with occasional oscillations. It would be unwise, however, to dismiss the other possibilities out of hand. One can only assert with considerable confidence that alliance or war are exceedingly unlikely.

How would the most probable scenario affect Southeast Asia in the period immediately ahead? On the positive side, it should make the USSR more anxious to see a political solution achieved in Indochina, one basically acceptable to both China and the ASEAN community, and indeed, there is modest evidence that Moscow's current orientation is in that direction—with what degree of success, only time will tell. It is not without reason that Hanoi—and New Delhi—evidence quiet concern about the steadfastness with which Moscow will support their respective causes against Beijing.

In addition, limited détente should sustain the interest of both major communist states in continued improvement of relations with the noncommunist states of the region, and correspondingly, limit their willingness to abet communist guerrilla movements. Each would wish to augment its economic and political position in the region.

There is ample evidence to indicate that such goals are being actively pursued. Soviet officials have toured Southeast Asia expressing the desire to increase economic intercourse with the ASEAN community, and also offering such cultural opportunities as invitations to students for schooling in the Soviet Union. Invitations have also been extended to ASEAN leaders to visit the USSR and have talks with Gorbachev and other Soviet officials. The Thais have accepted these offers. Soviet efforts appear concentrated upon governments, not upon opposition elements. Despite stories of assistance to the New People's Army in the Philippines—reports vigorously denied by Moscow—there is no evidence that either the Soviet government or the Communist Party of the Soviet Union is making any substantial effort to reestablish the type of close "fraternal ties" involving aid with the communist movements of the region. Such ties, it will be recalled, had been badly frayed by the Sino-Soviet split, with most of the East Asian communist parties and guerrilla movements affiliating with the Chinese. Soviet influence and support was largely confined to certain urban labor and intellectual circles, such as the Philippines (as well as Australia and New Zealand).

Soviet overtures up to date have produced very modest results. Future gains almost certainly hinge upon the fate of Soviet domestic reforms, political as well as economic. However, Moscow in the Gorbachev era can be expected to continue a two-pronged approach to Southeast Asia. On the one hand, it will seek to safeguard its alliance with Vietnam while at the same time offering private counsel to Hanoi with respect both to Vietnam's domestic economic policies and regional relations including the Cambodian issue. On the other hand, it will seek to move from a very minimal relationship with the noncommunist societies of the area to relations having economic and cultural components of at least moderate significance.

Meanwhile, in recent years, China has also placed great emphasis upon improving its relations with the nations comprising ASEAN, as is well known. In repeated trips to the region, Chinese leaders have pledged that their goal is expanded economic and cultural relations with the ASEAN societies based upon the five principles of peaceful coexistence. Even toward the two ASEAN states having no diplomatic relations with the PRC (Indonesia and Singapore), China has been exceedingly generous in political terms, ignoring anticommunist or anti-PRC manifestations and pursuing economic-cultural relations. Active assistance to the communist movements of the region has ended, with Chinese leaders insisting that the only ties between the CCP and the regional Communist parties are "moral" ones. Toward Vietnam, on the other hand, Beijing remains adamantly hostile, insisting that no negotiations can take place until the Vietnamese withdraw from Cambodia.

Understandably, virtually all of the Southeast Asian states harbor some doubts or misgivings regarding both the Soviet Union and China, current friendly overtures from these two nations notwithstanding. The USSR gives no indication of withdrawing from its newly achieved bases in Vietnam. On the contrary, it is expanding its strategic presence in the region. Thus, in conjunction with Vietnam, it is perceived to be a potential threat by some Thai and other ASEAN leaders. Beyond this, the Russians remain very foreign culturally as well as distant geographically to the people of Southeast Asia. While this can be an asset in terms of the limited concern evoked by their appearance, it also inhibits close ties. China, on the other hand, is seen by many Southeast Asians not as another Third World country, but as a nearby major power long desirous of exercising a sphere of influence over the region, possibly with the support of a portion of the overseas Chinese.

Maximum Sino-Soviet accommodation, even assuming that it would fall well short of alliance, has obvious negative potentials for Southeast Asia, including Vietnam. It would provide the principals with a greatly increased flexibility to deal with all of the smaller states in accordance with their perceived national interests. This would be particularly true of China, given its near presence. One result would be a heightened dependency within Southeast Asia upon the United States—and the constant apprehension over the uncertainties of American policy. The strains upon ASEAN would be severe since each state within the association would be confronted with separate tactical as well as strategic decisions in its relations with the PRC and the USSR, depending upon the timing and precise nature of the issues presented and the pressures mounted. Vietnam and its current satellites, Laos and Cambodia, would have to adjust to China.

Yet minimal accommodation would also pose substantial problems. A sizable degree of hostility between the USSR and the PRC would put greater pressure upon smaller states in the region—and especially states strategically important to one or both of the contestants—to align themselves more firmly. The maintenance of large Russian and Chinese defense forces, moreover, would not only inhibit progress toward global arms limitation, but would result in the type of regional tension likely to force other nations to step up military expenditures with resulting pressures upon their domestic economies. In sum, it seems clear that normalcy without warmth between the Soviet Union and China is the preferable scenario for Southeast Asia as well as the most likely one.

Sino-American Relations

Turning to future U.S.-PRC relations, one can also discern three possible scenarios. The most likely is what I earlier termed "tilted nonalignment," namely, a continuation of the relationship that has been under way since the early 1980s. China would use the appropriate rhetoric: opposition to "superpower hegemonism," adherence to the five principles of peaceful coexistence, support for and identification with the Third World, and a call for the complete elimination of nuclear weapons. It would play strongly upon nationalist themes, and continue to denounce both the United States and the USSR for specific acts that it considered transgressions (not in China's national interests). Yet whether the measure be economic, cultural, or strategic, China's tilt would be decidedly toward the United States. The effort to interest foreign investors in key priorities such as energy, transport, and telecommunications along with high-technology industries, would be directed at Americans along with Japanese and West Europeans. A stream of Chinese—at increasingly more specialized, advanced stages of training—would make their way to the United States (at present, 20,000 versus approximately 200 in the Soviet Union). And the low-level strategic relationship that has now gotten under way would be maintained, with a steady PRC effort to upgrade the weaponry and military technology obtained from the United States.[9]

There are two elemental reasons why this is the most probable scenario of the future: neither country poses a threat to the other; and China's current economic course dictates an ever closer interaction with the advanced industrial nations and, complementary to this, growing participation in the Pacific-Asian economic order. At the same time, China will want to preserve the symbolism of independence and non-alignment both for political and strategic reasons. China has a very limited capacity to project either economic or military power; hence, it must find a policy that maximizes its political strength without overextending its financial or strategic resources. Yet that policy must also serve its security and economic interests. Tilted nonalignment is appropriate to the times.

Under certain conditions, however, one can envisage a different scenario. What would produce a tilt toward the Soviet Union? One possibility would be a crisis over Taiwan that pitted the PRC against the United States. It is this risk that Beijing constantly holds up before Washington. A declaration of independence or large-scale violence on Taiwan might force the PRC to act, it is asserted, suddenly precipitating a crisis in PRC-U.S. relations that no one would want. (It is rarely mentioned that Beijing's use of force would also cost it heavily with virtually all other Pacific-Asian nations, including Japan and the ASEAN states.) Another and possibly more likely source of trouble lies in the economic realm. Should the United States adopt strongly protectionist policies or tighten up the sales of high-technology products for security reasons, the repercussions upon PRC-U.S. relations could be decidedly unpleasant. If Soviet economic reforms, meanwhile, were in concert with those of China, economic relations might expand on a scale not presently envisaged. Even under these conditions, Beijing would almost certainly retain its strong economic ties with Japan, augmented by those with West Europe.

Finally, a third possibility is a closer alignment with the PRC of the type envisaged by Deng Xiaoping and some elements of the Carter administration at the time of the exchange of diplomatic recognition in 1979. Such a development would occur as the counterpart to an intensification of tension between the PRC and the USSR as set forth in our earlier scenario of minimal accommodation. While stopping short of a

---

[9]For one perspective on Soviet and Chinese strategic views, see Banning N. Garrett and Bonnie S. Glaser, *War and Peace: The Views from Moscow and Beijing* (Berkeley: Institute of International Studies, University of California, 1984).

full-fledged mutual security agreement in all probability, it would be manifested in heightened U.S. arms supplies to China, economic assistance, and mutual consultation on a wide range of matters including defense strategies. For China, it would represent a higher-cost, higher-risk foreign policy, hence, likely to be accepted only through perceived necessity.

Once again, how would each of these alternative scenarios affect the nations of Southeast Asia? Tilted nonalignment between the PRC and the United States has several advantages: it gives the U.S. limited leverage in persuading China to take ASEAN interests into account in determining its policies when there is some divergence between Chinese policies and those of some or all of the ASEAN states. It underwrites a united front against Vietnamese expansionism, and hopefully at some point will help to induce a political settlement on the Cambodian issue which, together with the extension of more independent policies on the part of Laos, will produce a situation in Indochina more suitable to the interests of the ASEAN community. On the negative side, there is a concern rather widely shared in Southeast Asia that the United States is prone to place its bilateral relations with the PRC ahead of those with the noncommunist states of Southeast Asia, giving priority to its global strategic interests. Indeed, evidence can be found from the past to give substance to this concern, and since many Southeast Asians see China as a long-range threat, military and economic assistance from the United States and Japan to China stirs both fear and resentment.

These apprehensions would be greatly heightened if the strategic ties between the U.S. and the PRC were to be strengthened as envisaged in our third scenario. But a sharp cleavage between these two countries would also bring adverse repercussions to the ASEAN community. The latter states would be forced into more sharply profiled alignments, and the PRC would once again be tempted to shift its emphasis in some cases from state-to-state to people-to-people or comrade-to-comrade relations. American leverage on PRC policies, while perhaps not high under any conditions, would be nonexistent, and security problems for every state in the region would mount. Thus, tilted nonalignment is not only the preferable policy at present for the United States and the PRC; it is also the preferable policy for ASEAN.

U.S.-USSR Relations

When the forty-year history of U.S.-USSR relations since World War II is surveyed, one paramount question is posed: what part constitutes historical inevitability; what part, human error or, put differently, leadership shortsightedness? A case can be made for an intricate mix of these two central elements, with the quotient a judgmental matter.[10]

After the war, Stalin, in his determination to punish his enemies and to secure for the Soviet Union a buffer state system that would protect his country from another devastating war, went further than the tsars in expanding the Soviet empire. He accomplished this, moreover, at a time when the USSR was only a regional power, significantly inferior in total military strength—and strategic reach—to the United States, economically in a shambles, and with its political appeal having already passed its zenith, at least for Western peoples. Yet the Soviet Union possessed a massive land army and, assisted by developments in China, it was in a position to make a bid to dominate the Eurasian continent. Such a move, the United States was determined to stop. Poland, Czechoslovakia, and Greece were the first warning signs— would West Europe be overrun?

The U.S. policy adopted was labeled "containment"—a policy that had its economic, political, and military dimensions. It was the first comprehensive security plan, a program extended to previous enemies as well as wartime allies. On balance, it was successful, but at considerable cost, with American resources dispersed on a wide front. The focus, however, was upon West Europe and East Asia. Confronted with American power, Soviet leaders reacted with caution. They wanted no direct conflict with a power superior in every category. Russian resources, however, were marshaled to engage in a forced march toward military parity with the United States. To this end, great sacrifices were imposed upon the Soviet people and, at Stalin's death, considerable progress had been made. Khrushchev, cognizant of serious economic and social problems that cried out for attention, was anxious to undertake internal reforms that would require some reordering of Soviet resources. He had no intention of abandoning competition with the United States. On the contrary, he hoped to broaden its scope by driving his people to build a modern nation in every sense. This was the underlying rationale for détente, and in his determination to pursue that course, Khrushchev paid substantial prices, the foremost of which was Soviet relations with Mao's China.

Détente in this period became a victim of a host of incidents: the U2 affair, the Kennedy-Khrushchev Vienna meeting and, above all, the Cuban missile crisis, with the domestic politics of both nations progres-

---

[10]For varying perspectives, see the writings of Seweryn Bialer, George Breslauer, Zbigniew Brzezinski, Alexander Dallin, Jerry Hough, William Hyland, George Kennan, Richard Pipes, Dimitri Simes, Strobe Talbott, and Robert C. Tucker.

sively working against it. Throughout this period and beyond, the United States maintained a strategic edge, innovating in weaponry, with the Soviet Union seeking to catch up, most frequently counting upon quantitative gains rather than qualitative advances. It was in this setting that SALT I was consummated, and in the middle Brezhnev reign, a new era of détente opened.

The 1970s seemed to promise an overall strategic equilibrium between the U.S. and the USSR, an equilibrium from which the difficult task of scaling down arms could commence. Notwithstanding the sizable loss of American credibility as a result of Washington's abandonment of South Vietnam, the United States was positioning itself between the Soviet Union and China advantageously, practicing "evenhandedness." The ratification of SALT II and the diplomatic recognition of the PRC were scheduled to take place simultaneously, with Most Favored Nation economic treatment of both nations to follow. The Soviet invasion of Afghanistan destroyed this plan and, in its aftermath, massive publicity was accorded to the fact that the Soviets had greatly expanded their military arsenal in the 1970s while the United States had largely halted its buildup, with the Russians finally achieving the strategic equivalence they had long sought. The age of bipolarism had indeed arrived and the political fallout in the United States was heavy. The Carter administration was forced to change course, dedicating the United States to a resumption of heavy defense expenditures to reverse or contain the trend.

Ronald Reagan came to office strongly committed to a continuation and expansion of that policy. Negotiations would be undertaken with the USSR from strength, and until that strength had been acquired, no concessions would be forthcoming. At a certain political cost internationally, this policy was rigorously followed. It produced results. Confronted with the prospects of a costly, endless arms race, and facing a president who enjoyed great popularity with his people, Soviet leaders—after a period of political malaise—were not only induced to return to the bargaining table, but to advance serious proposals for arms reductions involving significant concessions, and ultimately, in September 1987, to reach with the United States the first strategic arms reduction agreement since SALT II.[11]

The capacity of the two superpowers to reach a limited but significant agreement on arms limitation stems from many factors. Above all,

---

[11]The dimensions of the domestic economy challenge facing the USSR are set forth by Timothy J. Colton, *The Dilemma of Reform in the Soviet Union,* rev. ed. (New York: Council on Foreign Relations, 1986).

it is testimony to the urgent need of both the USSR and the U.S. to direct more of their resources to pressing domestic concerns. In and of itself, this initial agreement will do little if anything to reduce military expenditures on either side, but it is a first step in what it is hoped will be a process encompassing conventional as well as strategic weaponry, and ultimately having both a major economic and political impact on the policies of both societies. Other factors were involved: Gorbachev's desire to enhance his domestic standing; Reagan's hope to cap his presidency with a dramatic act auguring an era of peace. The fact is also that in the recent past American-Soviet relations have been played out on a global stage, with each of the principal actors having to be increasingly conscious of world opinion.

It remains necessary to project possible U.S.-USSR scenarios for the future, seeking to place current events in perspective. Global war appears to have a very low probability despite the overkill possessed by both countries—or, more accurately perhaps, because of that overkill. Without going into the arcane debate over whether a nuclear war is "winnable," the fact is that American and Soviet leaders both recognize that such a war would permanently alter civilization and render their own societies shrunken cesspools of misery. The game of chicken remains a threat, but it will almost certainly be played for lower stakes than those of thermonuclear war.

Despite the new arms agreement, one cannot rule out the possibility that future events will conspire to worsen U.S.-USSR relations once again, with repercussions upon every key region, economic and political as well as strategic. Such a course would be marked by another escalation of the arms race at ever more sophisticated levels, with periods of imbalance unfavorable to one of the two central actors, thereby heightening the risk of irrational acts. The situation could be exacerbated by superpower intervention in those societies having high levels of instability, especially the authoritarian-pluralist societies attempting to undergo a transition toward greater political openness. A serious global economic crisis capped by the inability of the advanced industrial world including the United States to adjust satisfactorily to the current global economic revolution would add to the crisis. Similarly, the continued failure of socialist societies to consummate the leap into modernity, epitomized by the failure of Soviet reforms, would have equally ominous potentialities since it would tempt the strengthening of those restrictive policies and institutions characteristic of Stalinism at its worst. Even under these conditions, global nuclear war would probably be prevented, but the odds against it happening would shrink, and violence in all other forms would be endemic.

An opposite scenario warrants brief attention, one that can be labeled maximal accommodation, to borrow the phrase applied to one Sino-Soviet scenario. Such an outcome would require significant changes, both domestic and international. On the domestic front, the USSR under Gorbachev would undergo the type of structural reforms that facilitated its more active and constructive participation in the global marketplace. A political evolution, moreover, would ultimately accompany the economic changes that gradually altered the polity from Leninism to authoritarian-pluralism, thus reducing somewhat the inhibitions in political discourse, especially at the unofficial levels, and making the society more susceptible to influences from divergent sources at home and abroad.

Another development would be the acceptance of the USSR as a legitimate participant in conferences devoted to handling regional crises, and the satisfactory performance of both the USSR and the U.S. in such roles. In this fashion, targets of opportunity for superpower intervention would be reduced, with mechanisms for handling future as well as existing civil-international conflicts developed. Finally, cumulative, sweeping strategic and conventional arms reductions would occur on a basis that preserved the minimal security needs of both powers and other nations as well.

A final scenario is that of a gradual thaw, resulting in a relatively stable combination of competition and cooperation between the U.S. and the USSR. Such a development would include an agreement or series of agreements on partial strategic arms limitations; a political resolution of current hot wars in Afghanistan and Cambodia acceptable to the key parties concerned (in Afghanistan, that seems to be under way, but with uncertain results; Cambodian remains unresolved); avoidance of new situations where troubles within a given country or region resulted in direct superpower confrontation; and the gradual expansion of U.S.-USSR economic and cultural relations. It is to be noted that the realization of this scenario is not completely in the hands of Washington and Moscow. Events in states and regions of vital strategic importance to one or both of these nations will also determine its feasibility. However, domestic and international pressures combine at present to encourage limited American-Russian accommodation and, most particularly, some arms limitation agreement.

Once again, what are the implications of each of these scenarios for Southeast Asia? Of the four alternatives sketched, the gradual thaw scenario is clearly the most advantageous. It would imply the continued presence of the major powers within the region, but coexisting at a lower level of tension. It would enable some points of cooperation with respect to East Asia, as currently exist in Sino-American relations. And it would reduce, although not eliminate, the raison d'être for superpower intervention in domestic crises within the region. The shift from alliance to alignment would continue, with a higher premium upon the self-reliance of the lesser powers. Economic and social concerns could be given greater weight, with the purely military aspects of regional and national security somewhat reduced in terms of proportionate attention and cost.

The disadvantages and dangers of war or of a heightened level of U.S.-USSR tension are too obvious to need elaboration. No area including Southeast Asia could escape the consequences of either of these developments. However, maximal accommodation might also pose some risks from a Southeast Asian perspective. At certain points in the past, critics—notably the Chinese—have warned against a Soviet-American condominium of the world, with the two superpowers reaching agreements over the heads of their allies and others, having profound implications. While this risk seems much exaggerated, the events of Reykjavik rekindled precisely these fears among Washington's European allies. In any case, however, maximal accommodation does not seem to be on the immediate horizon.

Conclusion

As was indicated at the outset of this essay, this is a period of unprecedented fluidity in all major state relations, and the shifts in relations between and among the United States, the Soviet Union, and the People's Republic of China in recent years are eloquent testimony to that fact. It is also a time when the nature of relations between the superpowers and their allies—large and small—are undergoing multiple changes. The lessened dependence of the smaller states upon the larger states, and the greatly increased costs and risks of absolute security guarantees from the latter to the former have combined to induce an accelerating shift from alliance to alignment, with all of the complexities which the management of alignments involves.

It is not surprising, therefore, that every state—and especially the major powers—is exercising greater caution in making and executing international commitments. Total involvement of an official nature is to be avoided. Hence, the proliferation of clandestine, quasi-official efforts—"volunteers," client state involvements, arms shipments, mercenaries, terrorism—and a host of other policies intended to limit the risk for the government and state involved. In such operations, highly authoritarian groups and governments may have a signal advantage since they can preserve secrecy better and create their own justifications with minimal internal dissent.

If the road ahead is murky, a few general trends appear to be distinct. For most societies, economic development now occupies top priority, and that includes a wide range of states from the advanced industrial nations to the states that are still highly traditional. Meanwhile, the prospects for political convergence across a wide spectrum seem less promising than earlier writers suggested. At the same time, modifications in some Leninist polities, and the heightened struggle in many authoritarian-pluralist societies for increased openness, indicate an unprecedented degree of political ferment. Nor are Western-style democracies exempt from the possibility of structural alterations, with the excesses of total freedom the target.

Given the current domestic challenges, economic, social, and political, virtually every nation—including the major powers—is seeking lower-cost, lower-risk foreign policies. Scientific-technological developments in some respects mitigate against this quest, pushing leaders into the unknown without adequate safeguards or tested policies. Yet despite the formidable obstacles, major power accommodation—partial, tentative, and based on minimal trust, at least at first—would appear to be in the offing. And among the available alternatives, this is the best one for the smaller states, including those of Southeast Asia.

Contributors

Zainuddin A. Bahari is a fellow in Security and International Relations, Institute of Strategic and International Studies, Kuala Lumpur.

Chan Ngor Chong is research associate at the Institute of Strategic and International Studies, Kuala Lumpur.

Chia Siow-Yue is associate professor of economics, National University of Singapore.

Chin Kin Wah is Senior Lecturer in the Department of Political Science, the National University of Singapore.

Soedjati Djiwandono is Head, Department of International Relations, Centre at the Center of Strategic and International Studies, Jakarta.

Harlan W. Jencks is a research associate at the Center for Chinese Studies, University of California, Berkeley, and adjunct professor of National Security Affairs at the Naval Postgraduate School, Monterey, California.

Joyce K. Kallgren is the associate director of the Institute of East Asian Studies, University of California, Berkeley, and professor of political science at the University of California, Davis.

Stephen Leong is professor of history at the University of Malaya, Kuala Lumpur.

Kenneth Lieberthal is director of the Center of Chinese Studies, University of Michigan, Ann Arbor.

Edgardo B. Maranan teaches in the Philippines Studies Program, Asian Center, University of the Philippines.

Sukhumbhand Paribatra is director of the Southeast Asian Security Studies Program of the Institute of Security and International Studies, Chulalongkorn University, Bangkok.

Douglas Pike is director of the Indochina Studies Project, University of California, Berkeley.

Abhinya Rathanamongkolmas teaches in the Department of Political Science, Chulalongkorn University, Bangkok.

Edward W. Ross is Assistant for China, Office of Secretary of Defense, International Security Affairs, Washington, D.C.

Robert S. Ross is visiting assistant professor and postdoctoral fellow at the Henry M. Jackson School of International Studies, University of Washington, Seattle.

Robert A. Scalapino is Robson Research Professor of Government, Department of Political Science, and director of the Institute of East Asian Studies, University of California, Berkeley.

Hadi Soesastro is deputy director of the Centre of Strategic and International Studies, Jakarta.

Noordin Sopiee is director of the Institute of Strategic and International Studies, Kuala Lumpur.

Reynaldo Ty y Racaza teaches in the department of political science, University of the Philippines.

Jusuf Wanandi is executive director of the Centre of Strategic and International Studies, Jakarta.

K. C. Yeh is senior economist at the Rand Corporation, Santa Monica, California.

RECENT INSTITUTE OF ASIAN STUDIES PUBLICATIONS

CHINA RESEARCH MONOGRAPHS (CRM)

25. Rudolph G. Wagner, *Reenacting the Heavenly Vision: The Role of Religion in the Taiping Rebellion*, 1984, reprinted 1987, 134pp., $12.00.
31. Robert Y. Eng, *Economic Imperialism in China, Silk Production and Exports, 1861–1932*, 1986, 243pp., $15.00.
32. Judith M. Boltz, *A Survey of Taoist Literature, Tenth to Seventeenth Centuries*, 1987, 417pp., $20.00.
33. Yue Daiyun, *Intellectuals in Chinese Fiction*, translated by Deborah Rudolph and Yeh Wen-hsing, 1988, 143pp., $10.00.
34. Constance Squires Meaney, *Stability and the Industrial Elite in China and the Soviet Union*, 1988, 160pp., $15.00.

KOREA RESEARCH MONOGRAPHS (KRM)

11. Robert A. Scalapino and Hongkoo Lee, eds., *North Korea in a Regional and Global Context*, 1986, 405pp., $20.00.
12. Laurel Kendall and Griffin Dix, eds., *Religion and Ritual in Korean Society*, 1987, 223pp., $15.00.
13. Vipan Chandra, *Imperialism, Resistance, and Reform in Late Nineteenth-Century Korea: Enlightenment and the Independence Club*, 1988, 240pp., $17.00.
14. Seok Choong Song, *Explorations in Korean Syntax and Semantics*, 1988, 384pp., $20.00.
15. Robert A. Scalapino and Dalchoong Kim, eds., *Asian Communism: Continuity and Transition*, 1988, 416pp., $20.00.

JAPAN RESEARCH MONOGRAPHS (JRM)

8. Yung H. Park, *Bureaucrats and Ministers in Contemporary Japanese Government*, 1986, 192pp., $15.00.
9. Victoria V. Vernon, *Daughters of the Moon: Wish, Will, and Social Constraint in Fiction by Modern Japanese Women*, 1988, 245pp., $12.00.

INDOCHINA RESEARCH MONOGRAPHS (IRM)

1. William J. Duiker, *China and Vietnam: The Roots of Conflict*, 1986, 123pp., $10.00.
2. Allan E. Goodman, *The Search for a Negotiated Settlement of the Vietnam War*, 1986, 136pp., $10.00.
3. Tran Tri Vu, *Lost Years: My 1,632 Days in Vietnamese Reeducation Camps*, 1988, 288pp., $15.00.
4. Ta Van Tai, *The Vietnamese Tradition of Human Rights*, 1988, 320pp., $17.00.

RESEARCH PAPERS AND POLICY STUDIES (RPPS)

12. R. Sean Randolph, *The United States and Thailand: Alliance Dynamics, 1950–1985*, 1986, 245pp., $15.00.
14. Robert A. Scalapino, Seizaburo Sato, and Jusuf Wanandi, eds., *Asian Economic Development—Present and Future*, 1985, reprinted 1988, 241pp., $20.00.
15. Robert A. Scalapino, Seizaburo Sato, and Jusuf Wanandi, eds., *Asian Political Institutionalization*, 1986, 312pp., $20.00.
16. Robert A. Scalapino, Seizaburo Sato, and Jusuf Wanandi, eds., *Internal and External Security Issues in Asia*, 1986, 273pp., $20.00.
17. Robert A. Scalapino and Chen Qimao, eds., *Pacific-Asian Issues: American and Chinese Views*, 1986, 289pp., $20.00.
18. Karl D. Jackson, Sukhumbhand Paribatra, and J. Soedjati Djiwandono, eds., *ASEAN in Regional and Global Context*, 1986, 357pp., $20.00.
19. Robert A. Scalapino and Han Sung-joo, eds., *United States-Korea Relations*, 1986, 226pp., $20.00.
20. Karl D. Jackson and Wiwat Mungkandi, eds., *United States-Thailand Relations*, 1986, 332pp., $20.00.
21. Joyce K. Kallgren and Denis Fred Simon, eds., *Educational Exchanges: Essays on the Sino-American Experience*, 1987, 257pp., $15.00.